For Grace Wagnecke [illegible]
warm regards, an[illegible]
the most pleasant [illegible]
of KIARS.
Tom Gleason

A Liberal EDUCATION

A Liberal EDUCATION

Abbott Gleason

TidePool Press
Cambridge, Massachusetts

Published in the United States in 2010 by TidePool Press

For information, address TidePool Press
6 Maple Avenue, Cambridge, Massachusetts 02139
www.tidepoolpress.com

Printed in the United States

Library of Congress Cataloging-in-Publication Data

Gleason, Abbott.
A Liberal Education
Abbott Gleason—First Edition
p. cm.

ISBN 0-9755557-4-3/978-0-9755557-4-3
1. Gleason, Abbott Family 2. World Politics—20th Century
3. Brown University 4. United States—Biography I. Title

2009943456

In memory of

John Claiborne Davis, Dean Stambaugh,
John Lax and Adam Ulam

Acknowledgments

Sarah Gleason was an essential critic, and she also bore up extremely well under the regime of self absorption this project entailed within our household. Sheela Raman was a tremendous help on the whole manuscript and so were Deborah Cohen and Antonia Bryson. I am grateful to Philip Tilney for finding out a bit about my grandfather Gleason. Thanks to Andrea Petersen, to Peggy Anderson and Jane Barnes for several good stories I had forgotten, to Jonathan Beecher, Rebecca Birnbaum, Dan Brock, John Claiborne Davis, Lesley Davison, John Dittmer, Christopher Ely, Monroe Engel, David Engerman, Svetlana Evdokimova, Margaret Gleason, Lauren Faulkner, Mary Gluck, Peter Kenez, Christina Koningisor, Fred Leventhal, Karen Lynch, Jack McNees, Andy Rosen, Blair Ruble, Wendy Strothman, William Taubman, Jack Thomas and Sandy Walker for reading portions and drafts and making valuable suggestions. Thanks to Chris Boldt, John Woodford, Allen Graubard, Rose Mary Harbison and John Mudd for sharing their memories of Freedom Summer. Thanks to Leszek Balcerowicz for discussions about the end of the Soviet Union and to Nelson Aldrich for conversations about Eliot House. Thanks to Betsy West for introducing me to Jock Herron!

Contents

To become a human being is an art.

—"Mensch werden ist eine Kunst." Novalis, quoted in Jack Zipes, ed., *Victorian Fairy Tales*, Methuen, New York and London, 1987, p. xxvii.

A liberal is a man too broadminded to take his own side in a quarrel.

—Robert Frost, quoted by Guy Davenport (*The Geography of the Imagination*) and many others.

Now the question immediately arises: what sort of hope could ever justify the statement that, on the basis of that hope and simply because it exists, we are redeemed.

—Benedict XVI, *Spe Salvi*.

Foreword

To FILCH THE TERMS W.H. Auden employed about autobiographies and apply them to my own case, Sancho Panza and the Don engaged in a long and inconclusive struggle over who would grasp the pen (or occupy the uncomfortable chair at the computer) in the making of this account.[1] It's not even clear to me who was who. There was certainly no Henry Adams figure, to emphasize the writer's singularity. And, to evoke a favorite Russian author, the writer is anything but a hero of his time, although he was certainly marked by it.

When it comes to talking about what the author did with his life, does Quixote or Panza gets to do the "master narrative"? And how will his antagonist get to respond? With rude noises, or a lawyerly brief? In the midst of a descriptive mosaic of the Don's determined decisions to reform, hopes for the future, and the rueful realization of yet another setback—all of a sudden, there is that little alter ego again, grinning knowingly and reminding the author that he has given himself a bit of an artistic façade after all. "Whew! For a while I was afraid you were going to tell it like it really was!"

The integrity of these reminiscences suffers from a number of gradual and abrupt alterations in the consciousness of the author as he tried and tried to grow up and then remember afterwards what the process was like. What results is, most obviously, the old

[1] "Every autobiography is concerned with two characters, a Don Quixote, the Ego, and a Sancho Panza, the self." See "Hic et Ille," *The Dyer's Hand*, Random House, New York, 1962.

man's attempt to recapture the elusive personae of the child and the young man, to understand the angers, passions and fears of long ago. Then there is his effort to present his mature self as if it were somehow achieved, although we are never really finished until we're finished. Authorial points of view come and go, failures are defined, redefined and reinterpreted.

The multiple shadows that constitute our author do agree on a couple of things. We don't want to bore people or settle scores. We do want to amuse people and stir reflection. So this account is artificially full of stories, anecdotes, vignettes, snapshots, distilled from the fuzziness and defensive confusion of old memories. The existentially disparate team of autobiographers also agreed to club together and present a self and subjects with which the reader could in some wise identify—positively or negatively. Some conservatives will feast on the falsity of our interpretations of events; others will notice the infrequent appearances of God and Church. Radicals can criticize the timidity, indecisiveness and conventionality of the author(s). We hope that there is something for almost everybody here.

One conclusion may be worth suggesting at the outset. Fear and self-loathing are often disparaged by people regarded as knowledgeable about human development. But the author's experience suggests that this is an oversimplification. At least in moderation, they can lead to somewhat better odds for a useful life. Woody Allen is famous for suggesting that just showing up is 80% of the battle. In my experience, showing up scared was even more likely to help, provided you weren't scared out of your wits.

Some of the things written here are sources of modest satisfaction. Marriage and family life crucially shaped the arc of my education. Some recollections evoke shame or embarrassment, some amusement or wonder. There are surely things that memory has mislaid or suppressed, about which I have not written or cannot write, or cannot find words to express. These very same events and characters could provoke many other treatments, some darker, some farcical, some more introspective and perhaps more edifying. Perhaps if this collection doesn't fly we can have another go. But probably not.

Abbott Gleason
Leningrad – St. Petersburg – Providence, R.I.

74 Sparks Street, Cambridge, Massachusetts, c. 1940

74 Sparks Street

Across from the front door of my grandparents' house in Cambridge, Massachusetts, beyond the long curve of the driveway, was a grove of trees and an overgrown, dank, wild garden, hyperbolically known as "the wilderness", where I was often sent out to play. From as early as I can remember, I loved visiting the big house at 74 Sparks Street. It was of the kind known as a Queen Anne cottage, taking its name from the late nineteenth-century "Queen Anne" movement, inspired by the English Pre-Raphaelites. Described by their historian as "architectural cocktails," these dark, heavy brick and slate-shingled behemoths seem anything but cottages, at least in the American context.[1] Rows of them lined Sparks Street, up and down, dwarfing their well-dressed inhabitants out for a stroll to Harvard Square.

Vehicular traffic on Sparks Street in the 1940s was quite sparse, and the elderly lady next door, Mrs. Dodge, had an ancient electric car in which at intervals she would slowly set out for parts unknown. I still recall my amazement at seeing this large black antique moving silently down the street with its elderly driver erect at the wheel. Because it was driven by Mrs. Dodge, I always think of it as a Dodge, but of course it wasn't. Sparks Street, which seemed so enormous to me when I was three, has shrunk and is now one way, with dotted lines indicating that motor vehicles must share the

[1] Mark Girouard, *Sweetness and Light*, Oxford, Clarendon, 1977, p. 2.

space with a bike path. The "wilderness" is no longer there today, having been replaced by a larger expanse of driveway and a basket for shooting hoops. There is a new garage and the house where my grandparents lived is a light gray, rather than its former lugubrious dark red. Even its bulk, however, is dwarfed by the enormous trees surrounding it.

Inside 74 Sparks were seven portraits of Oliver Cromwell, scattered about the first and second floors, each of which I would greet in turn upon our family's arrival: "Hello, Cromwell." Although I can't recall them in detail, these dark canvases in their gold frames impressed me with their importance. My grandfather, known to my generation as "Baba" (pronounced BAA-baw), much appreciated my precocious interest in his academic specialty, although he himself did not care for Cromwell, whom he considered a precursor of fascism. Many years later I had to endure a long and severe lecture on my grandfather's politics from Christopher Hill, a great English student of the English Revolution from a more leftist generation. Like other English Marxists of his day, Hill considered Cromwell a type of revolutionary and was permanently incensed that a scholar of my grandfather's prominence should have made such a pernicious error. Although Hill was (barely) too polite to say so, it was my grandfather who was, in his view, if not quite a fascist, at least a dreadful reactionary.

After greeting the seven Cromwells, I would go upstairs to say hello to my grandparents, who by the mid-nineteen-forties were increasingly confined to the second floor. The formidable Professor Abbott liked to pose philosophical conundrums to his grandchildren, and occasionally I would score. "What is time?" he demanded on one occasion. "Time," I told him without hesitation, "is the wastebasket of days." An emphasis on time past, as appropriate to a family of historians, although the wastebasket idea was less than Proustian.

I loved Baba's workroom in the basement, where he made furniture as an avocation, and also his big study, reeking of cigar

Wilbur C. H. Abbott and Mary Ellen Smith, c. 1891

smoke, his enormous desk piled high with stacks of papers, and the enormous rubber plants at the windows. I also loved the sets of books that filled the shelves on the dimly lit first floor. For some reason, a large set of the complete works of Francis Bacon by the front stairs particularly enticed me. "One day it will be yours," my mother told me encouragingly. But I couldn't wait. On a rainy day my parents returned from a trip to Harvard Square to find me tearing the pages out of the volumes, one by one. After the ensuing confrontation, I modified my early and ecstatic approach to primary source material.

On the landing of the same stairs was an enormous console Victrola which you wound up with a crank. Of course it played only seventy-eight rpms. Most seemed to come from some unimaginably earlier period. Nora Bayes singing "Sally Green (The Village Vamp)" was my favorite tune when I was about four. It must have been recorded around the end of the First World War. I certainly didn't know from vamps at that time.

The rooms upstairs seemed enormous, dark and bare to me, and all smelled of cigar smoke. They signally lacked the cosy domesticity of our house in Amherst, which seemed small and cluttered by comparison. I was especially impressed by the bathroom with its enormous, old-fashioned tub, with a real sponge in the soap dish. I had trouble believing that it could ever have been a living thing. Taking a bath was an adventure.

I was fascinated by meals, too, which were much more formal than at our house, where we had no maid. Underneath the table was a buzzer, concealed by the rug. When a course was finished, my grandmother would press it with her foot, and the Swedish maid, a charming woman named Sigrid (I called her "See-see" because Sigrid was too hard), would come in and clear. During the day, I would sometimes crawl under the table and make the buzzer go off myself. But nobody came into the dining room, to my annoyance.

My birth was a painful and uncomfortable experience for my mother, then thirty-six years old. Many years later, she recalled being rushed to Mt. Auburn Hospital in the pouring rain the night before and being given a dose of castor oil:

> I remember I spent a very uncomfortable night on a floodlit operating table surrounded by men in white coats and drugged almost to insensibility. I do remember, however, that about 1:00 or 2:00 A.M. I told them firmly that I had had enough, I was tired and I was going home. They asked me in the morning if I remembered this impractical decision, which I did. It still seemed the sensible thing to do. It was not until the afternoon when the drugs had worn off that I recollected why I was there and asked to meet you.

Improbably enough, she reported, I was "the prize baby in the nursery at that time, and for the two weeks we stayed in the hospital ... the only baby who never cried, and the nurses called you 'widget'."

After coming home from Mt. Auburn Hospital, I lived in a clothes basket for a couple of months in Harvard's Adams House, where

Mary Eleanor Abbott Gleason with Tom, c. 1940

my father was Acting Senior Tutor. There my grandfather visited me. He had previously told my mother that he wanted me to be named after his father: Thomas Washington Abbott Gleason. What a moniker! But—perhaps for the first time in her life—my mother, Mary Eleanor Abbott Gleason—disobeyed her father. She allegedly wanted me at first to be named for my father: Sarell (a mysterious name that had turned up in the Gleason family) Everett Gleason III. But when my father objected strenuously, I was simply given my mother's maiden name—Abbott—for a first name. But my grandfather characteristically refused to admit defeat. Peering down into the basket he observed that it would be impossible to call such a little baby "Abbott". Smiling, perhaps a little grimly, at my mother and father he announced that he was going to call the little baby

BIBLIOTHÈQUE NATIONALE

N° [illegible]

Départ^ts des imprimés, Mss

M. S. Everett Gleason

Titres ou profession : A.B. ; A.M. Harvard

Adresse 46 rue Jacob Paris

Signature : S. E. Gleason, Jr

S. Everett Gleason, card from the Biblioteque Nationale, c. 1931

"Tommy". He did and it stuck. I was "Tommy" at home, but "Abbott" in school until the third grade, when I discovered that the most obnoxious kid in the class was named Costello. (The comedy team of Abbott and Costello was just hitting its stride about then.) From that year on I was "Tommy", then "Tom", in school as well. I never liked "Abbott" as a name. "Tom", on the other hand, suited me down to the ground.

My father had decided to stay on in Cambridge, following his graduation from Harvard College in 1927, and take a Ph.D. degree in medieval history. He worked under the scholar then esteemed as the most distinguished medievalist in the United States, Charles Homer Haskins, discoverer of the "renaissance of the twelfth century". Secondarily he worked with a younger professor, not much older than he: Charles Holt Taylor, who with his charming wife Dede (Fidelia) became lifelong friends of both my parents and me. I recall my father telling a characteristic anecdote about the passionately academic Haskins. When he was sending my father off to Paris to work on his doctoral dissertation, it suddenly occurred to Haskins to say "now Gleason—while you're there, don't spend all your time in the archives! Take some time off; get to know the people a little." Then he suddenly felt he had gone too far. He paused for a moment uncertainly and then smiled broadly as he found the formulation he was searching for. "Take Christmas Day off!"

My father was a graduate student and instructor just at the time Harvard College was building its new residential "houses", and what is today our dining room table was rescued by my father from Memorial Hall, where the whole university used to enjoy collective dining facilities before the early 1930s. Most of the more advanced graduate students and instructors were subsequently assigned to one of these new residential units as "tutors". James Phinney Baxter III, later President of Williams College, was Master of Adams House at the time my father was on the tutorial staff there, and was something of a name-dropper. A few years later, when we were living in Washington D.C., Baxter came to our house for dinner. After listening for awhile to his virtual monologue about his influential contacts in the capital, I turned to my father and said admiringly, "Daddy, Mr. Baxter knows everybody!" My parents kept their faces straight but appreciated my ingenuous response. I must have been six or so at the time.

Shortly after my birth, however, Baxter took the year off and the Professor of Classical Greek Philosophy, Raphael Demos, became Acting Master of Adams House and my father Acting Senior Tutor, a position with both administrative and scholarly responsibilities. With considerable nervousness, my parents undertook, as was expected, to give a tea once a week for undergraduate and graduate members of the house. Student attendance was irregular, but the brilliant senior, Arthur Schlesinger, Jr. and his fiancée came faithfully every week, something my father remembered with gratitude for the rest of his life, even though he considered "young Arthur" too pugnacious and dogmatic a liberal, a doghouse in which I was also to find myself a good deal later.

My father's liberalism was tempered by his respect for tradition, as well as his upward mobility within traditional structures, while Arthur Jr., born into the Harvard establishment (Arthur Sr. was a distinguished member of the History Department), felt no qualms about criticizing the authorities and their institutions. His spirited liberalism gave him a place a few years later in the prominent comic strip, *Li'l Abner*, drawn by Al Capp, then a New Deal liberal. Capp was more famous for creating the Shmoos, symbols of welfare state liberalism—vulnerable, defenseless creatures, dying to be eaten by people who needed them: material emblems of the welfare state, a sardonic paean to Roosevelt's domestic policies. Arthur himself appeared as a small, bespectacled, professorial type. Young Arthur and another moderately left professor, H. Stuart Hughes, whose father, Charles Evans Hughes had been a distinguished jurist, both worked with my father in the Office of Strategic Services (OSS) during World War II and my father would often remember their "extreme" liberalism; oddly enough, he seems to have been unaware of Herbert Marcuse, Otto Kirchheimer and Franz Neuman, real radicals and charter members of the "Frankfurt School", who were also at OSS during the Second World War.

In those days, Harvard and Radcliffe students were taught separately, at least in large-enrollment courses, and as an instructor and assistant professor my father taught the basic European History survey at Radcliffe. His comrade-in-arms was Crane Brinton, well known subsequently for a classic account of the French Jacobins, as well as a famous study of the rise and fall of revolutions, based not on Marx but on Italian elite theory as popularized by Vilfredo Pareto and Gaetano Mosca. My father liked and admired Brinton, and very much envied Brinton's self-confidence and apparently casual attitude toward his lectures. As my father was toiling away, agonizing about exactly how to put some difficult point, he would hear Brinton chuckling away in his adjoining office, and occasionally laughing out loud, as he polished some bon mot or other. A brilliant writer, Brinton worked more on style than on research. My father became a very good public speaker, but never lost a certain anxiety about proper preparation, something I inherited from him.

Gleasons had been around Massachusetts for a long time but had never amounted to much, with the exception of Roswell Gleason, a well-known Boston area pewter maker of the mid-late nineteenth century, and Herbert Wendell Gleason, whose fine black-and-white photographs accompanied fancy editions of Thoreau's works in the first two decades of the twentieth. The first Thomas Gleason, born in Northamptonshire in 1607, arrived in the Massachusetts Bay Colony in the 1640s. Nothing of his occupation or profession is known, but the Gleason family history notes tersely that he was apparently of an "arbitrary disposition." It was not long before he revealed the ill temper and bad judgment that would occasionally flare up in later generations as well, becoming terminally enmeshed in a major lawsuit with Governor Winthrop and the town of Charlestown over a large tract of land on the west side of "Mysticke Pond". "All of [his] resources were swallowed up in the litigation and the case was unsettled when he died in 1686," the Gleason Genealogy commented somberly.[2]

To jump ahead several generations, I never knew my grandfather Gleason, the first Sarell Everett Gleason.[3] Born about 1880, he died in the spring of 1938, just a few months before I was born. My father was extremely reticent about him, leading to subsequent family speculation that he had done something criminal or perhaps been a suicide. All my father would say was that he died in a hotel room somewhere in Florida. But his death certificate indicates that he died of a cerebral arteriosclerosis. He was buried in Bay Pines National Cemetery in Bay Pines, Florida, where records indicate that he was a navy quartermaster in the First World War. One story, perhaps apocryphal, had attached itself to him. He was supposed

[2]John Barber White, *Genealogy of the Descendants of Thomas Gleason of Watertown, Mass.*, Press of the Nicholas Print, Haverhill. MA, 1909, p. 20.

[3]My father was actually Sarell Everett Gleason, Jr., but he never used the Jr., for some reason.

to have owned a substantial bloc of Coca-Cola shares, when this bestselling beverage-of-the-future was still a patent medicine. Not believing in the future of newfangled things called soft drinks, he apparently sold his shares sometime around 1900, about the time that cocaine disappeared from Coca Cola. Linking the first Thomas Gleason's failure with my grandfather's, I would be seized by the counter-factual fantasy, from time to time, of living in a mansion in West Cambridge or Watertown—much of which had been passed down to me from my litigious forebear—and playing a major role in American corporate capitalism as one of the influential stockholders in the Coca Cola Bottling Company. I was particularly susceptible to this fantasy when I found myself grading fifty final exams on the history of the Soviet Union. Whether or not my grandfather Gleason's failure to grasp the brass ring was as dramatic as this anecdote suggests, he was definitely not a success in business and my grandmother divorced him some time prior to the First World War. My father was really brought up by Henry C. Baxter, a good-natured Chicagoan in the textile business, who became my grandmother's second husband.

Baxter was a rough and ready type, with a thoroughly business attitude toward the world, quite different from that of my genteel parents. They, for example, were continually upset and scandalized by my bad behavior at various schools that I attended early on. Although my grades were good, I scored poorly in what was called "deportment". I was often in fights. My attention wandered in class. I was rude to the teachers, showing them almost no deference—a problem that dogged me in various arenas for a long time. Most revealing of all, I couldn't keep my mouth shut. I "answered back" when rebuked. By the age of ten, I was doing a little bit better. "Tommy sometimes admits that he is not entirely correct in his statements," ran one report card, whose author was clearly attempting to put the best possible face on a bad situation. My parents lectured me and tried to shame me into better behavior. But my "Grandpa" Baxter just winked at my difficulties. "Just keep gettin' those A's," he would whisper, slipping me a silver dollar after my report card had been condemned by my parents.

His language and that of his wife, my grandmother, was much cruder than that of my parents. They were prone to mild anti-Semitism and anti-Catholicism, especially my grandmother. When we lived in Cambridge, she was amazed that my parents would simply let me go out to play on a Saturday or Sunday afternoon. "Why Everett," my grandmother would remonstrate, "Tommy might play with a little Catholic boy." Despite my grandmother's disapproval of the Irish, she was an outspoken admirer of the two prominent Hoovers of her era, Herbert and J. Edgar, frequently citing the conservative economics of the one and the anti-communism of the other. My parents were embarrassed by her casual bigotry, but if they ever replied to remarks like this, I was not aware of it. They gently indicated to me that I didn't need to worry about anything like that.

There is some evidence that my bad behavior began early on. When my sister Ellen was born just after my third birthday, I failed to welcome her enthusiastically and our sibling rivalry was off and running. Years later, when I met Sheila Gilmore, married to Professor Myron Gilmore, who taught Renaissance History at Harvard during these years, she told me in detail about how my mother would have to leave dinner parties because the baby sitter couldn't cope with my tantrums. Locking me in some sparsely furnished room until I came to my senses would clearly have been Mrs. Gilmore's answer. No doubt she was right, but my mother was soft-hearted (or perhaps embarrassed) and often went home from the party to calm me down. "We never thought you'd amount to anything," Mrs. Gilmore observed crisply, to conclude the conversation. She was the daughter of the distinguished English philosopher, Alfred North Whitehead, and not accustomed to pulling any punches. Other of my parents' contemporaries were less outspoken, but I was clearly regarded as a difficult and unpromising little boy. In retrospect I think that my terror at being left alone by my

Mary Eleanor Gleason with daughter Ellen, age six months, 1942

mother was connected to a fear of being abandoned which became a deep part of my psyche very early.

Why did I act up? As nearly as I can recall, when life didn't go well, or when impulses were thwarted, I felt myself to be an innocent victim, thus allowing me to revenge myself on whomever was available. Sometimes my friends, often my parents, most often of all my little sister. Of what or whom I was originally a victim is an interesting question, to which I have no real answer. An old-fashioned Freudian would surely guess that my sister's arrival precipitated matters. I must have been fighting to regain status with my mother in the wake of this disturbing event. Over time, however, as my behavior was slow to improve, the answer became, in part, my father's anger and the two of us became caught in a rather troubled relationship involving rebellion, defiance and my growing sense of injustice, which I was very slow to get under control. But my mother's love, so frequently on display, also suggested to me that I didn't

Tom, age four, 1942

need to observe the rules, which were fundamentally for others. As so many small boys have, I challenged my father, with my mother's love the prize.

My mother spoiled her children, especially me, and not only by going home from parties when I was throwing a furious tantrum. She had a sweet humor and was a most resourceful parent. She had the wonderful habit of buying presents for her children all the year round and holding them in reserve for when they were needed. The result was that when I or my sister was sick, there was always something hidden for us on the closet shelf: a new Oz book, or something by Edith Nesbit, or Hans Christian Andersen. Or perhaps *The Iliad for Boys and Girls.* Later on she read her children (separately) *Tom Sawyer* and *Huckleberry Finn*, both probably before we were ready for them, just because she couldn't wait to have us love them as she did. She closely monitored what we read, not for purposes of censorship, but in order to be sure that she worked in all of her favorites and whatever she could discover of a more recent vintage of which she—with her Victorian-Edwardian taste—approved.

It took me a long time to realize it, but I inherited a good deal of that taste, as well as the inclination to spoil children and students. To her I owe my love of romantic adventure stories: Robert Louis Stevenson's *Black Arrow*; Rudyard Kipling's stories; Conan Doyle's *Sherlock Holmes*, of course, but also his historical novels like *The White Company*; John Buchan's thrillers; G.K. Chesterton's Father Brown stories and the farcical tales of Jeeves, Bertie Wooster and Aunt Agatha.

All of this high-minded search for adventure (excluding Jeeves and Bertie Wooster, of course) deeply messed up my credentials as either a radical or a modernist, and I've never quite recovered. I have much too great an affection for Victorian and Edwardian England, at least in imaginative form. Mine was really a late Victorian childhood, a peculiar base for a life in my own time. My parents, from as early as I can remember, seemed archaic figures, and later on I was always afraid of being out-of-it. Their clothes were always formal and old-fashioned, and their slang likewise seemed from at least a generation back. "So unlike our own dear queen," my father would exclaim at some lapse in taste or modern turn of phrase. My friends, if present, would stop and stare, and I would cringe.

My boyhood frame of reference was more Anglo than American, and my family frame of reference closer to the 1920s than the 1940s and 1950s, which contributed to my confusion about who I was. My parents' extreme gentility set them apart from many of their contemporaries. This had the effect of directing my subsequent adolescent rebellion not only against the constraints of the 1950s, but in particular against their Victorianism. When consummated, this rebellion would bring me—not to the frontiers of my own generation but finally into my parents' generation, from which they had regressed. My emotions were always mixed about how to react to the fact that my parents seemed to me, and others, to properly belong to some earlier time. I was often embarrassed, but also more at home with formality than I realized until late in life. My efforts to become a laid-back lefty were always confused and inhibited by my uncertain sense of what age I belonged to and by what standards I should measure myself.

At the deepest level, my tastes were formed by folk and fairy tales, most especially those of English romanticism. John Ruskin, the Scottish visionary George MacDonald, and William Morris were writers whom I took in along with my mother's milk and have never given up reading. In line with the folk- and fairy tale tradition, I rejected the two successful elder brothers and identified with the youngest brother, who disappointed everyone and stayed at home until the time came to perform the heroic deed. I was much more comfortable in the fourteenth-century England of Conan Doyle's *White Company* than in the schools to which I was sent as a child, and could hardly wait to get back from school to return to a world that suited me better. J.R.R. Tolkien's *The Hobbit*, was a particular passion, followed of course by *The Lord of the Rings*. I thought that life was a quest, but didn't know how to establish that quest in my bourgeois life, other than by attaching myself to a hundred literary quests. There was something quixotic about my dilemmas.

When later I tried to overlay this unstable foundation with literary and artistic modernism, I created an even more peculiar Rube Goldberg structure, full of rickety conveyor belts and distorting mirrors. So my tastes and inclinations always remained fragmented and eclectic, if not actually incoherent, and childhood-centered. Growing up was hard. As the fairy tale authority Jack Zipes wrote in 1987:

> The [Victorian] fairy tale itself exhibited possibilities for the young to transform themselves and society into those Arcadian dreams conceived in childhood that the writers did not want to leave behind them. The artwork of the fairy tale assumed a religious quality in its apparent denial of the material world.[4]

[4] Jack Zipes, *Victorian Fairy Tales*, Methuen, New York and London, 1987, p. xxvii.

Cyril Connolly put it more simply when he wrote that "it was the English disease 'to go through life always looking back to childhood'".[5] No doubt it was a paradox: to be reluctant to leave a childhood in which I imagined myself the hero of fantasy narratives but was in actuality so often a negative minor figure.

My mother was also ingenious about games, largely word games, to be sure, but also something we called "head, body and legs," in which you folded over a piece of drawing paper and drew one of the three vertical segments of various human figures, without knowing from which figure the other two parts were drawn. There were hours of amusement in this. She would also give us a big word like "transcendentally," "panegyrical" or "dromedary" and we would compete to see how many little words we could make out of the available letters. Like her father and brother, she loved anything involving anagrams, palindromes, codes, or word play of any kind. She loved making things, was reluctant to buy them. When we did show-and-tell at school, most of my classmates would bring something bought in a store, but my mother insisted, almost invariably, that we make something. What I brought in always seemed to me childishly amateur and wholly inadequate. It took me a long time to understand where she was coming from.

My parents married late. My father was thirty-two and my mother was thirty-five, a very advanced age for marriage in the 1930s, especially for a woman. Interestingly, I never heard any tales of courtship, but clearly the Harvard History Department was a central arena. Until her marriage my mother had lived with her parents at Sparks Street and been a portrait painter with a studio in Harvard Square; she had also taught art at a young ladies' school of some kind in Florence for a time. I remember visits to her former studio in Brattle Square. On one such occasion I saw a tall man in a

[5] Cyril Connolly, quoted in Martin Green, *Children of the Sun*, New York, Basic Books, 1976, p. 131. Baudelaire, on the other hand, said that "genius is no more than childhood recaptured at will." Cf. Richard Wolin, "A Metaphysical Materialist," *The Nation*, Vol. 283, No. 12 (October 16, 2006), p. 31.

white suit, with a long white beard on the sidewalk in the center of Harvard Square. Waving his white cane, he plunged into the traffic, seemingly without looking, as the oncoming cars screeched to a halt. "Always remember you saw him," my mother said, displaying my family's characteristic reverence for all things Harvard. "That is George Lyman Kittredge." Kittredge was one of the lions of the English Department in the early part of the twentieth century. Since he died in the summer of 1941, my sighting must have been just before his death, when I was three. Kittredge was the student of Francis J. Child, the great collector of ballads, whose course he took over at Child's retirement. This gave rise to a turn of the century witticism later told to me by my friend Adam Ulam. A Radcliffe student is supposed to have written to her parents to tell them: "last semester I was under Kittredge, this semester I am with Child."

Without a real original artistic style of her own, my mother, known to her friends as Kitty, drew very well and could produce caricatures, cartoons, and her own versions of classic styles with great facility. To watch a drawing take shape under her hand was a marvel to me, a first dim inkling of the pleasures of making something and a sense of the miraculous about it. After her marriage she gave up her portrait career to devote herself to her children, something that with hindsight I regretted and for which I no doubt blamed my father to some degree. She also wrote stories for my sister and me, some of them quite ambitious fairy tales, set in contemporary America, but with surprising entrances into magical kingdoms, not unlike those in the subsequent Narnia stories of C.S. Lewis, though without religious dogmatism or pedagogical purpose. She knew the classic canon of fairy tales remarkably well, and loved Victorian imitations, like Ruskin's *King of the Golden River* and comic narratives like Thackeray's *Rose and the Ring*. When my children were young and my mother much enfeebled due to a series of strokes, she still made delightful alphabet books for them in the style of Edward Lear, whom she also loved, both as a wistful poet and as an eccentric but brilliant draftsman. Charming as they were, however, they seemed to belong to some world long past, which my children found hard to approach.

But not everything suffered from mystical archaism. A signature book in our household was Kenneth Grahame's *The Wind in the Willows*, which my mother would sometimes read aloud just to calm me down. "Am I more like Mole or Toad," Anne Fadiman asked herself at age six.[6] I also wanted badly at that age to be the child-like but noble Mole, but feared correctly that I was the insecure and boastful Toad (although at this point I am an Old Mole).

My mother had the first of her strokes in 1947, when she was only forty-five, and some element of joy and stability was subtracted from our household. My father became permanently concerned about her health and more disposed to be severe about my acting up, which he felt further endangered her. He became more brittle and prone to anger—a punishing bourgeois gentleman, as I later learned to conceive of him. He had a great deal of charm and wit, but when it was turned my way it seemed laced with mockery and a severity, which he denied indignantly when I accused him of it. I knew from early on that I didn't want to be like him, so I looked around for other ideals—identities, as we would say today.

I have never been quite able to understand my father's transition from his parents' agreeable but philistine manners to the formal and Victorian liberal gentleman that I knew. Certainly the locus of the transition was Harvard. My best guess is that my father found the sartorial formality, the erudite and somewhat archaic range of reference and the amour propre of the Harvard faculty of that day very much worth emulating. Some of this was connected to his marriage to a professor's daughter; some almost certainly happened when he roomed with subsequent Professor Mason Hammond, who taught Roman history at Harvard for many decades and was the epitome of the Boston Brahmin. Anglophilia was rampant in those circles.

[6]Anne Fadiman, *Rereadings*, New York, Farrar, Strauss and Giroux, 2006, p. xv.

As I grew older I gradually became conscious of the quite striking cultural differences between my parents and my grandparents on the Baxter-Gleason side, but it was a long time before it dawned on me that my father had deliberately assumed an upper-class identity that was far from native to him. Something of the sort must also have been true of my grandfather Abbott, whose large house and extreme social conservatism were far from the Indiana drugstore of his childhood. Academia was surely a ladder of social mobility, among other things, for these professors. Their pride in the status they had gained disposed them to various kinds of conservatism.

My maternal grandfather, Wilbur Cortez Holliday Abbott, was by all reports a hard man, although I have no personal recollection of anything like that. He was born into a poor family in Kokomo, Indiana, in 1870 and put himself through Wabash College, by selling his features, poems and stories to small-town Indiana newspapers. He was the big man on campus as an undergraduate, and later on in his career would occasionally send back essays to local publications on congenial subjects like the differences between Oxford and Cambridge slang, which no doubt impressed a later generation of Wabash students. Abbott appears to have entered college late because he went blind for several years when he was in his teens; only when he had recovered his sight could he continue his education. This peculiar bout of blindness appeared to his son and daughter to have been psychosomatic.

His life was certainly full of conflict. His father, whose namesake I was to have been, owned a small drugstore in Noblesville, Indiana, and never forgave his son for going off to college instead of taking over the store.In the teeth of his father's unrelenting objections, Abbott excelled at Wabash and then went to Cornell to do graduate work in English. There he was persuaded to change his field to History and go to Oxford for two years, where he took his B. Litt. and developed a lifelong interest in seventeenth-century England.

Wilbur C.H. "Baba" Abbott, c. 1926

His father died while Abbott was at Cornell, whereupon he sold the Noblesville drugstore and took upon himself the full support of his invalid, chronically querulous and perhaps drug-addicted mother, Eleanor Laura Holliday, even bringing her to Oxford with him.

His closest friend at Oxford was the conservative political theorist Ernest Barker, whom I met later in England.[7] "He's a pretty boy, Mary Eleanor," Barker said to my mother, eying me critically when we met for the first time in 1956, "but not as pretty as my grandson." That was Nicholas Barker, whom I encountered many years later in Providence, over the dinner table at the house of my friends, Becky

[7] Barker was one of the two principal models for the ubiquitous and manipulative Oxford don, Professor Sillery, in Anthony Powell's novel sequence. See Julian Anderson and Keith Marshall, "Models for Characters in Anthony Powell's A Dance to the Music of Time", <anthonypowell.org.uk/dancewho.htm-37k>.

and Tim More. Neither of us was as pretty by then as we may once have been. Ernest Barker was generous to Abbott in his memoirs:

> [Abbott] had a dry American humour, mixed with the gravity of a senior, the experience of a traveler and the devotion of a researcher. He associated readily with us undergraduates, and took a lively interest in our ways of thought and fashions of speech. He was a good host, who would entertain us sumptuously (at any rate to my thinking) in Buol's restaurant; he could tell us of Indiana and Cornell University: He could talk of the reign of Charles II as if he were living in good King Charles'golden days. In his own field of history, he brought me into touch with a higher scholarship, and I do not think it is extravagant, so far as my own experience is concerned, to say of him that he brought 'owls to Athens' and imported into Oxford a new sort of study of history.[8]

An early example, perhaps, of those provincial, ambitious Americans invading the English universities, more driven by research interests than their self-assured British counterparts, although Barker was anything but unproductive!

Abbott returned from Europe with almost no money and had to borrow train fare to get himself and his mother to Ann Arbor, Michigan, for his first academic position, pausing in Indiana to marry his sweetheart, Margaret Ellen Smith, to whom he had long been engaged. He held a series of posts over the next twenty years, ending at Harvard, where he was one of the most actively conservative professors during the 1930s. Along with Paul Elmer More and Irving Babbitt he took pride in being a scourge of all social radicalism. Over the course of his long career, from Michigan and Kansas to Harvard, Abbott became more and more an Eminent Victorian—an American version of the unreconstructed conservatives that Lytton Strachey lampooned. His style became more and more portentous and prophetic of civilization's decline as his career developed. In his numerous book reviews, he took angry and foreboding

[8] Ernest Barker, *Age and Youth*, Oxford University Press, London and New York, 1953, pp. 324-325.

note of the rise of radicalism in Europe and the United States and repeatedly expressed his fear that the United States might follow the increasing number of European states into dictatorship. A passionate Anglophile, he was wrathful about German nationalism, but reserved his most Cassandra-like lamentations for Marxism and as a historian paid close attention to the rise of Marxist historiography. He had a special interest in the French Revolution, the radicalism of whose historiography both repelled and fascinated him. He particularly detested the Marxist French historian Albert Mathiez, whose biography of Robespierre produced a conservative (but far from unintelligent) jeremiad from Abbott which began:

> The development of proletarianism, the emphasis on the "common man"—on the mass, rather than on the individual; the voice of God speaking through the actions of the mob; the spread of the idea that revolution is a natural political process rather than an exceptional phenomenon; the greater familiarity with its once sinister countenance, have long indicated that the emergence of its prophets into the rather favorable light of history was at hand. Like vice, it was once "a creature of such dreadful mien, that to be hated need but to be seen."[9]

Alas for the present age [the 1920s], in which "embrace" of terror replaced our natural abhorrence of it. In the future, he concluded, we shall probably fall lower still, though he found that "hardly conceivable."

Despite his severity, however, in a family setting he never lost his taste for the homespun Midwestern humor of his childhood. He and my mother, his daughter, loved James Whitcomb Riley, and she read us "Little Orphan Annie" and "Raggedy Man" over and over again when we were little. His ne'er do well cousin, Robert Cortes Holliday, chronically short of money, produced biographies of family friends, Booth Tarkington and Joyce Kilmer, though he too left the Midwest and passed himself off as a "man about town" in New

[9] W.C. Abbott, "Hail the Terrorists," *The Saturday Review of Literature*, January 16, 1929, pp. 679-680.

York. "Cousin Robert" as he was invariably known, died penniless, leaving only a collection of canes and walking sticks, a number of which somehow came down to me.

Abbott could also be quite intimidating to his students, even if they displayed no leftist tendencies. When I went to teach at Brown University in September, 1968, I met William Church, the distinguished historian of sixteenth- and seventeenth-century France, who had been a graduate student at Harvard in the 1930s. Church was not, as far as I could see, a timid or fearful man, but he remembered old Abbott with terror. "I was afraid to take your grandfather's seminar," he told me, his eyes distending slightly at the memory. "I avoided him." Certainly no one was good enough to marry Abbott's two children. Both their spouses had vivid and unpleasant memories of their failure to satisfy his high standards for in-laws.

But Abbott did have a sense of humor, which could appear almost like a softer side at times. He had a student, a sweet but timid young man, of considerable wealth inherited from his mill-owning family in Worcester, Massachusetts. In his eleven years in graduate school, L. James Knowles had never found the courage to take his preliminary exams. My grandfather became exasperated, as he liked Jimmy Knowles and believed that he knew more about the mores of upper-class Georgian England than anyone else he knew, professor or student. (In those days very few professors of European history—a more conservative field than American history—knew or cared much about how the working class lived. Certainly my grandfather didn't.)

But years passed and still timorous Jimmy Knowles showed no sign of being "ready" to take his preliminary examinations, the ordeal that had to precede the writing of the doctoral dissertation. Exasperated at Knowles' insecurity, my grandfather, according to family lore, decided to give him his examinations in such a way that he would not know he was taking them. So he threw a big cocktail party at Sparks Street; among the guests were the three professors —Wilbur K. "Kitch" Jordan, Elliot Perkins, David Owen and Abbott himself—who were to examine Jimmy Knowles for approximately half an hour each.[10] With a glass in his hand, among the press of the guests, Jimmy at first did not notice that he seemed to be having long and rather academic conversations with several of his professors. He had apparently passed one field and was well into the second before he noticed what was going on. He fled immediately and never did take his exams, eventually settling for the life of a gentleman farmer. In later years, he became exceptionally fond of my parents and was a familiar figure at our house. I vividly recall his enormous figure with his back to our fireplace, always with a glass in his hand. He gave my sister and me spectacular Christmas presents, of quite a different kind from the usual gifts we received. One I remember was a replica of Queen Elizabeth's coronation coach, with more than a hundred soldiers from various regiments, as well as courtiers, coachmen and religious dignitaries. I was allowed to play with this precious object only under close supervision. At some point when I was older it was given to a museum. He gave my sister a beautiful Georgian English desk, among other things.

My grandfather's best student was Jack Hexter, who received his Ph.D. on the eve of the Second World War and taught for many years at Yale and Washington University in St. Louis. Hexter was a poor Jewish kid from Memphis, Tennessee; my grandfather, originally a poor kid himself, was all too aware by this time of the advantages of material prosperity and social position. One day, as Hexter was walking through Harvard Yard, Abbott hailed him. "Look here, Hexter," he said. "You're the best student I've ever had." "Or ever will have," he might have added. "But what kind of a first name is 'Jack' for a serious scholar? Now look here, Hexter. My full name is Wilbur Cortez Holliday Abbott, but I've never used the Holliday—it's one name too many. I'm happy to give it to you. Then you can become J. Holliday Hexter, which will be a proper name for a successful historian. No more 'Jack'."

[10] This anecdote is probably apocryphal, but relevant here if only as an aspect of family lore.

Hexter was touched, as he later told me, but also insulted. American Academia before World War II was a snobbish place where Jews were just beginning to find a niche, especially if they were not from established families: Morgenthaus or Strauses. Hexter ended by half accepting my grandfather's offer. He did not become "J. Holliday Hexter" (small wonder), but he did add the letter H to his name, and his published work all appeared over the name J.H. Hexter. He remained Jack to his friends.

Years later, when Brown University was giving Hexter an honorary degree, its then president, Barnaby Keeney, an old friend of Hexter's, began to tell this story on a dais in front of the commencement crowd. Hexter leaned over toward Keeney and hissed, "Barney you bastard, shut up"! Unfortunately Hexter's mike was on, so the hiss came out a bellow, and echoed across the commencement site on the Brown Green, where thousands of people were momentarily diverted from the solemnities.

My grandfather never really felt at home in the age of the automobile, and although he did drive for a few years his children had to take the keys away at some point. I have a memory about this episode, but I have the feeling I may have associated old Abbott with an urban legend, related either by my mother or my uncle. "If you get into trouble on the highway," he was supposed to have said, "just give the car its head, and it will see you through." I'd like to believe he said this but it doesn't quite compute for this energetic activist who was devoted to tools, some of them powered by electricity.

Toward the end of his life, Professor Abbott was photographed in dark suits, with a watch chain and fob across his considerable girth. But I have a photograph of him at about age forty-five, during the First World War. He is formally dressed, but leaning forward eagerly and aggressively with a mildly ferocious expression on his face. Was he looking for Randolph Bourne, Louise Bryant or some other dangerous "red"—or just thinking about getting his manuscript to the publisher and getting on in the world? Family correspondence gives intimations of unfinished and unpublished

Grandmother "Mimi" Abbott, c. 1900

books of detective fiction, contemporary literature, economics and public affairs. Like his grandson he aspired to be a writer, as well as a historian.[11]

My visits to Sparks Street, which increasingly seemed like a visit to a museum of antiquities, ended in 1947, when both of my grandparents died, my grandfather of leukemia, my grandmother of the last in a series of strokes a few months later. Unfortunately, my favorite song of that year, learned at school, was an old (1876)

[11] Abbott was of course appalled by anything he regarded as appeasement of the forces of disorder in the world. Here is part of a Kipling parody he wrote

chestnut called "My Grandfather's Clock," and my mother was deathly afraid that I would sing the climactic lines "and the clock stopped, never to run again, when the old man died" to my dying grandfather.

After his death in February, 74 Sparks Street became a quiet and sad place where all of a sudden I hated to go. My grandmother now sat alone in the second-floor sitting room where we had so often visited both of them and stared out the window toward Sparks Street. Instead of reading me the Oz books in her sweet Midwestern voice, as she had done ever since I could remember, she just wept and held me in her arms, repeating over and over again, "Oh Tommy, I love you so." With the lack of empathy characteristic of a nine-year-old boy I only wanted to escape from her sorrow, which I totally failed to comprehend, although I obscurely felt that something awful had happened. That same year, my mother had her first stroke.

As sometimes happened among the Abbotts, my grandmother was a far more gentle and empathetic person than her husband and no doubt humanized him somewhat during his long climb to academic success, but remained in the shadows. She was a very beautiful woman in her youth. The wedding photograph I have of her on my bedroom wall reveals her shyness, sweetness, a certain resolution in the tilt of her chin, and her extraordinarily tiny waist.

on the eve of the Second World War. The occasion was a strike by young women students at a Burmese university.

By the old Moulmein pagoda
Lookin' eastward to the sea
There's a Burma girl a sittin'
For her ideology.
An' her mind don't run to kissin'
An' her glances seem to say
"Watch your step you British bobby
On the road to Mandalay."

'Er petticoat is yaller,
But her views are bally pink,
An I'd take a lot o' pleasure,
Could I land 'er in the clink.
For this blinkin' world is changin'
Where the spicy breezes sound,
And nothin's what it useter be
When Rudyard was around.

It was published, but I don't know where, because the only source I have is a yellowing newspaper clipping in an old manila envelope...

Tom Gleason with his parents, 1945

Wartime Washington

Harvard kept on offering my father one-year appointments and no tenure, so just before I was born he accepted a tenured position as an associate professor at Amherst College, then as now small and top-of-the-line, but more traditional in those days and definitely WASPier. We moved to western Massachusetts in September, just in time for the first semester of the academic year 1938-39 and to experience the full fury of the famous hurricane of that fall. We spent three happy years at 72 Woodside Avenue, a small house belonging to Amherst, lived in still by Amherst faculty. There I learned to sing "Lord Geoffrey Amherst was a soldier of the King and he came from across the sea." But of course I learned Harvard songs as well. Several places in "Fair Harvard" were mysterious to me. I heard the first line as a peculiar royalist appeal: "Fair Harvard, thy sons to thy jubilee throne, and with blessings surrender the oar." What sort of ceremony was this surrender of the oar at (or to?) the jubilee throne? I simply accepted this as some adult thing that didn't concern me. It was many years before I discovered my mistake.[1]

My first complete sentence, however, was "I am an Amherst College man." Had it not been for the Second World War, I might have grown up in this beautiful small college town. Amherst gave my father an associate professorship, but they did not raise his salary. He continued to get the same $4,500 per year that he received

[1] "Fair Harvard thy sons to thy jubilee throng
And with blessings surrender thee o'er."

in his last year of teaching at Harvard. But in those days this salary enabled our young faculty family to hire a cook and someone to take care of raucous Baby Tommy.

From our new base in Amherst we commuted to Cambridge three or four times a year to see my grandparents at Sparks Street. We had a sweet-natured Norwegian elkhound named Duna, short for the "Iduna" of Norse mythology. (Her brother, Loki, named for the most mischievous of the Norse gods, was killed by a passing car when still a puppy.) Duna lacked aggressive impulses almost entirely. When a mouse invaded the pantry just off the kitchen, my mother locked Duna in and hoped that she would take care of the intruder somehow. She did. When my mother cautiously opened the door several hours later, Duna was asleep on the floor and there was no sign of either the mouse or an epic battle. When Duna got up and waddled out the door, wagging her tale, the essence of the drama was revealed. She had gone to sleep on the mouse and squashed it flat.

In those early days, we took Massachusetts Route 2 from Amherst to Cambridge, a long drive for a little boy and a dog, both prone to carsickness. By the time our 1936 Packard had reached the neighboring town of Athol, one or the other of us, and most of the time both, had thrown up, usually out the window, but not always. The Packard stank, and the boy and his dog made it worse.

During those early years my growing inclination to disobedience led to an episode that I was lucky to survive. I was often taken for walks in the nearby Tuckerman Trail Bird Sanctuary, something like a mile from our house, a wild garden with trails and a pond. I was of course absolutely forbidden to go by myself, a prohibition which I characteristically defied at the age of four on a cold day in February. I knew very well how to get to the pond and immediately walked right out on the ice. I fell in, but managed to drag myself out and get home in a dripping, freezing snowsuit. I have no memory of what was a terrifying episode to my parents. All they knew is that I turned up, weeping icy tears, at our front door on Woodside Avenue.

"Oh mummy," I wailed as my astonished mother opened the door, "I'm so vewy misewable." But alive. At the time, I had no idea of how to swim, and was wearing a very heavy pair of galoshes in addition to the snowsuit. I have a mental picture of the shore, seen from somewhere out in the middle of the pond, but almost certainly it is a later reconstruction.

I was a brazen liar. When caught stealing cookies, I would deny what I had done even when caught red-handed and stick to my lies indefinitely. I remember distinctly how outraged I felt at having to tell the truth. It often took hours, or even days, for my mother to shame me into a confession. With all of my argumentativeness, lying and defiant behavior, my mother was forced to become something of a local specialist on discipline. When the professor's wife who lived across the street complained that her hand got sore spanking her daughter, my mother recommended a hairbrush as the implement of choice. But the professor's wife seems to have used the wrong side of the hairbrush, complaining later to my mother that her daughter's bottom was now "full of holes."

The Amherst College History Department was plagued by factions, as many History Departments have been over the years. My parents learned of this when Mrs. Lawrence Packard, the wife of one of the faction leaders (we were much engaged with a variety of Packards in those days), approached my mother in the checkout line at the local grocery store and said ominously, "What a pity you and your husband are making the wrong friends." This forthright comment referred to the fact that my parents had almost immediately upon arrival become friendly with a gregarious and fun-loving professor of European history named Dwight Salmon (I called him "Sandman"), not realizing that he was in the midst of a long feud with the Packards, who represented the publishing rather than the teaching faction in the department. Wives were of course expected to feud along with their husbands. (Female faculty members were extremely scarce in those days. Professor Rose Oliver, who came on board in the 1960s, seems to have been the first tenured woman

Mary Eleanor "Kitty" Gleason, age forty-one, 1943

at Amherst.) My father was not disposed to mend his ways, but his diplomatic skills—remarkable, when he chose to call upon them—helped him with the publishing faction, as did the appearance of his Ph.D. dissertation as a monograph with Harvard University Press. Whatever role he might ultimately have taken on in the dispute was interrupted by the outbreak of the Second World War and his enlistment in the army.

At Amherst, I continued my early interest in history. On the landing of their front stairs the Salmons had a bust of Julius Caesar, for whom I had the same formalistic respect as I did for the seven Cromwells in Cambridge. I called him "Dodus" Caesar, and made sure to pay my respects when we went to the Salmons, as we often did.

Pearl Harbor meant the end of my father's bucolic career as a small-town history professor. Upon enlisting in the Army, he became a "consultant" with the Army Air Force in 1942 and moved to Washington in January, 1943, while my mother, sister and I remained temporarily in Amherst. What this consulting entailed never became known to my mother or me. The three of us spent the summer of 1943 at Spring Farm, some two hours away in Connecticut. My father was able to get away from Washington only for brief visits; our family was finally reunited that fall in Washington, where we remained for three years.

The first nine months of 1943 were lonesome for my mother, who missed her husband enormously. She wrote a touching poem which has survived in her letters. Entitled "To an Absent Husband" it runs:

You live your life abroad, while I
Live your life here, my sweet.
Observe—your life is multiplied
But still is incomplete.
Your two lives do not meet.

Thus all rules arithmetical
Are utterly undone.
What is an axiom to do
If two are less than one?
Besides, where is the fun?

The scores of letters they exchanged reveal her efforts to maintain a marriage and household largely by mail. It wasn't easy. The winter weather was awful, and so was my behavior. Every other meal seems to have resembled a nursery food fight. Both my sister and I were sick all the time. I was also ready to wander away as soon as my mother's back was turned, even for a second, although I did not repeat the Tuckerman Trail Pond episode. The summer brought only a slight improvement. My mother's parents were not well enough to spend much time at the farm, and my aunt and uncle, Charles and Louise Abbott, were now the proprietors of "the big house". My mother was in a complicated situation, in which she lived in some indefinite space between being co-proprietress and guest in her brother and sister-in-law's house, until the Gleason family moved into a house of their own elsewhere on the farm a year later.

To complicate matters further the health and spirits of my grandparents were also beginning to deteriorate. My grandfather was fond of doggerel and he wrote a characteristic piece for his daughter that summer, somewhat in the manner of James Whitcomb Riley:

> Said the big red rooster to the little red hen,
> "You ain't laid an egg in I don't know when."
> Said the little red hen to the big red rooster,
> "You don't come to see me the way you useter."

It sympathetically but intrusively (as was my grandfather's wont) described her situation.

The family's move to Washington in the fall of 1943 came as a great relief to everyone. Academics were flocking to the nation's capital—the older ones into military intelligence, or serving as historians for various branches of the service, or into more active kinds of military involvement. My parents had been hatching plans to share houses with Charles Taylor, the Harvard historian, and also with the Salmons, but in the end all three families were able to afford establishments of their own. During our time in the District of Columbia (1942-45) we lived in three different houses, as many wartime transients did, and I went to three different schools. Being a new kid three years in a row did nothing to stabilize my volatile personality. I recall getting into a fight and getting hit in the head with a child's little metal shovel. As I lay on my bed, with a big bandage on my head, my mother alternately scolded me gently and read *The Wind in the Willows.*

When my mother, my sister and I returned for summers to the Farm we lived first in a small house down the road and after a year moved into the old and original farmhouse, a wonderful early eighteenth-century structure that had been beautifully restored. Charles and Louise Abbott remained in "the big house." Both families needed the extra space, particularly the Abbotts, whose family soon grew to seven. There we spent summers until my parents' permanent return to Washington in 1950, when we sold our stake in the Farm.

Only one of our Washington houses was memorable. That one was situated on a substantial estate called Rosedale, located unexpectedly in the middle of Cleveland Park, about three blocks north of the Washington National Cathedral. It was only a square block in size, but it was a very large square block and the whole thing belonged to the Coonley family, the same one for whom Frank Lloyd Wright had built the Coonley House and the little Coonley Playhouse in Chicago decades earlier. Elizabeth Coonley, later Faulkner, was the little daughter for whom Wright had built the playhouse. She had been my mother's college roommate at Vassar, and they remained lifelong friends. She was known as "Bussie" and she was one of the most devastatingly charming women I ever knew. She was a remarkable combination of deep kindness and practicality, of simultaneous shrewdness and unworldliness, of upper-class tastes and practiced, all-encompassing generosity. She was something of a social lion in Washington, seemingly effortlessly. In the most gracious way in the world she appeared always to do as she pleased, but what she pleased to do was always the right thing. Her mother was a Christian Scientist and Elizabeth Coonley Faulkner was left seriously deaf in her youth because of a case of German measles which was not treated due to her mother's Christian Science beliefs, to whichBussie remained forever after opposed. She was, however, a pious Episcopalian and a devoted churchwoman. Her husband, Waldron Faulkner was an architect who worked in an Art Deco style, primarily on institutional projects in the Washington area: the Lisner Auditorium and the hospital for George Washington University, the dormitories for the National Cathedral School, and the considerably later Providence

Hospital. They were stylish patricians, civic minded and loyal, with a deep talent for friendship.

The Faulkners had built two houses for themselves on the Rosedale estate, virtually out of sight of the older, original building, lived in by the now elderly Mrs. Coonley. These were also in an Art Deco style, with painted brick exteriors, and we lived in one of them for nine months while we were looking for a house, to my parents' intense pleasure, and to mine. The house was far and away the closest thing to a "modern" house that I had yet experienced, though it was a very conservative brand of modernism. When I subsequently became aware of the underlying assumptions of modern architecture I realized that the Faulkner houses were created to reconcile the middle class to modernism, rather than to provide a challenge. In both houses, the ornamentation was sparse; the floors were dark and elegant linoleum. I remember being struck by the trim in the Faulkner house, which was aluminum. Ours was the smaller of the two houses, but it opened onto a small garden, which gave way in turn to the farther reaches of the estate. Rosedale as it existed then is scarcely in evidence today. Some land has been sold off and built on, and the Faulkners' two architect sons built houses next to their parents. Avery and Win were happy to teach me about Mies van der Rohe and Le Corbusier (whom they sometimes called "Corbu") and to explain the greatness of Mies' Barcelona Pavillion for the 1928 World's Fair.

Frank Lloyd Wright was a byword among the Faulkners, not only because architecture was the family profession, but also because of Bussie's familial connection with the great man. As I grew older, the fact that Wright (always referred to by everybody as "Mr. Wright") was a household word in their family began to stimulate me in the direction of modern architecture. I learned from their two boys, Avery and Winthrop, a decade or so older than me, who also became skilled and successful architects.

At thirty-seven my father was too old for combat duty, so he was offered a commission in army intelligence, and later a position

Everett Gleason (left), having "attained his majority", OSS, c. 1945

in the Office of Strategic Studies (OSS), the nerve center of the American intelligence community during the war years. There he became a major, which he and my mother referred to facetiously as "attaining his majority" and ultimately became Chief of the Current Intelligence Staff, under the aegis of the Research and Analysis Branch (known as the "chairborne division" for its numerous deskbound professors), directed by his friend and future collaborator, William L. Langer.[2] In addition, at some point in his wartime service he became involved in a super secret organization called the Joint Intelligence Committee, which produced

[2] Barry Katz, *Foreign Intelligence: Research and Analysis in the Office of Strategic Services, 1942-1945*, Cambridge, MA, 1989, Harvard University Press, quoted in David Engerman, "Know Your Enemy: How America's Soviet Experts Fought the Cold War" (unpublished ms.), p. 11.

intelligence reports for the Joint Chiefs of Staff and other "higher authorities" and seems to have collaborated with a similar organization in Great Britain.[3] Everett Gleason was in fact the representative of the OSS on the JIC. It was family lore that his work with the Joint Chiefs was so secret that he had to take sleeping pills so he wouldn't talk in his sleep and spill the beans—whatever sorts of beans they may precisely have been—to my mother. Whether this was a regular procedure or an occasional practice I have no way of knowing. Their letters from 1943 do indicate that he told her almost nothing about his work, at least in writing. They are almost entirely bound up with domestic details and gossip about family and friends. Both seem to have suffered deeply from the separation, especially my mother. Affectionate sign-offs were lavish and lengthy.

My father appears to have spent most of the remainder of the war in Washington, with, officially at least, only a European trip in the summer of 1945, which entailed consultation with colleagues in British intelligence (and perhaps elsewhere in Europe) about the establishment of a centralized intelligence agency after the war.[4] Of course outsiders never knew for sure where intelligence officers went. He seems to have been very highly regarded by his OSS colleagues. Longtime CIA official Ray Cline told me personally in 1980 or '81 of his admiration for Everett Gleason, and he wrote appreciatively of him in his memoirs.[5] As the war drew toward a close, the

[3] Larry A. Valero, "The American Joint Intelligence Committee and Estimates of the Soviet Union, 1945-1947," *Studies in Intelligence*, No. 9, Summer 2000 (unpaginated). The Joint Chiefs was "still an ad hoc body with no legal sanction for its existence" until after the war. Steven Ross, *American War Plans 1945-1950*, Frank Cass, London, 1996, p. ix.

[4] Thomas Troy, *Donovan and the CIA: A History of the Establishment of the Central Intelligence Agency*, University Publications of America, Frederick, MD, 1981, p. 289.

[5] Cline remembered my father as "an Amherst professor with Harvard training, an extremely able man with a flare for bureaucratic management." Ray S. Cline,

creation of a postwar intelligence agency became the major project of General William ("Wild Bill") Donovan, the head of OSS, and my father was intimately involved in Donovan's lobbying efforts on behalf of what was ultimately to become the CIA.[6] Donovan believed that there should be an essential continuity between his OSS and the future Central Intelligence Agency. My father thoroughly concurred in that judgment, and he was one of the two men who drafted Donovan's memo on the subject to President Roosevelt.[7] My father was given the Legion of Merit by General Donovan at the end of the war, and I have a snapshot of my mother and me standing proudly with him (Wild Bill was mysteriously absent). I'm not sure that I actually remember the occasion—at the Pentagon—or merely remember the many times I saw the photograph. It was surely one of the high points in my father's life. He never ceased to treasure his ties with the intelligence community, and they may well have been broader and deeper than I have ever known. But he was very close-mouthed about them.

Rosedale was a wonderful place for a six-year-old. The garden was extensive, with greenhouses, kitchen and herb gardens and lawns and enormous old trees. Partly because of our family reading habits, I connect the greenhouses and cucumber frames (or what I have imagined to be cucumber frames) with the watercolors of Beatrix Potter and the epic struggle between Peter Rabbit and Mr. MacGregor. I was definitely a Peter Rabbit figure at this point, giving the Mr. MacGregors of the world all they could handle.

The Faulkner's daughter Celia was the girl next door, an older

Secrets, Spies and Scholars, Washington, D.C., Acropolis Books, 1976, p. 55. Cline was also trained in history at Harvard, where he was a member of the Society of Fellows.

[6] Cline, *Secrets, Spies and Scholars*, p. 82.

[7] David F. Rudgers, *Creating the Secret State. The Origins of the Central Intelligence Agency 1943-1947*, University Press of Kansas, p. 21; Cline, *Secrets, Spies and Scholars*, p. 87; Troy, *Donovan*, p. 248.

woman of nine when I was seven. I did everything I could to get myself into expeditions in which she was involved, usually movies or sometimes children's theater. We both loved a Saturday morning radio program called "Let's Pretend", sponsored by Cream of Wheat, a cereal which I deeply disliked and much later discovered was distinctly related to hominy grits. "Let's Pretend" ("what a dorky title", a later generation of children would say) originated in New York—a fabulous place known to me only by reputation—but on one occasion Celia and I set out to visit it, to be present in the studio for our favorite show, which was nothing more than the reading of stories over the air. I can't recall whether we were intercepted between Cleveland Park and Union Station or closer to home, but at this point my love of dangerous adventure, not to speak of my spontaneity, was undiminished.

During our year at Rosedale I was fortunate to have a roommate, my very first. Dwight Salmon, my father's colleague from Amherst, had become a captain in the army, engaged like other of my father's colleagues in writing aspects of the history of the war. Charles Taylor from Harvard was another. Nothing came of plans for the Salmons and the Gleasons to share a house, but he shared one of the twin beds in my room for many months until he and his wife, Irene, found a place of their own. He was man of great humor and good nature, and I was very proud to be sharing quarters with an officer, as I was very much an enlisted man at this stage. I felt my lowly wartime status keenly when I went to have my tonsils out in 1943 at the Walter Reed army hospital, not long after our arrival in Washington. All the war wounded who were recuperating there had red cotton pajamas, standard government issue, to convalesce in. I alone lacked them, being only equipped with devastatingly childish sleepers, doubtless with little feet attached. But my resourceful mother, never in those days at a loss, found me a red courduroy suit, so I could lounge the corridors with the convalescing warriors, unashamed.

One of my deepest fascinations that year was fire and my passion almost led to a conflagration at Rosedale. Along with my friend Chris Clague, who lived a few blocks away, I lit a grass fire at the corner of Newark and 36th Streets and then ran home. From the window of our house, a block away, I saw the blaze begin to spread. Like many another arsonist, I couldn't stay away from the blaze I had started, but when I had approached to watch, I was spotted by the police and seen to flee into our house. A short time later I was brought down from my room to confront the law, in mortal terror. According to my parents, I expected to be given life in prison, but in the event was let off with a reprimand.

Even this episode didn't cure me or Chris. Only a few days later, we lit a fire on the closet floor of the lodger at their house, a Russian émigré economist who worked for Chris' father, Ewan Clague, the Commissioner of the Bureau of Labor Statistics. We burned up a pair of shoes and singed the cuffs on a couple of suits before this new blaze was brought under control. Finally Chris' mother, a progressive-minded pediatrician, dealt with us by commissioning us to light all the fires—the stove, the cigarettes and everything else—so long as it was in the presence of adults. Her utilitarian and secular but benevolent aegis was my first experience with "progressive" attitudes toward education. Under her tutelage Chris and I finally got bored with fires, as we were intended to do, to everybody's relief. Years later Chris became a member of President Jimmy Carter's Council of Economic Advisers, and, later, an eminent economist at the University of Maryland. His early activities as an apprentice arsonist do not seem to have arisen to haunt him. Or me either, for that matter.

For our final year in Washington, we moved—for some reason—out of the Faulkners' sumptuous cottage into a small row house in Georgetown. There I had more of my early encounters with the media. I saw my first movie—Walt Disney's *Pinnochio*, which thrilled but also scared me. There were no late afternoon television programs in those days, of course, but there were comparable radio programs, and I was allowed to eat my supper on a tray in front of the radio, as the succession of fifteen-minute radio serials—"Jack Armstrong," "Sky King," and "Terry and the Pirates"—flashed by. One of the shows—it may have been "Jack Armstrong," offered its youthful viewers a Piper Cub airplane, if you sent in postage and a certain number of Wheaties box tops. I struggled through the awful Wheaties and sent in my boxtops, all the time wondering where we were going to put the plane, as we were no longer living at Rosedale, but in a small row house with almost no back yard. But the problem was solved when a small model arrived in the mail, rather than the full-sized plane that I was anxiously expecting. It was easy to keep in my room. I was very, very disappointed.

I fought the war very much as most small boys did, doing endless drawings of battles, especially of the air war. I also wrote and illustrated an epic struggle between some heroic rabbits and their evil enemies, the Jam-Wams, which I carefully bound into books. I also treasured a large comic book collection. As many American kids did in those days, I sang racist songs about the Japanese, whom I always drew as short with buck teeth: "Hi ho, hi ho, it's off to work we go. We'll slap those Japs right off their mats, hi ho." I think I imagined the "mats" as similar to those that we lay down on for rest period at school. Why this was the preferred military action against Japan I never inquired.

My supper arrangements had the advantage of enabling me to eat the evening meal out of the sight of my parents which delighted them as much me, my table manners being what they were. There were many things I didn't like in those days, principally liver, squash and brussels sprouts, and when my parents were in the dining room, out of range of "Terry and the Pirates," I would secrete brussels sprouts, pieces of liver and other detritus in the back of the large console radio in front of which I was seated. There they dried up and dwindled to a fraction of their former size, but of course there were hundreds of dried vegetables by the time that the movers came in 1946, when we were returning to Cambridge. When they lifted the radio up, out rattled enough dried lima beans, sprouts and minute nuggets of liver to have filled a small troop ship. My crimes were discovered, but fortunately the statute of limitations had expired.

On the eve of our move to Cambridge, my parents were still very concerned by my behavior. My mother wrote a letter to my elementary school and kept a copy of it:

> We felt that [the school's] summary of Abbott's abilities and weaknesses is excellent, though in some ways more generous than ours would have been. We realize and regret his nervous, restless and impatient temperament, which results in his poor control of actions, his carelessness, untidiness and extreme roughness. The ability to concentrate came to him slowly, but, when interested, he has improved greatly in this respect, helped, no doubt, by his great desire to excel. His respect for authority in the home is not impressive, but he is more willing to submit to group regulations without argument. He has a sense of honor, but his honesty in our experience is not above question in spite of definite efforts to improve. We do feel that his intelligence is of such an order that he should do well in his work, and we are glad to see that his progress is satisfactory.

My memory of my episodes of wickedness is vestigial, but somewhere I retain a sense of being seized by some outside power which dictated my smart-ass remarks and kept me in its grip for some time, before abruptly vanishing and leaving me suddenly realizing what I had done and overwhelmed by shame.

Haying at Spring Farm, c. 1940

Spring Farm

Between 1938 and 1950, we spent summers on Spring Farm, north of Pomfret, Connecticut, a small town almost equidistant from Hartford, Boston and Providence. My grandfather Abbott had bought the farm in the early nineteen-thirties, unceremoniously expelling the squatters who were living in its several ramshackle houses. He then turned it into a summer place for his family: his son Charles Abbott with his wife Louise; and his daughter, Mary Eleanor Abbott with her husband Everett Gleason. The Abbott children ultimately numbered five and the Gleason children two, my sister Ellen and I. During World War II, both the Abbotts and the Gleasons were in Washington, D.C., but returned to Pomfret for as much of each summer as they could, given the various academic and military pressures they were facing.

Over the years the farm grew considerably in size, but at that point it was a hundred-acre paradise for academics and their families in the summer and on weekends. It contained brooks, ponds, an abandoned settlement (the so-called "lost village"; how many of them must there be in rural New England!) and an equally abandoned "old orchard." By the time I can begin to remember the farm, my grandfather had retired from his Harvard professorship, but was still working on his masterpiece, the four-volume *Writings and*

Note: Portions of the material in this chapter appeared in a different format as "Peanut Butter" in *Blair & Ketchum's Country Journal*, July, 1975, pp. 59-61; and in *The Providence Sunday Journal*, Sept., 7, 1975, Section E., p. 1.

Speeches of Oliver Cromwell, which replaced Thomas Carlyle's edition, and is still today the most complete collection of Cromwell's work.[1]

Until 1944, everybody lived in a large, square, early nineteenth-century house, known in a traditional and rather immodest way as "the big house", a term more common in the South than in New England. My grandparents had filled it with antiques, bought at auctions over the years, and its bookshelves overflowed with seventeenth-century English history, detective stories, thrillers and fairy tales. Several of the bathrooms were ancient, with wooden-framed bathtubs that had stretched tin interiors. When the water pressure was good, the running of a tub sounded like a lawnmower being pushed at full speed along a rocky beach.

With so many men, women, children, nursemaids and dogs all jammed in together, the big house saw a certain amount of tension and quarreling and occasionally must have resembled a "Big House" in the John Dillinger sense of the term. But in my child's perspective, it was an idyllic time. Even before the war was over, the Gleasons moved out to another smaller house on the property, and then into the earliest farmhouse, built in the 1740s and by this time beautifully restored by Jimmy Knowles. The house had been the Ben Grosvenor Inn in the nineteenth century. Reputedly the Mormon founder Joseph Smith had slept there on one occasion, on his way to New York state. I would occasionally sleep walk and my nocturnal journeys were sometimes facetiously ascribed to Mormon influence.

Our move relieved the congestion. After the War, my Uncle Charles returned to the Harvard Business School and my father was working for much of the time in Cambridge on two fat volumes with William L. Langer on the United States entry into World

[1] It was published in four volumes over the decade 1937-1947, and reissued in 1988. Judging by my parents' correspondence, Harvard Press required a subsidy to publish it, but it remains overwhelmingly the best documentary source for Cromwell's public face even today.

War II. The train ride from Boston to the stations at Pomfret (a few trains stopped there) and Putnam, the larger nearby milltown, was relatively brief and much used by Abbotts and Gleasons.

Until the end of the war, there was no thought of making the farm pay its way, and indeed almost everything there seemed at least a decade or two behind the times. Workhorses named Billy and Jerry and even a team of massive white oxen lingered, long after tractors and hayloaders were the rule on the more serious farms in the neighborhood. All the men on the farm and many friends from Pomfret participated in the haying. Guest workers included the highly skilled woodcarver, Gregory Wiggins, who made wonderful small carvings for my parents, some of which I still have. His master work was the marvellous choir stalls in the Trinity College Chapel in Hartford, which mingle carvings of St. Thomas Aquinas and Albertus Magnus on the pews with Babe Ruth and Dwight Eisenhower. I believe he did similar work at St. Paul's School, of which he was an alumnus. My grandfather's erstwhile graduate student, Jimmy Knowles, was also a charter member. The haying was all done manually, with pitchforks, and many a wobbly load slid or toppled off the wagon before it could be brought home to the barn. Farm work was usually over in time for drinks at the Big House before the sun had sunk over the yardarm.

Wiggins, like my grandfather Abbott, was very conservative. As may be seen in the following little ditty he sent to his professor friend, both men mourned the end of Abbott Lawrence Lowell's tenure as president of Harvard and the coming of the more liberal James Bryant Conant:

> Of all the men I meet or see
> Named Smith or Forbes or Cabot,
> The man with whom I most agree
> Is Wilbur Cortez Abbott.
> In many ways his thought concurs
> With mine, which forms a link.
> He says quite frankly he prefers
> A perfume to a stink

He hates the Benny Goodman craze
And thinks the Russians mean.
And actually prefers, he says,
Abe Lincoln to Stalin!
I like all this—I like the whole—
I like the parts component.
In fact I'd say he had a soul.
(We both agree on Conant.)
And so I'm sure that he'll agree
That, as the times are queer,
It's well a times to have a spree,
And take a bit o' cheer!

My summer days were full of books. My grandfather had collected a virtually complete set of the colored "Fairy Books", edited by Andrew Lang, and these, along with the Oz books, became my first favorites, together with the enthralling Victorian classics by George MacDonald and almost anything about Norse mythology which I much preferred to Greek. Norse things were taken seriously in these households. Our dogs got Norse names, and my father read me popular Victorian versions of the eddas and sagas. Greek mythology at first seemed confusing and somewhat ethereal, but I soon got into that as well.

There was a tiny Pomfret public library, more or less across the street from Pomfret School, and there a group of children from Spring Farm would be taken every week or two to stock up on books. The librarian was a quiet, rather severe, white-haired woman named Miss Burdick, who sat at a sparsely equipped little desk, with hand stamps, and a small electric fan playing on her, and checked out our books. Many of the children's books dated from my grandparents' time—as did Miss Burdick—although the adult selections were more up to date. But I read the Tom Swift books, as well as a set of stories called The Baseball Joe books; the author was someone for whom Christy Mathewson and Rube Waddell were contemporaries (not Ted Williams and Stan Musial), but I devoured the entire series, despite the peculiar uniforms worn by the players

The Abbott and Gleason families at Spring Farm, c. 1940

in the illustrations, to say nothing of slang that was half a century out of date and romances in which I was not interested. So my taste in reading began with out-of-date literature that most of my contemporaries didn't know and to some extent it continued that way ever after. Walking into that quiet little library was a thrill. I have never entirely lost that early excitement that the sight of row upon row of books on a library shelf gave me.

The farm machinery and the reading were old-fashioned, and so was the domestic technology. There was one early refrigerator in a corner of the big kitchen, but most of the cooling was supplied by enormous "ice boxes" on the back porch. Several times a week, a truck drove up from Putnam early in the morning and a spry, well built man hopped out and, wielding enormous tongs on his hip, left something like a hundred pounds of ice in blocks (I called them "bergs") in the great chests and drove away. His arrival, around 5:00 AM, was a signal for me to jump out of bed and throw on my jeans and head over to the barn for morning milking. There were cows (and chickens, pigs and other animals) but the term "herd" would have been an exaggeration in those early days for an unrationalized bunch of Guernseys, Jerseys, Ayrshires and every conceivable combination. Whether the milk was sold or merely consumed locally at this stage, I cannot remember. There were many blueberrying expeditions up to "the hill" behind the barn and other sites, some of them involving better than a dozen people and three generations. At the end of the summer there was a massive process of "canning," putting up preserves and vegetables of all sorts. Even root beer was bottled in the kitchen of the Big House. I have lost track of precisely which roots were used, but the product was excellent. The director of culinary operations was neither my aunt nor my mother, but a large and jolly woman named Emma Feige (pronounced "Feej"), who was also in charge of the growing Abbott family, and to a lesser extent the entire household. She was a great organizer of games; she (and her sister Elizabeth) led the blueberrying; on Sunday she played the piano and we sang hymns. She could be peremptory, but generally the children saw her as tending to mitigate official severity. She could stand up to my irritable aunt and on occasion did ("Now Mrs. Abbott. . .!")

As my grandfather's health deteriorated in the mid- and latter 1940s, my uncle took charge of Spring Farm, and modernization began. My Uncle Charles had much in common with my grandfather, including his autocratic propensities, his explosive temper, his sometimes mordant sense of humor and his skill as a raconteur. After he became the founding dean of the University of Virginia Business School later in his life, he lovingly collected dean jokes, with which he would sometimes regale me when our paths crossed. One I particularly liked concerned A. Lawrence Lowell, still President of Harvard in the early 1930s, a figure of striking self-confidence. An alumnus from New York, my uncle would relate with a straight face, but his eyes twinkling, called up Lowell in high excitement. "We have a potential major gift for Harvard," he reported. "To make the ask, we'd like to have you send down someone prominent in the university. We were thinking that a witty dean would be best." To which Lowell is supposed to have replied. "Don't have a witty dean, but I have two deans who are half-wits, and I'll send them both." Lowell, it should be remembered, was the man whose secretary reported to a visitor at Harvard that he was unavailable for a meeting. "The president," said the secretary smoothly, "is in Washington, meeting with Mr. Roosevelt."

With all of his love of university lore and tradition, my uncle, the business school professor, was a fiscal conservative and he intended to make the farm pay for itself, which his father had never attempted. So a more modern and activist farmer replaced the languid and picturesque figures who had been in charge previously—pudgy Mr. Streeter, who looked a little like W.C. Fields, and sad-eyed Mr. Baker, whom I recall identifying as the Carpenter in *Through the Looking Glass*. The number of cows increased and a move began toward creating a real herd of Ayrshires, lowland Scottish cattle that gave less milk than Holsteins but with a higher butterfat content, which in those days was considered a good thing. We got a tractor; the workhorses and oxen disappeared. Cindy, a good natured horse for the children to ride, and Billy, a grumpy donkey with a colorful, elaborately carved Sicilian cart with moth eaten plumes, were imported for the children. The haymaking and other farmwork was now mostly in the hands of professionals.

The new farmer, whom I will call Mr. Angell, was my first hero. He was a lean, wiry man of great energy, with what seemed to me immense biceps. I never tired of surreptitiously eyeballing them and wondering if my sticklike arms would ever look like that. I knew they never would. Mr. Angell taught me to swear. I was amazed to hear him call a bull a "leap-jeeping sonofabitch," but I was soon at work learning a whole new vocabulary, to the consternation of my parents. I called everything a frigging this or that, although I didn't know what the word meant and nobody was in a hurry to explain it. My vocabulary was hard to control, since I was basing it on my current hero. Eventually my parents were reduced to allowing me certain words at the farm, while making them absolutely off limits "in the city."[2] On occasion my mouth was washed out with soap, a common punishment in those days, which caused me particular indignation when done by my aunt rather than my mother.[3] I trailed Mr. Angell everywhere, copied his clothes as best I could, got up at 5:00 A.M. to be on hand for milking and other chores and hated to come in for dinner when evening chores were not yet finished. When I discovered that he was a Red Sox fan, I promptly abandoned my incipient interest in the then-Boston Braves and rooted—from that day to this—for the Sox! Occasional group trips to Fenway Park in 1947 began my lifetime of fandom. When Mr. Angell hired me to work for him for $1.00 per day at the age of eleven I was overjoyed.

Mr. Angell had two daughters a couple of years older than me and a son, Ben, exactly my age. We were soon close friends and remained so until my family moved to Washington, D.C., in 1950, when we sold our share of the farm to the Abbotts. But our active friendship didn't survive. As adults we became very different people; perhaps we always were.

From the moment we arrived at the farm in early June I spent as much time with the Angells, father and son, as I could manage. From early on—perhaps as early as nine or ten—Ben did a lot of real farm work, and I learned to do the same, or at least to want to do the same. Bringing in the hay was great fun; digging postholes was boring and hard. The worst was spending two or three hours "picking

[2] The attempt to distinguish between city and country as a way of disciplining my vocabulary was not entirely successful. As late as the sixth grade one of my Browne and Nichols report cards commented a little primly that "Tommy…has acquired and uses a vocabulary not usually acceptable."

[3] I was somewhat gentler with my own son. When he was four or five he used the f-word for the first time. When we asked him what he meant, he thought for awhile and then said "Indian", the most exciting thing he could think of. Our boarder of that time, Wendy Strothman, remembers my cautioning Nick about its use. His usage is not a tribute to his father's discretion!

up stone," which meant taking the large rocks that came up every winter into the fields from New England's endlessly rocky soil and heaving them onto the back of a farm truck and then dumping them somewhere. I began to learn how to drive the ancient truck, which was fun but scary, and I would often stall the truck while taking on hay, which threw me into agonies of humiliation, in front of Ben and Mr. Angell, who would smile at each other. I was generally allowed to drive only as a last resort and of course only in the fields.

The milking machines we then had were relatively primitive. They had to be taken off the cow before she was completely milked, and then we kids would take the rest by hand. This process was known as "stripping" the cows and it was exciting to learn to milk by hand. In the school I went to in Cambridge, almost nobody knew how to milk a cow and I felt very superior to have acquired this remarkable skill, even though it was only called upon in the summer months.

Spending as much time with the Angell family as I did, I began to become dimly aware of some of the realities of social class in America, a subject never spoken of at home. The first thing I noticed was how differently the Angell family interacted from the way mine did. Although the family was entirely intact, quarrels among all members—husband and wife, parents and children, children among themselves—were noisy, open and often lengthy. The kids were all cuffed around a lot and what seemed to me real beatings sometimes happened. Ben also sassed and swore at his parents in ways that filled me with terror and secret admiration—even though he always got the worst of the confrontations that followed. Mr. and Mrs. Angell were also not averse to occasional screaming arguments in front of me, something I found particularly astonishing, since I had virtually never seen adults disagree. Whatever differences my own parents might have, they were never revealed "in front of the children." And although I was sometimes spanked and more often cuffed, I was never beaten. Shaming was the predominant mode of discipline in the Gleason household. Needless to say

I required it much more often than my good-natured and acquiescent little sister, which did not improve our quarrelsome relations. Ben and I seldom fought; he was so much stronger and braver than I that the result was a foregone conclusion. By comparison I was babyish.

My father greeted Mr. Angell with great cordiality when they met, but there was always a mutual formality that I couldn't fathom. Surely my father would want to get to know this remarkable man better. Compared to Mr. Angell, my father's build was pathetic. But summer after summer they called each other Mister. The Angells never came to our house, nor did we, as a family, go to theirs. On at least one occasion, I asked my father why. He said something about differing interests, not having much in common, despite the fact that Mr. Angell was a splendid man, and so on. I knew my father wasn't lying, but I sensed that there was more to it than that.

By about the age of ten or eleven, I had begun to dislike the genteel society of my parents and my aunt and uncle, for reasons I couldn't exactly have put into words, except perhaps to say that it seemed soft and insufficiently masculine, perhaps infantile. By comparison with Mr. Angell's strength and vitality, my father seemed sedentary, cerebral and worst of all, prissy. I resented being hauled off, divested of my manure-stained dungarees, to a birthday party where all the boys would be wearing shorts and the girls frilly party dresses, and where there would be potato races and pin the tail on the donkey instead of fishing and snake hunting in the back pasture and woods. I almost never saw those children except on such occasions. This did not prevent me from developing secret crushes on several of the girls. But potato races were the worst! I felt emasculated by them, although I didn't yet know the word. Even worse, I wasn't very good at them.

Ben and his father would often be on hand as I was driven away to those dreaded parties. I was embarrassed, unwilling to go and unwilling to have them see me go, just as I instinctively kept The Red Fairy Book or the archaic Baseball Joe stories out of Ben's sight. Sometimes they would grin at each other as we left, seeming to know something that I didn't. Then they would turn back to the farm work that I longed to be doing. I knew that if it weren't for the birthday party—how I hated what seemed to me the babyish phrase "birthday party"—I could be going with them too, riding on the back of the old truck with Ben.

When I returned from my afternoon excursion, chores would usually be in full swing. I vaguely sensed that I had to overcome some distance that had opened up between Ben and me in particular. Over time I would be successful, but I would feel again that there was something about life and about me that they knew and accepted and that I didn't know. I might have been able to figure more of it out if I had put my mind to it, but I rejected the idea. I really didn't want to know.

A kind of unhappy illumination came one day when I was, perhaps, eleven. One of Ben's friends, a lean quiet boy named Russell, was spending a Saturday at the farm. This in itself was unusual. I knew of course that Ben had school friends. He would talk about them or we would run into them around town. But they didn't ordinarily "come over to play" the way my friends did when I was in Cambridge. We were not yet old enough to drive, except around the farm, and most of these kids were already working, one way or another. But that Saturday Russell came. I sensed immediately that he neither liked nor trusted me. And Ben, who was ordinarily a very loyal friend, and exceedingly tolerant of my city-bred ignorance, tacitly allied himself with Russell against me. Clearly I embarrassed him. And although nothing overt happened, I was uncomfortable all day and felt abandoned. An hour before chore time, we came back from somewhere in the woods and I said enthusiastically, "Let's go and have peanut butter sandwiches at my house." Ben agreed, turning to Russell and saying, "You should see how much peanut butter Tom puts in his sandwiches!" Russell gave me a long, level stare of dislike. "Yeah," he said, between his teeth, "He has all the peanut butter he wants."

It was a horrible moment. I was suddenly forced to be aware that I had things that Ben and Russell did not have, that I was in some way privileged, that it was unjust and yet I couldn't help it, indeed do anything about it at all. If I handed out big sandwiches, that merely demonstrated my utterly undeserved position of material superiority. Ben and Russell were both, I knew, stronger and more worldly wise than I was. By applying the primitive Darwinism of children, I could see that their strength and cleverness should have given them the lions' share of the peanut butter. I was privileged in some unfair way that I didn't understand, but passionately wanted to repudiate. If, on the other hand, I didn't provide the advertised enormous gooey sandwich, I would merely be ungenerous. Nobody would be fooled.

I cannot remember what happened then. I only recall my intense longing for Russell to go home, to leave Ben and me to our friendship, to let me slip back into my position as acolyte of the Angell family. Of course he did eventually go home. But I could never quite forget what had happened and the unhappy knowledge and consciousness I had gained.

In 1950, we sold not only our house but also our share of the farm to my aunt and uncle's family. My father was going to join the staff of the National Security Council in Washington. The Cold War was in full swing. Long weeks or months at the farm would be impossible for my father, and my mother had no desire to run a household with two small children, far away from her husband, for the better part of three months. She had already had the first of the series of strokes which would eventually kill her, and although she had recovered, she was never again in her former good health. So my summers at the farm came to an end. A very sad end for me, for I have never loved a particular place so much.

There were also sublimated political issues. The two families were not entirely comfortable with each other politically. The Abbotts were—like my grandparents—very conservative, my parents more liberal, Rooseveltian internationalists. The Abbott children were treated with somewhat greater severity and there were tensions about who was punished, how, and by whom. The Abbotts undoubtedly believed that the Gleason children were spoiled, especially me, and they had some grounds for thinking this. I was just unwilling to accept criticism and argued about virtually everything. I had no idea of deference, despite my parents' best efforts.

Relations between the Abbotts and the Gleasons were never broken off. A period of coolness ensued, however, although my cousin Louise lived with us at a later period while she went to private school in Washington. By that time, Charles Abbott had left Harvard and become the founding Dean of the Colgate Darden School of Business Administration at the University of Virginia, and the rest of the Abbotts were living in Charlottesville. The conservatism of Virginia was very much to the Abbotts' taste.

Later on, the generosity of the Abbotts led to a restoration of closer relations. After my father suddenly died of cancer in 1974, the Abbotts took my mother back into the "big house," where she remained until her death four years later, thus obviating a series of awful choices for me, involving nursing homes or moving an increasingly ill woman into our house, where there were two young children and two working parents.

Harvard Square, Cambridge, Massachusetts, 1940s

14 Craigie Street and Beyond

My father was decommissioned on October 30, 1945. As late as July of that year he wrote to my mother from London of his intent to return to Amherst, but he soon changed his mind. After an interval during which he worked for the Department of State as a "Planner for the Intelligence Section" (this mysterious term may relate to the transfer of the Research & Analysis Branch of OSS to the Department of State), my family returned to Cambridge, where my father had contracted to co-author an account of America's entry into World War II with the distinguished historian of modern Europe, William L. Langer, of Harvard, with whom he had worked at OSS. My father did not become a Harvard faculty member, but a Fellow of the Council on Foreign Relations, which supported the authors in their research to the tune of $140,000 over four years. This was a very large sum at the time, but World War II loomed very large in the consciousness of Americans. So at the end of the summer of 1946 we moved into a spacious Victorian house on Craigie Street in Cambridge, about a five-minute walk from the Radcliffe campus and about fifteen minutes from Harvard Square. We lived there for almost four years. It was a rambling, pleasant, slightly dumpy house, about which I still have pleasant dreams every so often, returning to my old room, with its high ceilings, big windows and outdoor, second-floor porch. About our various conservatively furnished, comfortable, old-fashioned houses, I might echo what the critic Walter Benjamin wrote of the furniture that surrounded him as a child: "Here reigned a species of things that was, no matter how compliantly it bowed to the minor whims of fashion, in the main so wholly convinced of itself and its permanence that it took no account of wear, inheritance or moves, remaining forever equally near to and far from its ending, which seemed the ending of all things."[1]

In one respect the choice by the Council on Foreign Relations of the two authors was a curious one. Langer was primarily a historian of pre-World War I Europe. My father was a medievalist. Neither was really experienced in American history. On the other hand, they had both lived through the war as members of OSS, and Langer was actually finishing up an account of American relations with Vichy France, about which more in a moment. Langer was also a figure of great influence in the guild of historians in the United States. I suspect Langer did the choosing in this instance, and he was well aware from their work together of how well my father wrote.

And indeed the Council's choice was vindicated, although the task was enormous, and the authors barely managed to take the story up to Pearl Harbor.[2] The volumes that they produced (*The Challenge to Isolation* and *The Undeclared War*) turned out to be very successful and were awarded the Bancroft Prize, the most prestigious award for new books in American history, then as now.

[1]Adam Kirsch, "The Philosopher Stoned: What Drugs Taught Walter Benjamin," *The New Yorker*, August 21, 2006.

[2]For Langer's account of the collaboration, see his *In and Out of the Ivory Tower*, Neale Watson Academic Publications, New York, 1977, passim. Money was evidently an issue as well. My father maintained in his letter of resignation that "had any suitable academic job turned up" he would have taken it, and could have then continued to work on the United States and the war, but the Council on Foreign Relations was clearly not minded to give my father and Langer any additional funding. By a "suitable academic job" my father must have meant a position in the Harvard History Department. He would not have accepted anything in the Boston area but Harvard, and he could perfectly well have returned to Amherst, which was eager to have him and was less than one hundred miles from Cambridge. My father's romance with Harvard continued.

Saturday Review *cover featuring a drawing of (left to right) William L. Langer and S. Everett Gleason, authors of* The Challenge to Isolation, *January 19, 1952*

Historians of twentieth-century America tell me that the two volumes by Langer and Gleason have not lost their usefulness even today, although they were criticized by Roosevelt's enemies as representing a very establishment view of the war. Broadly speaking, that is to say, the authors supported the participation of the United States in World War II and refused to endorse a general view that Roosevelt "manipulated" political events and "lied America into war," as one revisionist, Charles Tansill, put it. There was also the issue of access. My father and Langer always maintained that they had not had any special treatment by the authorities, but serious questions have been raised about that.[3]

[3] David Engerman of Brandeis University, for example, working in the Langer papers, unearthed a letter to Langer from Dean Acheson (dated April 17, 1946)

I always hoped that my father would write more over the course of his career. He was a conscientious researcher and an elegant writer. Finally he confessed to me, toward the end of his life, that although he loved university life, he did not enjoy writing, good as he was at it. His minutes of National Security Council meetings are described by scholars who have used them as extensive, lucid and fair-minded.[4] I suspect him of having been a perfectionist, although we never talked about that. But he was certainly reverential about his position and the importance of the work he did and in his writing did his best to render the complexities of arguments in ample detail, something which he did not always do at home.

Cambridge, more than fifty years ago, was a far smaller and more intimate place than today, and far less ostentatious and glitzy. There was much less vehicular traffic and more mom-and-pop stores. At Egan's Market, a mile or so out Concord Avenue from Harvard Square, Mr. Egan sat behind the meat counter in his white coat, or circulated and chatted cordially with his classy clientele, all upper-middle-class ladies and children. He was the proprietor and seldom soiled his hands with the actual business of the shoppers. Harvard Square itself was devoid of tall buildings or anything in steel and glass. Even a seven- or eight-year-old boy could range freely through Cambridge streets on foot or bike, although it was a year or two before I was allowed to go to Harvard Square by myself and then certainly not on a bicycle. Many people did not lock their doors, and boy's baseball gloves were not yet much more than leather rags. Haircuts cost $1.00. The Saturday morning movie at the University Theater (now the Harvard Square Theater)

saying "It is also understood that the notes which you take from classified papers in the Dept will be turned over to the Dept or disposed of in some other manner after compilation of your book so that such notes may not be used by unauthorized persons."

[4] Robert R. Bowie and Richard H. Immerman, *Waging Peace: How Eisenhower Shaped an Enduring Cold War Strategy*, New York and Oxford, Oxford University Press, 1998.

cost fourteen cents. Between the feature and the serial, there was a ticket stub drawing on stage, and the winners were given a little sack containing a hundred pennies. It seemed a princely sum, and I was an exultant winner on several occasions—not surprisingly, as I went almost every Saturday, except in the summers, for almost four years.

I loved the trackless trolleys that took you into Harvard Square via Huron Avenue (pronounced like "Urine Avenue" by born and bred Cantabridgians), and especially the subways that ran into Boston. In those days, the Red Line ended in a dismal suburb called Ashmont, where I had never been and about which I wondered endlessly to myself. What would it be like to go all the way to the end of the line? What was out there? I thought of it as in some fashion the end of the known world, and I longed to see it. Finally my father gave in and we rode all the way out to the end of the line and back. Great was my disappointment to discover that Ashmont was just another place, and there was nothing in any way interesting or striking about it.

I had two interlocking circles of particular friends in Cambridge in the late 1940s. One involved the step-children of Professor Langer, Evan and George Nelson, and Evan Nelson's friend, Johnny Tribou, who lived with his irascible father in one of Cambridge's many six-story brick apartment houses, this one almost directly across the street from our house. Evan and John Tribou were close friends, and their activities centered around the usual military-adventurous fantasies of little boys, to which I also gravitated. Much of this activity took place in a large, semi-wooded vacant lot behind the Henry W. Longfellow House, known to us all as "Sherwood," after Robin Hood's famous redoubt. There we made spindly bows and arrows and tomahawks, painted our faces and bodies and played games somewhere on the borderline between late medieval England and late nineteenth-century Texas.

On rainy days we often sought refuge at the Langers' house, but there we were under pressure to play more quietly than we liked in the playroom at the top of the house. Mrs. Langer often told us to be more quiet because of someone (something, as it turned out), called "Our Vichy Gamble." Now at this time there was a famous daily radio soap opera called "Our Gal Sunday," which asked the provocative question as to whether "Sunday," a beautiful girl from "a small mining town in Colorado" could "find happiness with a wealthy and titled Englishman." I had no clue as to why finding happiness with a wealthy and titled Englishman should be a problem for someone from Colorado, but I accepted that it must be difficult because nobody seemed to find the question odd. I often listened to that program when I was sick and stayed home from school, and I imagined that "Our Vichy Gamble" was a similar person. Why she lived in the Langers' house or what connection she had with them I never discovered. The fact that I never saw her did not stir me to reflection. The only thing that I knew for sure about her was that she hated any sort of loud noise, but I developed a picture in my mind of a beautiful woman who was always in bed in one of the extra rooms on the Langer's second floor, below the playroom. After a while she was no longer spoken of, but I accepted this, too, as children will, and don't remember wondering what she was now doing, whether she too was trying to find happiness with a wealthy and titled Englishman or had just gone off somewhere, perhaps to Colorado.

Years later—circa 1955 when I was a junior in prep school in Washington, D.C.—I was looking developing a bibliography for a paper, and my eye fell upon Langer's name. Lo and behold, he had written a book about American policy toward France in the war years entitled *Our Vichy Gamble*! I instantly recalled the mysterious lodger at the Langer's house and realized why she needed so much quiet attention.

Through the Langers I also encountered Russia for the first time —in a very pre-revolutionary form. Evan Nelson taught me an occasionally famous piece of doggerel, apparently the work of a nineteenth-century balladeer named Percy French. Generally known as "Abdul Abulbul Amir" (there are almost as many spellings as there are add-on verses by other hands), it describes the epic encounter of a leading soldier in the Tsar's army with a ferocious Turkish fighter. I was charmed by these verses and memorized a brief version of the poem:

> The sons of the Prophet are hardy and bold
> And quite unaccustomed to fear
> But of all, the most reckless of life or of limb
> Was Abdul Abulbul Amir. (...)
>
> The heroes were plenty and well known to fame
> That fought in the ranks of the Czar.
> But the greatest of these was a man by the name
> Of Ivan Skavinsky Skavar.

So my first encounter with the Russian soldier was culturally nearer the Crimean than the Cold War, but the later theme of "Russian backwardness," which would prove an important subject for me was already present, in the Gilbert & Sullivan-style condescension of the author. Other Russian moments, somewhat less archaic, are also lodged oddly in my mind: Coming home from school one afternoon in 1949 and learning from the afternoon paper that "Stalin had the bomb"; or hearing on the radio in June of the following year, when I was just short of twelve, that South Korea had been invaded. On that occasion, we were visiting my Baxter grandparents on Cape Cod, and were on the train back to Washington within a few hours.

Langer was a powerful and imposing figure, although not a big man, and he exuded energy. He was always the quintessential Harvard professor for me. When I arrived back in Cambridge several years later, to begin college, I met him walking in the Harvard Yard, "Waaaal Tommy," he half drawled, half bawled. (His accent was extraordinary.) "I'd forgotten you were a freshman." After exchanging a few pleasantries about my family, he invited me to come to tea with him and his wife in the familiar house at number 1 Berkeley Street. Trying to be "a nice young man" (a very recent aspiration in my life at that time), I replied "oh, why don't I come and see you in your office hours?" There was a second or two of silence, and then Langer replied: "Waaaal, Tommy, I don't *have* office hours for undergraduates! I used to—every Thursday afternoon at Berkeley Street, from 4:30 until 5:00. But ya know, Tommy—no one ever came!"

Having Langer know my name was not always an advantage. Promptly at nine o' clock he would shut the door to his lecture room and begin his lecture on the European state system in the nineteenth century. No one could enter the room after the door had been closed. I was, then as now, a chronic latecomer. Sometimes if the door were merely ajar, I would try to slip in, but he invariably saw me. Those he didn't know he simply told to stay outside, but to me he gave a little lecture. "Gosh, Tommy, can't you *ever* be on time? No, you *can't* come in, you'll have to sit on the floor in the hall."

Langer read most of the major European languages, but he had no ear for them and spoke all of them with a ferocious Boston accent. The following anecdote used to circulate about him. In his graduate seminar he got an excellent paper from a second-year graduate student. "Mr. Jones!" Langer shouted. "This is an excellent paper! You used French and German sources and some Italian documents and even the Ottoman sources. But, Mr. Jones (his expression turning more severe), I notice that you haven't used any Romanian sources." Poor Mr. Jones squirmed. "But Professor Langer, I don't read Romanian". Langer looked at him for a moment. "Ya *don't*?" he asked, I imagine a bit pityingly. "Have ya ever *tried*?"

Langer, it must be said, read voraciously himself, in virtually all areas of modern European history. My subsequent Ph.D. dissertation was on nineteenth-century Russian intellectual history, an area far from his specialty on political and diplomatic history and I had no particular contact with him when I was a graduate student. But he read my dissertation, *European and Muscovite*, when it appeared as a book, and was eager to engage me in conversation about it. Somewhere along the line he had had time to learn to read

Russian—or perhaps he just began to read it, the way he presumably had with Romanian. He had a deep and steady commitment to understanding the past in what he believed were its own terms, which could be discovered if you worked at it. And work at it he did.

Langer had been very committed to the American side in the World War II, though several of the few scholars who had taken a long-term pro-German stance accused him of having adopted his somewhat Wilsonian positions only in the late 1930s, when he wrote an essay for the *New York Times Magazine* on "the faith of Woodrow Wilson." My father, a great admirer of Langer, always denied that his colleague had changed his previous rather pro-German views opportunistically. Both men were bitter at isolationists, including the distinguished Charles Beard, who accused them of whitewashing Roosevelt and called them "court historians." Neither Langer nor my father minded being part of the Establishment—indeed they gloried in it—but they resented the idea that they were in any way courtiers.

My closest friend in those early Cambridge years was Mark DeVoto, who lived around the corner from us, also on Berkeley Street. He was the son of Bernard DeVoto, the great historian-journalist-conservationist, and Avis, a brisk, charming woman, who later gained recognition as a close associate of Julia Child, the famous "French Chef." Mark was something of a musical prodigy and, like me, a great reader, so our activities revolved more around books and stamp-collecting than games of the cowboys and Indians variety. Together Mark and I read all existing Hardy Boys books and then decided that more must be written, and if the mysterious Franklin W. Dixon could do it, so could we. (Little did we know that Dixon, like us, was actually a committee.) In order to define the scope of our activities, we decided to write the titles first and when we had done that to turn to what would be the simple project of creating books to go with them. The result, of course, was that we ended up with hundreds of titles, but no books, as that aspect of our work turned out to be more laborious than we had imagined.

Mark DeVoto, c. 1947

For a time, images from the Hardy Boys books dominated our imaginations. We were on constant alert for criminal malefactors, whom we suspected must be following us, and for secret panels leading to secret rooms in our houses. We spent a great deal of time looking and did find a way to get under the raised front porch of our Craigie Street house and from there into the cellar. This was quite exciting and we figured that this route into the basement was probably being used by mysterious criminals whom we had not yet discovered. Mark approached my parents about this as they were having their evening cocktail. "Mrs. Gleason," he said, eying my mother in his intense and unblinking way. "Do you realize there are MEN IN YOUR WALLS?" My mother was startled. No, she had not realized that. She promised us to look into it, but we knew instinctively that she was a skeptic.

Mark and I had virtually neighboring rooms at Harvard a few years later and Mark, who was a great sight-reader of keyboard music, often used our piano. I remember being awakened around four in the morning (undergraduates didn't usually go to bed as late in those days as they do now, so we were all sound asleep) by Mark and George Nelson playing a four-hand sonata by Schubert or Mozart in the next room. "Oh," said Mark, as I and several of my roommates staggered out of the adjoining rooms in our pajamas, "we had no idea you were asleep." This despite the silent, darkened room in which the piano stood. Mark subsequently became a considerable composer and the principal American scholar of the modernist Alban Berg.

The scourge of the denizens of "Sherwood" was the gardener/caretaker of the Longfellow property, a Mr. MacGregor figure named Gaffney, who lay in wait for us trespassers and was constantly shouting at us, chasing us and threatening to have us arrested if we were caught on the property again. But we had a powerful answer for the Gaffney problem. Mark's house was only a hundred yards from one of the fences that separated "Sherwood" from the Episcopal Theological Seminary (now the Episcopal Divinity School) and Berkeley Street. So when we ran away from Gaffney we would seek sanctuary in the DeVotos' house. This was a particularly effective gambit, as Bernard, or "Benny" as he was known, worked at home, and, like the mysterious Vichy Gamble, demanded silence so he could concentrate on the wonderful works of popular history he was creating—things like *Year of Decision* and *Across the Wide Missouri*. Gaffney would inevitably come steaming up to the DeVotos' front door—he never learned—and ring the bell, pulling Benny up from his desk and breaking his concentration. He would meet Gaffney on his front porch in a rage. "I don't give a ---, what they did. Who cares if they play there! Get out of here, don't come back or I'll have you arrested for trespassing!" Mark and I would be lying on the second floor, peering around the corner of the newel post at the top of the stairs, listening to our champion send the deflated Gaffney away with a flea in his ear.

I have many pleasant memories of the DeVoto household and

some about which I feel repentant. One rainy day, bored with going over our stamp albums, Mark and I decided to set what we called a tiger trap for poor Avis DeVoto. We pulled the hot-air register out of the floor and put a rug over the top of the opening. Then Mark called his mother and asked her in an innocent voice to come to his room. Of course, she went sprawling and more or less sprained her ankle. I was sent home. It was a mean and stupid little prank, but at the time we thought it was funny.

I often stayed for dinner at the DeVotos. I am sorry to say that I was too young to appreciate the savor of Bernard DeVoto's conversation about politics or the environment, but I remember how interested I was to hear adults telling mildly off-color stories for the first time, as well as my first dirty—not really so dirty—limerick:

> There was a young lady named Alice
> Who pee'd in a Methodist Chalice.
> She did this dark deed out of very great need
> And not for sectarian malice.

I didn't know what "sectarian malice" might be, but my strait-laced parents never joked about peeing in a Methodist chalice, or anything like that.

Mark DeVoto has continued to be a friend to this day. By a remarkable coincidence, when his father Bernard DeVoto died in 1953, he was replaced as the writer of the "Easy Chair" column in *Harper's* magazine by my future father-in-law, John Fischer. So the family of my future wife, Sarah Fischer (whom of course I did not then know), was also close to the DeVotos.

Our nemesis on the streets of Cambridge was a big, rangy kid named Dmitrii. He had no last name that any of us younger boys knew, but he was always on the lookout for us, and I remember him always approaching on a dead run. Given my later professional involvement with things Russian, it is interesting to recall the dread that my first Russian acquaintance inspired in me; even today the name inspires ancient and far away feelings of fear. We often encountered Dmitrii as we walked to school. In those days, what is today Buckingham, Browne & Nichols was still two separate institutions. My sister walked to Buckingham, scarcely two blocks from our house, while the walk to Browne & Nichols on the Charles River was more like a mile. Often we would encounter tough public school kids, like Dmitrii, who instantly recognized a group of little WASP preppies (the term did not yet exist) and often challenged us to fight—starting with that old, old challenge, "hey whaddaya lookin' at?" Most of the time we ran, but once in a while we would have to stand and fight and almost invariably got the worst of it—in those days, nothing more than bruises, black eyes, bloody noses and humiliation. My father disapproved of my fighting, but especially when we got the worst of it.

I was fairly big for my age, and while at Browne & Nichols had a moderately traumatic experience on that account. The upper school had a wrestling team, but no one light enough to wrestle the lowest weight class—105 pounds—so I was on several occasions pressed into service. I was a sixth grader wrestling with boys perhaps five years older than I was, and invariably much stronger. My instructions were to avoid being pinned. If I could manage to lose only by a decision, there would be a net benefit for the team, since having your wrestler pinned led to the same loss of five points as a forfeit. These wrestling matches were intimidating and I dreaded them, especially given the public arena in which they took place. Barely avoiding a pin was useful for the team but hardly glorious. I rejoiced in being intimidating to other sixth graders, but of course was no match for kids five years older.

I had a more diverse group of acquaintances in the choir of Christ Church, where I sang every Sunday between the ages of nine and eleven. Almost all the boys in the choir went to public schools; here I met my first black kids. Christ Church was a beautiful eighteenth-century wooden structure, where my parents had been married, and where they were again parishioners in the late 1940s. The rector was a somewhat fulsome preacher named Gardner Day, known to my parents and some others as "Heavenly Day." At choir rehearsal, as well as at Browne & Nichols, my big mouth was continually opening, and my acting out, though more cautious, continued. So I often found myself in scrapes with bigger and tougher kids, whom I couldn't prevent myself from sassing, and I usually ran home from choir rehearsal as fast as I could, trying to get a two-minute jump on the bigger kids who would be hot on my trail. But it was my first actual job, and all of the boys were paid a couple of bucks a week, depending on how many services we sang. Our choirmaster was a man named Alfred Nash Patterson, whom all the boys respected. There were many of us who feared that boy sopranos were sissies (a point that some of our friends insisted on), but Mr. Patterson was a big, strong, handsome man with a commanding presence, and the fact that he was our leader was reassuring. Just before we moved back to Washington, he was replaced by a very nice woman, and talented musician, named Marion Boron, but she could not keep order the way Mr. Patterson had. I remember when she decided to play the complete organ works of Bach, and put up a poster in churches and Harvard buildings locally, reading "Bach's Organ Works". Some wag added in ball point pen underneath, "So does mine, but I don't advertise it."

The academic invasion of Washington, D.C., by professors eager to help in the war effort continued during the Cold War. It was not until the 1960s, during and immediately after the Kennedy administration, that academia and Washington had a serious falling out. My father was part of the academic transition between the anti-Hitler and anti-Stalin efforts. At some point in the summer or fall of 1949, he decided to accept an appointment as Deputy Secretary of the National Security Council from President Truman, an important job in the days before there was a National Security Adviser.[5]

[5] David Engerman reminds me that the starchy Boston lawyer Robert Cutler played the role of national security adviser to a certain extent during the latter phases of the Eisenhower administration, and was followed by Admiral Lewis

He decided to join the NSC rather than returning to academia, a fateful decision in his career.[6]

In retrospect, a fresh start was almost certainly a good thing. I had continued to be obstreperous in class at Browne & Nichols and my bad behavior was a staple of my report cards. In the late 1990s, some of those report cards turned up in a box of letters and amazed and delighted my children, who couldn't believe what a bad boy their father had been early on. "In and about school Tommy has exhibited a lack of courtesy many times, especially if he does not have his way," read my final Browne & Nichols report card solemnly. In athletics I displayed "a depressing lack of sportsmanship."

So we moved again, and once more I was an outsider, a "new boy" in a new school.

In Washington I was accepted at the Episcopal St. Albans School, with the understanding that I would sing in the choir at the nearby Washington Cathedral; but my voice was changing, and my days as a boy soprano were over. As a tenor I was adequate but not more, definitely a couple of notches below my former ability in the top register. Of course I was delighted not to be a soprano any longer.

Fortunately, my father had a love of Georgetown some years before it became fashionable, when many government employees regarded it as a "negro slum." To my father it seemed like Beacon Hill. It was one of the few integrated neighborhoods in the District of Columbia, although whites already occupied most of the larger and more solid houses. The Gleasons moved into a substantial row house, almost directly across from the front entrance of Dumbarton Oaks, at the corner of 31st and R streets, for which we

Strauss. But these appointments were by no means of comparable importance to the position occupied by a Brzezinski or a Kissinger in later administrations.

[6] Private correspondence between my parents suggests mid-1949 as the time the decision was made, but my father did not inform the Council on Foreign Relations officially that the project was terminated until February 13, 1950. (Letter to Walter Mallory, in my possession)

certainly paid under $30,000. There my parents continued to live until my father died in 1974.

A block away ran 32nd Street, parallel to our street, for some four or five blocks. It had probably originally been merely an alley behind 31st Street. Its population was almost entirely black. I had almost no contact with the inhabitants, nor, as I remember, did my parents, but I have no memory of racial hostility. By the time of the Kennedy administration almost all the blacks had moved away and their houses had been "restored," rebuilt or gutted. The populations of the two streets became indistinguishable, and white. Traces of Georgetown's mixed-race past were observable only in its churches. Many of its parishes continued to be largely African-American, evident every Sunday at services, but not during the week.

Dumbarton Oaks, right across the street from us, played a substantial role in our family life. It was the former estate of a retired foreign service officer named Robert Woods Bliss, who had donated it to Harvard in 1940. The residence was built in 1800 and extensively altered in the years that followed. My father, always worshipful about Harvard, was delighted to be across the street from its major southern outpost. There were a number of important collections of books, manuscripts and objects there: pre-Columbian, Byzantine and garden history being the principal ones. My parents walked often in the formal gardens, which a twelve-year old boy was of course slow to appreciate, but there was a contiguous "wild garden" called Dumbarton Oaks Park which to some extent took the place of my lost Sherwood Forest in Cambridge. There was even a Gaffney figure, although I never knew his name. In my later schoolboy years, I used to climb over the wall and roam the gardens at night with friends, until the night watchman chased us away. Once or twice we even dared to plunge into the beautiful swimming pool behind the mansion. Right next to Dumbarton Oaks was Montrose Park, where I shot hoops and played tennis on weekends.

My parents participated only at the edges in the swell of social popularity and renown that attached to living in Georgetown in those later times, when most of its Afro-American inhabitants had sold their houses for big profits and moved on. This was partly because my mother and father were a bit too old, and partly because my father came gradually to prefer a smaller and more intimate social circle, as my mother, now weakened by repeated strokes, had always done. Although he knew such intelligence community stars as Tracy Barnes, Frank Wisner and Kermit Roosevelt, he never became an intimate friend of any of them, and he never aspired to be invited to dinner parties by Joseph Alsop, who lived around the corner. He became steadily more conservative across the fifties and sixties, and gradually developed the attitudes of a loyal staffer in the great adventure of the Cold War, secure in the knowledge that he had an important job, but content to labor loyally in the shadows. Arthur Schlesinger, Jr. remembered my father as instinctively critical of authority, if not always publicly so, but that Everett Gleason gradually disappeared over the course of the Cold War. In the 1960s, however, his support for the powers that be accelerated, as loyal "cold warriors" became controversial. My father and I were to fall out dramatically over the Viet Nam War, the final and most shocking instance of my bad behavior.

Tom, senior year photo, St. Albans, 1956

St. Albans

When I arrived in Washington, D.C., in September, 1950, I was a bright, rebellious, spoiled, undisciplined and rather mouthy kid, with an unpredictable inclination to bully smaller children one minute and try to ingratiate myself with them the next. I was a volatile mixture of childish needs and narcissistic fears and fantasies, rebellious but cowardly. My father and I clashed frequently at home, mostly over issues of authority. I was disobedient both at home and at school, argumentative and insulting, and would not back down. I was never beaten, but I was cuffed around a good deal and spent a great deal of time shut in my room, where I nursed my grievances for long hours. My father compounded my rage with witty and sarcastic claims that my problem was not being treated severely enough, rather than the reverse. My mother tried to mediate, and my sense that she was not entirely on my father's side probably encouraged my defiance. My responses to this regime were complicated. I developed an identification with losers and victims that I never entirely lost thereafter, but I also feared being a "loser" myself. So while I struggled ineptly for success, my sympathetic identification was often with those who didn't have it. And just as I felt I needed to be championed, I dreamed of championing others.

But as time passed in my new surroundings, I began to set myself a different kind of ideal, perhaps in response to shaming and pressure both at home and at school, where I was also much criticized by teachers. My fear of humiliation and failure drove me to try to change. As a fanatical Red Sox fan from the age of ten, I took for an ideal the quiet and mature second baseman, Bobby Doerr, rather than the supremely volcanic and talented Ted Williams. I longed to be one of those people, like Doerr, who somehow achieved respect without constantly shoving themselves into the limelight. A major personality change was involved, although of course I didn't realize that, or at least conceive of it so abstractly. How to change myself? A mystery. Among historical figures from the general baseball world, I idolized Lou Gehrig, for the same reasons, rather than Babe Ruth. No doubt I was quite directly challenged to emulate such figures by my family, constantly stressed out as they were by my antics. After every failure I lectured myself, and I turned my parents' shaming techniques on myself. Having boasted or lied, I would grind my teeth at my failure to live up to my emerging ideal and vow to do better next time. Gradually, so, so gradually, I improved, shoving that nasty, vain little boy down under the water into the mud somewhere. But from that day to this, I dream about him and his failures.

By the time I graduated from St. Albans six years later, these idealistic yearnings to be a trustworthy "team player" were beginning to take on some flesh. I was slowly growing better at dealing with the world around me. I had much greater self-control, as well as the beginnings of self-knowledge. I was finding my own way in the company of boys of my own age—with many a setback—and was beginning to with girls. I was still torn, as we would say today, between the society of nerds and jocks, but I was at least minimally aware of the contours of my conflict. I largely preferred the nerds but was embarrassed by my preference, and tried to counter it by devoting myself to sports, specifically soccer and tennis, and seeking out the society of athletes, to whom I often had little to say. I would seek them out, then fall silent when they began some casual conversation. So most of the jocky school leaders tolerated me, but not too much more. I was most at home with the rare individuals who combined athletics with studiousness and some aestheticism.

There were more of those in the class behind me, especially the future novelist John Casey, who became a lifelong friend, and the handsome rogue Steve Truitt, the grandson of Vice President Alban Barkley.

I was deeply influenced in my early days at St. Albans by the sports stories—especially the baseball stories—of a writer named John R. Tunis, now almost forgotten. The teams he related to and fictionalized were the Yankees, Dodgers and Cardinals between 1935 and the early fifties. The popular literature on baseball still seems richer than that of any other sport in America, but football and to a lesser extent basketball have certainly caught up a bit in the years since then. Tunis had an excellent ear for the baseball slang of the period, but especially significant for me, he was an unabashed liberal idealist. He dealt with racism and anti-Semitism in baseball, completely new subjects for me, but saw most ball players as at least touched by heroism, as I did. He performed the great service for me of making generosity and fairness ideals to which I longed to respond. Books like Tunis' *The Kid from Tompkinsville* and especially *The Kid Comes Back* prepared me for the adult classics that were to form my ideas of how to behave—like George Orwell's *Road to Wigan Pier*. Roy Tucker, the centerfielder who came back from a World War II back injury to play in the World Series, was the first of my many liberal literary heroes. He was a hero, but a man among men: the first intimation of my later "band of brothers" fantasies.

I had also become seriously interested in painting and architecture. The latter I imbibed in part from our friends the Faulkners, for whose architectural firm I worked as an office boy in the summers. The young architects there, several of whom had ties to Frank Lloyd Wright, also showed me the work of Mies van der Rohe and Philip Johnson, and explained to me what was great about it. Waldron and Bussie Faulkner's sons, Avery and Winthrop, themselves both young architects, were among my first teachers. My interest in modern architecture developed alongside my interest in modern painting. But home environments prevented me from ever losing my love of the gothic and baroque. My father's taste for medieval architecture had already taken root.

I also discovered that I was a liberal in politics and identified instinctively with underdogs, undoubtedly based on my personal experience. This was uncomfortable for someone who also aspired to membership in the jock elite. St. Albans, the private Episcopal boys' school connected to the Washington Cathedral, was the arena where all these largely affirmative developments took place and to a considerable degree were fostered. I owe the school a great deal, one way or another.

St. Albans was, nevertheless, in many ways a very snobbish place. When later in my life I became a devotee of George Orwell's essays, I recognized a considerable kinship between the portrait he gave of St. Cyprian's (under the pseudonym of "Crossgates") in his memorable essay, "Such, Such Were the Joys," and St. Albans. There was an undiscriminating admiration for elite English public schools among many of the teachers (whom we called "masters"). Instead of "grades" (as in seventh grade) we had "forms" (as in "first form"). We ate lunch in a "refectory"; at the entrance to the main school building was a large tree which had begun life as a slip from England's famous Glastonbury Thorn. The ecclesiastical architecture and gothic windows added to the impression. "Looks like a minor English public school" was the verdict of a not unsympathetic British visitor. The dress code was conservative, even for the time. Coats and ties every day. The only exception was for letter sweaters, won for participation in a competitive sport. No jacket was required with such a sweater. No jeans; chinos were tolerated; grey flannel trousers were preferred. Nearly everyone had a blue blazer.

I entered St. Albans at a time of transition. Canon Albert Hawley Lucas, a Philadelphia patrician, known behind his back (but generally affectionately) as "the Chief," had just retired. His replacement was another Philadelphia native, who also became a Canon of the Washington Cathedral, Charles Martin. The two men were

Canon Charles Martin, Headmaster of St. Albans
from The Albanian, *Tom Gleason's senior yearbook, 1956*

quite different, but both were muscular Christians, with strong interests in athletics and perhaps a belief that the desired afterlife was easier for jocks to achieve than nerds. Neither were intellectuals, nor people of any great subtlety of mind. Charles Martin was a rather hot-tempered and stubborn but deeply pious man who did not seem to have toadied very much to the influential social elite of Washington that patronized the school. His "Letters from the Headmaster's Study" were widely read and admired by most of the school's parents of that time. They appeared perhaps a half dozen times a year and dealt with the usual moral dilemmas of schoolboys and their solutions were orthodox, but they were written in a straightforward way and with obvious sincerity. Orthodox as

Canon Martin's opinions were, he had a gut sympathy for boys who strayed from the path, as I had occasion to notice. An alumnus from a few years later than I recently made the interesting suggestion in a commemoration of Canon Martin that this emotional man, who had been a famous college wrestler, had to struggle quite hard with some inner demons of his own:

> If you were rebellious as a boy you always felt you traveled some back road to the canon's heart. Despite his decorum, despite his certainty about right and wrong, the man sympathized with outrage. ...Yet his official position left little room for rambunctiousness. He carried himself reined in against an excess of spirit which threatened to overwhelm.[1]

He was famous for telling parents that he was more interested in getting their children "into the Kingdom of Heaven" than into Harvard, an anecdote that redounded to his credit. But one may wonder if he had been less successful at getting them into Harvard (and Princeton in particular) whether some of the approval might have been withdrawn. Princeton first, followed long afterward by heaven was, after all, what was wanted.

Canon Martin was often theologically at sea, but he sometimes struck just the right note with students. When one of St. Albans' few Jewish students won the poetry prize, "the Canon" as he was known (or "Pope Charlie") presented him with a copy of Martin Buber's *I and Thou*, an appropriate and rather sophisticated gift for 1955, which the student warmly remembered a half century later.

Lucas was a charismatic extrovert who liked to have his hands on everything, Martin more inclined to delegate. But both men created a stable framework for the school and hired a pretty good faculty. Even so, both men's values emphasized points of view from my rather Victorian past, with which I was increasingly in conflict —don't break the rules, and we all know what they are—so that it

[1] Charles W. "Toby" Thompson, "On Failing to Recognize Canon Martin," *St. Albans Bulletin*, Winter, 2006-2007, p. 26.

was only gradually and in retrospect that I was able to give them their due.

The headmaster of the lower school, whom I encountered on my first day in the seventh grade, was a man named Alfred Randall True. Virtually every morning when we arrived at school, he was standing outside the front door, greeting students and the parents who dropped them off. He was a quiet man, with an extraordinary ability to project the empathy that he undoubtedly felt for almost all of his charges. Some masters probably regarded him as an exasperating goody-goody, but he exuded a remarkable mixture of fairness and sympathy which I have never since encountered to that degree in the groves of academe. For a new kid, the sight of Mr. True (the name sounds like something out of *A Pilgrim's Progress*) greeting the boys as they arrived at school was very reassuring, almost the only thing that was in that first year.

Racial intolerance was quite widespread at St. Albans. I experienced anti-Semitism for the first time there, and hostility to blacks was commonplace and openly expressed. There were no black students at St. Albans. African-Americans were generally spoken of at school as if they were both stupid and inherently comical. Minstrel show or *Amos 'n Andy* imitations of black speech were a staple of conversation among the boys. If somebody did someone else a favor, it was standard to reply sarcastically "mighty white of you." Another racist expression was common too, although more often on the lips of teachers than students: "nigger in the woodpile," meaning in the way it was used casually at the school that something was out of place. Almost no students at the school knew any black people at all, apart from servants, so the racism existed at an almost totally white, show biz or fantasy level. Of course I picked up the "n word," not knowing any better, and my using it at home provoked a crisis. I cannot remember exactly what I said, but I was immediately summoned to face both parents and read a stern lecture, about which they were obviously deadly serious, although, for once, there was no shaming involved. I don't believe I used the word a second time.

My parents were firm about racial prejudice, but of course they knew no black people socially either. When on rare occasions they encountered them in a social or semi-social situation they treated them with an exaggerated politeness which eventually came to seem almost as embarrassing to me as racial hostility. I began to be fascinated by black culture, knowing virtually nothing about it and—along with a couple of friends—tried my hand at black talk.

St. Albans was in no way unusual in the racism that prevailed there, and it was probably no worse than other private schools or upper-class circles. Washington, D.C., in the early 1950s was very much a southern city, with the federal government as it were dropped on top of its southern substructure. Public education was segregated and so was almost every aspect of city life, including theaters and restaurants. When the decision of the Supreme Court on Brown vs. Board of Education was announced in class in 1954, one seventh-grader I knew well immediately announced that his parents would pull him from the school and no doubt there were other similar declarations. The Episcopal Bishop of Washington, Angus Dun, was a strong liberal, but was quite often criticized and mocked, by teachers as well as students, for his progressive views. When, several years after my time, he pioneered the coming of black students to St. Albans, he was often referred to as "Black Angus." My parents thought very highly of him, partly because he was known to be a friend of Reinhold Niebuhr, whom my father admired.

Contempt for black people among whites was so widespread and readily expressed that any kind of public opposition to it was likely to result in various degrees of ridicule or even ostracism. The term "nigger-lover" was used relatively often and made me feel both frightened and as if I were off in some kind of goody-goody land if I objected to it, which I could bring myself to do only sometimes. I wasn't strong enough to endure much of the group hostility that ensued, especially in early grades. As I was already coming to regard my parents as Victorian fuddy-duddies, the last thing I wanted was to be projecting their out-of-it values in the world of school, where I desperately wanted to fit in. At the same time, on the issue of racism I knew they were right. Incidentally, we never used the term "racism." We talked about "prejudice," and "being prejudiced." Students—and my memory may be imprecise here—were generally reticent about using such terminology in front of the teachers, but I don't recall any student being rebuked for it either. Certainly there was no sermonizing about it in my time, although once a year a black employee of the school came to chapel and sang "Were You there When They Crucified my Lord?". Some people made fun of him, some people were touched. I can't recall any discussion about whether more was required of us than this condescending gesture, a very thinly veiled expression of racial and class superiority.

On one occasion my mother's almost total naiveté on matters of race led to a situation of considerable embarrassment for me. Having given up the farm as a summer place, my parents bought a small cottage at a posh resort on Chesapeake Bay called Gibson Island, entirely because the Faulkners summered there. My father came down infrequently; it was mostly my mother, sister and me. My mother, who had played golf during early summers in Hanover, New Hampshire, was determined that I should learn the game. The way she and my uncle had learned was by caddying at the Hanover (New Hampshire) Country Club during World War I, and so in the summer of 1951, at the age of thirteen I became a caddy.

The problem was that my mother didn't realize where she was. All the other caddies were black kids from outside this gated island community. They were amazed to see the son of a "member" of the club in the caddy shack, and they shunned me. The run of the golfers raised their eyebrows but paid little attention to this unusual spectacle. But some few resented it, presumably understanding it as a premature form of "race mixing," and others thought it hilarious. The golf pro used to bring people back to see the white kid in the caddy shack. He sometimes asked if I were Jewish. When I said "no sir," with a puzzled look, everybody would roar with laughter.

Some of the members called the caddies obscene names (I remember "watermelon head") and chewed them out in the most humiliating way. With me, they didn't know quite what to do. I was, after all, the son of a member. After a month or so, I tried to explain to my mother what I thought was going on. She didn't really get it, but I didn't have to caddy any more, and instead was given regular lessons.

A good many of the St. Albans masters were gay,—perhaps as many as a dozen, counting both the upper and lower school—and most of the students were aware of it. There seemed to be very little homosexual activity, beyond occasional surreptitious fondling or pinching, although there were occasional anecdotes about serious seduction. In retrospect what seems interesting is how little significance was attributed to the situation, in a decade supposedly so repressive. Kids joked about it, but as far as I knew did not complain. I just accepted it, as most students seem to have. Mr. Hogan, the Latin teacher, used to pinch our earlobes and play footsie, rather often. It wouldn't have occurred to me—and I think to most students in his classes—to complain about it. Were parents aware that teachers had crushes on some students? In at least a few cases, yes. But if there were discussions between parents and school authorities, we didn't know it, or at least it was not talked about seriously among students that I knew. In retrospect that seems kind of odd, but this version of "don't ask, don't tell" seemed to work. Perhaps there was some general understanding among parents that teachers in this sort of school were likely to be gay. The term "gay" was of course not generally known at the time. "Queer" was what we usually said.

The McCarthyism of the early Cold War years probably added to the generally conservative atmosphere at St. Albans, although when it came to national politics the school was far from monolithic. Mark Lindley, the son of the liberal *Newsweek* columnist, Ernest K. Lindley, was the leader of the Liberal side in the school's "Government Club," and the two sons of the *Washington Post*'s Alfred

Friendly, Sr., were in my classes and in fact lived on my street. They were two of my first friends at the new school. Political liberalism at St. Albans was reflected in our school arguments about Senator McCarthy, for there were plenty of students with connections to the Truman as well as the Eisenhower administrations, and there were probably more students against McCarthy than in favor of him. Most didn't care.

St. Albans felt strange to me at first; adjustments were hard, and I was an outlier for much of my first year, but of course I was desperate for social success and would have done anything to achieve it. On one of the first days at my new school, early, that is, in my seventh grade year, I had to go to the bathroom and was excused from class, but couldn't find the toilet. After opening door after door, to find them all full of students in class (and being too shy or dumbstruck to ask where the john was), I was reduced to peeing in the janitor's sink that was located in a kind of little closet just off the main hall, I was so desperate. I was still young enough so that wetting my pants was a real memory. Just as I was fully launched, however, the bell rang, and all of the classrooms emptied out into the corridors. Soon there were shouts of "hey, look at this!" and "some kid's peeing in the sink" and a small crowd gathered, to snicker at me. Much of my first year seemed to go like that. My desperate desire to fit in warred against my inveterate desire to challenge the accepted order of things. It was not until a couple of years later that I made any progress on this conundrum.

My seventh-grade teacher, a wonderful character named Stanley Sofield, helped me get through that year. Mr. Sofield had the most eccentric, mixed up lesson plan that can be imagined for twelve-year old boys. Much of his pedagogy consisted of general knowledge quizzes, which he called "hash tests," which might have questions about everything from classical antiquity to politics, boys' books, popular songs, or professional baseball. Those with the best grades were awarded nickel Hershey bars for prizes. Mr. Sofield also read to us a great deal, but seldom from approved literature. His favorite stories were by Damon Runyon, which he read with a magnificent New York mob accent. Sofield, I later realized, may have heard Damon Runyon himself read them, as he had often done over the radio. He also liked stories about "Sam Small, the Flying Yorkshireman," by Eric Knight (who had also written the original *Lassie Come Home*); and the charming minstrelsy of Roark Bradford's *Ol' Man Adam an' his Chillun*. Racing forms appeared from time to time on his desk; we were given to understand that he spent time at the track, and we also learned a certain amount about the horses, despite our young ages. He also wrote musical shows for his students. In class he was likely to refer to us as "gentlemen," but in other moods we were his "babies," especially on the athletic field. Anything he called us was okay. He could negotiate varying levels of authority and democracy with an unerring instinct for the needs of the moment. As a result, he was loved the way few teachers ever are, but also respected for his eccentricity, his array of talents, and for his own brand of integrity. I longed desperately for his favor, but didn't really make his inside circle. But there was improvement. I had done a good job, Sofield told my parents, and wrote on my report card that I had learned "at least partially, that unwarranted remonstrances are somewhat ridiculous."

The teaching at St. Albans in both the lower school and the upper school was quite uneven, however. English was taught to seniors by an ineffective authoritarian who had us read very little literature or serious criticism, but dictated to us a long, petrified chronicle paraphrasing major works of literature, almost entirely in terms of plot summaries. He did it in a wheezing, sing-song voice, beginning most sentences with a long drawn-out "oooooooh." "Oooooh, Cafritz," he would moan hoarsely. "Where did the Red Cross Knight go after he left the Bower of Bliss?" A class session of such questions (and the brief answers they elicited) constituted our contact with Spenser's "Faerie Queene," which I had great difficulty for many years in seeing in other than burlesque terms.

On the other hand, there was John Davis. Mr. Davis stooped and peered nearsightedly at the world through thick glasses. He was not politically sympathetic with my burgeoning liberalism, although he chose to ascribe it to naiveté rather than malevolence. He was very much an Anglophile and a conservative and sniffed at any infiltration of "public school" costumes or points of view into the world of St. Albans. He especially disparaged the satin athletic warmup jackets that many of us liked. But his teaching opened doors for me and did more than anything else, apart from pervasive family influence, to point me in the direction my career would ultimately take. Mr. Davis was the first teacher I had ever experienced who really introduced me to the pleasures of history, made it fun. His classes made me peer into the future and imagine what writing history might actually be like. For example, there was the final examination in his English history class, which I took as a junior. The entire examination consisted of a single sentence: "Trace the growth of English liberties." We had an entire day, beginning at nine in the morning and being required only to turn our papers in by five in the afternoon. We could write any amount and work anywhere within the borders of the Washington Cathedral; for lunch we were allowed to leave the Cathedral grounds for the drugstore across Wisconsin Avenue. We were of course on our honor not to talk to anybody about our work in progress.

"Trace the growth of English liberties." Even at the time I knew it was a much taller order than any I had ever received up until then—too tall, perhaps, even if you had all day, which I did. It was only later that I understood that we were being given the same assignment that the great Whig historians, from Macaulay to Trevelyan and beyond, had spent their careers and indeed their lives grappling with. I would go on to find historians in college who thought that the Whig tradition was exhausted, and probably from a scholarly point of view they were right.[2] But it was more than enough for

[2] The idea that history is progressive and that we and the world we live in are the best that has yet come along.

John Davis, Teacher, St. Albans School, from The Albanian, *1954*

us to handle, and indeed our primary and secondary texts were all geared to the Whig point of view. The notion that nineteenth-century English liberalism marked the goal toward which humanity had been striving for centuries seemed to be perfectly all right with Mr. Davis, although I later learned that he had a more complex view of the world than that.

I was disconcerted by this one-sentence examination, indeed scared by it, but I was not really surprised. I had already come to understand that Mr. Davis' courses were not entirely like the ones I had experienced up to then at St. Albans and at schools I had gone to earlier. You did have to know "the facts"—and if you couldn't give a relatively comprehensive five-sentence version of Wat Tyler's Rebellion, or if you thought that Jane Seymour was one of Gladstone's discarded mistresses, you were in trouble. But Mr. Davis' English history course pointed the way beyond the memory work with which I was so familiar, to a stage in my historical studies when I would have to make sense of things for myself. It was challenging, at times frightening, as intellectual work would be in college and graduate school. So I can see, in retrospect, that his course had some of the qualities of a rite of passage for me.

I learned some very practical things from him about what made a good teacher. As he did in other areas of human existence, Mr. Davis knew that miracle, mystery and authority have—or can have—an important place in teaching. He deliberately made himself interesting, mysterious to us, his students, in a way that few other teachers were able to do, or perhaps cared to. There was something monarchical about him that piqued our interest—one-on-one encounters could have something of the character of a royal audience. Sometimes the king was disposed to be gracious, sometimes cool, occasionally frosty, even threatening and once in a great while, apoplectic. Although he was never, that I remember, actually unfair (in the way that a seventeen-year-old could recognize), he could be capricious, again as one imagined the sovereign might be. To put it in a nutshell, he introduced me to the theatricality of teaching, something I have often thought about in my own teaching career, and to the notion that a good teacher ought to think about his or her persona. To cite a provocative parallel (one that would surely annoy him), like Mel Brooks in *History of the World Part I*, John Davis could remind you that "it's GOOD to be the king." But most of his students deeply respected his intelligence and understood, if subliminally, that he had qualities of mind that were most unusual at St. Albans.

Another wonderful man who made a big difference in my life was Dean Stambaugh, the art teacher, a lanky, balding Pennsylvanian, who had studied art with the American painter Hobson Pittman at

Penn State University.[3] One of the things that was marvelous about him was that he treated all those who were really serious about painting as if they were real artists. As I had no idea of what "being an artist" might mean, to be given this kind of identity, however temporarily and tenuously, was important and challenged me to think about what it in fact entailed. Criticism from him was more like "crits" in an art school studio than ordinary secondary school teaching. "If it were mine," Mr. Stambaugh would often begin his discussion of your picture, "if it were mine, I might"—and then would follow some useful, generally rather technical piece of advice. He always spoke carefully and clearly, pursing his lips very slightly, alternately giving your picture the most intense scrutiny and looking you disconcertingly in the eye.

If it were mine. Why has that phrase stuck in my mind all these years? Perhaps because when I heard it I felt that Mr. Stambaugh was taking me seriously and at that time being taken seriously was very, very important to me. He was suggesting that my painting was a complex piece of work, like his own, and that he could imagine himself having painted it. To that extent, and to that extent only, he set us on a plane of equality. But his use of the phrase also suggested that I might have something quite different in mind from anything he could suggest, which I ought to realize. He could not tell me in any absolute terms how to improve my picture. Described in these terms, his technique reduces itself to an elementary, if benevolent, pedagogical device, but actually it was immensely effective with almost forty years of student painters, some of whom went on to be artists, architects or designers of note. "If it were mine," that is, reflected Mr. Stambaugh's belief, which we all imbibed at a young age, that art was a highly personal affair, and that even the least of us was capable of surprising solutions in our painting that no one could have anticipated. And above all, art was serious. Almost no

[3] Portions of the material on Dean Stambaugh appeared in a somewhat different form in Smith Hempstone, ed., *An Illustrated History of St. Albans School*, Glastonbury Press, Washington D.C., 1981, pp. 88-89.

one who encountered him in the classroom—at least in the lower grades—had ever given a thought to such a fantastic idea.

Mr. Stambaugh would also talk about whether your picture "worked" or not, which was also in its way a revelation. It added a dimension that in retrospect seems almost banal, but at the time was important. A picture had to have a certain consistency; it had parts, and all of them had to be in some kind of harmonious order. It was in some way a system, even analogous to a machine. It had to function. Almost without noticing I took in this new point of view.

Until I met Mr. Stambaugh, it never occurred to me that excelling at everything I did was not the only possible goal in life. Of course I never remotely lived up to any such notion, but I really thought in some ritual way that I ought to try to be very good at everything that attracted me. Mr. Stambaugh attacked that idea in the most deadly serious way, launching repeated and extremely sarcastic attacks on what he regarded as a fatuous ideal: the "all around boy." This came as a considerable shock to me, and to other students. At first, I just thought it was part of his "differentness," relating to the vague sense that I got from Mr. Stambaugh early on that (unlike at least the publicly expressed views of most of the other masters at the school) not every aspect of the world as it was pleased him. I felt obscurely his long intense struggle to make the painting of pictures an acceptable part of the world of adolescent boys. I felt his bitterness at his merely partial success.

There is a great deal to be said on both sides of the issue of being a generalist or a specialist, but when I was fourteen or fifteen, I had never heard a case made for working passionately and intensely at one thing—if necessary to the point of neglecting other things, good things, important things. Undoubtedly this was because orthodox pedagogy took the view that we were all far too young to be told any such thing. So Dean Stambaugh provided me and other boys with an early sense that in life we would be forced to choose (not between good and evil—everyone told us that) but between good and almost-as-good, or worse yet, between things that might be equally good. When Mr. Stambaugh lectured me and other boys severely about wasting our time playing baseball or singing in the glee club, we knew that most, if not all, other teachers at the school would deeply disapprove of what he was saying. Seeing such open disagreement among the teachers was interesting in its own right and vaguely disturbing. But—though it made me uncomfortable —I was also eventually forced to see something of what was right about his view, in the work of student painters (and other kinds of enthusiasts) who were neglecting much else of what they were supposed to be doing in school, but already getting into shows at the Corcoran Gallery or the Baltimore Museum.

Mr. Stambaugh was often disapproving, sometimes irritable and occasionally really angry—more often at other teachers, but occasionally at us, but he seldom said anything stronger than "dammit," so that his rare outbursts were all the more impressive. On one occasion he was in a rage with someone or other and he said in his most flat, dismissive voice, "Well you know, he's just not worth a fart in a mitten!" I think he was slightly amused and perhaps bemused too when all of us present began to roar with laughter. Despite his small town Pennsylvania background, Mr. Stambaugh dressed beautifully and quite formally, and we all thought of him as the essence of civilized elegance and sophistication. It was wonderfully incongruous to hear such a homely expression on his lips.

Mr. Stambaugh prided himself on liking modern art, and he really did, up to a point—actually quite a specific point. He admired Matisse and Picasso, loved Georges Braque, Pierre Bonnard and Edouard Vuillard. Amadeo Modigliani and Chaim Soutine were appreciated. I well remember the phased process of coming to see Soutine as far more than merely a messy colorist who couldn't draw and wondering why Modigliani's nudes didn't have regular eyes. The Americans Marsden Hartley, Stuart Davis and John Marin were lovingly shown to us and their merits extolled. But the heart of his taste was the School of Paris, and around 1940 he lost his appetite for much of what was being done, particularly in New York. He could

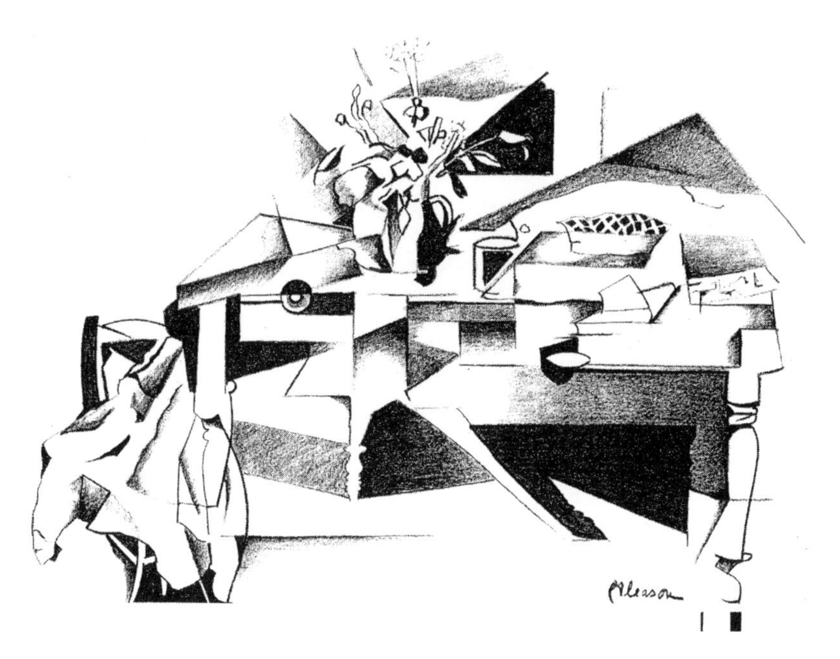

Richard's Studio by Tom Gleason, 1961

find no merit in Pollock, de Kooning or Arshile Gorky, and we were actively taught to dislike them; worse, we were told that they were charlatans and so were the people who championed them. His own lovely landscapes resembled oils by the Barbizon School of the pre-Impressionist period. In retrospect this taste seems a bit narrow and predictable, but at the time, we believed that he was unlocking the mysteries of modern art to us, which added to his mystique in our eyes. After all, many of us—not me—came from places where all modern art was laughed at or execrated.

Apart from Mr. Stambaugh's art room, the place which primarily formed my taste in modern painting and helped me to understand, among other things, that New York painting after 1940 was not the work of frauds or charlatans, was the Phillips Gallery. Duncan Phillips was an heir to the enormous resources of the

Laughlin Steel Corporation. In the intimate setting of what had been his residence, less than a block from Dupont Circle, was one of the greatest small collections of painting in the United States. In fact there were not many places in Washington, D.C. in the fifties where great modern painting could be seen. There was also the Corcoran Gallery, but the Phillips had the more spectacular masterpieces. At the Phillips, Goya and El Greco shared quarters with the American abstractionist Arthur Dove and the painter of seascapes, John Marin. There I saw Renoir's "Luncheon at the Boating Party," his greatest painting. There I saw my first Rothko, my first Pollock and my first Gorky. Although Mr. Stambaugh didn't like them, he probably pulled his punches a little bit because of his respect for Phillips, and at any rate, I saw these pictures over and over again, and began to understand their relationship to different kinds of painting that I understood better. Duncan Phillips himself was still alive in the fifties, but only occasionally seen. His wife Marjorie was represented in the collection by a daub of a still life, which suggested to us schoolboys who haunted the place that even our similarly routine work might grow into something out of the ordinary.

Presumably most of us cherish places in their lives that have some kind of archetypal meaning for us that we never lose: the essentials of an old house—or a beautiful and very modern one—a vision of an artist's studio, a comfortable study full of books and couches in which good conversation is natural. One of my archetypal milieus is Dean Stambaugh's art room. When I imagine it—or rooms like it—it is generally large and rectangular, and crowded with life. It is a human workroom, primarily, smelling of turpentine, full of brushes, painting knives, palettes, cans and jars of chemicals. In various corners of the room are old tobacco tins, vases, pieces of fabric, pieces of old silvery wood, flowers, fruit (some artificial, some real), large pineapple juice cans, and other splendid objects. Mr. Stambaugh taught us a lot about objects. Some are assembled into still life form, others are just lying around, waiting to be organized.

In the corners stand various large indoor plants, some distinctly exotic if not actually carnivorous. At one end of the room sit several big, indoor birdcages, full of large doves and smaller, more brightly colored finches. The strains of romantic music, often Italian opera, fill the air. (Mr. Stambaugh was never one for modern music.) My love for Sibelius and Dvorak dates from the St. Albans art room.

Finally and most important, of course, are the pictures—finished, half finished, or just begun—ranging from the daubs of beginners to the work of talented young painters, ready for shows and galleries. Even these latter are not quite as original as I once thought they were, but almost all of them are personal, and as a group they are as original as such a body of schoolboy art is ever likely to be.

That art room gave me a sense of studio and workplace that I have never lost. Years later I tacked up a photograph of Brancusi's studio on my office wall in grad school because it seemed a so much more attractive work space than the one I was occupying, writing a history Ph.D. After a couple of weeks of looking at it, I realized its kinship with the St. Albans art room and the linked nature of the images of work space. The St. Albans art room also gave me a sense of how a person's style, taste and culture could take on tangible form—how one could make a place to live, and then proceed to inhabit it. And as with other places precious to me, I have returned to it in my mind all my life.

Black music was my other great discovery between the ages of thirteen and eighteen. I was first caught in the seventh grade by the sound of forties big band music: Benny Goodman and Glenn Miller. This was a relatively common enthusiasm among American teenagers, even as late as the early 1950s, but with me it didn't last long. One day I heard a traditional New Orleans front line on a record—it was the Bunk Johnson band, later fronted by George Lewis after Bunk's death. The tunes, which I remember to this day, were *Tishomingo Blues* and *When the Saints Go Marching In*. It was a revelation and I remember it as instantaneous. One minute I was listening to Miller, Goodman and Shaw, the next minute I was completely enthralled by the three-instrument counterpoint of a New Orleans front line. It was an epiphany, really the first time anything like that had happened to me. I was probably not yet fourteen, but I felt that I had seen far down into the way things were in the world, and I knew I was changed forever. Jazz quickly filled up my afternoons, evenings and weekends. To this day, I have some trouble understanding how such a passion could strike so fast, and so permanently. Years later, when I was relatively well read on jazz, I discovered for how many others, perhaps especially in Europe, suddenly hearing jazz had the quality of religious conversion. I had a modest, entirely ordinary musical ability, but there was no existential precedent for my falling in love with jazz, a passion that endures until today and I am sure will continue until the very end.

There were two places in Washington where in 1953 you could hear jazz that was a kind of mix of Dixieland and swing, the closest thing I could find anywhere nearby that approximated the music of New Orleans. One was a place called The Bayou, on Georgetown's waterfront under the K Street Freeway to Key Bridge from downtown. The other spot was the Charles Hotel, on the edge of a black neighborhood some distance out 16th Street. The Charles was unusual in that it had a racially mixed band on a regular basis. In 1954 around Washington blacks and whites played together at sessions or on a sitting-in basis, but serious musical integration was not yet really established. Black clubs were located in black neighborhoods, where whites rarely went, and white clubs in white neighborhoods had few black patrons. The Charles Hotel was one of the few exceptions.

One of the first black musicians I got to know and whose playing I admired was the trombonist, Slide Harris (his name was listed in the DC phone directory as "Harris, Slide"). He was rumored to have played with Duke Ellington, but I later discovered that he had in fact played with Lucky Millinder and other black swing bands of the 1940s. It took me many months, but after numerous rather fumbling and generally perfunctory conversations with him between sets I finally worked up the courage to ask him to a session at our house (with my parents away for the weekend, of course). To my enormous pleasure, he accepted, after a moment of hesitation, and came several times in the year or so that followed.

"Slide" was a quiet, obliging person. When I mixed him a gin and soda (instead of a gin and tonic) at one of these sessions, he drank as much as he could manage and didn't mention my gaffe. I was fifteen and this was the first drink I had ever mixed. I had no idea of mixers; soda and tonic looked the same to me. But he was his own man. At another session a few years later, the trumpet player, Jimmy McPartland, called him "Slip," not "Slide," several times on the bandstand. Finally, Slide confronted him. "If you're not gonna get my name right, don't call me no more," he said. I was also friendly with the regular trumpet player at the Charles, Kinny Focher. He was partly immobilized by a bad leg and wore a heavy brace; he had a tendency, perhaps stemming from that, to overblow, but that was not uncommon with Dixieland bands of that day and the Charles Hotel group made some inspiring music, as I heard it.

I spent even more time at the Bayou, partly because it was only seven blocks from my house and it was easy for me to get there on foot, and I began hanging out at these clubs well before I was old enough to drive. The regular band (called, naturally, the "Dixie Six") at the Bayou featured a fluent Goodman-style clarinet named Wally Garner, who had gone to the University of Virginia, and the leader was a passionate clone of the Dixieland cornetist "Wild Bill" Davison; ours was "Wild Bill" Whelan. I liked to spend Sundays there, from 3:00 in the afternoon, when the band started, until 10:00 at night, regardless of homework. (Sunday lunch was the big meal of the day at our house; supper was a free for all.) Sometimes big stars from New York came down and sat in. Being of an academic turn of mind, I tried to learn the entire repertoire that these bands played, even writing the titles down in chronological order, and trying to pick them out on the piano at home. I would also go to the Bayou during the week for a couple of hours at night, often

Wally Garner and Roy Lamson, composite photo, c. 1960

sneaking out of the house after my parents had gone to bed. At that time, I neither smoked nor drank, so I would consume Coke after Coke and listen to the band. When an occasional policeman would stop by to check up on who was there, the generally friendly waitresses would tell me to go into the men's room until the cops were gone. Eighteen was the legal drinking age in Washington, and I was three years younger than that. A certain amount of marijuana was also smoked on the premises, but I never got deep into that.

I became part of a group of wannabees that hung around the

Bayou, all of them older than I, and my parents were scandalized when these disreputable bohemians began to come to the house (and on occasion deplete the liquor closet). My father liked traditional jazz, but knew nothing about it. He had grown up in Evanston, Illinois, but had never heard any Chicago jazz in person. He had never gone to hear Louis Armstrong at the Dreamland Café. I could hardly express my indignation. What a missed opportunity! He didn't even know who Bix Beiderbecke was!

On the other hand, my father thoroughly approved of another jazz friend, Johnny Eaton, who had gone to Yale and was quite able to deal with my parents on their terms. Johnny ultimately devoted his career to jazz and has made several fine solo piano records for Hank O'Neal at Chiaroscuro Records. Eaton was at that time (around 1960) a stride piano player, although following Art Tatum and Earl Hines into more modern styles, and he did me the inestimable service of introducing me to Willie "the Lion" Smith and Ralph Sutton, but most especially to the unique Art Tatum. My favorite disc of Johnny's was a record session with the Charles Hotel band, featuring "Wild Bill" Davison visiting on trumpet, "Slide" on trombone and Johnny on piano. It was recorded at the Manassas Jazz Festival, near the Civil War battlefield, and is called "Wild Bill at Bull Run." I often play it and it brings back those wonderful days and nights, when I lived to hear new music and a great ensemble chorus could make me almost sick with excitement.

Another musician who helped bridge the jazz gap between my parents and me was Roy Lamson, a disciple of clarinetist Pee Wee Russell and also an English professor at Williams and later at MIT. Roy had been a tutor in Harvard's Adams House with my father at Harvard in the late 'thirties, and after the war continued to have reserve military responsibilities every June in Washington. He always stayed with us, and my prestige always benefited when Roy sat in at the Charles or the Bayou in my company. He was known to my friends as "Pee Wee Russell's father"; although his hair was white he was actually a bit younger than Pee Wee, whom he several times took care of when Pee Wee was suffering from physical ailments, alcohol or both.

Being incorrigibly bookish, I also read extensively about the history of jazz and blues, decked my basement quarters with photos and album jackets, drew and painted musicians (and sometimes imagined myself teaching a history of jazz, something I finally did for a semester at Brown University more than twenty years later). When I came across a new name I hunted through record stores and discographies for example of their playing. I tried to get my St. Albans schoolmates interested in my musical enthusiasms, with no better than moderate success. I read everything I could find about Louis Armstrong and Bix Beiderbecke, Duke Ellington, Count Basie and Eddie Condon and his friends, the white followers of Bix, who lionized Louis. By some mysterious process, on Sunday nights late, I was able to pull in a New Orleans station on my little radio that broadcast live jazz from the Parisian Room in the Crescent City. The band, led by cornetist Tony Almerico, was not remarkable, but the vocalist was the venerable Lizzie Miles, who made me realize that not all the great blues singers were available only on the old 78 rpms that I collected so zealously. I tried to be next to the radio on as many Sunday nights as I could (starting at ten or eleven) to hear her sing.

But jazz, during those years, was changing. Soon I began to notice new kinds of more abstract looking cover art, and new names that I had barely heard of: Dizzy Gillespie, Miles Davis, Bud Powell, Fats Navarro, and, above all, Charlie "Bird" Parker. As I was reading everything I could find about jazz, I also began to read about the sessions at Harlem in the forties—at Minton's and Clark Monroe's Uptown House, and the new music that was worked out there. It took me a long time to begin really to hear bebop. I had a lot of troubles relating the chord changes to the improvised notes, which except for ballads, seemed screechy and tuneless and too fast for my ear and brain to process. But gradually I began to hear the music.

One great advantage in getting to like the more modern forms of jazz was that there was so much more of it around. There were little clubs all over Washington, and although most of them had a largely black clientele, young whites in some numbers were beginning to get interested in the music too. One kid only two or three years older than I got a job with the Woody Herman band, which for some reason had a number of alumni in the DC area, and there were other examples. There were also clubs downtown where blacks and whites both went, and which booked nationally known bands. The Bohemian Caverns, near Howard University, was one, and perhaps Davis' Patio Lounge was another. Bill Potts, sometime arranger for Woody Herman, was the house piano player at Olivia Davis'. I heard Clifford Brown at the Bohemian Caverns, which featured plaster stalactites and stalagmites, a few weeks before he died in an automobile accident on the Pennsylvania Turnpike just as I was graduating from St. Albans. Charlie Byrd, the guitar player was a regular at a small club called the Showboat for many years. But there were scores of local clubs where small groups played, mostly made up of beginners and locals. In retrospect, from a time when so much jazz training is quasi-academic and so much jazz has a repertory flavor, one marvels at all that energy and the passion and commitment that bebop aroused in so many urban young people, white and especially black. How hard they practiced and what wonderful schools all those little local clubs were.

Unexpectedly, I met the man who might have been the most talented of all these young local musicians not at a bar in southwest Washington, but right at St. Albans—a young Greek-American with what seemed to his schoolmates the tongue-twister name of Alex Lagoudakis (mispronounced by us "Lock-a-DOCK-us, and twisted into all sorts of devilish little-boy variants behind his back), who became a tenth-grader—known under our British system as a "fourth former"—the year I went into the ninth grade or third form. Alex was a distinct presence at St. Albans. He was reputed to be the strongest schoolboy in Washington, and perhaps, he was. Light, at less than 190 pounds, he made an enormous difference to our football team, despite the fact that he had a hard time seeing without his glasses. As I recall, this was the pre-contact lense era. No opposing linemen could do much with him, as in addition to his massive strength, he was amazingly quick. He was also a formidable wrestler and did beautiful naturalistic torsos in clay for art class.

Initially our relations were not good. Like others at school, Alex resented my tendency to shoot off my mouth in class, and after an exchange in which he believed that I had intended to insult him in biology class, he knocked me down in the hall outside the classroom, in the absolutely shortest of my many fights. As sometimes happened, from that inauspicious beginning, a friendship blossomed. He was somewhat abashed at having taken care of me so decisively with two punches, and I was eager to get to know him. His strength was so much greater than that of anybody else in the school that I suffered no loss of prestige in being beaten up by him. Jazz was the medium, as Alex was probably the best white bebop drummer in Washington. Because of his great strength, as well as his musicianship and a certain emotional unpredictability, he could go anywhere he wanted in the black jazz world without interference.

Alex was a charter member of young jazz musical circles in Washington, apart from myself and a bass player from Wilson High School, the only person, so far as I knew, who actually went to black clubs. He frequently played in sessions and had gigs at clubs all over Washington, and I trailed him around to many of these places, sometimes after an evening of the usual private school party social life, in which Alex was only sometimes involved. In addition, he often would come over and play with other musicians in our basement, a bit later with Johnny Eaton. The latter was disconcertingly of the swing era for Alex's taste, but he liked Johnny, and I was in seventh heaven when my two new friends would play together (sometimes with others) when my parents were engaged elsewhere. Once in awhile I would try to keep up with some of the lesser musicians on drums.

Tom Gleason (lower right) and friends working on the St. Albans yearbook, 1956

Both with Alex and without him, I explored other popular music venues, theaters and revues as well as clubs. I loved black talk, especially the bebop slang of that day. One night when I was driving a carful of musicians home from some club, I narrowly missed a car coming out of a side street. "Watch it, man," said Alex sharply. "I ain't got eyes to get hung by that boat." Meaning he didn't want an accident.

There was a segregated musical theater scene in the District of Columbia, and as I got older I began to venture to the Howard Theatre and other places where there was gospel, stand-up comedy and small band music, usually on the border between jazz and rock and roll. Sometimes I would invite other friends from school and occasionally they would come. These evenings could be uncomfortable. I wanted to go to black theaters, but I often drew stares and sometimes open hostility. My white friends from St. Albans were even more ill at ease. Our little world was so segregated. I didn't tell all that many people of my trips out into the black world.

Black culture was, to a young WASP not entirely at ease with himself, so expressive, so uninhibited, so wide open. It was fascinating in its extroversion, physicality and spontaneity, but also frightening, partly because of the way it opened up questions of social class as well as race. The songs that I was used to had titles like "Dancing on the Ceiling" or "I Get a Kick Out of You." It was a bit of a transition to "Pig Meat Papa" or "Black Snake Moan," as sung by Leadbelly or Blind Lemon Jefferson. On one occasion, a white friend I had brought with me suddenly burst into hysterical and frightened laughter during the show at the Howard Theatre. He couldn't stop, and we had to leave.

Much later I realized that I was experiencing an abbreviated and late version of the fascination with black culture that mildly rebellious young whites had been going through for much of the twentieth century, first in the U.S. and then in Europe. Although I lacked the courage to acknowledge it, part of me really wanted to be black, a fantasy partly about music, partly about strength and toughness.

In those early days, the stylistic contrast between New Orleans jazz, swing and bebop seemed very sharp, to the point that fans of one style literally couldn't believe that you could really like music outside that particular "bag," as we used to say. But I noticed as the years passed, the contrasts seemed less sharp. As "free jazz" became the frontier style, the differences between swing and bebop dwindled. As a composer friend of mine, John Harbison, several times reminded me, something very important happened in black music around 1945 with the emergence of bebop. Jazz became less rural, less amiable, and took a long step away from popular culture. Required technique was far more formidable. Musicians quickly became less disposed to produce entertainment for white folks.

In the fall of 1955 I applied to Harvard, Yale and Brown (where several of my cousins on my father's side had gone). Harvard was my first choice. College admissions were relatively stress-free. The then Dean of Admissions at Harvard, Wilbur Bender, was another old roommate of my father's, and when he visited Washington he stayed with us. By this time my behavior was less and less a problem; I had even been elected to what was the equivalent of student government—I had become a "prefect" in my senior year at anglophile St. Albans. My last notorious escapade was a suspension in my tenth grade year for showing rude and open skepticism about the Resistance war stories of our French teacher and refusing to accept his reprimand. Years later I was amazed to be told by John Davis that Mr. de Marne was regarded by some of his colleagues as a blowhard, and that my rudeness provoked some secret sympathy from the faculty, although to my knowledge no one intervened on my behalf.

Another escapade also attracted some similar approval. In my senior year, a donor had given the Washington Cathedral a gaudy, gilded statue of George Washington riding the racehorse Man O' War, which was located in a very public place: at the foot of a flight of steps running down from the south transept of the Cathedral. It was badly sculpted and its bright gold color made it seem even more a joke. Both the horse and rider were widely mocked for vulgarity and incompetence in the execution, especially by artistic cognoscenti, such as Dean Stambaugh. So one night I and a friend whose name I will not mention, brought a pint of bright Chinese red paint and a ladder to the statue, climbed up onto the pedestal and painted Man O' War's genitalia and tail, as well as the tip of Washington's sword. On Monday, Canon Martin addressed the entire school and called for the malefactors to turn themselves in, but we never did. I haven't been back to look at the awful statue in many years, but as I recall at some point the gilding was removed and this cornball object at least ceased to draw so much attention to itself.

Tom and feline roomate, Siegfried, in the Eliot House courtyard, 1958

Harvard College

... dreaming of justice, yet himself a source of injustice ...
—Albert Camus

HARVARD WAS A PHYSICALLY FAR MORE modest place fifty years ago than today. Room furnishings for freshmen in the Harvard Yard were extremely spartan: ancient double-decker beds, rickety chairs, a table. You could buy a rug some blocks away at a down-at-the-heel auction house. TVs and refrigerators brought from home were very rare and seemed ostentatious. Dormitory floorboards were old and dirty. Food quality was far below the restaurant-grade standards about which students still complain. They should have experienced the "mystery meat" that Harvard freshmen were served in 1956! Athletic facilities were not very different from secondary school. Lockers were old and battered; showers were antique. Co-ed dorms would have seemed like something out of science fiction or *Mad* magazine.

Cambridge was rather similar. Harvard Square and Brattle Square were predominantly shabby-genteel rather than glitzy; no steel and glass facades to be seen anywhere. The tower of Memorial Hall had just burned at the beginning of the past summer, and would not be repaired for decades. It's hard to escape the conclusion that the whole culture even of the rich was a good deal more austere and less materialistically pretentious than today (although undoubtedly more snobbish), except perhaps for a tiny handful at the very top. Old-fashioned gentility still prevailed in many Cambridge quarters; silver tea services might be brought out when faculty wives entertained students on a Tuesday or Thursday afternoon, just as in my parents' time. Americans were part of a consumer culture no doubt, but consumption was still comparatively inconspicuous, and students were not catered to remotely the way they are today. The idea of using luxurious student accommodations to compete with other universities would have seemed bizarre and sybaritic to the administrators of that time.

Harvard kids were as a group very smart; and it was a considerably more cosmopolitan world from what I had known at St. Albans. The future math majors next door threw many Greek letters into their conversations and there was much talk of Kierkegaard and Marx, which made my roommates and me feel like the relative provincials we were. I knew both Karl and Groucho by name but had only read *The Communist Manifesto* and never seen *Monkey Business*. That would soon change.

My roommates in my freshman year at Harvard were two of my close friends from St. Albans. Richard (Rick) Harkness was the son of the well known NBC radio newscaster, also named Richard Harkness, and Andrew Rosen was the son of a political scientist from the University of Chicago, now, like my father, turned government bureaucrat. Andy was probably less at sea than I was in the first weeks and months of freshman year. He was a serious modern poet, knew about Sartre and Camus (I was just beginning to find out) and played very nice blues guitar. He sang Leadbelly songs particularly well. I vividly remember him singing "Bourgeois Blues":

> White folks in Washington, know just how
> Call a colored man a nigger, just to see him bow.
> Lord, an' a bourgeois man, in a bourgeois town.
> I got the bourgeois blues,
> I'm gonna spread the news all aroun'.

I was very much of that opinion at the time. With Andy I also had my first conversations about what it was like to be Jewish and about anti-Semitism, a subject of which I had become barely aware at

St. Albans, but had not thought much about. When I found Andy brooding in our room on a cloudy Sunday afternoon and asked him what was on his mind, he replied that he was thinking about what it was like to be Jewish. His answer was almost unintelligible to me. Although I had been church-connected all my life, my Christianity had been shallow and routine until then, something which has changed in various ways since. I sometimes thought about whether God existed, occasionally about whether Christianity was true, and even what "true" might mean in this context, but never what it was "like" to be Christian, which then seemed to me analogous to Andy's peculiar question. Andy's Jewishness was something I had barely noticed at St. Albans. There were so many more Jews at Harvard that Andy began to seem if not part of a cohort, at least a member of a discernable group.

In those days there was nothing called "the Holocaust" and I was barely aware of what had happened to European Jews at the hands of the Nazis. That is to say, I knew that millions of Jews had been killed but somehow failed to carry this knowledge further. The subject was undeniably horrifying but it was remote, and it never occurred to me that any contemporary of mine would be likely to brood about it, let alone derive an identity from it, not that I had any idea yet of what deriving an identity from events or circumstances might be. In some ways World War II seemed further away to me in 1956 than it would thirty or even fifty years later.

In fact, I knew almost nothing about Jews. My family was essentially devoid of prejudice, but also of information. I knew that Jews wrote the Old Testament, which had been superseded by the New, although of course there was continuity between them, but again this subject was academic to me and remote. I knew that some kind of prejudiced people disliked Jews, considered them money-grubbing and imitated them with a disgusting accent and talked about shekels while rubbing their hands together. But I had never known anybody who looked or sounded remotely like this stereotype. I was aware that Jews were sometimes called Christ-killers, but I had no idea of the extent or virulence of such ideas. Hostility to blacks had been much more a part of my world, although I remember noticing that there had been some overlap between anti-black racists and anti-Semites at St. Albans. Some of the little I knew about anti-Semitism came from such unlikely and meager sources as John R. Tunis' baseball stories. As far as contemporary Jewish culture was concerned, I was a blank page.

Because I had known Andy at St. Albans, contact with him did not make me conscious that friendship between Christians and Jews—at college or elsewhere—was in any way remarkable, or even a subject about which to think. My understanding of the history and importance of anti-Semitism took some time to develop. I did pick up over the course of my first two years at Harvard a sense that Harvard was more Jewish than either Yale or Princeton, and after a while I began to feel that I was in a world that was far more Jewish than anything I had experienced before. All of which is to say that I began to develop an idea that the social world was different if it contained a significant Jewish presence—which meant that I began simultaneously to be able to understand my own world as a particularly non-Jewish, or WASP one. It was many years, however, before I had any idea at all about how places developed—or didn't—a Jewish presence. Or about relative admissions policies, quotas, or of how much more Jewish Harvard was in the mid-fifties than its best known competitors.[1] I discovered only gradually how many American worlds had been closed to Jews but were now opening up. Many, if not most of my WASP contemporaries were as ignorant as I was, or more so. Several knew only that Jews were, as Jack Womack later related to me, "in the Bible." Many were never aware of having met, let alone known, a Jew.

[1] An excellent account of the ups and downs of admission policies can be found in Jerome Karabel, *The Chosen. The Hidden History of Admission and Exclusion at Harvard, Yale and Princeton*, Boston and New York, Houghton Mifflin, 2005. See also Susanne Klingenstein, *Jews in the American Academy*, 1900-1946, New Haven, Yale University Press, 1991.

Over the course of my years at Harvard I became fascinated by Jewish jokes: the self-mockery, the complex and, to me, extraordinary sense of being the eternal underdog but nevertheless smarter than one's tormentors, the self-consciousness. As I began to find my way in a more Jewish world I experienced a disconcerting sense of how shaped I had been—despite my rebelliousness and bad behavior—by the world of the Episcopal Church and its educational practices. Often the new acquaintances I was making poked fun—usually gentle—at my prep school friends and habits. I was sometimes called "the Abbott of St. Albans." Some of my new friends came from a leftwing political milieu which was quite new to me. The whole history of the organized Left in the United States—a continent I had not hitherto explored—began to come into view.

It was not just Jewish traditions and points of view of which I was ignorant. I had never heard of James T. Farrell or read anything by Eugene O'Neill or James Joyce. None of the few Catholics I had known ever talked about their particular experiences growing up in the United States. Except for my rather superficial romance with black culture, I was completely a product of what used to be called "the genteel tradition in America."

Over the next several years I became increasingly aware that a mixed group of Jews and Gentiles rooming together and hanging out was not an absolutely everyday affair, but I had little sense at the time of Harvard's mixed record on "the Jewish problem" and anti-Semitic discrimination in admissions. As far as I can tell, there was no longer a Jewish quota at Harvard, but the University acted discreetly to limit the numbers of Jewish students.[2] Any serious knowledge of or even interest in these things was a long-term development for me.

Almost immediately, however, I began to meet some remarkable people, who were to detonate some time bombs under large parts of my prep school point of view, a destruction that I was soon actively

[2] Karabel, *The Chosen*, pp. 193-194.

seeking. I continued to pursue the will o' the wisp of serious athletics, which was in one respect fortunate, as it was through our mutual membership on the Harvard freshman soccer team that I met John Harbison, with whom I would room during my final three undergraduate years. He was a musical Wunderkind, but clothed in the ordinary American schoolboy costume: short hair, interests in school and sports, and girls. In their sophomore year, Harvard students left "the Yard" and moved into a "House," modeled rather approximately on Oxford and Cambridge colleges. Our house was Eliot and our "housemaster" was John Finley, the widely known Professor of Greek Literature and arbiter of traditional Harvard elegance. His lectures and even his ordinary conversation were laced with references to classical heroes and Homeric phraseology. "Ah, Harbison," he said, welcoming us to Eliot House, where we had elected to live. "A member of the large Exeter contingent, I believe." "No, sir," John replied, circumstantially, "a member of the small Princeton High School contingent." Later Finley dropped by our small room with its double-decker bunk bed. "Gentlemen," he observed, eying our quarters keenly, "this room should prove an eminent test of compatibility."

John loved jazz, and after soccer practice we would linger in record stores on our way back across the bridge to Harvard Square and listen to music. Record albums in that happy time were not sealed. Then we would eat at the Freshman Union, after which I would go to the library and fall asleep, often for two or three hours. Real studying didn't begin until 10:00 pm or so.

At the beginning of sophomore year, Harbison brought with him into our new Eliot House quarters his freshman year roommates, Stevens Garlick, inevitably known during our undergraduate years as "Onions"; Stockton Keith "Socks" Garver, now an art historian; cellist Harlow Russell; and Sheldon Lubow, a hard-working concert pianist-in-training, who died tragically young. Over the next three years a remarkable group of people joined us as roommates in Eliot House. Eventually there was a group of some ten people who actually roomed together, surrounded by a large penumbra of others with varyingly close ties. Almost all of us were interested in the arts and humanities, especially music, writing, philosophy and theater.

There was a lot of mutual attraction, but I believe in the end John Harbison was the center of the group, because we all knew that he was one of the most remarkable people that any of us were ever going to know. People liked John and wanted to be his friend, but at times he seemed a being of another order to me, and I think to others as well. Not only did his musical talent seem boundless, but he was amazingly articulate about music as well. Most of us were simply in awe of him. At any rate, all of John Harbison's roommates and friends who had any sense for music learned an enormous amount from contact with him, by attending the concerts of the Bach Society Orchestra, which he conducted brilliantly, and other concerts at which he performed and at which his music was played. Living with him and looking at his desk, covered with drafts of pieces he was composing, gave me an exhilarating sense of being present as art—perhaps major art—was coming into existence. And in my room, no less! I would ask John endless questions about the music that went on to our stereo turntable, trying to remember and think about what I heard him say. So much new music, so little time: the Mozart viola quintets, countless Bach cantatas, the *Musical Offering*, Schubert's *Winterreise*...

Through John we met other composers, like the extreme modernist, Fred Rzewski, who dropped into our room late one evening to ask John to play one of his pieces with the Bach Society Orchestra which John conducted. The piece seemed pretty far out even to John. After Rzewski had gone, he shook his head as he skimmed the score. "Look at this Gleason," he said, "for the second movement, the conductor is supposed to stand on the podium for nine minutes and fifteen seconds (or some such time) with his baton raised, but nobody plays anything." I guess we all snickered like philistines. And when Rzewski dropped by a couple of nights later to find out whether John would do his piece, Harbison told him that the Bach society was programmed up for the rest of the year. "But," he said, "I really like the second movement. I think we can squeeze it in at our March concert. Maybe at intermission." Rzewski hesitated. John kept an absolutely straight face. Rzewski didn't know whether he was being kidded or not. So he left without saying much more. Neither the second movement nor any other part of the piece was performed by the Bach Society that year, but there doesn't seem to have been any lasting ill feeling, as the two men's music was often performed together in subsequent years.

John seemed to have been able to learn almost any musical instrument within a very short period of time. He played piano, of course, and was a fine jazz pianist, on the cusp between swing and bebop. He played in a number of different jazz groups, and through him I met other jazz musicians: the alto sax player, John Brust, now a distinguished brain specialist at Physicians and Surgeons in New York; the fine trombonist Herb Gardner; and the stride piano player Henry "Thins" Francis[3], then still largely a trumpet player, who became a lifelong friend. I remember a late-night session at the Harvard radio station, at the beginning of which Francis sat for what seemed like hours, playing Count Basie-like intros for the horn players who had not yet arrived. One by one they made the scene, as we used to say, and the session gradually took shape. People would walk into one of Francis' intros, get out their horns and start to play. Almost everybody knew all the tunes. Or they played the blues. In retrospect, the arrival of the soloists came to seem like the beginning of post-college life and adulthood.

It wasn't exactly Harlem, but the relaxed atmosphere of the jam session gave me a sense of the creative process that has always stuck with me: individual contributions … ensembles, relaxed music, chatter, more music, jokes, more music … everybody together. After working briefly for the management consulting firm, Arthur

[3] "Thins" Francis in relation to "Fats" Waller.

D. Little, Francis gave it up to become a professional jazz piano player and is still going strong as he turns seventy.

John's father, E. Harris Harbison, a Reformation historian known as Jinks, was a stalwart of the Princeton History Department and a beloved figure in Princeton circles, a devout Christian and a man of wry wit and deep humor. It was unanimously agreed that he was one of Princeton's greatest teachers ever. A number of people told me that had he not come down with an illness akin to Parkinson's Disease, he would likely have become president of Princeton. His influence on John was strong, but not easy to define, although religion was part of it. John took Christianity very seriously in those days. Certainly both father and son expressed themselves in a low-keyed, non-melodramatic conversational style that was straightforward, occasionally confessional, and laced with humor. Eloquence was always subtle and understated. Boasting in their presence would have seemed extremely tasteless—an excellent environment for me.

Jinks was interested in music, including non-classical music, and the house was filled with it. John played chamber music on viola, but jazz on brass instruments like valve trombone and, in his early days, tuba. I remember a charming story that his mother, Jan told me. John had been pressed into service at a very young age with the Princeton University marching band for a football game, one of the undergrad tuba players being sick. John was so small that although he could play the tuba it was very heavy for him to march with it. But on the Saturday of the football game he found mysteriously that he could hardly get a sound out of the instrument. He blew and blew, and suddenly the mystery was solved. A box lunch popped out of the bell of the instrument, where some prankster had stuffed it.

John knew an enormous amount of music, jazz and classical. As a little boy he had written compositions in the style of the Bach sons, but when we met he was writing in an idiom that owed something to Bartok. Stravinsky became an influence later, and later still the

Tom Gleason and John Harbison, c. 1996
Photo by Sarah Gleason

austere, linear vocal music of Heinrich Schütz. His music achieved a deep connection with musical tradition but always contributed original elements from the contemporary and revealed the stamp of a powerful musical personality. It seems appropriate that today, at the height of his career, he should have been adopted by New England as a specifically Boston composer, perhaps a nationalist declaration of independence vis-à-vis the dominant New York musical world. It may also be due in part to his being so steeped in musical tradition, without ever having his own musical personality submerged, as well as to his many years of connection with MIT, where he has been a professor in the humanities faculty.

Over time John's literary talents helped him discover a dazzling array of texts from many cultures to set to music. Has any composer ever chosen better texts to set? Poetry figured briefly as a possible alternative career for John. I remember him saying that he thought he might support his composing through his poetry, perhaps within a university English Department. Has a major composer ever before thought he might support his musical habit by writing poetry? John might actually have done it, too.

My friendship with John vastly strengthened my love of baroque music. It also opened the world of the pre-baroque to me, as well as the modernist music of the twentieth century, about which I knew virtually nothing: Bartok, Stravinsky, Webern and Schoenberg. I came to love Bartok in particular, linking him in my mind with Camus' *Myth of Sisyphus* and *The Plague*, both of which became favorite books during my undergraduate years. Goodness knows what Bartok had to do with the slightly sentimental neo-stoicism I was developing à la Camus, but Bartok's "Concerto for Orchestra" seemed to sketch out a life course which I felt would be mine in some way. Having never had any deep feeling about God, I decided he was dead, and immediately began to miss him. Years later I discovered a yellowing sheet of lined paper on which I had written lines from Georg Lukàcs' *The Soul and the Forms* which expressed my point of view in the sort of anguished language that appealed to me at the time:

> I hope that a judgment by God will illuminate the different struggles which he sees in the world before him, and will reveal the ultimate truth. But the world around him still follows the same path, indifferent to both questions and answers. No word comes from either created or natural things and the race is not to the swift nor battle to the strong. The clear voice of the judgment of God no longer sounds out above the march of human destiny, for the voice which once gave life to all has fallen silent. Man must live alone and by himself. The voice of the judge has fallen silent forever, and this is why men will always be vanquished, doomed to destruction in victory even more than defeat.

I found a visual equivalent of this point of view in Anne's vision of Christ in Iris Murdoch's wonderful novel, *Nuns and Soldiers*.

Read many years later, it reminded me powerfully of my painful early religious struggles.

All ten or eleven of us hung out with musicians and were undoubtedly regarded as a little weird—especially those of us who could have passed for "normal." The sixties, however, would drastically redefine social nonconformity; by later standards we were pretty conventional. We dressed in jeans or chinos, not looking particularly bohemian; we were interested in girls and sports, but went around with people who would be called nerds today, like my old friend, Mark DeVoto, but we also had preppy friends. We enjoyed our composite, artsy, ethnically diverse identity, even taking, it seems to me in retrospect, a bit of false pride in it. This kind of nonconformity turned out to have been pretty easy. But there were no African-Americans in our group and only a few score in our class. I never knew any of them very well, although I made desultory efforts to get acquainted.

I remember riding into Boston on the subway with Harbison, as he studied a score that he would conduct with the Bach Society Orchestra in a few weeks. As he went over and over certain places in the score, it turned out he was giving a different performance of the passages in his head. "Can you actually *hear* the differences," I asked naively. When he said that he could in effect perform the music differently in his mind, thinking about how he would eventually perform it in the concert hall, it seemed miraculous to me.

Like other Harvard undergraduates from time immemorial, I learned more from my contemporaries than in class. There were two philosophers in our group of roomates, Allen Graubard and John E. (Jack) McNees. In 1958, the latter wrote a scalding account of Princeton bicker, the process by which students were selected for membership in one of the Princeton eating clubs, for the *Harvard Crimson*, entitled "The Quest at Princeton for the Cocktail Soul."[4]

[4] *Harvard Crimson*, February 21, 1958. The club selection process in 1958 became known as the "dirty bicker," partly, I believe, because of McNees' article.

McNees did not neglect the anti-Semitic elements in the selection process. He did his account in a semi-documentary style derived from the novelist John dos Passos' work, interspersing his prose with personal encounters with students. He contrasted the jubilant and well-dressed recipients of membership, with the abject failures, sitting huddled on the back porch of Ivy Club, waiting to be grudgingly accepted by some club or other, so that nobody could claim that anyone had not been given a bid.[5] To dramatize that contrast he inserted quotations from Woodrow Wilson in his text on what he hoped Princeton would become. His account stirred a major controversy at Princeton and among the Princeton alumni, and must have played some role in the eventual democratization of "bicker" and the club system generally. We were in awe of both McNees' journalistic talents and his ability to he apply them in the real world. I think he had a real influence on many of our subsequent careers and the kind of activism we later undertook. He was an intellectual polymath and a superb conversationalist.

In his philosophy studies, McNees was torn between Marx and Nietzsche in ways that anticipated the subsequent philosophical landscape of the sixties. He admired Marx's radical democratism and Nietzsche's determination, in some non-barbarous way, to transcend traditional ethical norms. Many of us expected him to write a remarkable book exposing the flaccid fifties, against which we were most of us in revolt one way or another, or at least felt we were supposed to be. We expected it to be informed by philosophy, yet to have profound political and social implications. Years later when I read Iris Murdoch's *The Book and the Brotherhood*, it seemed to me that McNees was in certain ways our David Crimond,

[5] Most, of course, were Jewish. The masters of Harvard houses apparently used a similar system in the 1930s to ensure that none of the Harvard houses had more than its share of Jewish students. At least the Jewish students at Harvard were not required to sit in a group before they were assigned somewhere. Morton and Phyllis Keller, *Making Harvard Modern. The Rise of America's University*, Oxford, Oxford University Press, 2001, pp. 49-50.

although none of us thought to give him money to free him up to write, as "the brotherhood" did in Murdoch's novel.

There must have been something about the cusp between the fifties and the sixties which led to such imaginings. We were almost as hostile to the Harvard final clubs as to the Princeton eating clubs, although the racism of the latter seemed far more explicit. Harbison and I were invited to be looked over at several club "punches," purposeful cocktail parties where we were to be examined for sociability, clothes and general demeanor, but neither of us ever went. Master Finley was quite put out with me for not even investigating his club, known as the A.D. I don't believe our Jewish roommates were ever "punched" by any club, although Graubard and McNees did join the intellectual Signet Society. I longed to be asked, but wasn't. Eventually my daughter Meg became its president many years later. I fantasized about her inviting me to join, simultaneously glorying in her triumph and hoping to be compensated for this ancient slight.

As it turned out, neither McNees nor Graubard became academic philosophers or career philosophy teachers. McNees recently retired as a Columbia University librarian and remains a deeply valued adviser to a variety of friends in literature, philosophy and film. Graubard became an educational activist during the sixties, producing a well known book called *Free the Children* and has continued to be interested in radical approaches to education, even in the uncongenial atmosphere of the early twenty-first century. His other major book, *Saving Remnants: Feeling Jewish in America*, dealt critically with matters of Jewish identity, stressing the freedom of choice which the United States has given its citizens to choose how to express ethnicity.[6]

Who was I? Like many another confused adolescent, I tended to reveal or foreground different aspects of my developing personality, depending on whom I was with. I instinctively used both black

[6] Written together with another friend, publisher Sara Bershtel.

and Jewish culture to critique my old-fashioned and bourgeois origins, toward which I was developing an almost physical aversion. Jews, according to my emerging, if inchoate, sense of them, were always smart, more likely to be original, indeed breakers of paradigms. They were unsentimental (except, sometimes, about their own world, and then in a heavily ironic fashion), mostly secular and often wildly funny in an irreverent way. I already sensed that I was too sentimental, and perhaps not smart enough, to become a good Jew in the somewhat parochial way I was coming to construct Jewishness. And I was too cerebral, preppy and puritanical for the black world—to say nothing of being white.

In some other ways, I was at a disadvantage as well. Music and philosophy were the twin signatures of our group, and I had little talent for either. The philosophy professor Marshall Cohen was probably the most important mentor to our group. I knew he liked me, but I felt I could never communicate with him on the same level as McNees and Graubard. Marshall had a remarkable knowledge of music. Knowing him helped produce my overall sense of the *Gestalt* of the Eliot House of my day, to which Master Finley also contributed the essential elements. The ideal individual exuded—but modestly, somehow—effortless and elegant intelligence; was simultaneously Jewish, aristocratic and Anglophilic, and at the same time was liberally committed to social justice; virile, yet with a touch of the homoerotic. I did not see myself as more than barely scraping by in terms of this extraordinarily confused and contradictory catalogue of virtues. Only at odd moments was I aware of the element of snobbery pervasive in it. Only over time did I become aware of how deeply the distinctive culture of Eliot House had been shaped by Finley's aestheticism, his cult of Oxford and Cambridge, his snobbery and his tendency to mythologize his surroundings, generally with elegant good humor.

Finley was a renowned public speaker—easily the best known orator at Harvard. On one occasion, Nathan Pusey, then president of the university, came to speak at the annual Eliot House dinner in honor of the former president, Charles W. Eliot. It was rumored that Finley had been passed over for Harvard's presidency in favor of Pusey; certainly there was no love lost between the two. Finley's introduction of Pusey was lengthy, but he never mentioned his guest, dilating instead on something like a dozen different students, comparing them extravagantly and affectionately, as was his wont, with Greek gods and classical heroes: Achilles, Patroclus, Aeschylus, Pericles, etc., etc. Finally, there was a long pause and Finley stared at Pusey. "And now," he said in a low flat tone, "our great man." Then another pause "who has always reminded me of ... George Washington."

Finley was extremely fond of comparing Eliot House to every kind of historical referent, from Leonidas and his three hundred Spartans at Thermopylae to the aviators in *Thirty Seconds Over Tokyo*. But he outdid himself on another social occasion during our senior year, comparing Eliot House to a current beer advertisement. "Eliot House is like the Ballantine three-ring sign," he proclaimed. "Purity" (pointing to a rather religious group, which I believe included the future head of the Episcopal Church in America), "body" (pointing to some football players), "and flavor" (pointing to us).

Another member of our gang whose struggles over identity were in certain ways like mine was John Casey, also from St. Albans, but the son of a former Democratic congressman. My impression was that John learned a lot about being Irish from books he encountered at Harvard. Educated for some years in a Swiss private school, his connection with Irish hardship seemed pretty attenuated. His mother was a starchy WASP from north of Boston. John used to regale us with anecdotes of his Uncle Drew Dudley frowning and observing plaintively on a summer evening, "John, I feel *a courant d'air*." But John was much more Irish after studying Irish culture at Harvard than at St. Albans. He later published a number of fine stories in the New Yorker and won the National Book Award in 1989 for his novel, *Spartina*, set on the Rhode Island coast.

Toward the end of his undergraduate years and his early years at

John Casey, c. 1972
Photo by Sarah Gleason

Harvard Law School, Casey wrote an exuberant, somewhat narcissistic autobiographical novel called *Michael Carey*, which reflected something of the development of an Irish aspect of his identity. It was never published, perhaps fortunately, but it certainly was a stage in the creation of his later fiction. He was also a figure in Harvard theater, and a noted wit. Especially after he'd had a couple, he liked to identify with the opening lines of Rafael Sabatini's picaresque popular novel, *Scaramouche*: "He was born with the gift of laughter and a sense that the world was mad." One of the best Harvard actresses of the day was the daughter of a Greek shipping tycoon. Someone asked her one day how far it was from the front to the back of the theater. "Oh, about the length of a good-sized yacht," she replied, thoroughly in character. Casey smiled broadly, "First time I ever heard the yacht used as a unit of measurement." Casey was also an accomplished actor, who lost his habitual stutter when on the stage. We were very much in synch in those days. On one occasion, perhaps a few years later, we were driving somewhere to a party perhaps, when Rossini's "William Tell Overture"—which had been part of the Lone Ranger radio program when we were kids, came on the car radio. We got so excited after a couple dozen bars that we pulled the car over and immersed ourselves in the music while it lasted.

Then there was John Hancock, a passionate Brecht enthusiast and one of the principal directors of the Harvard Dramatic Club in the late fifties and early sixties, who along with Casey led the theater wing of our collective. Hancock was a Chicagoan, with some of the hulking vitality of that city. I remember an occasion when he and I had gone into a local travel agency to get our airline tickets home for Christmas. "Okay," said the kid behind the counter, "put your John Hancock right here" and handed him a pen to write a check with. Hancock did as he was told, but it took us some ten minutes to persuade the clerk that his customer's name really was John Hancock.

Hancock and I used to eat late Sunday breakfasts at the down-at-the-heel Hayes-Bickford cafeteria in Harvard Square, known universally as "the Bick," which was also where actors and directors waited up all night until the reviews of their new shows were published in the *Crimson* or, less often, in the *Boston Globe*. On one occasion after we had consumed coffee, an order of toast, two fried eggs and a rasher of bacon, Hancock drew a deep breath, looked at me and said "Again?" So we did, and the word stuck, employed to indicate a gluttonous repetition of some pleasure or other. Hancock has subsequently directed theater in New York, Pittsburgh and San Francisco and made a number of movies, of which *Bang the Drum Slowly* (1973) was the most commercially successful. One of the stars was a then-unknown actor named Robert De Niro.

All this time I continued to paint. My style moved from impressionist through a Fauve period in my early Harvard years, through cubism to a derivative New York style. I took no courses, but during the winter I painted in the basement of Kirkland House, where

I was provided with a studio by my godfather, Charles Taylor, the medieval historian who as a young man had taught my father and was now Master of the house. For three years, I spent summers at the Penn State campus in the middle of Pennsylvania, where the American painter, Hobson Pittman, presided over the summer program. He had been the teacher of Dean Stambaugh, which was how I was drawn into his orbit. His own paintings were somewhat wan studies of flowers, or empty rooms with the door ajar, or luncheons on the grass, which seemed to have a vaguely Southern quality. Nevertheless, he was a shrewd critic of a wide variety of styles and made no effort to influence students in the direction of his own work. One of my principal problems with painting may have been that I liked so many pictures that I had a hard time deciding what it was that I myself wanted to do. There was also the small matter of talent. Disappointing Dean Stambaugh's hopes for me, I was becoming an "all around boy," largely out of necessity.

In the 1950s, State College, Pennsylvania, was a charming small town, especially in the summer, when the density of the student population lessened somewhat. There were many beautiful rural sites in the vicinity, some of which I painted. In my first summer there I stayed in a dorm, but never repeated the experience. I was lodged in the midst of football players who were taking courses they had presumably missed during their busy fall semester. They played cards deep into the night almost every night and arguments and fights were common, so it was rare that I got to sleep before three in the morning. This was particularly difficult, as Hobson Pittman liked to do his crits early in the morning, while the football players slept in. Eventually I took to sleeping outside, rolling a blanket in the bushes away from the campus walkways, but of course even when I could get to sleep early I was wakened by the sun. In subsequent years I rented rooms with other summer regulars.

Penn State also provided me with my first experience of gay culture. I had hitherto been extremely uncomfortable with any manifestation of homosexuality. As a seventh-grader, I thought I was being followed home from St. Albans on the streetcar by a skinny, almost emaciated university student who was lame and wore a brace and had dark, deepset eyes. He probably had polio. He used to appear on the streetcar stop nearest the school very often. In my fearful and, perhaps, self-centered way, I became convinced that he was waiting for me—loitering with intent. My parents were obviously upset by this possibility, which further frightened me although of course I didn't admit it. But at art school I became much more accustomed to being surrounded by gay liaisons. Public discussions of gay sex were natural, not rare. I learned what camp humor was, something that scarcely existed in the straight fifties world that I usually inhabited. I also got used to being propositioned fairly frequently and gradually developed some skill at fending off advances without feeling excruciatingly embarrassed for myself or for someone else. Some of my homophobia dissipated.

Plenty of my continuing education to the visual arts took place at Harvard as well. As a sophomore, I spent one memorable evening with Paul Sachs, the retired curator of prints and drawings at the Fogg Musuem, who lived in a spacious apartment on Memorial Drive, overlooking the Charles River. My mother's old friendships with people in Fine Arts opened many doors for me, but none more interesting than this. He was a small, dignified man, with a courtly manner, very meticulously attired. His formality in old age—he was almost eighty—initially concealed from me the passion and dynamism with which he had built his great collection for Harvard in his younger days. For two hours the distinguished collector showed me Goya, Degas and Delacroix drawings and other masterpieces from his distinguished collection, most of which had by this time been donated to the Fogg Museum. Meanwhile his elderly but still beautiful wife, dressed in a filmy night gown, sat at a small card table and played solitaire silently.

In my junior and senior years at Harvard I had an art-connected experience of a quite different, yet highly satisfying kind. I brought a Russian icon owned by my father to the Conservation

Department at the Fogg Museum, at that time run on a day-to-day basis by a motherly soul named Betty Jones. The needed restoration was beyond my means, but Miss Jones told me that she would show me what to do, and I could do it myself. This interesting project led eventually to a regular job at the Conservation Department. It was a fascinating experience. Some of my jobs were at the most basic level: polishing the Harvard silver collection or scrubbing down stone sculpture. But there were more interesting projects. I was actually allowed to take layers of varnish off some very fine old pictures, on one occasion even a large Audubon bird painting. And every few days, there would be staff consultations about pictures which had been brought in by outsiders to be authenticated. These sessions were particularly intriguing. I learned all the different ways there were to fake cracking on an old canvas and many other tricks of the forger. Working up at the top of the Fogg Museum in the Conservation Department was a delight. There was a tranquility and a focus there, a sense of living among beautiful things and taking care of them that satisfied me deeply.

And the art historians were in and out of the Fogg. Sydney Freedberg, the High Renaissance specialist, was memorable, a remarkable scholar and intellectual polymath. He was unusually accessible for a senior Harvard professor, and was great fun to talk to. Originally a local boy, he would explain his British accent with humor as "pure affectation": a summer in England was enough. A graduate student working for him always referred to him affectionately as "the fat cat," although his obesity was only figurative. This was the fascinating Dorothy Dean, an enormously witty African-American woman who, obsessed with gay men, was reputed to call herself "the spade of queens". Shortly thereafter she left Harvard for New York, where she became a member of Andy Warhol's entourage. After becoming famous as a diminutive bouncer at Max's Kansas City, she died at the young age of fifty-four in 1987, apparently of cancer. In my naiveté I dreamed of having sex with her.

Some of the faculty I knew in Eliot House seemed, and still seem in retrospect, like characters out of Evelyn Waugh or Anthony Powell. There was, for instance, the Frothingham Professor of the History of Religion, Arthur Darby Nock, who was reputed to live largely on vintage red wine and take-out fried chicken. Having once caught a glimpse of his living room, I can attest that there was copious evidence of both inside. There was a story that during World War II, when Eliot House was taken over by the military, Nock alone among the faculty tutors refused to vacate his room. The colonel in charge of the housing arrangements was annoyed. "I'll take care of this," he said. But when he knocked on the door, the professor confronted him in the nude. The colonel retreated and Nock supposedly remained in his rooms for the duration of the war.

Once in awhile, Nock would eat in the dining hall, occasionally with members of our group. He was famous for academic puns, in class and at the table ("One man's Mead is another man's Persian"), which he would follow up with an explosion of laughter which would momentarily silence conversation at across the dining hall. He was the author of an enormously erudite book on St. Paul, but his conversational style was rapid, rambling and jerky, though learned, and his accent was very difficult, so conversation with him seemed all but impossible. In retrospect I wonder if he suffered from Tourette Syndrome. In one of the (usually obscene) Christmas plays that Eliot House students produced just before winter vacation, I came in on all fours in a dog suit and lifted my leg on the Christmas tree. This made a great impression on Professor Nock, who for months afterwards would laugh out loud and lift his leg slightly when he encountered me on campus, somewhat to my embarrassment but to his vast amusement.

Then there was Ved Mehta, who became renowned in subsequent years as a staff writer for the *New Yorker*, specializing in profiles of historians and philosophers, as well as rather sentimental family memoirs. He lived in Eliot House for several semesters, and controversy raged among us about whether he was really blind or not, as he always represented himself to be. He had a way of putting down his coffee cup, just over his neighbor's knee, half on and half off the table, without ever missing the table entirely and spilling his coffee on you. His unerring ability to do this made us suspicious. He would also refer in a detailed way to how people were dressed. Did he have informants? Visions? We never found out.

My girlfriend of my final three years at Harvard was a lovely and talented musician named Betsy Hendry, now Elizabeth Vercoe, well known as a composer. She lived in Arlington, Virginia, a suburb of Washington, D.C., and I had known her very slightly in earlier years, as she went to National Cathedral School, the sister school of St. Albans. We met at a screening of *The Red Shoes* at the end of my freshman year, and I fell for her quickly, enchanted by her full-blown beauty. I fell deeply in love for the first time. In Arlington where she lived in a rambling old house, we roamed the banks of the Potomac, sometimes until nearly sunup that summer and for several summers to follow. Just before dawn I would walk back across the river to Washington in a state of non-alcoholic intoxication.

As with John Harbison, knowing Elizabeth continued my musical education, to say nothing of improving my ability to relate to other people, tempering my fluctuating self-esteem and generally improving my character by chastening some of my show-off tendencies. As she was entering Wellesley the following year, I also bought a Vespa motor scooter, which began a decade long infatuation with motor scooters and small motorcycles that ended only when my wife persuaded me in the late sixties that more than ten years without a serious accident was pressing my luck and I should quit while I was ahead.

Dating Elizabeth was an adventure in other than romantic ways, however, as her parents were extremely conservative, especially on racial questions. Although I was getting slightly better at keeping my mouth shut, I had not improved sufficiently to be able to keep my opinion about racial matters hidden, and they were horrified at what an "integrationist"—as the phrase then went—I was. Matters became so charged that I was threatened with a gun by Dr. Hendry in the driveway in front of his house and told never to see his daughter ever again. He confronted me with a .twenty-two rifle, backed up by his son with a baseball bat. I retreated down the drive, not really believing that he was going to shoot me, but of course not being absolutely sure. Oddly enough, this dramatic episode took place on my twenty-first birthday, so I returned almost immediately to a party put on by my parents, with most of the guests older people and family friends. There I discovered that a bottle of Napoleon brandy given to me at birth by my grandfather's student, Jimmy Knowles, for just this occasion, had turned to vinegar—probably at some point around 1820. Of course, no one knew this, so the flask of vinegar continued to pass from hand to hand throughout the nineteenth and much of the twentieth century at steadily increasing prices. It seemed somehow to characterize the whole day.

Elizabeth and I did not acquiesce in this forced separation and eventually she left her parents' roof and lived for a time with my friends the Clagues in Washington. Her parents refused to continue to pay for her college education, but a benevolent aunt stepped in and she stayed at Wellesley.

Betsy Hendry Vercoe's parents were not the only conservatives who lived on their lovely spacious property high on the south bank of the Potomac River. Purely by chance, I believe, the Hendrys had rented a small house on their property to a conservative of a rather different stripe named Bill French, and his young wife, and I soon met them. Bill French was one of the peculiar and extremely heterogeneous group of intellectuals and political agitators who formed a circle around Ezra Pound, then incarcerated in St. Elizabeth's Hospital to forestall his being tried for treason. These people included John Kasper, who served a prison sentence in Tennessee for protesting efforts at desegregation of schools. He was clearly linked to at least one school bombing. Then there was Sheri Martinelli, a nymphomaniac of sorts who passed herself off as a painter. My friend Guy Davenport used to do a very funny imitation of Pound receiving Sheri on his bunk at St. E's: "Sheh-reeee!

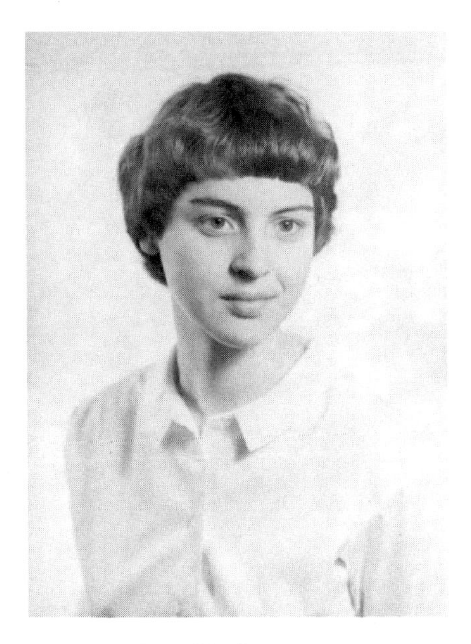

Betsy Hendry, c. 1954

Get up on the bed while I still have an erection!" (This last pronounced with a very fancy rolled "r," in high excitement, almost as if the word were "election"). There was also a thuggish real estate broker named John Châtel. The most respectable of them was an English professor from the University of Maryland named Michael Reck, who was a real scholar.

French was an extremely handsome and rather narcissistic man, with a passion for baroque and pre-baroque music, as well as the endemic anti-Semitism that enveloped the Pound circle. Having known almost nothing about Jews until a year or two before, I now met my first anti-Semite. French's views seemed utterly fantastic to me, but he was such a powerful personality, an impression enhanced by the mantle of Pound, that Betsy and I spent quite a lot of time with him and got to know him well. His taste in books and pictures was eclectic, a mix of romantic modernism, pre-Raphaelitism and almost anything Pound had recommended, including such funny-money fantasies as Pound's own tract, "Jefferson and/or Mussolini." Any of the modern Jewish-American writers that I was reading, especially J.D. Salinger and Saul Bellow, were violently rejected as degenerate, although the term was never very precisely defined.

French attracted a number of young disciples who fell under his spell to varying degrees. The several that I remember were not particularly well educated by orthodox standards—indeed were attracted to Bill by their mutual alienation from the educational culture of the fifties. Both were intelligent and handsome men, somewhat receptive to the Bill French repetition of Pound's clarion call for a historically oriented modernism, with the Jewish component excised. "Wipe your feet," French told his potential disciples, self-consciously echoing Pound—not that it was clear what might have been stuck to the boots of Wes Porter, an interesting and independent person, with whom I spent some time. Porter was a radical seeker in his own quiet, Southern American way. We used to go fishing and frog hunting—we called it "frog-gigging" because of the sharp gigs on long poles with which we stabbed the frogs—till all hours of the night. Handsome and attractive to women, Porter had never gone to college, but was very well-read in an unfocused sort of way: Japanese poetry, Western novels, European mysticism. I had just read Somerset Maugham's *The Razor's Edge* and had been very impressed by the hero's rejection of middle-class materialism and embrace of a life spent in search of knowledge, wherever it might be found. Wes seemed a more contemporary American version of Larry Darrell, the novel's protagonist. At times I agreed with Bill French at least that my organized, syllabus-based Harvard education seemed inauthentic and insipid compared to Wes's leisurely exploration of world culture on his own timetable.

Russia became a focal point of my interests in my sophomore year. Eliot House for some reason was full of professors interested in Russian things, one of numerous clusters of people with common interests in the Harvard house system. No doubt the group had taken shape gradually over several years. There was the great literary critic, Renato Poggioli; there was my future friend, Adam Ulam, then embarking on the remarkable career that would make him such a celebrated student of twentieth-century Russian and Soviet history and international relations; there was Hugh McLean who wrote on nineteenth-century Russian literature. All of these were then unmarried, so my roommates and I saw them often at dinner in Eliot House. Most immediately for me then was James Billington, who became my tutor for several years and had a large impact on my developing Russian interests. But he was married, so we saw him socially only at occasional lunches or when he invited us over to his house, which he generously did from time to time.

My interest in Russia developed on two tracks. First, the Cold War had made Soviet-American relations a constant subject of family conversation, although my father was always the soul of discretion about what he told his family about his work at the NSC. Second, I was overwhelmed by Russian literature in college, particularly by Dostoevsky and by James Billington's *mysterioso* skill as a lecturer. He was melodramatic on the podium, occasionally dropping his voice to a whisper, as he intimated that he was approaching some inexpressible romantic truth. I joked about him with my roommates, but he had snared me. And the other Russianists in Eliot House fanned the flames. The subject was vast and mysterious. Russia had everything I then needed: underdogs, mystical philosophy, revolutionary terrorism, extremes of wealth and poverty and suffering. "God how sad our Russia is," remarked Pushkin, after reading a notorious critique of Russia by his famous friend, Peter Chaadaev. I began, not very systematically, to learn the language in which this great literature was written.

Among the scholars involved with things Russian in Eliot House was a great Italian student of the European avant-garde, Renato Poggioli. He was a famous character around Harvard, of legendary wit, and he was by no means averse to pithy public obscenity. Stories about him abounded, especially among undergraduates and younger faculty. He was supposed to have attended a party given by the Harvard literary magazine, the *Advocate*, in honor of Dylan Thomas, who had just given a reading. According to the version of the story I heard from two young faculty members, Poggioli arrived late with a friend and began a quiet conversation at one end of the room, while Thomas was holding forth loudly to a circle of admirers at the other, at least three sheets to the windward. After a while, Thomas became aware that there was a holdout conversation in the vicinity. So he staggered up to Poggioli and asked aggressively "and what do *you* do?" "I compare literature," Poggioli replied drily. "And what do you compare it to," demanded Thomas. Poggioli looked the disheveled poet up and down. "Shit," he replied calmly.

Poggioli was also famous for a remark he was alleged to have made in a Harvard faculty meeting during a discussion of whether Harvard should accept government money under the National Defense Education Act, if the recipients had to sign a loyalty oath. A spokesman for the Harvard administration—it may have been McGeorge Bundy—had urged acceptance. Harvard was not administering a loyalty oath, merely sending the completed document which included the loyalty oath, back to Washington. In the end, Bundy said casually, it was just a matter of "who licks the stamps." Poggioli was on his feet. "Vaaary well," he declared to President Pusey, who was chairing the meeting, employing his trademark opening phrase. "I am a refugee from Fascist Italy, and I can tell you something, you lick the stamps now, you lick something else later!" This rhetoric became less unusual ten years later, during the sixties, but it was uncommon during my undergraduate years. His undergraduate fans were also told of an exchange with a hostile interlocutor in which Poggioli was alleged to have drawled in conclusion: "an Anglo-Saxon word does not come easily to my Latin lips, but fuck you." Needless to say, this was a man undergraduates could relate to.

It would of course be a mistake to see this extraordinary scholar as merely a master of the aggressive put-down. This man was familiar with five or six languages and cultures and wrote the first focused and important treatment in English of avant-gardism in the arts, a book which is still required reading for cultural historians today. His lectures on Russian literature were wonderful. At the beginning of his discussion of *War and Peace*, he would say—and how often his friend Adam Ulam would recall this—"It is not the war; it is not the peace. It is the spot on the child's shirt." Incidentally, both he and our group's principal mentor, Marshall Cohen, regarded Ortega y Gasset's *The Dehumanization of Art* as the first serious account of the artistic avant-garde and told us to read it. It began a new phase in my understanding of the history of painting. The gradual evolution of taste had been the only way I had apprehended the development of painting until then.

Adam Ulam, one of Poggioli's principal foils at dinner in Eliot House, was quite a different character. A man of considerable size and leonine good looks, he was switching his research interests from English socialism to Soviet politics and foreign policy when I met him—leaving, he liked to say, an empire in decline for one on the ascendant. As I later learned he could be a devoted friend, but he was awe-inspiring to me as an undergraduate, and I didn't get to know him very well. I do have a vivid memory of him, rather full of wine, shaking his head and saying over and over again, "no! no!" at a fancy Eliot House dinner where George F. Kennan was the speaker. Kennan, as sometimes was his wont, was suggesting that Americans might not be morally up to their increasingly awesome global responsibilities, a view from which Adam dissented vigorously. Adam had a low tolerance for what he regarded as pious or moralistic rhetoric, and Kennan's earnest style offended Adam's worldliness.

Martin Malia, the historian, probably paid more attention to the undergraduates than any of his distinguished colleagues, a tendency he decisively reversed in later years. He was just completing his great biography of the nineteenth-century Russian socialist, Alexander Herzen, which was a landmark in the cultural history

Young Russia *by Abbott (Tom) Gleason, pub. 1980*

of Russia and one of the best books ever written in English about Russia. Malia was then far more liberal than he became after enduring the sixties on the Berkeley campus, but he was a Catholic liberal who believed in natural law, and he was witty and compelling in debate, and committed to teaching us how little we knew about European history. It was the dawn of my understanding of the proposition that the first stage of knowledge is the understanding of how little you know.

James Billington, later the Librarian of Congress, was then an assistant professor at Harvard. He was handsome and charismatic and outfitted himself in a self-conscious aura of Russianness in a way that neither Ulam nor Malia nor any of the others did. He chose to regard our group of roommates as radical Russian intellectuals of the nineteenth century, and was in the habit of asking us the famous questions of that day: "What is to be done?" and "Who is to blame?" This treatment created a mix of amusement, interest and disapproval in our group, most of which had a much more contemporary notion of identity in mind, which anticipated the ideas of the American 1960s rather than harking back to the Russian 1860s. Billington's jocular treatment of us may nevertheless have supplied me with the germ of the comparison I later made between the two eras in my second book, *Young Russia*. Billington's lectures on the cultural history of Russia pulled me deep into the eighteenth and nineteenth centuries.

Billington was then engaged in the book that became his masterpiece, a giant canvas treating the early modern and modern phases of Russian culture, entitled *The Icon and the Axe*, eventually published several years after I had graduated from college. Because Billington's interests were at that time (1959-60) focused on the spiritual contours of Russian culture among the mystically inclined romantics of the reign of Alexander I, he suggested to me for an honors thesis a rather specialized and difficult topic in which he was interested: the influence of a Catholic counter-revolutionary Bavarian philosopher named Franz Xaver von Baader on a variety of Russian contacts around the time of the defeat of Napoleon. Baader was an important early figure in the transmission of German anti-revolutionary messianism to Russia. I had agreed to the topic because of its general significance, without knowing to what I was agreeing, and was struggling with the topic early in my senior year. At just that point, I had the great good fortune to meet a young Polish scholar named Andrzej Walicki who was spending the semester at Harvard. He was at that time twenty-nine and I was twenty[7], but he was considerably more than nine years ahead of me in his reading, his focus on Russian intellectual history, and his methodological maturity. He had his first book out in Poland, and

[7] Portions of this material appeared in different form in *Archiwum Historii Filozofii I Mysli Spolecznej*, Volume 44, Warsaw, 1999.

he was dividing his time between Harvard and the University of California at Berkeley in a kind of postdoctoral year. It was his first trip to the United States. He was tall, gawky, shy and a bit ill at ease upon first acquaintance, but we soon became good friends.

Andrzej Walicki was a somewhat exotic figure in the Harvard student world of 1959. Organized exchanges with the Communist world had not yet begun. Neither I nor any of my friends knew anyone from Poland; most had never met anyone from a Communist country. Andrzej, furthermore, was more reserved and formal than most Americans. "I am one quarter Manteuffel," he used to say, in elucidating his social style with reference to the stiffness of the Prussian aristocracy. When I introduced him to Jack McNees, he bowed formally from the waist, clicked his heels and said in a resonant voice, "Walicki." McNees assumed that "Walicki" was the Polish word for "hello" or "how are you?". So he smiled and also said "Walicki." This was a puzzle, but eventually the matter was straightened out.

Walicki was a very welcome appearance in my life for a number of reasons, but in the first instance because he knew about Baader, the only person in my life who really did. Baader was a rather important figure in the history of the European counter-revolution. But to the struggling and inexperienced history and philosophy student that I was then, he seemed hopelessly obscure. My roommates, many of whom were also writing honors theses, all seemed to have much more exciting topics. Graubard was writing on divergent historical explanations for the rise of German National Socialism. McNees was working on "Nietzsche's Critique of Liberalism" and there were other topics that could generate sympathetic comment in our circles. Philosophy tutors like our friend and mentor Marshall Cohen were encouraging and even excited about their work. But when I told people what I was writing about, conversation stopped instantly. I felt trapped in a topic that I had not yet understood and that would be too difficult for me. All the sources were in German, French and Russian, which I was only just beginning to learn. Only a few sentences existed on Baader in English. But when I told Walicki what I was doing, he was warmly responsive. "Baader!" he exclaimed, his face breaking into a broad smile. "He's extraordinarily interesting." He made me feel that my hitherto obscure subject was significant and took a supportive interest in my halting progress. He even subsequently cited my undergraduate honors thesis in his magisterial study of the Russian Slavophiles, published in 1964, elevating my little student essay to the status of master's thesis in his footnote.

During the months we spent together in Cambridge, Walicki virtually took over my education in everything that pertained to Russia. This was in part because of his interest in my subject, but he also had more time than the other Russianists, occupied with their own work and with limited time for students, in the Harvard manner. In helping me understand Baader he gave me my first clear explanation of the intellectual reaction against the French Revolution and helped me formulate a rudimentary social interpretation of romanticism. He explained to me the importance of pre-romanticism and Freemasonry in the late eighteenth century, and of occultism and mystics like Jacob Boehme and Emanuel Swedenborg. Without him I would have regarded these people as mere eccentrics. In effect, Walicki provided me the bibliography for my dissertation, beyond the readings that Billington had suggested. A young man whose early career had been spent trying to teach Russian history to mostly hostile Polish students, Walicki enjoyed my enthusiasm. He counts me as one of his first students.

That year marked the beginning of a considerable period of intellectual discipleship for me. Walicki introduced me to the work of Karl Mannheim and explained the significance of Mannheim's use of "styles of thought" in examining the rhetoric, vocabulary and conceptual apparatus of political thinkers of various traditions. He also helped me with Karl Marx, whom at the time he admired, albeit with distinct reservations. He was the first teacher I had ever met who had given me such a concrete sense of what sort of scholarly work I might want to do myself. He encouraged my interest in the Russian Slavophiles. Completed some eight years later, my doctoral dissertation on the creative founder of the group, Ivan Kireevskii, was greatly influenced by Walicki's encompassing *Slavophile Controversy*, a book which I staggered through in Polish.

Jim Billington was convinced that Walicki would never understand the United States unless he understood the American game of baseball. So he proposed that we take Walicki to see the Boston Red Sox play at Fenway Park, at a time, be it noted, when Ted Williams was still in the lineup, at the very end of his career. We did so, but things did not work out exactly as planned. Billington and I both threw ourselves into the game like the fans that we were, but Andrzej was bored to death. At the end of the first inning he said how interesting it had been, but surely it was now time to go. He expressed this wish in stronger terms at the end of the third inning and looked truly doleful when he discovered that his ordeal was only a third over. In desperation he seized the newspaper that we had bought because it had a scorecard on the back. He looked through it hopefully but then turned to me again: "Please, Tom," he begged, "where is the political news?" It was his first experience with an American tabloid newspaper, which of course normally had almost no political news. Somehow he managed to get through the next two hours, before being permitted to return to the Harvard Library. "Most interesting, but one time is enough," was his courteous verdict on baseball. He politely but firmly dismissed the idea that this excruciating experience would help him understand the United States in any way whatsoever.

My senior year, especially its concluding moments, was a mixed experience. Despite making several appalling mistranslations, my honors thesis on Baader, which had occasioned me such anguish, was well received. It helped me to understand the importance of perseverance and caused me to thank God one final time for the providential appearance of Walicki. I also did well on my honors examinations. Most of my roommates were applying for fellowships for the following year, and I was no exception. The first round of fellowship awards had been announced, and as yet none of us had gotten anything, but Dave Winter, a social relations major, not part of our set, had been awarded some sort of desirable fellowship. John Finley, the Master of Eliot House, seeing us sitting glumly at dinner, came and sat down at our table. "Well, well" he said cheerfully, "when Winter comes can spring be far behind?" And he turned out to be right. None of us who hoped to go to Europe was actually disappointed. I ended up with a German Government Fellowship, known as a DAAD, and decided to study German-Russian relations at the University of Heidelberg and learn German properly.

The end of the semester brought dislocation and setbacks, however. While I was finishing my honors thesis, I stopped attending most of my other classes. At the same, time I was breaking up with my girlfriend, Betsy. I felt that I was going to enter a whole new phase of my life after college, which might result in unheard of new adventures and experiences. Whatever the future might hold, I felt I needed to encounter it unaccompanied, or perhaps "unencumbered" was more what I shallowly and unfairly thought at the time.

When I returned to Eliot House from Logan Airport, where I had put Betsy on a plane and said good-bye, I encountered John Finley, the Master. "So sorry to hear the news, Tom," he shouted across the Eliot House courtyard. Thinking he was referring to my dissolved relationship, I wondered in amazement how he knew something I hardly yet knew myself. But it turned out it was my academic failure he was referring to, and a postcard in my mailbox broke the news to me a minute later. I had flunked second-year Russian. My parents arrived a couple of days later from London to discover that I was not graduating with my class. Instead, I spent Commencement week skulking around my grandfather Baxter's house in a Boston suburb, feeling sorry for myself. My parents were unexpectedly gracious, which was some relief. But then they flew back to London, leaving me in Cambridge to make up the missing course at the Harvard Summer School and recover my wounded self-esteem as best I could. It wasn't easy. My Eliot House cohort was widely viewed by younger faculty (and of course by ourselves) as a particularly promising group of undergraduates, from whom great things were expected. I was proud of my membership in this group, even while feeling it to be a little tenuous, and failing Russian entailed a major loss in status. In addition, the possibility of a career as a Russian historian was beginning to appeal to me, and flunking Russian seemed a particularly inauspicious augury.

Given my gloomy state in early June, the summer of 1960 proved a pleasant surprise. Through a connection in Harvard's Slavic Department, I lived in the house of Albert Lord, the author of *The Singer of Tales*, the book that made such a major contribution to understanding the nature of the oral epic in European culture. Lord studied the oral epic of the South Slavs and demonstrated that the singers employed essentially the same narrative method as Homer had so long ago. He and his wife, who taught classics at Connecticut College, took me on as a lodger, in return for a certain amount of baby-sitting and limited meal preparation. The boys, Nathan and Mark, for whom I was responsible were trusting and friendly, the company was good, the duties light. Members of the Harvard Slavic Department often gathered there. Almost across the street lived the dazzling Ellis sisters, the wittiest and most charming girls I knew at Radcliffe, Isabel, Deborah and Priscilla.

I was also reunited that summer with a childhood friend, Pat Lamson, now Chute. Before World War II, her father, Roy Lamson, the English professor-clarinetist, had been in Adams House with my father, Charles Taylor, Raphael Demos and others. He had also been my boon companion for several years at jazz clubs in Washington. After many years in the English Department of Williams College, Roy was teaching at MIT and together with his writer wife Peggy, shepherding a distinguished visitor, Aldous Huxley, around Cambridge. Pat remembered that being brought over to play with me when we were little was such a gut-wrenching event that she almost always threw up afterwards. She and her first husband were also attending the Harvard Summer School, and together we took a lecture course from the great Hans Morgenthau, and so I learned something about realism in political science from the horse's mouth.

Another reunion that summer was with John Casey, to whom I had become closer at Harvard. As a result of being active in Harvard Theater, John had neglected his studies and as a result had transferred from Harvard to the U.S. Army, at the strong suggestion of Harvard, vigorously seconded by his father. Having finished his hitch, he was getting in academic shape again at summer school before re-entering Harvard. We played an enjoyable game that summer, which we referred to as "the spirit of the tree." We climbed up into a maple tree on Massachusetts Avenue, behind the Harvard Library and tried to pick up girls from the upper branches as they went in and out of the library. "Stop," one of us would call, "the Spirit of the Tree would have speech with you!" The technique got girls' attention all right, but somehow there was always a letdown when the "Spirits of the Tree" revealed themselves.

Casey and I also spent many a pleasant evening talking with the writer and artist, Guy Davenport, who was just finishing his Ph.D. dissertation at Harvard on Ezra Pound's early cantos. Guy was a great raconteur and he regaled us with tales of everything from William Blake to his military service. He described reading Thomas Mann's *Joseph and his Brothers* by the light of a jukebox in the canteen during his military service in the Korean War, the only place he could find to read. Guy Davenport provided a bridge between two parts of my life that I had thought unbridgeable: the rather disreputable St. Elizabeth's circle of Ezra Pound and the world of Harvard. He was also a very gifted draughtsman, whether as a caricaturist ("Flaubert Digesting a Newly Received Idea") or in a semi-abstract mode that owed something to the drawings of Wyndham Lewis. The Grolier Bookshop in Harvard Square was a haunt for poets, and Guy did a wonderful drawing for the proprietor, Gordon Cairnie, of "Mr. and Mrs. William Blake (stark naked) walking in the garden and talking with God." Blake appears to be giving God his instructions for the day.

Guy did not much care for his thesis director, Professor Harry Levin, who quite understandably did not care for Pound. Guy considered Levin chilly and self-regarding, and he did a funny version of Levin's Russian wife, putting her husband to bed in the kitchen freezer, setting the packages of frozen beans and corn in just the right places to make his pillow and then leaning down into the freezer and saying in a heavy Russian accent before closing the top, "Haaary, are you cold enough?"

Guy developed a considerable homosexual crush on me, which I found both frightening and frustrating, as I wanted nothing more than to be his friend. His attempted epistolary seduction left me with a wonderful sequence of letters, drawings and his incomparable monologues on life and letters. His intellect and style were breathtakingly different from that of my liberal intellectual friends: classical, encyclopedic, taxonomic, cubist. He had imbibed Ezra Pound's deep feeling for calligraphy and ideograms and made visual music on the written page. His correspondence with me veered from archaic slang, to self-conscious Southernisms, many of them naively, innocently I am tempted to say, racist, to classical allusions. Many of the latter were in the original Greek, in the style of Pound's Cantos. He represented, as George Steiner later wrote, "a cultural omniverousness, an attempt at making a complete inventory of the world's aesthetic-poetic loot, which is radically American."[8]

I was fascinated by Davenport and by his sensibility. He enjoyed what were to him my highly orthodox. liberal opinions to some degree and lectured me slightly condescendingly from his conservative point of view:

> OK, down with hierarchy but WHUT do we do without hit? Who president of Harvard & will not the intelligence continue to

[8] George Steiner, "Rare Bird," *The New Yorker*, November 30, 1981, p. 199.

> make distinctions, huh? You are thinking of love and democracy and the fellowship of peers. Someone has to run the store and captain the futbol team and write books.[9]

But I sensed that he had a harder side that I never saw and could never escape the feeling that what he really wanted was to get his hands on me. But then I'd feel ashamed of that. I later stayed with him once over night in his Haverford, Pennsylvania, apartment, near the college where he was teaching. He later drew me a picture of a Vorticist-cubist angel, in the style of Wyndham Lewis. This was the angel, he told me, that had stood guard by my bed during the night that I had spent in Haverford.

In 1963, after a lengthy correspondence, rather evasive on my side, he dedicated *The Intelligence of Louis Agassiz* to me, but only "if I would share the gift" (ran his dedication) with a woman I did not know named Sara Dakin, who had allegedly taken her life, after having been spurned by a gay friend of Davenport's with whom she had fallen in love. This episode subtly increased my fear of homosexuality, still rather powerful even after three summers at art school.

The summer which I had so dreaded passed quickly and pleasantly and at the turn of August, I packed up and flew to London, as an intermediary step toward the University of Heidelberg. But I was still an uncertain wannabe, neither an "ancient nor a modern," neither Jew nor black, academic nor artist, preppy nor committed rebel. My experience of hard work had been episodic and my overall academic record uneven. All the big decisions were still ahead. But I was under much better control, had learned a bit more about the world over the previous four years and a little more about myself.

[9] Postcard, 15 March, 1962.

Tom in Wieblingen, Germany, 1961

European Interlude

In the fall of 1960, at the beginning of my senior year at Harvard, my father was appointed Cultural Affairs Officer at the American Embassy in London. That is why my year abroad began not in Germany, but in England, in a picturesque small house with antique furniture (and plumbing to match) on South Street in Mayfair, a couple of blocks from the American Embassy. Our rented house, number 23, had been nice enough to start with, but in the late 1940s, someone had redone the entire ground floor with paneling from one of London's Wren churches[1] that had been destroyed by German bombs, which gave it a really sumptuous look. The furniture was also lovely and the house was right on the corner of an old mews.

I was delighted to be able to spend several months there, exploring London's art galleries and bookstores and going to the theater three or four times a week at breathtakingly cheap prices, before heading off to Germany and encountering a new country where my knowledge of the language was relatively elementary. Over that year our London house became a watering hole for many of my roommates and friends who were also in Europe. Allen Graubard and Jack McNees were at Oxford; John Harbison and another friend, John Mudd, were in Berlin, Harbison at the Conservatory, Mudd at the Free University. We gathered for vacations of theater-going and sumptuous meals prepared by my parents' rather Germanic

[1]English architect Christopher Wren (1632-1723).

housekeeper, who was nicknamed "Mrs. Danvers," after the sinister custodian of Manderley in Daphne Du Maurier's then popular novel, *Rebecca*. She often made popovers for us, which she called "over pops." Concerned about how thin I was, she invariably remarked when I came home that I was looking "*Schmall ins Gesicht*," literally "small in the face" in German.

My parents, being unreconstructed Anglophiles, especially my father, were delighted to be living in London. Slightly over a decade at the National Security Council had been wearing for him and being Cultural Affairs Officer in London felt like a vacation in comparison and a half step back toward academia. He lectured at universities all over England on Anglo-American relations, on U.S. foreign policy and other topics which he knew well. My parents made a whole set of British friends, and renewed acquaintance with old ones, like my grandfather's friend, Ernest Barker.

The American ambassador to the Court of St. James at that time was John Hay Whitney, subsequently the publisher of the now defunct *New York Herald Tribune*[2], whom my father liked, but whose sheltered life enabled by his enormous wealth constantly amazed him. When Whitney hired my father, for instance, the ambassador met him at the house of William Clark, who lived around the corner from us in Washington and was one of my dad's best friends and was at that time Public Affairs Officer at the London embassy. When Bill Clark asked everybody what they wanted to drink, Whitney asked for a Scotch and soda. Bill came back a minute later and somewhat shamefacedly said he was out of Scotch. "So Jock, what can I get you?" he repeated. Whitney hesitated. "I think I will have Scotch, Bill," he said. Bill didn't know how to respond to this, so he blurted out, "But there isn't any." My father, listening to this happy hour drama play out, suddenly realized that Whitney had

[2]The story runs that after Whitney bought the paper, he was leaving the building where the business had been transacted and as he reached the street, a newsboy passed, shouting "get your New York Herald Tribune here." Whitney is supposed to have said "thanks, boy. I've got mine."

23 South Street, Mayfair, 1960

never, or at least very rarely, been in a situation where there actually wasn't any Scotch—it was merely a matter of sending out for some, or going down to another floor, or something of that sort. He literally could not understand the idea that Scotch was unavailable. What Whitney ended up settling for was not recorded.

Not long after arriving in London and starting work in the embassy, my parents were relaxing at home at about nine o'clock on Sunday evening, reading in their pajamas. They were early-to-bed people. Suddenly the phone rang. It was Mrs. Whitney for my mother. "Oh Kitty," she said brightly, "Jock and I have been so wanting to have you over, but we just haven't had a minute. What about coming over for a quick drink now?" My parents groaned inwardly, but of course they didn't say that they were already in bed. After the

Whitneys politely rejected their protestations, they agreed, got dressed and took a cab to Regent's Park. The drink didn't take long, but it turned out that the visit had another purpose. The writer Mary McCarthy was coming to London to lecture and was staying with the Whitneys, arriving sometime after 11:00 p.m. Since it was Sunday, there was no staff at the ambassador's residence, and Mary McCarthy's bed had not been made. The Whitneys, it appeared, did not know how to do such a thing, so they summoned my parents, who did. Once this feat was accomplished, my parents were allowed to return to bed. My father expected to find Mary McCarthy an unpalatable radical, but in the event they got on very well. No doubt the bed-making story helped break the ice. "I made your bed, but you'll have to lie in it," my father would no doubt have said.

Before I left for Germany I had one memorable adventure. An acquaintance of my father was Sir Basil Gray, curator of what was then called the Oriental Collection at the British Museum. My father told me that Gray had a daughter named Camilla, who was also interested in Russian things: Would I like to meet her? Of course I would. Then he told me that Sir Basil did not approve of higher education for women, so that Camilla had not attended a university. But being a person of great determination, she had simply gone to Cambridge and lived there for several years, attending lectures and getting to know various professors. What was most fascinating was that her field of interest was Russian modern art, a subject of great interest to me, but that I then knew almost nothing about, since there was no decent book in English taking a large view of the subject and my Russian still being pretty rudimentary. Camilla Gray was writing an account, which turned out to be a classic.

As a result of my father's fortunate intervention, I visited her several times at the British Museum where the family lived, and we had several long conversations. After her time at Cambridge, where her study of Russian modernism began, Camilla set out to consult with people like Alfred Barr and Meyer Schapiro in the United States and spent extended periods in Russia, where she interviewed surviving modernists like Mikhail Larionov and Natalia Goncharova, David Burliuk and Sonia Delaunay, as well as pioneer Russian art historians like Alexander Benois. The result was *The Russian Experiment in Art*, 1863-1922, published in 1963, a book which is still fresh and vital forty-five years after its initial publication. Camilla told me just a little about the book, but what she told me and the eventual arrival of the book itself lent an aura of mystery to Russian art for me, which it has never lost.

Unfortunately, I was due to leave soon for Germany and she for Russia. I was quite prepared to fall in love with her, although she was two years older than I. On what was to be the last time I saw her, she asked me if I would do her a rather unusual favor, as I "was about the right size." Mystified, I agreed. She then asked me to model some shirts and jackets that she was taking to someone in Russia. There, I assumed, correctly, went my romantic hopes. I tried on the clothes, which seemed a little Edwardian for my conservative taste, but were clearly going to fit. She never told me for whom they were intended. It was only later that I found out that they were for Sergei Prokofiev's son Oleg, an avant-garde painter whom she later married, after going to live permanently in the Soviet Union, a highly unusual thing for a Westerner to do in those days, particularly a member of what the Russians called "the creative intelligentsia," with no sympathy toward Communism.

The Soviet authorities, still quite unreconciled to modern art and almost insanely anxious to avoid any "kowtowing" to Western critics, were infuriated by the publication of *The Russian Experiment in Art* in 1963. As a result, Camilla and Oleg were kept apart for six years, before being allowed to marry in 1969. Sadly, she died of an unusual variety of hepatitis in 1971, after only two years of marriage, and I never saw her again. Oleg Prokofiev was allowed to bring her body back to England for burial, and he decided not to return to the Soviet Union. He died in England in 1998, but had the satisfaction by then of having his work exhibited in Russia. He had studied with Robert Falk, an important Russian modernist, and his painting and sculpture is represented in the collection of the Tretiakov Gallery in Moscow. I have been unable to discover any details of Camilla Gray's life in the period between the publication of her book in 1963 and her marriage to Prokofiev in 1969, in particular how the anger of Soviet officialdom was expressed, apart from the prohibition of their marriage.

A few days later I took the boat train from London to Heidelberg and arrived for the first of my two semesters in Germany. Upon arrival, I went to the foreign students department, where I was taken in charge by a very determined young woman who set out to find me a place to stay. Susanne, I think her name was, gave me a first small taste of German authoritarianism. "Du, Tom, pass auf!" ("You, Tom, pay attention!") she would invariably say, as soon as she had discovered that my German was not good enough to understand everything she said, and my attention span was too short for her lengthy and detailed instructions. But she soon found me lodgings with a German family in a suburb of Heidelberg. The streetcar, a block away, delivered me at the university after a fifteen-minute ride. But I eventually acquired a Vespa Grand Sport motor scooter, after a three-month struggle with the German bureaucracy over its purchase and transfer from Cologne to Heidelberg.

Dominated by the ruined castle, Heidelberg was indeed a charming city, although lacking the intellectual and cultural dynamism of Berlin. Its predominantly pinkish stone, its relative compactness, its situation on the banks of the Neckar River made it a delightful and manageable place to explore, although a great many Germans annoyed the American students by assuming that our presence in the city was inspired by the faded and cloying romanticism of Sigmund Romberg's *The Student Prince*, set in Heidelberg, rather than an interest in history or desire to learn German. The cobbled streets, the late medieval church and the "Old Bridge" across the river were exactly what I was looking for.

Living in a family introduced me to some of the mysteries of Germany—from the routines of everyday life to how ordinary

UNIVERSITÄT HEIDELBERG
STUDENTENAUSWEIS

für stud. phil.
Abbott Gleason
Vor- und Zuname (in Blockschrift ausfüllen)
geboren am 21. Juli 1938
zu Cambridge/Mass.
Wohnort der Eltern: London
des Ehegatten:
Staatsangehörigkeit: U.S.A.
31. Okt. 1960
(Immatrikulationstag)
DER REKTOR:

Sudent ID, University of Heidelberg, Germany, 1960

people remembered the Third Reich. I learned about the obligatory Sunday walk, which took place rain or shine and lasted some two hours or more. I had some interesting conversations. When I asked my German "father," who was a postal worker, what the best time of his life had been, he said "between 1933 and 1939." I was surprised. "How so," I enquired. "Because it was so peaceful", he said. I was stunned by his answer, but soon realized that for an apolitical little boy growing up in Germany, the late thirties could have been experienced as an interval of tranquility between the upheavals of the 1920s and the horrors of World War II.

I was not a model lodger. I was experimenting with a pipe and periodically showered my little room with sparks. The family retaliated by gradually removing articles of furniture which I had allegedly damaged, starting with the rug and ending with armchair, so that by the time I moved out my quarters looked more like a prisoner's cell than anything else, my furniture being reduced to a bed, a straight-backed chair, a desk and a waste basket. I considered myself a victim at the time, but my perspective has shifted over the years. After renting rooms in our house to students, and on one memorable occasion—never to be repeated—subletting our entire house for two years, my sympathies are now firmly with my German family.

At the university, I heard lectures by Werner Conze on German history and by the great historian of philosophy, Karl Löwith on the Kant and on the Left Hegelians. The authoritarianism of German academic culture of course astonished me. Professor Löwith was a diminutive figure with snow white hair, but compelling on the podium and a man of extraordinary good looks of a most delicate kind. His appearance belied his temper. On one occasion a student entered through the professor's door, which led directly to the podium, rather than via the door through which the students were supposed to file into the hall. Löwith, who followed him in, flew into a rage, collared the student and made him go out again through the professorial door and re-enter through the student entrance. This little display was quite surprising to an American student, especially since the brilliant Löwith, a Jewish student of Heidegger, had a reputation as a liberal and had spent the war years at the University of Chicago.

Years later I was reminded of this German academic formality by the great mathematician Peter Lax, who told me the following story. A young German female mathematician had fled her German university after 1933 and eventually received an appointment at the University of Chicago. As soon as she arrived, she set tirelessly to work to find a position for her Jewish professor who was now forbidden to teach in Germany. Eventually she succeeded, and in a few weeks she was able to greet him in the Chicago railroad station, at the head of a small delegation of academic dignitaries. "Ah, Hilde, how very nice to see you," he said in English, as they embraced on the platform. But he said quietly in German a second later, "When the Americans are around, I will call you Hilde and you will call me Stefan, but when we are alone, you will call me Herr Professor and I will call you Frau Professor Doktor."[3]

The principal academic I had come to study with was a distinguished Ukrainian professor of Russian literature name Dmitrii Chizhevsky, transliterated by the Germans as "Tschiżewskij." He was one of the world's leading authorities on Russian-German cultural relations and the main reason I had chosen Heidelberg as a place of study. He was also a remarkable character and provided me with additional education about the exalted status of academics in Europe. About a week after my arrival, I went to the Slavic Faculty with a letter of introduction to the great man from an American colleague. His assistant told me that Chizhevsky had just left for his apartment, and then he gave me a piece of extremely bad advice. "If you hurry along, you can probably catch him just as he's going in the door," said the young man pleasantly. And so it turned out. But when I tried to give my letter to the professor, he hurled it on the floor, told me to present it at his office, muttered something about intolerable rudeness and flung himself into his apartment and slammed the door in my face. And he had been a left socialist—a Menshevik—when he was young!

Part of the reason Chizhevsky had such an extreme reaction to my unintended breach of etiquette was because he had an exceedingly low opinion of Americans. When he taught at Harvard some years earlier he had very few undergraduate students. This was not

[3] A truncated version of this anecdote appears in Peter D. Lax, "The Bomb, Sputnik, Computers, and European Mathematicians," *The Bicentennial Tribute to American Mathematics*, The Mathematical Association of America, 1977, pp. 132-133.

surprising, as he never learned much spoken English and always lectured in Russian or German. He also, it seemed, believed in werewolves and other evil spirits, and several people in Cambridge later told me that he never went to the famous Cambridge outlet store called Lechmere, because he was convinced that the surrounding area was a werewolf haunt.

I never recovered from my bad start with Chizhevsky. I took his rather unstructured pro-seminar, but his conversations with me were always personal and disapproving. After holding forth on the importance of the steppe nomads in the Russian middle ages, Chizhevsky would turn to me and say in an irritable way. "Let's see what Mr. Gleason has to say about this. He's an American, and you know the Americans are really all nomads." My German was improving, but I usually found myself tongue-tied when invited to speak in such a fashion before a group of ten German students. In what way were the Americans nomads? In my ear the charge had something almost National Socialist about it. "Nomads" seemed to have some reference to words like "homeless" (*heimatslos*) and "outcast" (*vertriebene*) that I associated with anti-Semitic rhetoric.

Eventually, on a trip to Paris, I was picking through second-hand book bins on the banks of the Seine, when I came across a rather valuable document, a first French edition of Empress Catherine the Great's treatise on government known to scholars as her *Nakaz.* I bought it and presented it to Chizhevsky for the Heidelberg Library, which did not have it. He told me that he was glad that I was not venal and mercenary like most Americans, but our relationship remained chilly.

Another professor, Heinz Koeppler, had a group of students—most from his seminar—to dinner at a fancy local restaurant and told me the following anecdote. In the restaurant he was confronted by Dolph Sternberger, a prominent political scientist from the Heidelberg faculty. Addressing Koeppler as "Herr Koeppler" rather than as Professor, Doctor, or Professor-Doctor, more respectful forms of address for German academics, Sternberger spoke sarcastically of how since Koeppler had been away from Germany so long—he had fled during the Nazi period—he would have forgotten that it was not customary in Germany for professors and students to sit down at the same table at dinner!

But a certain propensity for getting myself adopted by hospitable families brought some warmth into my personal life. My parents, on the eve of my departure for Heidelberg, had told me to look up acquaintances of theirs from Washington, a couple named Sydney and Jameson Parker. Jameson had been a protégé of the Dulles family at the Eisenhower State Department. In Germany, he was serving in the American Embassy as an economic affairs officer. I called on the Parkers, and thereupon met some of the most delightful people that a student away from home could have hoped to meet. When I should have been working on my German, Polish or Russian (I was studying all three at once, confusingly, in German), I would ride my Vespa up the Rhine to the Parkers' house at Bad Godesberg and spend the evening in reminiscence about Washington, or the early lives of Sydney and Jameson, or the activities of their son Francis, later famous as a television actor under his father's name Jameson Parker (particularly in a show called *Simon and Simon*) and his sister, Judith. Jameson Parker was a man of ideas and projects. We might be sitting in his living room at four in the afternoon and he would say dreamily "if we left now, we could be in Brussels tonight for a late dinner." No sooner said than done. Everyone would be packed in half an hour, and we would be on the Autobahn in thirty-five minutes and in Brussels several hours later for dinner and a day of tourism to follow.

Jameson was from an old and—I had the impression—rather staid Baltimore family. Far from staid himself, he had many amusing stories about his parents. They often took Jameson and his sister abroad in the summer. His father, Sumner Parker, a manufacturer of decorative iron work, felt it necessary to do this in some style, so fancy and very formal clothes were purchased for European summer wear. But in order to save money, the senior Parkers made every effort to book a relatively inexpensive passage. Jameson recalled one occasion when they had gotten on board a quite scruffy looking vessel in New York, and woke up early the next morning to discover that the ship was taking on a load of coal in Fall River, which it proceeded to distribute at Halifax, St. John's, Newfoundland, and other depots along the way. The swanky outfits were suffused in coal dust by the time they arrived in England, and the captain's table was not at all what they had hoped for.

Sumner had married a woman who, if not an exotic dancer, was certainly from a very different social milieu than her husband. She was a woman of striking originality, and I soon had the opportunity to make her acquaintance. Recently widowed, she flew frequently to Bonn to see her son and daughter-in-law from the mansion she had constructed outside of Baltimore and dubbed "The Cloisters." She was known in the family as "sweetie," and one of her compelling reasons for traveling to Europe was to build up her remarkable art collection, about which I heard much but never had an opportunity to view.

Not that Mrs. Parker was dependent on trips to Europe to build her art collection. Back in Baltimore she had the remarkable good luck to discover a painting by Saint Luke, known from a passing scriptural reference as an artist. A most fortunate find, to say the least. No other works by St. Luke are known to have survived. She had been in a bar in Baltimore, she told me, and had caught sight of a barrel of oysters over near the bar. The barrel was covered by a piece of canvas, and she could see a man's leg painted on the canvas. "As soon as I saw it," she said, "I knew it was by Saint Luke." So she bought it and had it framed and hung up in the Cloisters. I never found just the right moment to ask her how she had become so familiar with Saint Luke's style, but of course I always wondered.

When I met her, Mrs. Parker's quest was to find and acquire for her collection one of the several medieval statues, most the subjects of devotional cults, known as Black Madonnas or Virgins. There was a famous one in Guadalupe, one at Chartres, and one in

Częstochowa in Poland, among other places. But Mrs. Parker believed that asking people was the best way to find out where things were, rather than trying to locate them from books. So as soon as she came down the steps from the transatlantic flight she said to a bemused Bonn-Cologne Airport official, "Excuse me, dear. I'm Mrs. Sumner Parker of Baltimore, Maryland. Can you tell me where the Black Madonna is?" Having failed to get satisfaction, she proceeded by taxi to her son's house, where a discussion ensued about how hard it would be to get the authorities at Chartres or Częstochowa to part with such a famous statue.

I was such a success with Mrs. Parker senior that by the time the weekend was coming to an end, she had offered me the position of curator of her art collection, and also of her "Muniment Room." I didn't know what a muniment room was, but Sydney and Jameson did. It turned out that Mrs. Parker understood "muniments" to be old family papers, and of course, the Parker family had some, but not a sufficient number to require a curator. In any event, I explained to Mrs. Parker that I was obliged to finish out my fellowship and I was then planning to enter graduate school. I wouldn't be on the job market for six or seven years at least, but that I would be happy to consider an offer further down the road. As it happened, however, I let this golden opportunity pass me by.

I heard many more stories about Mrs. Parker, over the course of the next several years. Something like a decade earlier, when her husband was still alive, she had become convinced of one of the durable indications of contemporary American decadence: that people were no longer able to quote poetry the way previous generations had, and that she had to do something about this deplorable development. So she persuaded Sumner to acquiesce to a scheme by which she arranged to have a number of prominent short poems carved in stone or slate and suspended by chains from the branches of some of the larger trees in the garden of the Cloisters. Everything was fine at first, and the poems were much admired by visitors, who attempted to commit them to memory over drinks on long summer evenings. Then, however, came Hurricane Carol, at the end of August, 1954. Although it struck Baltimore only a glancing blow, the winds were strong enough to set the stone poems swinging wildly on their chains. Several of them eventually came off, flew through the air and made contact with a neighbor's house, causing considerable damage. Thus ended a promising experiment in monumental or "concrete" poetry.

Mrs. Parker senior was not very careful about her money, and much of it passed into the hands of a fortune-hunter that her son and daughter-in-law always referred to as "lover boy." At her death, the house was taken by the city of Baltimore for back taxes. It experienced a phase as a museum—of children's art, I think. It is now a site for weddings, bar mitzvahs and other pleasant events. The papers in the muniment room were scattered to the four winds. Modern times are hostile to aristocrats, even newly fledged ones.

Sydney Sullivan Parker was one of the wittiest women I have ever met, partly because she was such a bewildering mixture of opposites. Her father was the famous newspaper columnist, Mark Sullivan, who although quite conservative and a great friend of Herbert Hoover, was an Irishman who had become a successful journalist in America and was well-acquainted with discrimination. Sydney's mother, however, was from an old Virginia family with very conservative attitudes of a much more traditionalist kind. Sydney and I fought constantly about politics, but without animosity. It was a kind of ritual exchange, almost a game that we would fall into every so often. Somehow her constant remarks about the "G. d. lower classes" seemed a fantastic aberration on the lips of this witty and affectionate woman.

She played the piano quite well and loved to find things for us to sing, from spirituals to madrigals, to show tunes. I well remember a wonderful Scottish ballad with quite complex chord changes, called "The Road To the Isles," referring to Bonnie Prince Charlie's escape route to the Hebrides. Both she and Jameson could quote poetry endlessly, from the Elizabethans to Eliot—although I largely failed to convince them of the merits of Ezra Pound—and we spent a great deal of time reading aloud. In retrospect I can see that the Parkers helped me rediscover my inner preppy. They were snobs, but lovable snobs and they were very kind to me. They cherished personal relations and believed in Forster's "Only connect." They were charming, accepting and self-indulgent, and started a thawing process in my slightly priggish and unrooted leftism, which proceeded by dribs and drabs. Their vulnerabilities and eccentricities were extremely endearing, and my long-suppressed sympathy for rootedness, inherited from my mother, began to stir.

Another charming family that I came to know in Heidelberg was that of John and Janet Fiske. John ran the Amerika Haus in Heidelberg, the task of which was to reintegrate the Germans into the postwar western world, so I often met German students there for informal discussions. The Fiskes had three children: Cindy, who was a bit younger than I, and the twins, Fred and Anne (known then as Nanny). John Fiske had gone out to teach in the Middle East after college and had spent a number of years teaching at what was then Robert College in Istanbul, before returning to Harvard to get his Ph.D. in Russian literature. But with a growing family to support, he had not taken an academic job after receiving his degree in 1947, but gone into the foreign service. He was a delightful, poetic soul, with a slightly apologetic manner, who in succeeding years had a series of fascinating if somewhat out of the way foreign service posts. I managed to visit him at most of them. He was U.S. consul in Bremen and Cultural Affairs officer in Rejkjavik, Iceland, and I managed to stay with him and his charming western wife Janet in both places. I never made it to the Congo, however, where he also served a somewhat beleaguered term as Cultural Attaché.

Something like a decade after going to teach at Brown, I was still in touch with the Fiskes, who had retired to the small academic community of Moscow, Idaho, but still spent summers on Cape Cod. One summer—maybe in the late 1970s—we hadn't managed to get out and see them, but they stopped in Providence to have dinner with us, on their way back to Boston to fly home. Was there anybody at Brown they would like to see at dinner, I asked? "Yes," John replied, "I'd like to see Alan Trueblood. He and I were in graduate school together." I barely knew Trueblood, a distinguished scholar of early modern Spanish drama and an excellent translator of Spanish poetry, but of course it was easy to call him up and say that his old friends the Fiskes were passing through Providence and would like to see him at dinner. There was a brief pause—in retrospect perhaps not hard to explain—and Trueblood said he would be pleased to come for dinner. So several days later, he arrived and we had a very pleasant dinner. John Fiske had written his Ph.D. dissertation on Dostoevsky's off again-on again career in the Soviet Union and Trueblood had written on Dostoevsky and Spanish writers, so the conversation was pleasant and lively, but soon after dinner, Trueblood excused himself and went home. The minute the door closed behind him, John Fiske turned to me and said "I've never seen that man before in my life." I later discovered that Trueblood had from the beginning not been sure that he knew a "John Fiske." Both men were too polite to broach the subject but made friendly conversation for a decent interval instead. I was never able to figure out whether they had forgotten each other or genuinely never known the person with whom they spent some three hours. I suspect the former, since Alan Trueblood is quite a distinctive name and they had been in graduate school at Harvard at approximately the same time.

Europe for me was not just the drizzle of London and the smoky mists of the Rhineland that year. I spent a good deal of time in Berlin with Harbison, where he was studying composition and conducting at the Hochschule für Musik. We had a similar attitude toward the authoritarianism of German culture. John told me in amazement about an incident he had experienced on the Kurfürstendamm in West Berlin. The going convention decreed that someone using a public telephone booth was allowed only one telephone call if another user was waiting. John had been physically hustled out of a phone booth, even though no one had nswered the first call he had tried to make.

We decided to stage our own version of this encounter. John went into the phone booth and I positioned myself outside. When he started to dial I burst in and pretended to knee him in the groin and we exchanged a few mock blows. I then ran off, leaving John groaning on the sidewalk. A German burgher hurried up. "Was ist los?" he enquired, as John continued to writhe on the pavement. "Ich ... ich habe ... ich habe zu lang telefoniert,"[4] John stammered. The onlookers shrugged and moved on. Their facial expressions made everything clear: what did the foreigner expect, in light of this flagrant breach of etiquette? "Das geht nicht in Deutschland, zweimal zu telefonieren!"[5]

John's landlady was a character out of Christopher Isherwood's Berlin stories, with a pinch of Brecht thrown in. She must have had a first name, but John and his American friends just called her "Frau Baum". She was maternal and intrusive, and in an overpowering way kind to her tenants and their friends. She often brought John ghastly snacks which—thanks to the development of indoor plumbing—he could quickly dispose of. She was thrilled to have a composer from America under her roof. John's initial German experience had been that the natives weren't very interested in American music, but when Frau Baum discovered that he was a musician she exclaimed, "Ach, I love American music!" Who were her favorites, John wondered. Aaron Copland's name flashed through his mind. "Prezley," she said enthusiastically.

Early in March I mounted my Vespa and set out for Italy, heading first for Florence, where I had another name to look up. He was Richard Maury, a couple of years older than I, also from Washington D.C., or at least its Takoma Park suburb. I had heard of him through Bill French and his wife Lois, in the Pound circle back

[4] "I telephoned too long."

[5] "You can't telephone twice in Germany."

in Washington, D.C. So I wondered if he would turn out to be some kind of fascist. Not at all. The Maurys were simply not interested in politics.

Richard and his wife Anne, a talented botanical illustrator, were settling down to what turned out to be a lifelong residence in Italy. They were immensely hospitable, and we quickly became friends. Richard was spectacularly handsome, with fiery red hair, and Anne was extremely pretty. They had several young children, all blonde, and they caused quite a stir when they walked together through downtown Florence—a renewal of the Viking invasions their dark-haired neighbors might have thought. We painted together around Florence for several weeks before I returned to Germany for the second semester.

I was at that time painting in a neo-cubist style, while Richard was working in a post-impressionist style that owed something to Gauguin. Over the years, however, his style became more and more conservative, so that by the end of the century he was painting in an extremely representational-realist style which has been described as Dutch. In the early days, Richard and Anne had hardly any money, and were often reduced to painting trays for tourists and doing other pseudo-artisanal, low-wage work. But as realist painting became more fashionable, Richard's work was discovered by New York galleries, and after years of poverty, they are now more than comfortable, still living in Florence.

Harbison visited Florence for part of the time, and we went daily to the Uffizi Gallery. There we discovered the wonderful Portinari triptych of the Nativity by the Netherlandish painter Hugo van der Goes, which I have gone to see every time I have been back in Florence and about which John wrote a wonderful poem. We had marevellous, lazy days of exploring Florence, painting, writing and hiking. John began to recover from a broken romance in Berlin. On one occasion we set off to hike to Fiesole too late in the day, and the sun set just as we arrived at the top. We got lost in the dark coming back, and it took us hours to find our way to the small pensione where we were staying. Harbison tried to write a poem about it, which wouldn't quite come. Later he wrote to me that:

> It makes no difference, since I have rethought the whole imagery of the adventure, the sun going just before we reached the top, the nostalgic conversation about past euphorias, getting lost coming home, until they all mean something else. That the sun had eluded us was clear, before and after we talked. That we talked about the good old days and the atmosphere of summer seemed appropriate. That we both depended on each other for certain things while getting lost was tangible but mysterious. All these things can be cleared up in the play of pure images, even the under-tension of a conversation. But what disturbs me about the day and the days around it is that perhaps they escaped uncomprehended. Was that the time somehow [of] our summer's hottest sun, will we ever be that high again? I have a fear that we will some day look back to that point or some like it, and say, it was good then,and has never been so good since.

On my way back from this mellow trip, I decided to try and call on Ezra Pound, then living in a castle in Alto Adige, a northern province of Italy, contested by its former Austrian owners as Südtirol. The castle was called Brunnenburg, and it was owned by Boris de Rachewiltz and his wife, Mary, daughter of Ezra Pound by Olga Rudge. I bore a letter of introduction from Guy Davenport, to wit:

> Dear Mr. Pound:
>
> XAIPE.[6] This is to introduce Tom Gleason. Son of the Republic's Cultural Attaché in London; Harvard; now on his way to Heidelberg. He would count it a gracious privilege to see you for a few minutes. He knew Bill French in Washington, and got in, though late, on the Gadfly circle in Cambridge. Next year I hope to make an appearance myself. I trust you are fine. Greetings to Mrs. Pound.
>
> Yours,
>
> Guy Davenport

[6] "Rejoice", in Greek. Title of a 1950 poem by e.e. cummings. *Gadfly* was a short-lived journal founded by Davenport while he was at Harvard.

Guy had given me instructions that I should write "weeks ahead, to Mizz Pound, to inquire whether the greatest of America's poets was in." I had not done that, partly because I was twenty-one years old and partly because I was not clear who "Mizz Pound" was. Was it Dorothy Shakespeare Pound or Olga Rudge? Wife or long-time companion? Precisely what family arrangements prevailed at the Schloss? When I arrived, Pound had gone to Rome, apparently to address a Fascist rally, or at least to be present at it. So after greeting my friend David Gordon, of the old Washington circle, I rode on.

For the second semester I relocated from the household of my first German family, partly because of the increasing sparseness of my room's furnishings, partly because of the heavy hand of my landlord, which he too frequently used on his children. My second family lived on the other side of Heidelberg, up the Neckar in a little hamlet called Peterstal. My landlord was a former painter, now employed by a wood-processing company, who steered me toward a number of small galleries and museums in the vicinity. It was altogether a more pleasant situation, and I contrived not to set the furniture or rugs on fire.

I was not the only lodger in his house. There was an interesting couple up stairs over my head, whose life experience enlarged mine significantly. This couple, somewhere around sixty in age, were laborers in a local factory. They were illiterate and had arrived in Heidelberg from somewhere in central Europe at the end of World War II. They had been born and brought up in one of those virtually all-German towns that could be found in so many Slavic nations and in Hungary. The young man had been drafted first into the Hungarian army and then made to serve the Germans. At the German surrender, he and his wife set out to walk to Germany, where they felt they belonged, although they seem to have known next to nothing about politics. After months on the road, they reached Heidelberg, all borders in between being essentially open at this time, and there they got factory jobs, which had kept them going ever since. Although they were illiterate, they did have a book about their German village, which listed all the various local social and sport organizations (*Vereine*) and on one list or another most of the inhabitants. They were eager to invite me up for meals, and would even put up with my American accent if I would read aloud to them about their former community, which I did many an evening. Experiences like this gave me a view of the desolation of the immediate postwar period which I could never have assimilated from books.

So did meeting a few Nazis and many Germans whose family members had been Nazis. Sometimes fellow students would discuss what seemed to me their remarkable lack of awareness and they sometimes used phrases that fascinated me: "My father was a bit brown"; or "my father believed a little bit in the brown shirt."[7] I had often fantasized about what it would be like when I met my first Nazi, these fantasies sometimes taking the form of physical combat, sometimes of violent arguments, in which my German mysteriously expanded into eloquence under the pressure of the encounter. But the actual event was an anticlimax. When I was hitchhiking back to Heidelberg from Berlin, a little old man in a tiny car pulled over and picked me up. "I was with Hitler from the first," he announced proudly, and went on to tell me what a great man he had been. Of course I argued with him, but I could hardly hit this tiny old man, and he went far out of his way to take me near Heidelberg so he could keep haranguing me. He gave me arguments that I had already heard many times: that Hitler was a bulwark against Bolshevism and that Weimar was run by the Jews, English and French, etc. I felt deflated when he finally let me out of the car, since I could neither silence him nor even effectively refute him with my still relatively rudimentary German. I had of course not foreseen that my first Nazi encounter would resemble this one.

[7] "*Mein Vater war ein bissel braun*"; "*Mein Vater hat ein bisschen in das braunes Hemd geglaubt.*"

Incidentally, I have occasionally read that as late as 1960-61, virtually no one in Germany would talk with foreigners about Hitler. It was my experience that any such generalization is a great exaggeration. I had all sorts of different kinds of discussions with many students, professors and virtual strangers about the Nazi period.

Before returning to the United States, I visited my undergraduate benefactor, Andrzej Walicki, in Poland, at his invitation. It was a pleasant trip of several weeks, the first part of which was spent in Warsaw, and the second part camping out in the Tatry Mountains near the Czech border. Warsaw was a wonderful place. The jazz was the best I had heard in Europe and I was amazed by the restoration of Warsaw's old neighborhoods. I had some phone numbers to call, and was able to play tennis as well as go club hopping. The days passed in a haze of music and talk among cordial strangers, who kept me up till all hours, plying me with drink and giving me a vivid sense of how anti-Russian most Poles were. I used various languages, as best I could, even my rotten French. With Walicki I spoke mostly English, with his wife, Russian. The Walickis lived in a development of small but comfortable houses, built to house Soviet construction workers who built the Palace of Culture, a large and hideous Stalinist skyscraper in downtown Warsaw. "Where is the most beautiful view in Warsaw?" went the joke. "From the Palace of Culture," was the answer, "because from there you can't see the Palace of Culture."

After a week and a half, we decided to round off my visit with some travel to the south of Poland. We would stay in camping grounds or sleep in peasant barns, cradling our sleeping bags on mounds of hay and listening to the soothing sounds of sleepy animals. It took me back to early summers on the farm. When I first met him in Cambridge, Andrzej had not yet learned to drive, but he had later done so. On his way home, passing through Paris, he had bought a small French Citroen, of the type known as a "deux chevaux"—two horses. As appropriate to a new driver, Andrzej was very cautious and our drive south from Warsaw proceeded at a leisurely

Tom Gleason, Andrzej Walicki, Poland, 1961

pace. But who was in a hurry? As we drove along, Andrzej, his wife and his cousin taught me Polish songs, political and non-political. On our first night out, Andrzej was heading for a camp ground of which he knew, but we slightly overran the turnoff and stopped. The road was too narrow to turn around, but there was little traffic. "Just back up," I urged him. "No," he said, with a mysterious sort of unease, "no, there's a better camp ground just a bit ahead. I think we'll go there." We drove along for quite a long time, though, before we came to another site. It was not until later in the trip that I discovered that Andrzej had learned well enough how to drive the car forward, but had not yet mastered reverse, a skill that did not elude him for long, however.

While we were hiking, mountain climbing and sleeping in peasant barns, the Berlin Wall was suddenly erected. The Polish press, however, did not immediately inform the Polish public what had happened, not wanting to concede that a barrier had been constructed to prevent defections, so we were left to figure out what had happened ourselves. "We'll be able to do it," Andrzej said firmly. "*Trybuna Ludu* (the principal Polish daily newspaper) is not *Pravda*. They will quote Western sources who suggest that the Soviet action might be at least understandable, if not actually justified." Sure enough, within just a few days, the commentaries of Walter Lippman and other Westerners that diverged from straightforward condemnation appeared at least in snippets in the Polish paper. From these it became clear to us that the border had been sealed and some sort of a physical barrier was being erected through the heart of Berlin.

My return trip from Warsaw through Berlin and on to Paris was memorable, taking place as it did only about two weeks after the wall had been erected, when international tension was very high. Most of the cars on the Warsaw-Berlin train ended their run in the East Berlin station, and then were taken off somewhere else. Just two cars were uncoupled and remained in East Berlin for an hour or so and then were slowly taken across the now more sharply demarcated border to West Berlin, where they were joined to another train going on to Paris. When we reached East Berlin, I was deep in conversation with some pleasant Hungarians I had met, in one of the cars not going on to Paris. Suddenly, there was a mild jolt, and our part of the train began to move out of the station again. I ran to the end of the train and saw the cars which were going on to West Berlin still sitting in the station, as the rest of the train gathered speed. In that Paris-bound car was my passport and two suitcases. Without thinking what I was doing, but instinctively rejecting a trip to some unknown destination in East Germany, I jumped off the train and walked back into the station. Only as I was hauling myself up onto the platform, did I see that it was crawling with East German police and soldiers. I suddenly realized the danger of my situation: an American without luggage or passport climbing from the railroad tracks onto the end of the platform. Miraculously, however, no one seemed to notice me and I was able to reboard one of the Paris cars without incident. My passport and tickets were in my bag, and before my excitement and terror had fully subsided we were back in "the West."

Only when I was back in my seat did I suddenly realize that I had left the East Germans a souvenir: a Harvard letter sweater, crimson, with a big white H on it. My father had been the manager of the 1927 Harvard track team, and now his sweater that he had given me was headed God only knew where—to the yards or maybe on to Leipzig. When I returned to Cambridge, I went to the Harvard Athletic Association and told them my pathetic tale, and they gave my father a replacement sweater.

For many months, I had been turning over in my mind what to do when my year in Germany was over. I thought of applying to art school at the Pennsylvania Academy where I knew some students and faculty, or for training in architecture. These possibilities seemed increasingly risky, as time became shorter and the necessity to make choices more compelling. I didn't have an adequate sense of myself as either a painter or an architect, but I knew I could be a reasonably good historian. So when deadline time was upon me, I applied to graduate school in history at Princeton, California-Berkeley and Harvard, and seduced by continuity, when the time came chose Harvard, even though I was not offered financial aid there. My academic record was sufficiently uneven that Jinks Harbison had to work fairly hard to persuade the Princeton History Department "to take a chance on me." But at that point, my career seemed far away, immersed as I was in day-to-day German reality. I made the best choice I could, a prudent one. But I had a fugitive sense that a scholarly career was second best, that some magic had gone out of my future when I didn't choose the arts. For me, that exciting, terrifying alternative has always been the road not taken.

Joel Henning, Tom Gleason, John Hancock, John Casey, 1963

Graduate School

On more than one occasion, hurricanes seemed to attend transitional stages in my life, beginning with my birth, just before the great storm of 1938. My return to Cambridge in September, 1962, took place in the middle of Hurricane Daisy, and as I drove into Harvard Square at 4:00 A.M. in a drenching downpour, I had the vivid fantasy that I had been found wanting in my first four years at Harvard and was repeating college. God had decided that I would have to "stay back."

I was also brooding about the fact that higher authorities—my father in particular—believed the time for intellectual freewheeling was over. I was now expected to grow up, a big part of which meant seeking, or at least becoming resigned to, a "professional" experience. My father was also disapproving that I had turned down good offers from Princeton and the University of California at Berkeley to return to Harvard. He was vividly aware of the mesmerizing romance of Harvard and Cambridge, since he had fallen under its spell himself. When he and Langer had exhausted the funding provided by the Council on Foreign Relations, he hoped to be asked to take a position at Harvard and continue his work with Langer. Only after that offer failed to materialize, he maintained, did he accept the position on the National Security Council. When he resigned as Cultural Affairs Officer in London in 1962, he had hoped to be invited to teach at Harvard, but wasn't. He was also hoping to be invited to join the CIA, but wasn't. He went so far as to write to

Allen Dulles and indicate his availability and remind Dulles gently how often he had told my father that if ever he were available how delighted the Agency would be to have him, etc., etc. But Dulles did not even answer his letter. After months of genteel but increasingly urgent job hunting he accepted a position as editor of the *Foreign Relations of the United States* (FRUS), the document series published by the State Department. It was really an excellent job for an academic-cum-bureaucrat in his late fifties who did not aspire to further scholarly work, but my father felt it to be a backwater, after the exciting days at the National Security Council and the pleasures of life in London.

Meanwhile, what exactly did a "professional experience" mean? As my graduate training began at Harvard, I quickly discovered that it was indeed a very different experience from Harvard College. From the vantage point of most undergraduates, a professor is a professor. Gradations within that lofty status mean little. But the nuances of the academic world began to be revealed to me in graduate school. The gulf between senior faculty and junior faculty at Harvard was enormous in the 1960s and apparently still is. Assistant professors were treated more like graduate students than younger colleagues. Only very rarely were people promoted from the untenured ranks at Harvard. Undergraduates mostly saw graduate students as a notch up in the world, but the faculty tended to regard undergraduate leaders as more interesting and certainly more glamorous than graduate students, who were preparing for an academic life and career. So in a complex way, becoming a graduate student entailed a loss in status, rather than the marginal improvement I had imagined.

Faculty interest in new graduate students seemed very limited in the early 1960s at Harvard. These were the days when the graduate adviser would say when meeting with incoming graduate students for the first time: "Look to your right, look to your left. One of the people you see won't be here a year from now." Judgments were quick and often brutal. Mentoring was sporadic and often whimsical.

When I went to see Professor Robert Lee Wolff, who was then in charge of the academic study of Russia before 1800 and asked him for a bibliography, he got red in the face and lectured me wrathfully on how I wasn't an undergraduate any more and had better take responsibility myself for what to read. He quickly dismissed me and said in an irritated way, "read...read (pause) Catherine [the Great]'s plays." It was only later that I realized the degree to which Wolff's interest in early Russia and the Balkans had receded over the years. His real interest had become the religious utopian works of nineteenth-century visionaries like the Scottish George MacDonald, author of *Lilith* and *Phantastes*. And he required a great deal of deference. I may have been slow to see how much. I often was.

The seminars I took were rewarding enough. My baptism of fire was a seminar on the German Revolution of 1918 given by Reginald Phelps, a junior dean and not a regular faculty member, but most knowledgeable and pleasant in an austere Yankee way. I read period newspapers in the Library of Congress and reams of documents published by the Communist International. In the spring I took a seminar by a soft-spoken and cordial Englishman named James Joll on international socialism between the wars. Otherwise I returned chastened to studying Russian and started to read earnestly on Russian history. It wasn't all that much fun, and I was still not psychologically committed to this as my life's work. Nor was I convinced that my Russian language would ever be good enough. My cohort, furthermore, was intimidatingly bright, fueling my fear that although I might be a quick study and a fast talker I would not turn out to have enough academic staying power or any real originality. Because I had run with a fast intellectual crowd as an undergraduate, one part of me imagined myself superior to plodding academics-in-training, but another part of me realized how little I really knew. Graduate school confirmed my split personality on this point.

This insidious mixture of boredom, irresolution and terror was considerably alleviated by two relationships. For the first two years of my graduate training, I lived on the third floor of a house owned by a delightful couple named Benjamin and Felicia Kaplan, just a block from the Radcliffe campus. And immediately next door lived Dan and Holly Field, both of my Harvard class but whom I had really not known when we were undergraduates. I had only a vivid image of Dan, standing in line at the Freshman Union, where we all ate in our freshman year. He seemed vaguely aloof, in my memory, and he was invariably reading an orange Penguin paperback, of the sort that could then only be purchased in the U.K.—Evelyn Waugh, I imagined, or Malcom Muggeridge—something very English. He was clearly a flaming anglophile, I muttered to myself. He had been an English major as an undergrad, I remembered, and a formidable drama critic for *The Harvard Crimson*.

I soon discovered just how superficial this image was. By the time we reconnected, it was Dan's second year of graduate school, and he knew considerably more Russian history and Russian than I did. But he shared his experience generously, and since he lived next door, I was soon spending a lot of time in the Fields' living room and, in the summer, their back yard. Field had an extremely dry wit that I cherished. His wife Holly was delightfully cordial and generous about putting another plate on the table on short notice. Dan's father was a well known law school professor and Holly's father a well known medical school professor. When I viewed their wedding pictures, with all this faculty in the background, they seemed the ultimate young Harvard couple to me: Dan being in graduate school and Holly teaching at the posh and proper Winsor School in Boston. Dan and Holly gave me an advanced course in friendship, and our lives have been intertwined from that day to this.

The Kaplan family provided a delightful nest for a lonesome and uncertain first-year graduate student. Benjamin Kaplan was then a professor at the Harvard Law School. He would was later become a judge on the Massachusetts Supreme Judicial Court—one of the first Jewish supreme court justices, if not the first. His wife, Felicia Lamport Kaplan, was a writer of comic verse. She produced three

Holly and Dan Field, 2005
Photo by Richard Field

volumes, each brilliantly illustrated by Edward Gorey, over the next several years. Her verse owed something to Ogden Nash, but was much more political. One of her numerous attacks on Ronald Reagan was a parody of Whitman called "Leaves of Crass." Felicia came from a wealthy Jewish family in New York and had written a charming memoir of her growing up entitled *Mink on Weekdays (and Ermine on Sundays)*, which had made the *New York Times* bestseller list for one week earlier in the 1950s, an achievement that was the subject of much jesting commentary about "best-selling authors."

The Kaplan and the Gleason families had become acquainted five years earlier, when we had adjacent cabins on the small Cunard liner that took us to Southampton for a summer of European travel. The Kaplans had two children, James, known as Jimmy, and Nancy, who were several years younger than I. During my undergraduate years, the Kaplans had been generous hosts, frequently inviting me to Bond Street for drinks or dinner. I fitted conveniently in between the generations, halfway between the kids and their parents, which gave me a kind of privileged position at 2 Bond Street. I was a senior adolescent (or immediate post-adolescent) to Nancy and Jimmy and an adult-in-training to the senior Kaplans. Both relationships were nourishing to someone no longer a promising child and not yet an adult with anything to his credit.

The life rhythms of Ben and Felicia were very different, especially their work rhythms. Ben worked largely during the day and Felicia largely at night, so there was always somebody conscious of the heartbeat of the household, except for the hours between 3:00 and 7:00 A.M. Felicia was a great entertainer, and all sorts of fascinating people were constantly on hand in the late afternoon or evening from the academic community or the theater world, and she was immensely generous in including me in the family social life. So was Ben, but he was concerned that I not lose track of my professional obligations, something I was intermittently not unwilling to do. "Keep your eye on the main chance," he would admonish me with just a hint of a wink, as we headed out in the morning. And occasionally "Did you remember the main chance today?", as we re-convened at the close of the day.

I was supposed to pay some nominal rent for occupying the third floor, which included a large study and a comfortable bed and bath. I wanted to pay something I regarded as decent (no more) by way of rent, such as $100 a month, but Felicia wanted me to live with them for free. So we compromised on $50, an absolute pittance. Not content with charging me this ultra-low rent, Felicia would try surreptitiously to return what I had paid, by leaving it on my bureau or even slipping it back in my wallet, if she spotted it. So we had an absolute reversal of the usual struggle between landlord and tenant over the rent.

Ben was liberal in his politics, but cautiously so. Felicia, on the other hand, was by the standards of the late fifties an ultra-liberal. I met many interesting people at their house, almost all of them on the Left. It was fascinating for me to meet James Wechsler, the former editor of the *New York Post*, a man who seemed to embody all the contradictions of the American Left. He had been a communist as a young man, then broken with communism. Summoned by Senator McCarthy before his Senate committee, he had named names and then repented of having done so. By the early sixties he was embroiled with his son in the sort of generational conflict that I had long been enmeshed in with my father. Talking with him at the Kaplans was a moving and educational experience for me. My father thought McCarthy a demagogue but was cautious about speaking out publicly against him. No such caution restrained tongues at the Kaplans. My father's caution meant little to me one way or another in the mid-fifties, but we quarreled over it later.

Politics was the one area where Felicia and I were not completely at one on the world and its ways. I, for instance, while not an expert, was of the view that Alger Hiss was probably guilty of espionage, while Felicia was deeply, passionately convinced of his innocence. Over the summer between my second and third year in graduate school, Tony Hiss, Alger's son and later an original and amusing writer for *The New Yorker* and other publications, Andrew (Andy) Weil, subsequently a well-known health guru, and I shared the Kaplan's house as sitters, purely by chance.[1] At the end of the summer, with the Kaplans returning from Martha's Vineyard, Alger Hiss came to pick up his son, and Felicia gave a lunch for him. She told me, frowning in an unaccustomed way, that she didn't know whether to invite me or not because of my view that Hiss had probably been guilty of espionage. I was indignant. "He's your guest, Felicia," I expostulated. "My opinion of his guilt or innocence doesn't matter. Of course I would never say anything which would offend him."

So Sunday came, and Sunday lunch. Hiss was urbane and charming and spoke of his experiences at Yalta. He recollected how

[1]My principal memory of Dr. Andrew Weil that summer is his considerable interest in exploding cake recipes—things that you could fob off on inexperienced housewives that would blow up in the oven—the very opposite of the classic disaster, the falling cake.

frequently Stalin had needed to telephone back to Moscow and discuss various points with his colleagues there before coming to any agreement with the Western powers. At this point I forgot myself. "No, no," I protested, politely enough at first. "By 1945, Stalin didn't have to consult with anyone before taking major decisions." We discussed the matter back and forth for several minutes. Perhaps my voice rose slightly. Then Hiss said gently but with some resonance, "Now isn't this interesting. Here's a nice young man preparing for his preliminary examinations in Russian history. He's read some books on the origins of the Cold War. And he's telling me what happened at Yalta. I was AT Yalta! I SAW Stalin leaving to make phone calls. I was there." A hush had fallen over the table. Felicia looked at me. She was furious. I was mortified. While I had been guarding the front door against the possibility of political argument, controversy had come in through a rear window. She was mad at me for several months. It was the only interruption in our friendship. But eventually she forgave me.[2] I never saw Alger Hiss again.

Felicia Kaplan was one of the great raconteurs I have known. Among the many stories that spring to mind is her account of the mating of her pampered russet cocker spaniel, Napoleon Bonaparte Lamport Kaplan, known as Nappie. Napoleon, who as far as local observers could ascertain, had never had sexual intercourse, was brought in the midst of a serene old age to a summer house on Martha's Vineyard, in response to an ad seeking a stud for a female in heat. Felicia brought him over. To her horror, all the neighborhood children and some of their parents were gathered to watch the

[2] An interesting footnote to this episode: according to decoded Soviet intelligence documents, the Soviet agent known as ALES, who was "probably" Alger Hiss, was awarded a Soviet medal just after Yalta. See Robert Louis Benson and Michael Warner, *Venona. Soviet Espionage and the American Response*, 1939-1957, Aegean Park Press, Laguna Hills, CA, 1996, p. 423. For a summary of recent views that cut the other way, see Victor Navasky, "Hiss in History," *The Nation*, April 30, 2007, p. 8. See also Tony Hiss, *The View from Alger's Window: A Son's Memoir*, New York, Knopf, 1999 and Arthur Schlesinger, Jr., *A Life in the 20th Century*, Vol. 1, *Innocent Beginnings*, 1917-1950, Houghton Mifflin, pp. 497-98.

operation in a theater-like gallery, which overhung the living room.

But Nappie was not interested and seemed to have no idea of what he was supposed to be about. After he had ignored the langorous female for some fifteen minutes, and with the crowd getting restive, her owner began to become desperate. "Mrs. Kaplan," he expostulated, "I think we're just going to have to show them how to do it." Felicia had a momentary vision of lying on the floor with a perfect stranger, before a rapt audience of local families and two uncomprehending cocker spaniels. But it turned out that all that her host had in mind was that she hoist Napoleon Bonaparte onto the haunches of his beautiful partner. But even that didn't work. The crowd broke up in disappointment. But as the perspiring and exasperated owners were filing out, Napoleon suddenly broke away, ran back, and did the job he came for. Perhaps the audience was too much for him. Anyway, Felicia went home with a check for the stud fee in her pocket.

Without many such pleasant interruptions, and certainly without any stud fees, I continued to move toward my Ph.D. exams as year one yielded to year two. My base of operations was not the History Department, but the Russian Research Center, now the Davis Center for Advanced Russian Studies, funded by a consortium of foundations, and devoted to the interdisciplinary "area studies" model of studying Russia and the Soviet Union. Early in the sixties the Center gave off the aura of a power center, both in the sense that it was a powerful command post in the network of American cold war fortresses, and in the sense that everyone there was powerful and important. Initially I was very intimidated.

The ethos at "the Center," as it was called, presented a moderately sharp contrast to relations with my largely left-wing friends. Everyone there was quite anti-Soviet, an attitude which I came to accept, and which presented a serious challenge to my other opinions more and more explicitly, as the sixties later became more radical. But the negative view of the Russian Revolution and what followed was so thoroughly grounded in primary sources that

I never questioned it. I was and remained a liberal, but uneasily evolving into a cold war liberal. Particular questions—such as the relationship between Lenin's and Stalin's Russia—could be debated, but during and after my time at the Center, I never deviated from the view that something had gone badly wrong with the Russian Revolution from day one or, in a historical sense, even before day one.

The professors devoted to studying the Soviet economy provided a particularly illustrious cohort at the Center. Probably the figure most deferred to was Alexander Gerschenkron, who was employed at Harvard as an economic historian, but was also a polymath, knowing a number of European literatures, economics, politics and much else. The consensus among the Center faculty was that Gerschenkron was among the handful of real geniuses at Harvard, although he had written, and would write, comparatively little. I quaked in his presence, but attended every public event in which he participated in order to gauge the breadth of his intellect and observe how a genius comported himself. Years later I managed to finagle an invitation to dinner for my wife and me with the Gerschenkrons. With my characteristic impetuosity I managed to step on Gerschenkron's toes by asserting that Vladimir Nabokov was a greater writer than Sir Walter Scott, a proposition impossible to either affirm or deny. But Gerschenkron disliked Nabokov, with whom he was engaged in a polemic over Pushkin, something which I didn't yet know. In the process of refuting me, Gerschenkron demonstrated a remarkable and detailed knowledge of some of the more obscure of Scott's writings and looked down his nose at me when it turned out that I hadn't read *Minstrelsy of the Scottish Border.* I never heard Gerschenkron refer to Scott before or after that evening. The only other professor in my intellectual world that I thought was in Gerschenkron's league was the sinologist, Benjamin Schwartz, a kind, slow-spoken, gentle man, but a person of subtle intellect and a breadth of reading almost as great as that of Gerschenkron.

Abram Bergson was another very highly regarded economist, known to his peers as perhaps the foremost student of Soviet-style command economies in the United States, and Joseph Berliner was beginning to become widely recognized as a kind of social historian of the Soviet economy. Berliner was also a man of extraordinary kindness and civility. His primary academic appointment was at Brandeis, but he spend as much time as possible at the Russian Research Center, where he had such a distinguished set of economist colleagues to interact with. Whenever he spoke in a seminar or in a lunchtime conversation, whatever the subject might be, everybody listened.

Most new graduate students feel weak and unimportant, but I may have felt especially so. I continued to struggle with the Russian language, and I did not have as much Russian history under my belt as other members of my cohort, as I had been such a dilettante in college. I had the sense, not entirely justified, that everyone at the Center was, by family or cultural tradition, from Eastern/Central Europe, or at least had spent a lot of time there. I felt myself to be an ignorant and rather conspicuous American WASP. Later in my career, my non-Jewishness would become a non-offensive joke. "We're going to call you Gleasman," decided the avuncular Allen Kassof, the head of the Soviet-American exchange organization a bit later.

Why was I so insecure? With my background, one might have supposed that I would fit right in. But Harvard was then a contested territory—between generations, ethnicities and political points of view. Gender contestation lay in the future, though not very far. My politics made me contemptuous of the old WASP Harvard. But politics also put me on the left of my teachers, except for the courtly radical Stuart Hughes, who seemed to me insufficiently anti-Soviet. Did I have the intellectual depth and the Sitzfleisch—a "big enough ass to keep myself anchored" in the vernacular—to be a scholar? The professor who would one day direct my dissertation, Richard Pipes, told Felicia Kaplan at a dinner party early in my second year that I was unlikely to get my degree, as I seemed to think that my connections to an older Harvard would see me through. I knew that wasn't true, but the incident didn't augur well for my future in Cambridge. Even in my second and third years I found it hard to give up my dilettante ways and work absolutely regularly, day in and day out. Now I can't stop.

Worse, I was, by this time, too much of a WASP to be a Jew, too much of a Jew to be a WASP, too radical for my Cold War liberal status, too traditional to be a modernist, too much of a modernist to be satisfied with artistic tradition, which I nevertheless venerated. Where and how could I find my niche? I was on edge all the time—and without a regular girlfriend for the first time in years.

I continued to think often of my former girlfriend, Elizabeth Hendry. My rather lonesome routines early in graduate school increased my sense that I might have missed the boat by breaking up with her. I had already gone through patches of missing her acutely during my year in Europe. In some confusion, I had written her twice. First I confirmed that we were broken up. Then I sent her a wonderful poem by Philip Larkin, "No Road," which expressed my ambivalent feelings exactly:

> Since we agreed to let the road between us
> Fall to disuse,
> And bricked our gates up, planted trees to screen us,
> And turned all time's eroding agents loose,
> Silence, and space, and strangers – our neglect
> Has not had much effect.
>
> Leaves drift unswept, perhaps; grass creeps unmown;
> No other change,
> So clear it stands, so little overgrown,
> Walking that way tonight would not seem strange,
> And still would be allowed. A little longer,
> And time will be the stronger.
>
> Drafting a world where no such road will run
> From you to me;

> To watch that world come up like a cold sun,
> Rewarding others, is my liberty.
> Not to prevent it is my will's fulfillment.
> Willing it, my ailment.[3]

She was justifiably upset and annoyed, "Why did you ever write a second letter—or do you regret it already—or could the same person have written both? Irritating as your first was, it did convince me that our relationship was no longer problematic for you, & that sufficed...". When she got engaged to an MIT composer, she invited me to meet him. Probably foolishly, I did so, which induced weeks more of misery and acute consciousness of the irrevocability of the past. Harbison wrote me sympathetically from Venice, where he and his new girlfriend, Rose Mary, were making contacts with Italian modern composers and being radicalized by American foreign policy blunders. "I understood feelingly the whole Betsy encounter," he wrote. "Decisions should not be reconsidered. And the imaginary alternatives can be very destructive...I hope your recovery is more or less complete." For a long time it was less, but I had made my bed. Now I had to lie in it. And get to work in it!

Harbison and Mark DeVoto were both graduate students in music at Princeton, and Harbison wrote amusingly about Mark's impetuous enthusiasims and spontaneous, sometimes unconsidered speech. They were both taking composition with Roger Sessions, and Mark had become enamored of the (relatively) little-known Swedish composer of the nineteenth century, Franz Berwald. In class after class, Mark would apparently ask Sessions about Berwald and ply him with scores. Finally, Sessions felt compelled to tell Mark in his deep-voiced soft-spoken way: "Mark, I don't know my

[3] Philip Larkin, *Collected Poems*, Farrar, Strauss and Giroux and the Marvell Press, New York and London, 1988, 1989, p. 47. Like so many other things, I owed my early knowledge of Larkin to John Harbison. As early as 1956, our freshman year, he said that there was this great young English poet, and I should get his book, *The Less Deceived*—which I did.

Berwald as I should." On another occasion, Harbison described to me the following exchange in class:

> DeVoto (to Sessions): "How did you feel at the performance of your 3rd Symphony in Boston when everybody booed?"
>
> Sessions: "I felt that such vocal expressions were salutary as emotional release for those present, and assumed they expressed a sort of approval. I look at clapping the same way."[4]

Thinking about the academic dimensions of my exacerbated sense of uncertainty then, I am also reminded of an anecdote my historian friend Peter Kenez told me a few years later, when he was working with new graduate students at the University of California, Santa Cruz. A South Asian student came to see him, because Kenez was in charge of "orienting" new graduate students. His visitor was in high dudgeon. "Professor Kenez," he said indignantly. "I didn't come to the United States to be oriented. I came here to be oxidized." Like him, I wasn't sure which point of the compass I occupied, which one I wanted to get to, or how to use a compass. Like pre-modern sailors, I was at the mercy of dead reckoning.

In my second year, Pipes, who had been on leave during my first, returned to the History Department and I took his seminar. We had only fleeting contact outside of class. Eventually my revised seminar paper on a well known Russian Jacobin was published in the *Slavic Review*, a respected journal in the field. I met Pipes a day or so later at the entrance to the Center lunch room. He took note of the paper's publication in a scholarly journal. "But nobody reads articles," he observed cheerfully, and went in to lunch. Other Center denizens were more cordial. On the administrative side there was Mary Towle, who in my early days ran the MA-level "Soviet Union program" and eventually directed the administration of the entire

[4] Letter from Harbison to Gleason, November 8, 1961.

Center. Mary was a relatively recent Radcliffe graduate, who was not an Olympian and not from Eastern Europe. It was nice to find someone with a pleasant smile, who looked you in the eye and wasn't chronically involved in extremely important activities which your question was interrupting. Later, when I got to know her better, I realized to what a degree Mary's presence at the Center helped humanize it, as did that of her successor, Christine Porto. We would laugh together at some of the more peculiar fellowship applications the Center received—and then I would laugh again, more ruefully, when I discovered that she had put one or another of them in the group office where Sarah (Sally) Meicklejohn, Dan Field and I were frantically trying to finish our dissertations and get on the job market.

Mary and I were also links in the long chain of semi-official writers of doggerel verse for Center parties. John Fiske, who later became a foreign service officer, was the first and probably the most accomplished of these versifiers, in the late 1940s. Mary Towle provided occasional verse for Christmas parties and other events during the 1980s. I was active in the middle and latter sixties. Robert Williams (now Emeritus from Davidson College) and I produced a comic epos in 1964, following the fall of Nikita Khrushchev. It began:

> 'Twas the night before Christmas and out in Skowhegan,
> Not a creature had heard of Brezhnev or Kosygin,

and continued in that vein:

> The experts were nestled all snug in their beds,
> while visions of monographs danced in their heads.
> And Mao with his H-Bomb and Chou with his missile
> had just licked the stamps on another epistle ...

Despite the towering intellect and encompassing erudition of Alexander Gerschenkron and the sympathy and intellectual perspicacity of Joe Berliner, the person who really unified the Russian

Research Center was Adam Bruno Ulam.[5] He was an unusual person to embody an institution, since by temperament he was skeptical of collectivities, and even his love for the Russian Research Center was expressed belatedly, indirectly, discreetly and shyly. Adam, the younger son in a middle-class Jewish professional family, had emigrated as a young man to the United States from Lwow, Poland, just two weeks before the Nazis attacked in the fall of 1939. His brother, Stanislaw, was then a Junior Fellow at Harvard, and Adam was entering Brown University as a freshman. Adam's mother had died of cancer in Vienna the previous year. He was never to see his father or sister again. Both perished at the hands of the Nazis, along with numerous other members of his less immediate family. Adam never returned to the land of his birth but graduated from Brown and after a year at the University of Wisconsin went on to take his Ph.D. in Government from Harvard.

The extent and details of his bereavement were almost completely unknown to his colleagues or students until the very end of his life. Much information emerged only posthumously. At the time I came to know him, first as an undergraduate in Eliot House, then as a graduate student, he was a rising professor at Harvard, full of charm and eccentricity, who never spoke of his past. We were aware of his scholarly ambition (he was ultimately to produce some nineteen books in his career), his towering physical stature, his extraordinary systemic intelligence, undergirded by a remarkable memory, his sense of humor (occasionally describable as gallows humor), and his tendency to befriend his younger colleagues and students. He was extremely handsome and something of a lady's man. He could be at times rather formal in his social style, but sometimes riotously informal. It was said that he once walked into his early morning lecture on the history of socialism in a dinner

[5] Portions of this material have appeared in different form in the *Proceedings of the American Philosophical Society*, Vol. 146, No. 4 (2002), pp. 416-418; and in *Occasional Paper #282* of the Kennan Institute for Advanced Russian Studies, "Remembering Adam Ulam," pp. 3-4.

jacket and wrote on the board "Professor Ulam will not meet his socialism class today." Then, without cracking a smile, he exited the classroom.

Adam's home was not Harvard's Government Department, populated, according to his slightly jaundiced view, by "social scientists," a term that made him smile, but the Russian Research Center. There he produced his nineteen books (including a novel), there he received the thousands of books and pamphlets that his research assistants brought him from Widener Library, and there he held forth every morning at "coffee," where he exchanged views and on occasion information with his colleagues. "Coffee" was a pleasure for most of his companions, but it was also thoroughly institutionalized, and attendance was virtually *de rigueur* for visitors at the Center, but particularly for his friends. There was never any question as to who was the presiding genius at this daily gathering, which could seem a Cold War version of a nineteenth-century salon. Adam was an institutional homebody, utterly dependent on his office, and almost as much so on his daily colloquies with his friends and colleagues.

Adam, a lover of Sherlock Holmes, had something in common with Sherlock's elder brother, the legendary "smarter brother," Mycroft. Conan Doyle told us that the sedentary Mycroft would have excelled Sherlock at detection, had he only had the energy to get out of his armchair at the Diogenes Club and do the field work. Here the parallel with Adam becomes more complicated. Adam was neither portly nor inactive, but his abilities and temperament were ideally suited to a universe in which the sources came to him, rather than his having to go to them. Travel in the physical world made him nervous, whereas the opposite was true for the world of books. And for that, his situation five minutes' walk from Widener Library was ideal. Not that he went to the library himself very often. Emissaries brought what he wanted to his desk. Adam did not go out to the world. He sucked it in and filtered it through a powerful and systematizing intellect that was Hegelian in scope, but

Adam Ulam and Tom, May, 1993. Adam has just received an honorary degree from Brown. Between them is a new Brown History Ph.D. from Taiwan, Ping-chen Hsiung.

Photo by Sarah Gleason

Bismarckian in its view of power and human folly.

Adam liked the idea that he only worked in a measured and regular portion of each day, filling the rest of his time with games and social life. To some considerable extent this aristocratic self-conception was true. He was a genuine hedonist and needed companionship on a regular basis. For many years his favorite venue for lunch was the so-called "long table" at one end of the main room of the Harvard Faculty Club, where a number of Harvard's older and more sociable hands gathered daily to exchange banter and gossip. Shop talk was rare and not encouraged. If he didn't lunch there, he would stroll to Harvard's intellectual social club, the Signet Society, where he would usually begin with "a martini, straight up, very dry, with an olive." Adam also loved tennis, and for many years his search for partners was constant. Tennis with him was demanding, as he didn't move particularly well on the court, and the most highly prized partners were those who could deliver the ball to his forehand in such a way that only a step or two was necessary to make contact. "So when did he do all that work?" asks a young colleague at Brown. I guess the answer has to be "all the rest of the time." As far as Adam was concerned, there were no Sundays or holidays. Vacations from work were as brief and few as he could manage.

His bent for society enabled a number of his younger colleagues to become quite close friends, to establish cross-generational relationships, which were quite unusual at Harvard. Both during his marriage to Mary Burgwine and after they were divorced, Adam remained strikingly dependent on younger friends, usually from the Center. I took full advantage of this opportunity to become friends with such a remarkable man.

Adam's mentoring was indirect. He was oddly shy of talking about personal matters. He did almost all his advising with humor and a kind of bantering rhetoric. His pursuit of women did not preclude his love of traditional, masculine society. He found it piquant that I was a preppie WASP in this field. It was a tiny pinch of spice in a world that needed it. At his death, I inherited a beautiful scotch glass, monogrammed with his initials, passed along to me by Christine Porto.

Another mandarin, who turned out to be more approachable than he seemed was Merle Fainsod, Adam Ulam's senior colleague in the Government Department. Fainsod was almost a generation older than emerging authorities like Ulam and Pipes, then in their early forties, and had been in the Government Department at Harvard since the late 1930s. He was the author of *How Russia Is Ruled*, the regnant text for the study of the Soviet Union during the fifties and early sixties. Fainsod was a shy man of great formality, with a charming and effervescent wife named Jonny, who helped make his social existence easier. Fortunately the Fainsods were friends with the Kaplans, and the fact that I could see them in the Kaplans' living room as well as in seminar situations helped him unbend.

Fainsod was also the author of another remarkable book, *Smolensk Under Soviet Rule*, which retains much of its interest to this day. The "Smolensk Archive" was a rich compendium of Soviet source material for the city and region, looted by the Germans on their drive toward Moscow. The Archive fell into American hands after Germany's defeat and was deposited in the National Archives. The vast array of Party documents on local events, political objectives and difficulties in town and countryside contained in the archive enabled Fainsod, who was the first to employ it systematically, to create the only essentially local history of a Soviet region which existed until almost the end of the Cold War. Fainsod, like other scholars of his generation, was subsequently accused of employing the so-called "totalitarian model," meaning an approach which was too much top-down and assumed that all local politics originated in directives from the center. But even younger scholars of the next two generations found—sometimes grudgingly—his work a model of cautious fairness and accuracy. He not only noted the decrees emanating from the Kremlin, but looked carefully at how they were implemented and what their ramifications were as far out into the provinces as he could see.

I regarded Fainsod with the same respect that others of the younger generation did, and although we had pleasant, slightly formal conversations at the Kaplans, I was unprepared for him to sit next to me on a plane coming back from an academic conference and tell me he was reading with interest my newly completed dissertation. Unfortunately he died soon thereafter (1972), so I was not able to pursue a deeper relationship with a man, whose name was a byword for fairness and rather formal courtesy.

Fortunately I did get to know Alexander Inkeles, the senior partner in Harvard's famous "Soviet Interview Project," in which hundreds of what were then called "displaced persons" were interviewed and thousands more submitted questionnaires. This remarkable project was made possible by the chaotic population transfers of the immediate postwar period and supplied an extremely important empirical base for a generation of research on the Soviet Union. Inkeles, a lively and spirited liberal, was seriously harassed by a radical graduate student (from Columbia, as I recall) during the political agitation at Harvard in the late sixties and left Harvard for Stanford, partly as a result. This mysterious radical showed up in Inkeles' class over and over again, disputing his academic assertions, and disrobing on at least one occasion to make a point.

One of the most remarkable biographies among the first generation of Cold War scholars belonged to Alexander Erlich. He was the son of a prominent Polish-Jewish radical, Henryk Erlich, an original member of the Jewish labor organization in Poland, the Bund, who participated in the Russian Revolution before returning to Poland in 1918. Alex grew up in a family in which revolutionary traditions could not have been stronger, and went back to the very beginning of the twentieth century. When the Nazis invaded Poland in September, 1939, Henryk Erlich and his colleague Viktor Alter were the leaders of the Bund, and to escape certain death at the hands of the Nazis they fled to the Soviet Union, where they were arrested, released in a general amnesty for Polish citizens in the Soviet Union, then re-arrested and ultimately executed on Stalin's orders. His son Alexander somehow escaped arrest and managed to make his way to the Russian Pacific, from where he was able to reach San Francisco by boat. Eventually he was discovered by American Jewish labor leaders—for whom his father's murder had become a cause celèbre—working as a stackboy in the library of the New School for Social Research in New York. He was assisted by Jewish labor leaders in obtaining a Ph.D. in economics from Columbia. After spending several fellowship years at the Russian Research Center at Harvard, he eventually became a professor at Columbia, specializing in the Soviet economy. By a rather similar route, his brother Victor Erlich became a professor of Russian literature at Yale.

The reader could be forgiven for supposing that Alex Erlich, with such a background, would have ended up a resounding conservative, or at least an ambivalent one, like Adam Ulam. Nothing could be further from the truth. Alex remained a passionate leftist all his life, a man of the deepest democratic commitment. He wrote comparatively little—a wonderful book about the 'twenties debates in the Soviet Union over industrial policy, and a number of articles on essentially the same subject—but everything he wrote was clear and deeply thought through—indeed agonized through.

Alex's hostility to most forms of hierarchy was legendary, as was his commitment to the idea that the powerless of the world ought to be protected as far as possible from the powerful. In the Harvard of that day especially, many of us idolized him. Stories about Alex abounded, of course. When he first lived in Cambridge as a fellow at the Center, his daughter at a relatively young age wanted to ride to the local public school on a bicycle. Alex was in a quandary. He believed she was entitled to do this, and he believed it would be wrong to forbid her, but at the same time he was terrified of an accident. And she had to ride several blocks on Massachusetts Avenue, then as now one of Cambridge's busiest streets. So he found a convoluted but somewhat characteristic compromise. He would call a cab, timed to arrive at his house just a moment after his daughter left on her bike for Peabody School. He would then trail her to the school in the cab, and return home when she arrived safely, as she fortunately always did.

By pure chance, I shared an office with this paragon during two of the years he spent at the Center in the mid-1960s. Until those years I had never had any idea that a distinguished senior colleague could treat a graduate student with such warm and natural friendliness, sharing lunches, incidental conversation, evening meals and every other ritual of everyday life in the most natural way in the world. I swore an oath to do the same, if I ever got my degree and a job. His wife Rachel, a Yiddish teacher known to her friends as Shoshka, shared Alex's views, but lacked his gentleness and ease with people. She was constantly liable to attacks of indignation at the injustice of the world and corresponding outbursts of uninhibited joy when, against all expectation, things turned out well.

Not that Alex was always gentle. I recall an occasion when a mutual friend, Mark Pinson, came bursting into our office, full of excitement. "Gleason," he said, "there's a genuine Polish Hassidic rabbi giving a talk in (of all places) the parish house of the Unitarian Church in Harvard Square. You don't want to miss this. Let's go." Indeed I didn't want to miss it. But in order not to be rude, I asked Alex if he wanted to go too. Alex hesitated. He was a faithful socialist (his politics formed as a member of the Jewish Bund in Poland) and his memories of the Hassidism were not particularly cordial—mostly fights between Bundist kids and Hassidic kids after school during his childhood. And, of course, Alex was passionately secular. "Well, Tom...". But in the end he decided to go, perhaps to be polite, perhaps to look after me on this voyage into alien territory.

The parish house was jammed, so we ended up sitting uncomfortably on the floor, as the rabbi began to speak. He started by giving examples about how to read the Torah properly. Before reading each passage, he would say, "*This* is how the gentiles read the Torah", and then read the passage hurriedly, or with pauses in odd places or with his voice quavering. But we didn't stay long enough for me to understand the principles behind correct or incorrect readings. Alex was outraged at this mockery of "gentiles." Whoever precisely was meant, Alex understood that I was definitely one. "Come on, Tom," he roared. "We are getting out of here. If a gentile had said this about a Jew, B'nai Brith would already be here." And he dragged me to my feet and plunged into the crowd, undoubtedly stepping on a few feet and perhaps fingers, in his hurry to get out of the building. He was angry about this for several days.

Of course his reaction was excessive and rooted in the conflicts of his Warsaw childhood, but it also derived from his lifelong concern for anyone whom he could regard as the "insulted and injured." Throughout this time the civil rights movement was becoming more central to the American political scene and Alex was in demonstrations, from New York to Washington. And on a number of occasions, despite his rather frail health, he would take a bus for many hours to Memphis or Birmingham, to march on behalf of the rights of black Americans. On one occasion, I saw in a movie theater newsreel his slight, balding figure, stooped, and wearing his inevitable gabardine overcoat, toiling slowly at the end of a column of demonstrators, somewhere in the Deep South.

Raised bilingual in Polish and Yiddish, Alex made himself into a decent writer in English, but only with great effort, and he struggled with spoken English his whole career. "Can you fix me up with a spoon," he called across the lunch table at the Center on one occasion. "Sure Alex," came the reply, "but it seems a funny way to ask." "I'm working on idioms with 'fix' this week," was his explanation.

As the academic year 1967-68 dawned, I was struggling to finish my dissertation and Alex was back in Columbia. Despite his disapproval of some of the actions of the Columbia student strikers, his sympathies remained with the Left, although his friendships ranged across the entire Columbia faculty. When his friend Richard Hofstadter replaced the beleagured President Grayson Kirk as the regular Columbia Commencement speaker, Alex Erlich spoke at the radical counter-commencement ceremony on the steps of Lowe Library.

As future years were to reveal, I had a remarkable cohort at the Center during the seven years I was there (1962-1968). Robert Williams, William Rosenberg, Daniel Field, Peter Kenez, Michael Hittle, Sarah Terry, Nina Tumarkin—all went on to have highly successful careers in Russian or East European History and Politics. In-ho Lee, also a member of our cohort, was a brilliant young Korean woman who had attended Wellesley College and then gone on to do her graduate work in Russian history at Harvard. In her career she turned out to be a pioneer in a number of ways. She did a great deal to develop the study of Russia in South Korea; but she also became an educational reformer and a women's rights activist. Eventually she became the Korean ambassador to Finland and then to the Russian Federation after 1991, a major civil rights breakthrough for a woman, in the Korean context.

Another close friend from those years was a historian of the Soviet economy named Lenny Kirsch. He was perhaps a half a generation older than Dan Field and me, but gravitated more toward his younger colleagues than toward the Olympians who were his teachers—Bergson, Berliner et al—as he shared our general awe of them. Lenny was from a lower-middle-class Jewish family in Pittsburgh and although they were not working-class, he had a strong sense of social justice and a democratic socialist point of view. He enjoyed regaling us with tales about growing up in his poor neighborhood in Pittsburgh. On one occasion, as part of a gang from the wrong side of the tracks, he roamed through a wealthy neighborhood on "Beggar's Night," the night before Halloween. It was Friday. The kids found a mansion where the owners had left the garden hose connected to a faucet on the side of the house. Lenny and his gang took the nozzle of the hose, stuck it through the mail slot on the front door, turned on the faucet and fled. On his way to school on Monday, Lenny detoured slightly to pass the victimized household. To his amazement (and horror, I think), the hose was still in the mail slot. The family appeared to be away for some extended period of time.

Lenny's wife was a charming Russian woman named Lena, who was kind enough to try and help me with my spoken Russian. She was from a family that lived in the north of Russia and her parents had spent time in the camps. Lenny and Lena told the following anecdote about their betrothal. They had gotten to know each other at the university in Moscow, but the time came when Lenny had to make a trip to the village and formally ask Lena's family for her hand in marriage. He was not looking forward to the meeting. Lena was not Jewish, and the possibility of hostility and anti-Semitism in this faraway rural location seemed quite real. But his visit with her family went extremely well, and toward the close of his visit, he was interviewed by Lena's grandmother, the matriarch of the family. She greeted him cordially. She naturally regretted, she said, that her granddaughter was going so far away, but she could see that Lenny was a good man and it would be wonderful for her to live in America. But one thing, she concluded, puzzled her, and she wanted to ask Lenny about it: "Why did you kill Christ?"[6]

Later on, the town of Newton, Massachusetts, where Lenny lived, set up an exchange with a comparable Russian city. Lenny, as a Russian speaker, was asked to escort the Soviet visitor, some kind of reliable official, around town. At the dinner in the visitor's honor, conversation languished. The good burghers of Newton found it hard to get conversation going with an unknown Soviet:

Burgher # 1: "(Ahem) Dr. _____, do you live well in Russia?"
Soviet Visitor: "Yes of course, very well."
(Silence)
Burgher #2: "Uh, do you have a house or an apartment?"
Soviet Visitor: "An apartment."
(Short silence)
Burgher #3: "A big apartment?"
Soviet Visitor: "Oh yes, very big. Two bedrooms and a chicken.
(Long silence)
Burgher #2: "Just one chicken?"
Soviet Visitor: "Why we would need two chicken?"

At this point Lenny realized that to people who read English but don't speak it, "kitchen" and "chicken" were easily confused.

Lenny was a heavy smoker and did not watch his weight and his life was cut short by heart trouble. One day in the early 1970s he passed out in a store. After an agonizing period when he went in and out of the hospital for months, he suddenly had a massive heart attack. This was the first time I recall the death of someone I thought of as a virtual contemporary, and I was haunted by it for a long time thereafter. Mortality was suddenly and terrifyingly

[6] There is an affectionate portrait of Lenny and Lena in Moscow in Loren Graham, *Moscow Stories*, Bloomington, Indiana University Press, 2006, pp. 44-53.

revealed. The whole Center turned out for his funeral and many of us were in tears. Almost simultaneously, my wife and I dreamed that Lenny came to say good-bye to us.

One of the complex pleasures of continuing with my education in Cambridge was the ongoing participation in the now larger group of friends that derived from my undergraduate roommates and our circle. It was nice to have an intellectual focus quite distinct from Russian history, but it probably perpetuated a certain dilettantish character to my life longer than was good for me. When you have brilliant friends, it can be too easy to participate vicariously in their lives and neglect your own. But of course people were coming and going. Old friends went elsewhere and newcomers arrived as the 1960s drew toward their end. One of our undergraduate mentors, Marshall Cohen, subsequently the founding editor of the journal *Philosophy and Public Affairs*, left for the University of Chicago. And an old friend of Marshall's, Stanley Cavell, came to Harvard from Berkeley, and took over certain of Marshall's mentoring activities. Stanley was a brilliant lecturer and his Humanities 5 course created a swirl of intellectual energy in which many of my friends were involved.

A newcomer to our circle was John Womack, known as Jack. He had been a Harvard undergraduate, but a class ahead of us. He was from Oklahoma and very much a radical. His undergraduate dissertation on Oklahoma's so-called Green Corn Rebellion of 1917, a mixed race uprising against the emergent white elite in the state, had created a sensation. It seemed to combine the virtues of a genuine populist account with an adherence to rigorous academic standards. For those in search of "radical history" it seemed an important model. In 1962-63 he returned to Cambridge from a Rhodes Scholarship at Oxford. Initially Womack intended to do German history. But circumstances gave him an unusual opportunity. The Harvard History Department decided to introduce Latin American history as a regular part of the curriculum. Surveying the available talent, they decided that no one out there was quite up to Harvard standards and that they had better train some of their own graduate students. Generous financial offers were made to several if they would change their fields to Latin America. Womack took advantage of this opportunity and made the switch. Both he and Thomas Skidmore, later a colleague of mine at Brown, received the concluding phase of their Harvard graduate education essentially free, for shifting into the new area that Harvard wanted to develop. Womack became a Mexicanist, Skidmore a Brazilianist. Womack went on to write a brilliant and highly personal first book on Emiliano Zapata and to become famous as the only self-proclaimed Marxist ever to chair the Harvard History Department. Skidmore became the leading foreign Brazilianist of his generation. A saturnine personality at times, he was one of the very wittiest academics I ever knew, and a very good friend to me.

During this period, our group of friends began to mingle with a large milieu of young scholars, some five to ten years older than we were. In addition to Skidmore, they included two brilliant young students of French politics and culture, Stanley Hoffmann and Nicholas Wahl, who gave a course together at Harvard, "The Government and Politics of Modern France." We were certainly flattered to go to parties with them, and no doubt we occasionally spoke as if they were members of our group. Nick Wahl, in particular, was amused by the pretensions of these wannabe leftists, hardly more than undergraduates, and on Halloween in 1962, he wrote me a sardonic note from Oxford, where he was teaching for a term:

> I discovered at the Conservative Party conference a booth selling party pins of various kinds and a couple of them inspired me to create a series of monthly prizes for virtue to be bestowed upon members of the Group. I am asking you to serve as Curator of the Happy Few Virtues Foundation and to:
>
> (a) bestow the enclosed prizes on the first recipients, nominated by me herewith.
> (b) organize the process by which, each month, a new recipient is chosen.

> There are two prizes, one for women, one for men. The prize for women is the Hélène de Portes Prize, bestowed upon that member of the group who in any given month has provided the greatest emotional support to the group in general or some of its members in particular. The recipient of this award is to be considered, in the manner of Hélène de Portes, as the Egeria of the group.[7]
>
> The prize for men is the Rhodes-Manqué Award, bestowed upon that member of the group who in any given month displays qualities of leadership and energy that, while in accord with the values of Cecil Rhodes, would never be enlisted in any of his causes.
>
> As first recipients of these honors, I name Enid Bok[8] to the Hélène de Portes Prize and Alan Graubard to the Rhodes Manqué Award. I hereby commission you to bestow the honors in appropriate circumstances and to report to me when it has been done.
>
> It is not impossible that further virtues prizes may be established in the months to come. Meanwhile give everyone my best and assure them that their turn may come if they support and lead in the months ahead.

A bit prolix, but I'm afraid that the "Happy Few Virtues Foundation" caught something of our group's ambiance: intelligent and idealistic, to be sure, but also naïve, self-regarding and childishly ambitious.

Another new arrival, in the fall of 1962 was the art critic and historian Michael Fried, also returning from a Rhodes, after graduating

[7] Hélène de Portes, as I almost certainly didn't know at the time, was the mistress of Henri Reynaud, who tried to escape by car with millions of francs as the Vichy regime was coming to power in France, but was killed in an accident, which Reynaud had the misfortune to survive. Egeria was a minor Roman deity, known for dispensing good advice.

[8] One of the few female members of our group, Enid was an extremely successful foundation executive, usually referred to under her married name of Enid Schoettle.

from Princeton with an undergraduate degree in English literature and spending another year in London. Fried was extraordinary for his theoretical audacity and for his intellectual passion, both of which have become legendary among his contemporaries. His championing of the "stain painters" and his catalogue essays on several of them brought him to an academic frontier at an extraordinarily early age. His achievement and the controversial public recognition he was accorded were awe-inspiring. It seemed to me and I think to others, that while we were still trying to scope out intellectual directions, Fried had taken off from the art criticism of Clement Greenberg and already established himself as the most brilliant critic in his generation.[9]

He was to me a thoroughly intimidating figure, of course, in the violence and absolutism of his judgments and in the absolute certainty of his rightness, as was Greenberg.[10] Fried later wrote about his early essays (and in a sense his early persona) that: "I already felt that somehow the writer's response to important work ought to have something of the same intensity and challenge to expectations that the work itself has ... Everything I've written about art has always been marked by that desire to match the intensity of the work of art."[11] No one I had ever met hated sentimentality with such passion or defined it so broadly.

There was an enormous amount of emancipated Jewish energy in our group. There had been, in fact, since our undergraduate days, but Fried embodied it more fully than anyone else, in his capacity for enthusiasm and rage alike. I remember praising in his

[9] "Three American Painters: Kenneth Noland, Jules Olitski, Frank Stella".

[10] "Everything Clement Greenberg wrote as an art critic was exactly what Baudelaire said criticism should be: partial, passionate, political—embodying 'an exclusive point of view, provided always the one adopted opens up the widest horizons.'" See Barry Schwabsky, "Modern Love," *The Nation*, Vol. 283, No. 12 (October 16, 2006), p. 25.

[11] Amy Newman, *Challenging Art: Artforum 1962-1974*, Soho Press, New York, p. 10.

presence a somewhat conventional poem by W.D. Snodgrass about a divorced father's gradually and poignantly attenuating relationship with his daughter, called "Heart's Needle." At my timid words of praise, Fried's face turned bright red. "Heart's Needle is absolute SHIT, Gleason, complete SHIT," he croaked through clenched teeth. I had unguardedly allowed my Edwardian/Georgian sensibility to express itself. There were great things and there was shit, and I was one of the large majority who couldn't tell the difference. Fried in later years modified some of his more categorical formulations, deepened his perspective and, of course, became a great art historian. It also turned out a bit later, however, that Snodgrass attracted some heavyweight support. Robert Lowell, after initially criticizing his former student for writing such "tear-jerking stuff," changed his mind and called "Heart's Needle" a "break-through for modern poetry."[12]

The contributions of American Jews to twentieth-century culture was one of the big stories of American history (and European no doubt), particularly in the arts and sciences. Looking back, it seems to me that this emergence of young talent out of a sometimes provincial, but invariably quite Jewish milieu into a larger arena was an absolutely dominant aspect of our group dynamics. It created an explosive energy, highly antinomian and very ideological and self-confident. It was deeply anti-bourgeois, perhaps even more hostile to Jewish philistinism than to gentile, as much of Philip Roth's early fiction suggests. The provincial clannishness of traditional Jewish culture was mercilessly satirized, perhaps with even greater passion than the traditionally anti-Semitic world of WASP gentility. This mocking and passionate spirit gave life especially to the humanities, but saturated them in a sometimes unstable blend of moralism and philosophy, dogmatism and questioning, personalism and abstraction. Not that everybody in our group was like

[12] William McDonald, "W.D. Snodgrass, 83, a Poet of Intensely Autobiographical Themes," *New York Times*, January 15, 2009, p. 22.

that, of course. Harbison stood out on the basis of sheer talent and his modernism was deeply rooted in tradition. Casey was Irish, with links to traditional WASP culture. McNees was a self-defined exile from lower middle-class southwestern Protestantism. Womack was a similar case, a provincial radical whose western Left populism provided a salty harmony with the East Coast urban Jewish shtick of Graubard, Fried and others. I think we were all aware of the explosive emergence of Jewish talent in our university world, but the subject was just beginning to be examined and understood. Jewish quotas to American universities were just beginning to be widely discussed and condemned. And intellectual Jewish opinion was almost entirely on the Left and heavily secular. I simply did not—perhaps could not—imagine a world in which educated, right-wing Jews would become a major force.

There was a deep connection between my friends and their larger world and the *Partisan Review* generation that had preceded them. Even before the end of our undergraduate years many of us had most every issue of Partisan Review going back to the end of the thirties, and we read them to pieces. The connection between Clement Greenberg and Michael Fried was very deep, and everybody admired Dwight McDonald. But our cohort was a little more ideologically stable than our greater, if more volatile, predecessors, whose experience of outsider-hood was deeper.[13] A great many of the Irving Kristol-James Burnham-Norman Podhoretz generation ended up on the far right, although some, like Dwight McDonald and Irving Howe were truer to their original values. As far as I know, none of our group ended up on the far right, although many of us slid a bit.

[13] An interesting perspective on my generational experience may be found in David Hollinger, "Jewish Intellectuals and the De-Christianization of American Public Culture in the Twentieth Century," in Harry S. Stout and D.G. Hart, eds., *New Directions in American Religious History*, Oxford University Press, New York and Oxford, 1997, pp. 462-481. Thanks to Gordon Wood for this reference.

Over time I felt my overwhelming attraction to this world attenuating. For one thing, I didn't have the sheer brilliance to be part of it as I longed to be. The bourgeois world in various ways refused to let me go, and indeed this was to some degree true of most of us. But I discovered that for a person of my level of talent, a solid routine of work and the self-discipline that went with it was crucial. I would have to go to school with my mentors like Andrzej Walicki for longer and assimilate their work more fully, before I could make my own contribution, whatever it might be. I might do "good work" but I was unlikely to be a paradigm-breaker—which was the *beau ideal* of most of my brilliant friends. And if you're not a paradigm-breaker, what you achieve is going to be cumulative. It means you go to work every day. And the sheer competitiveness, which was such an important strand in the fabric of their lives, I began to find discouraging rather than inspiring. And if I were going to find a more bourgeois identity, I didn't want it to be that of Sancho Panza.

Tom Gleason and musicians in New Orleans, 1964

Civil Rights

The sheriff got exactly what he meant by trouble, and things changed. It wasn't exactly my doing, of course, but I was a part of it.[1]

Somewhere below the level of consciousness, I invariably identified with those whom I imagined had been unfairly punished or otherwise mistreated. This instinctive reaction, in combination with my passion for black culture, led me inexorably to the civil rights movement around 1960. My involvement with organized civil rights activity went back to my senior year in college when the "movement" in the United States as well as student radical activity in general was just beginning to heat up. Part of the literature which had made the rounds of my undergraduate group of friends was about American racism, so we were to some degree prepared for the developments of the early sixties. In addition, of course, the Jews in our group had prepared the non-Jews to think about race in a way that I certainly never had before. This was a very influential stage in my education, the more difficult to describe because it was so gradual and incremental. Then, in February of 1960, our senior year, the sit-in movement began, and from Greensboro, North Carolina, spread rapidly across the country. All of us were paying attention.

Much of the sit-in activity was directed against Woolworth's, in particular their lunch counters. One small, auxiliary part of this growing movement was an organized effort to picket northern Woolworth Five and Ten Cent Stores (as they were called in those far

[1] Sue Moon, "Beloved Community: Mississippi Revisited," *Turning Wheel. Journal of the Buddhist Peace Fellowship*, Fall, 1994, p. 26.

off times) until their lunch counters in the South were desegregated. Their northern lunch counters of course were not segregated, but Woolworth's conformed to southern custom in the South. The picketing happened mostly around northern colleges and universities, among them Harvard. Organization meetings among students and a few faculty got picketing going in Harvard Square and Central Square. The two "captains" of the picketing at the Harvard Square Woolworth's were Charles Parsons and I. Charlie, as he was then known, was at that time a notably laconic but brilliant graduate student in philosophy. He is now the Edgar Pierce Professor in the Harvard Philosophy Department, where he teaches mathematical logic and Kant. John Woodford, an African-American freshman, who later went with us to Tougaloo, was among the picketers, as was Amon Horn, the most radical African-American student at Harvard. Amon had studied in Prague, I remember, and perhaps Moscow, and had become a dedicated Marxist-Leninist, the only one I knew as an undergraduate.

Charles and I knew each other from Eliot House. We had our work cut out for us in organizing the picket lines, the first most of us had ever participated in. Our student colleagues were in general not a problem, but the possibility of making a contribution to civil rights without straying farther afield than Harvard Square attracted a number of local people from the Old Left. These stalwarts could be difficult. Professor and Mrs. Dirk Struik were a case in point. Struik was a distinguished specialist on early American science who taught at MIT. He and his wife were both militant Marxists, and it galled them when well dressed Cambridge matrons crossed our picket line to pick up some item or other in Woolworth's. Mrs. Struik, in particular, sometimes lost her cool and directed ominous, ideologically charged speeches at picket-line-crossers. Then Charles or I would have to drop our signs and prevent Mrs. Struik's fiery rhetoric about the imminent coming of revolution from getting out of hand. Eventually we even tried framing our objections to her speeches in Comintern slogans that we imagined might have a favorable impact on Communists: "no, no, Mrs. Struik, this is the popular front from ABOVE." She was generally apologetic afterwards and the whole picketing business was so exotic and peculiar at this early date that it may have hardly mattered what the picketers were shouting at passersby. Most people had no idea of what to make of us, and we felt strange and awkward at being on a picket line at all. The Harvard Square demonstrations petered out in May when we graduated, but that same month on the campus of Atlanta University the first meeting was held which led to the founding of the Student Non-violent Coordinating Committee (SNCC).

By the time I returned from Europe in the fall of 1961, things had developed considerably further. Martin Luther King, Jr., whose public career had begun with the Montgomery bus boycott in 1955, was emerging as a major figure in the movement. Freedom rides had been going on since early May, with the Congress of Racial Equality (CORE) taking the lead in getting them started. As I was entering my second year of graduate school in September, 1962, James Meredith was being admitted to the University of Mississippi, escorted by federal troops.

SNCC—called "Snick" by young contemporaries—was on the minds of a good many undergraduate and graduate students in Cambridge in the fall of 1962. I was trying to focus on my studies and on becoming enthusiastic about academic history, but I also began attending meetings and sporadically contributing to SNCC, as well as organizing fundraisers in the houses of Boston-area sympathizers. In the winter of 1963 a number of us worked on a food drive for poor blacks in Mississippi who had been cut off by the state from the distribution of surplus food. It wasn't much, but I was pretty absorbed by academia for the next couple of years and it was all I felt I could do. We went on marches, of course, and most of us were on the mall in Washington for King's "I Have a Dream" speech in August of 1963.

But of course other tragic events played their role in taking our minds off graduate education. I was walking across the Harvard

Yard on that November day in 1963 when the Memorial Church bell in Harvard Yard began to toll. John Casey met me at the door of our rooms, a few blocks away. "They've shot the president," he said, with tears in his eyes. He didn't say who "they" were and I was initially too shocked to ask. It was the most powerful eruption of the public world into our private lives that we had ever experienced. It was also the beginning of my consciousness of what a violent country the United States was, something I somehow had managed not to notice until then. The assassination of the President had a subtle but unmistakable effect on the civil rights movement: it increased the vague consciousness shared by most of us that the United States was moving toward a crisis. And it was in our polarizing world that important decisions would be made. This was true, but not in the way that I envisaged.

That self-absorption induced by graduate school got harder to maintain in the winter and early spring of 1964. My initial anxieties about graduate school had been routinized to some degree; and because I still had a range of friends who were not in graduate school, or were in other departments, or further along, I felt I had some social existence outside of the History Department and the Russian Research Center. It was therefore easier to think about politics and especially racial politics, than it initially had been. Or, perhaps, it was a welcome relapse into my pre-professional past.

By the turn of the year 1964, there was increasing discussion of something called "Freedom Summer," which would entail a large influx of civil rights activists into Mississippi the following summer. Some of the SNCC field secretaries began to circulate around the country, especially to universities, with an eye to recruiting students, both black and white, to go south in a couple of months. I remember meeting two of the first white figures in SNCC when they came to speak and recruit at Harvard in January—the legendary SNCC field secretary Bob Zellner and his wife Dotty (Miller) Zellner. They spoke to a crowd in Sanders Theater about what the organizers hoped for in the upcoming summer. Dotty was enthusiastic about a white activist of whom I had never heard until that evening: Allard Lowenstein, who was asserting a leading role for himself in the organization of the summer's activities. Soon, however, the Zellners and Bob Moses broke with Lowenstein not only over his attempt to dictate to SNCC about organizational matters, but also over his attempt to exclude organizations that he regarded as too close to the Communist Party, like the National Lawyer's Guild.

One of my old friends from undergraduate days took the lead in organizing a summer project involving Harvard. This was John Mudd, whom John Harbison and I had known since the fall of 1956 when we all met on the Harvard freshman soccer team, where Mudd started on the forward line. Both as a soccer player and an organizer, John Mudd was a man of enormous energy and infectious enthusiasm, with a loud and uninhibited laugh and a three-pack a-day cigarette (non-filtered) habit. Imagine if the Mickey Rooney of the Rooney-Judy Garland films of the late 1940s had been somewhat bigger and jockier, but with a comparable sense of purpose and organizational enthusiasm—to say nothing of an enormous capacity for work.

Mudd had also spent the year 1960-61 in Germany, at the Free University, studying politics, and I had seen him several times in Berlin. He was at that time close to another remarkable man: Guido Goldman, the son of the Zionist activist and subsequent critic of Israel, Nahum Goldmann. Along with David Ben-Gurion, Nahum Goldmann was probably the leading spokesperson for the whole Zionist project at this point and he was currently the President of the World Jewish Congress. Not surprisingly, Guido Goldman seemed even at a young age to have a remarkable array of acquaintances. One of them was the civil rights activist Robert Moses. During the winter of 1962-63, he had stayed with Mudd and Goldman in their apartment at 1039 Massachusetts Avenue. Moses suggested a visit to Mississippi over the coming summer to see the SNCC project that was then underway in Greenwood. Goldman went to Europe instead, but Mudd and Allen Graubard flew down to Jackson and then went on to Greenwood by bus. After reconnoitering with some of the local white officialdom who turned out to be not entirely unfriendly, Mudd and Graubard, joined by a young African-American lawyer named Marian Wright (now Marian Wright Edelman), met a number of SNCC people, and then went by Tougaloo College, the only place in the state where blacks and whites could meet without harassment. Graubard remembers Marian Wright as suggesting Tougaloo as a possible base of operations for a project the following summer, but of course nothing like "freedom summer" had yet been thought of. In late August, the three of them traveled with a group of SNCC people going up to Washington for what turned out to be Martin Luther King's "I Have a Dream" speech on the Mall, where I was also present.

The following spring, Moses came to Cambridge to recruit a squad of Harvard people for the "Freedom Summer" project, which by this time was taking shape. Privately, debate had already been underway for months in civil rights circles about whether attempting to mobilize the nation by bringing large numbers of whites into Mississippi was too sensationalist or risky, or would detract from the gritty, daily struggle of "local people."[2] Some had misgivings. Others thought having thousands of their children there might focus the attention of the American middle class on what was going on in the deep South as nothing else could. After being of two minds about this, Moses had decided that if the United States was willing to countenance the murder of "local people," the country needed to be made to focus its attention on Mississippi in a new way. "Freedom Summer" might just do that. Moses, incidentally, with his record of having put himself at physical risk so many times and his soft-spoken habits of speech, could dominate a crowd of civil rights people the way no one else could, even Martin Luther

[2] I take the phrase from John Dittmer's landmark study of Freedom Summer and much else in Mississippi, *Local People: The Struggle for Civil Rights in Mississippi*, University of Illinois Press, 1994.

King. His style proclaimed to us in the most total way: no bullshit!!

Moses spoke to a group of us in Mudd's rooms at 1039 about coming to Mississippi. But he urged us not just to join what he projected to be a fairly disorganized stream of unprepared and disoriented liberals, streaming into Mississippi and looking for something to do. In the event, there were more than three hundred of them. We should do something better thought out and organized, he told us. And he mentioned Tougaloo College, an institution that I do not remember having heard of until that moment.

Tougaloo had been founded in 1869 by the American Missionary Society, which bought a five-hundred acre plantation north of Jackson, Mississippi, and there established a school, later a college, to provide education and "industrial training" for African-Americans. By the summer of 1964, Tougaloo had become notorious in Mississippi. Since the late 1940s, Tougaloo chaplains, faculty and students had episodically participated in civil rights projects, and Tougaloo students and faculty had been inspired to renewed activity by the sit-ins and freedom rides of 1960-61. A faculty member, John Salter, and the chaplain, Ed King, had been particularly active. A Jewish refugee from Nazi Germany, Ernest Borinski, had tirelessly tried to promote dialogue between blacks and whites from his base on the Tougaloo faculty. In the increasingly tense racial climate of the early sixties, Tougaloo had come to be regarded by whites as a hotbed of race-mixing and communism. Blacks and whites even pronounced the name of the college differently. Whites called it "TUG-aloo," blacks "TOO-galoo." Whites from Jackson were in the habit of driving their cars around the outskirts of campus, and shooting in the general direction of the administration buildings, particularly after they got off work on Friday afternoon. One Tougaloo faculty member had put up a steel screen in his baby's bedroom which faced the road to protect against the shooting.

Moses suggested that wealthy and well connected Harvard students and faculty should raise some money, give the Tougaloo faculty the summer off to rest and recuperate, and take over summer school teaching—plus participate in local civil rights activities. As John Mudd recalls, the idea at first was to set up a program of seminars for pre-freshman, to prepare them for entering college. From there, the project evolved into providing scholarship money to existing faculty and our group taking over the bulk of the summer instruction.

Moses' idea seemed a good one and we began to discuss how to implement it. Mudd wrote to the President of Tougaloo, A. Daniel Beittel, about the possibility of a group of Harvard graduate students and faculty coming to the campus for the summer and doing a mix of teaching and civil rights work. Beittel was interested and encouraging. So the next question was all important and posed itself quickly: how to fund such a venture?

Somehow or other, a decision was made by Mudd and Marian Wright, to approach a man named Charles Merrill for help with funding our summer activities. Merrill was the son of one of the founding partners of the Merrill Lynch brokerage house, and it was alleged in our ranks that in response to his father's highly conservative politics, which had drawn the ire of Franklin Roosevelt, his son had become an outspoken liberal. In 1957, Merrill had founded a progressive private secondary institution, the Commonwealth School, located in Boston's Back Bay. He knew Marian Wright from his membership on the board of Spelman College and it was thought —correctly as it turned out—that our proposal to take over summer instruction at Tougaloo might find favor with him. So Wright and Mudd contacted him, and discussions ensued. Eventually the Commonwealth Foundation gave us $15,000. Other donors provided us an additional $7,000, all of which made it possible for us to provide a brief summer sabbatical for most of the Tougaloo faculty and fund our own teaching activities. We were all volunteers and brought our own books to supplement what we ordered for the courses we taught and to loan to students for out-of-class reading.

But first I had to pass my preliminary examinations. I was beginning to feel more confident about doing so. It seemed to me that I had read an enormous amount of Russian history, but with the advantage of hindsight I can see how spotty my knowledge really was and how superficial my grasp of important historiography was as well. I never really learned Russian history until I had been teaching it for four or five years. In early May, I took the examinations and passed them, though not with particular distinction. One episode stands out in my memory. When I exited from Richard Pipes' office after my two-hour ordeal had taken place I found myself in the main administrative offices of the Russian Research Center. Mysteriously, a party was in full swing. A waitress came up to me and stuck a tray of champagne glasses under my nose. For a second, I had the absurd illusion that it was to celebrate my rite of passage. But a second later I noticed that nobody was looking at me. In fact the party was in honor of Helen Parsons, then the administrative head of the Center and her husband, the famous sociologist Talcott Parsons, who were off on a trip to Moscow. Dreams of glory. I went home and sat by the telephone until, some hours later, the message came through that I had passed.

By the time I was over that academic hurdle, the summer activities in Mississippi were taking on final form. I went home to Washington, traded cars with my father, and headed down to Jackson, Mississippi, and on to Tougaloo. My father had an inconspicuous tan Rambler, while I had a tiny blue Saab sedan—the three-cycle-engine Saab in those days was more like a power lawnmower than a luxury car—which would have been conspicuous anywhere in the deep South, where foreign cars were rare, particularly small ones. My parents were not opposed to my going, although they were frightened and somewhat concerned about my not demonstrating due diligence in graduate school. The days of my father's and my worst conflicts lay ahead, as the Viet Nam War heated up.

As we expected, we found that Tougaloo was very much a movement-oriented institution. The sit-ins around Jackson had been sparked by Tougaloo students and faculty—and even President Beittel had participated. The Jackson sit-ins began in early 1963, more than a year before we arrived at Tougaloo, but Memphis Norman, one of the leaders, still had his arm in a cast, I believe, from having been beaten months earlier.

Eventually we put together a fairly large group to go and teach at Tougaloo. The loosely related cadre that grew out of the Eliot House roommates provided the focal point, but many of them brought in other individuals and occasionally couples. I recruited my oldest friend, Chris Clague, with whom I had set fires in Washington in the mid-1940s, and his wife Monique. Chris was then working on his Ph.D. in Economics at Harvard. John Mudd recruited Elaine DeLott (Baker), who continued working in the South well into 1965.[3] Christopher Ann Boldt and Patrica Collinge from Radcliffe did theater. Chris Boldt was a slim, willowy blonde with something of an ingénue manner but an admirable habit of straightforward and apparently spontaneous speech and an ability to get to the heart of the matter. Peter Herman taught English, as did his then wife Dr. Judith Lewis Herman. Both were just out of Harvard. Bill Rintala, now a prominent litigator in California, found out about the project in his first year at Harvard Law School and signed up. John Harbison and his violinist wife Rose Mary put on classical concerts, and taught music, including jazz. John's brilliant sister Helen came too, and her fiancé, the historian of modern Iran, Ervand Abrahamian, known to us for some reason as "Jed." Helen, a fine cellist with a subtle and ironical intelligence, died tragically young of cancer.

Allen Graubard recruited a talented student in political philosophy, Mickey Morgan. He, Elaine DeLott, Chris Boldt, and Patty Collinge were our only undergraduates, having just completed their junior years. A year later Mickey became a Rhodes Scholar. John Woodford, who had just graduated from Harvard, was the only African-American in the group; he went on to a journalism career

[3] Elaine has told her story in Constance Curry et al., eds: *Deep In Our Hearts. Nine White Women in the Freedom Movement*, Athens (Ga.), 2000.

at the University of Michigan. George Ranney, sometime candidate for Congress from Illinois and his wife Vicky came at the suggestion of Marshall Cohen. Barry Gewen, recently an editor of the *New York Sunday Times Book Review*, was also part of the group. Not including the professors, most of whom came for briefer periods of time, there were twenty-five of us.[4]

In addition to the formal courses at Tougaloo there were ten evenings devoted to seeing and discussing European and American films, and ten live concerts, all involving the Harbisons, but also featuring much student talent. And there were play-readings too. John Mudd remembers how John, Rosie and Helen intermingled jazz and classical music and a little musical history:

> I remember a memorable time when Rosie was going to play the Bach "Chaconne", with John sitting at the piano saying to the audience of students and others in the sweltering auditorium. "You know the theme [he said]. It's something like the the Ohio State fight song. This is how that sounds. [he played the tune.] Here's what Monk would do with it," and he pounded the keyboard with elbows and fingers.[5] "And here's what Bach did to the same theme." I think I and everyone else were spellbound. And then Rosie did her impeccable thing. John didn't preach down to the kids from some lofty classical heights. He knew Little Richard, Monk and Bach and made it accessible to all of us.[6]

Although most of the full-time teachers were graduate students, a number of faculty members came down for more or less brief periods and gave what amounted to mini-courses, though we didn't use the term. The philosopher Stanley Cavell lectured on American movies. The warm-hearted playwright from Harvard's English

[4] [John Mudd] *Experiment in Education—Tougaloo College, Preliminary Evaluation, September, 1964*, p. 1.

[5] Some research indicates that Thelonius Monk rarely used his elbows on the piano.

[6] Letter from John Mudd to the author, August 26, 2003.

Department, William Alfred, author of *Hogan's Goat*, lectured on American theater. Patty Collinge and Chris Boldt persuaded English Professor Monroe Engel to come down and teach a novel for several weeks. It was supposed to be a Dickens novel, but metamorphosed into Faulkner's *Light in August* by the time Monroe actually got into the classroom.[7] He was joined by Al Leibowitz from Tufts. A well known political philosopher, Yosal Rogat, from the University of Chicago, spent most of the summer with us, teaching a course on legal decision making, and Michael Lipton, a Fellow of All Souls at Oxford, led a seminar on economic development.

Generally we taught things we had some knowledge of, but many of us got a foretaste of our academic future when we would not always have the privilege of teaching things we knew. I taught a seminar on the Russian Revolution, intensive second-year German for Mississippi public school teachers, and studio art, the only time in my life that I have had that pleasure. Somewhat to my surprise, my students were not particularly enthusiastic about the Russian Revolution, even its radiant hopes, not to speak of its disappointing reality. I had been absorbed by every aspect of revolution for so long that I had lost sight of the fact that it could appear sinister, arcane or boring to most Americans.

In fact, I and many others were expecting the Tougaloo students to be somewhat more radical—to use the word extremely vaguely—than they turned out to be. As fairly radical and mostly white bohemians, we dressed very informally—T-shirts and jeans in the Mississippi heat. Only the dining room and faculty lounge were air-conditioned. Certainly we had no sense of dress code for the classroom, nor any idea that such a thing might be necessary. But

[7] Monroe later (June 30, 2008) wrote me that "after I had agreed to teach *Light in August* in my seminar, I got a call [from the bookstore] saying that there wasn't a copy of the novel available anywhere in Jackson, and I had to call Jason Epstein [the publisher] and ask him to arrange to have twenty or so copies put on my flight in New York. These were just indications of the atmosphere in which we were all trying to do something useful."

Young dancers in Tougaloo, Mississippi, 1964

before many days had passed, meetings had to be arranged between the teachers and the students. A number of them thought we were so badly dressed because we didn't take black students seriously and weren't bothering to dress properly, as they assumed we would have done for white students. We were horrified, of course, at the very idea, but there were some wry smiles. We explained as best we could, and the students took in our explanations as best they could. But on the semiotics of clothes we were worlds apart. The students were well and neatly dressed—"for success", as we would say today—while we were also dressed for success, differently defined. The only times all summer when we wore jackets and ties or suits was at Sunday lunch in the Tougaloo cafeteria, and when we were sending integrated groups to try and get served in Jackson area restaurants.

Then everybody dressed up. Many of the other outsiders who streamed into the state were considerably more semiotically extreme than we were, with longer hair and bandanas, not to speak of baggy overalls that looked like castoffs from the Grand Ol' Opry. We had been at work for several weeks when the first contingent arrived, and Chris Boldt remembers how exotic and "inappropriate" their costumes seemed.

There were fewer faculty members around, but my memory is that they too were offended at our clothing and our use of first names. John Dittmer, the author of a prize-winning study[8] of Freedom Summer, became the academic dean three months after arriving at Tougaloo in 1967. When he returned many years later to receive an honorary degree, students he had known back then still called him "Dean Dittmer."

For the northerners among us in particular, the damp heat was extraordinarily oppressive and helped to define the atmosphere of the whole experience. The air seemed thick with moisture and could give us a disconcerting feeling of operating under water. Most of the time everyone slowed down a little, with the possible exception of John Mudd. It took us hours to cool down after playing basketball. Many of us had moments of disorientation.[9]

At any rate, the most spirited student in my seminar, Eloys Long, was unequivocally negative about the Russian Revolution. She had a tendency at first to regard me as one of its latter-day agents, although she eventually relented and realized that I was no worse than a liberal. Students in other courses resented being asked to read Karl Marx. It was subversive, remote and hard. C. Wright Mills wasn't much better. Our informality upset them too. Most were either uneasy or downright hostile at being asked to call us by

[8] John Dittmer, *Local People: The Struggle for Civil Rights in Mississippi*, University of Illinois Press, Urbana and Chicago, 1994. It won the Bancroft Prize, the most important academic prize for works on American history.

[9] As Chris Boldt reminded me in an email of February 7, 2006.

our first names. And it seemed strange to play basketball with us after class. To some, our syllabi, as well as our clothes, seemed to confirm what the local white Mississippians were saying about us: these are northern white radicals, subversives who don't know how to act and want to destroy the social order.

We spent an enormous amount of time with the students – in class, playing basketball, or just hanging out. This kind of informal contact certainly had an impact on the way I came to prefer teaching in later years. The social world of the Tougaloo students did seem very conservative to us, though. To my surprise, these middle-class black students were more or less as fraternity-minded as white southern students, and just as interested in beauty contests and similar pageantry, while we considered such things an aspect of white oppression. After stirring initial hostility by joking about beauty contests, most of us learned to keep our mouths shut, even me.

Despite lurid stories circulated in conservative circles, sexual contact between the largely white faculty and the black students and the Tougaloo staff was minimal. There were occasional episodes. Several of us in a certain sense "kept company" with students of the opposite sex in a social way, but such sexual contact as there may have been was extremely discrete. I was in awe of the beauty of one junior, but the six years difference in our ages seemed prohibitive to me at that time. I was notably lacking in the sexual boldness of the era that was dawning.

The threat of violence hung over us all summer, and we were scared a good deal of the time, especially when we left the relative safety of the Tougaloo campus. When shots were fired into the campus, the chaplain, Ed King, would ring the chapel bell and we would assemble there and he or others might speak, and there would be singing. One of my most vivid memories of the summer was all the singing of freedom songs. Like many of us, I was self-conscious at first about group singing, but gradually got over it.

Then, on June 21, came what turned out after several days of suspense to be the murder of the three civil rights workers, James Chaney, Andrew Goodman and Michael Schwerner. We had no connection with them and I don't believe anybody in our group knew them, but all of us were now afraid. A day or two later, we received an invitation from a white state legislator (whose name I have forgotten) to meet at his house for coffee and conversation. He wouldn't come out to Tougaloo and joked about what it would mean to his reputation if he were seen there. Several of us went, as part of our assignment was to work in "the white community," variously defined. Our host was an amusing raconteur and represented himself as a moderate, but his jokes seemed to us mostly gallows humor. Although there had been no public word about what had happened to the three, our host gave us an account that, although vague, squared in every important respect with the account that emerged later and much more gradually. Word had spread quickly among local whites, although it took a lot longer for broader circles to learn of the cooperation between the sheriff and his deputy and local Klan circles.

Despite the fact that we had a great deal to do with our teaching at Tougaloo, most of us visited the headquarters of COFO (The Council of Federated Organizations, which included SNCC, CORE, the NAACP and others) in Jackson fairly often. We were consumed with curiosity and some no doubt wanted the glory of being able to say or at least imply we had "worked" there. We did mostly routine clerical work, however, in connection with the expansion of "freedom schools" or just hung out, meeting Stokely Carmichael and other future luminaries there.

After the civil rights bill was passed on July 1, interracial groups of faculty and students began to go to local restaurants and demand to be served. There was a general move sponsored by national civil rights organizations to test whether access of blacks to public accommodations in Mississippi would now be permitted. The record was mixed. Some delegations of out-of-state dignitaries were in fact served in restaurants or allowed to stay in previously segregated hotels, but our mixed-race groups of students and faculty never succeeded in getting a meal in a restaurant around Jackson. We usually sat at tables or counters until the proprietor or staff decided to close the restaurant down. Frequently we were jeered or called names, or spat on, occasionally even punched. John Mudd recalls one group being sprayed with bug spray until they couldn't breathe and had to leave. But I don't believe that anyone from a Tougaloo group was severely beaten that summer.

On one occasion, however, an integrated group was pulled over by a police car coming back from a dinner-dance place in a black neighborhood outside of Jackson. We had my Rambler, but Allen Graubard was driving for some reason—probably because I had had a beer. We were all extremely careful about drinking and driving. When the cops approached the car, Allen sat motionless in the driver's seat, but as the owner of the car, I started to get out. When I reached inside my jacket pocket to pull out my wallet, the cops all drew their guns and began to scream at me to get back in the car. I did as I was told. They then pushed Graubard onto the hood and frisked him. I was terrified at their rage, but I later realized that they were also scared, and may well have thought that I was actually going to pull out a gun. Who in white Mississippi knew what these communists might do? Probably fortunately, the cops were from Jackson, not members of the state highway patrol. They shined their flashlights into the car and discovered that there were five people in there, of mixed race and gender, but students of some kind. Eventually they calmed down a bit when they found out that we were from Tougaloo and after a long whispered confab, they decided just to give us a warning and let us go. "Don't come back here again," one of them said to one of the whites. "You can get your throat cut." Meaning, we suddenly realized, that the black neighborhood was dangerous for whites. We were much more worried about getting shot by police than "having our throats cut."

Another encounter was scarier yet. After preparing our teaching for the next day, we were in the habit of going out for coffee and chocolate or black bottom pie at one of the few Jackson area restaurants that was open 24 hours a day. It was one of a national chain called "Toddle House," which was later put out of business by the interstate highway system and the rise of fast food. One evening as we were eating at the counter, three Mississippi troopers came swinging through the door and saw us. They knew right away by our clothes that we were "agitators." There was a moment of silence. Then they surrounded us. One of them said to the waitress between clenched teeth, "Seen any niggers in here." The waitress replied in her usual sing-song, "No, sir." Seen any white niggers?" I can't remember what she actually answered, but she didn't finger us. We tried to continue eating our pie, but mine stuck in my throat. There was further provocative conversation between them. Then they for some reason decided to leave, with one final threat. "If you see any nigger-lovers," one said to the waitress, "you call us." "I surely will," she replied demurely. When we left a few minutes later, she said, as she always did, "Y'all come back." But this time as we were going out the door, I noticed a rifle leaning against the wall in the corner. Whether it had always been there and I had just never noticed it before I don't know.

Trips to New Orleans, several hours away by car, provided our principal weekend relief. Preservation Hall was a discovery of the summer for me, although I had learned the name from recordings. It had been founded in 1961, but its pre-history goes far back in New Orleans history.[10] During the 1950s the building had been an art gallery and kind of community gathering place, owned by a local eccentric named Larry Borenstein, allegedly a great-nephew of Trotsky. A tradition of jam sessions began to develop there toward

[10] The best place to start learning about Preservation Hall and the music played there is William Carter's wonderful *Preservation Hall* (W.W. Norton, New York, 1991). The text is knowledgeable and the photographs of several generations of musicians are memorable. Most of my knowledge of the early history of Preservation Hall is based on Carter's book, plus my own conversations with Allan Jaffe.

the end of the decade, at which point the place became known informally as "kitty hall," because the musicians were paid by passing the hat to raise a kitty. In 1961, Borenstein left temporarily for California to get married, and the management of one of his buildings—a beautiful but run-down eighteenth-century structure, 126 St. Peter Street—passed temporarily into the hands of two rather impractical partners. They developed it as a site for jam sessions and after experimenting with "Perseverance Hall" and "Authenticity Hall," renamed it Preservation Hall. But although they loved the music and put bands of older New Orleans musicians in the hall up to six nights a week, they proved unable, during the summer of 1961, to get along with Borenstein, who remained the owner. And so, in September, Preservation Hall was delivered into the hands of a new manager, a recent arrival in New Orleans named Allan Jaffe, and his wife Sandra; they leased the building from Borenstein. Only in 1984 did they finally buy it. Allan and Sandra Jaffe were in charge when we arrived in late June, 1964, on our first weekend visit.

The Jaffes were the real creators of Preservation Hall. Allan Jaffe remained in charge of its activities until his early death in 1987, and Sandra Jaffe continues to manage Preservation Hall, together with their son, Ben. Allan was a bit of an enigma to me that summer. He was from a small town in Pennsylvania, had gone to Penn and ended up in New Orleans, he told us, because he loved the music. Like me, his passion had crystallized hearing Bunk Johnson records in his adolescence. His college roommate was a cousin of Stan Rubin, who ran a commercial but very popular Dixieland band out of Princeton, called the "Tigertown Five." Jaffe was a tuba player, I later learned, but I never heard him play that summer. But he had been a business major at Penn and he had a lot of experience in booking, which stood him in good stead in his new career.

Jaffe was obviously not a southerner and he loved New Orleans jazz, so I naively expected him to be sympathetic to the civil rights movement. Maybe he was in some ways—he let us sleep on mattresses in the top floor garret of Preservation Hall—but never admitted it to us. He chose to take a very white southern line in conversation, and actually introduced us to people as "agitators" ("I'd like you to meet some of these agitators you've been hearing about."), and generally said that we were doing more harm than good. Rightly or wrongly, though, I attributed his way of talking to a certain contrarianism and a determination not to parrot what might be expected of him rather than straightforward conviction. Nevertheless, he introduced me to Raymond Burke, a well known white New Orleans clarinetist, who, when not playing music, was the proprietor of a local antique store, and he also took me to meet Jim Robinson, the great tailgate trombonist, whom I plied with questions for several hours over a couple of bottles of wine. The tourists from Tougaloo marched in the "second line" of several New Orleans funerals, one featuring the Eureka Brass Band, certainly the greatest New Orleans marching band of its day. We heard the great husband and wife team, Billie and Dede Pierce, and "Sweet Emma the Bell Gal," a tiny, foul-mouthed black woman with a beautiful child's voice, who always had a garter with bells on it around her upper leg; the bells jingled as she stomped her way through "Ain't Gonna Give Nobody None of My Jelly Roll" or "Big Butter and Egg Man." Two of the young women in our group went up to Sweet Emma and asked her what a "jelly roll" was. She cackled and said "it's a piece of cake, darlings."[11]

The hall itself was extremely plain, inside and out, with oil paintings of musicians on the walls. There were no tables—you sat in rows of old chairs, or stood behind in a standing room section. You could ask for tunes you wanted to hear. "Traditional" requests were $1.00, non-traditional tunes cost $2.00, and "When the Saints Go Marching In" cost $5.00. No food or drink was served, so you had to buy a drink down the street, which you were allowed to bring in. Or you could put a dime in the coke machine which stood just outside

[11] Thanks to Allen Graubard for remembering this.

the entrance. Sandra Jaffe collected your donation in a basket at the door. The band generally quit at 11:00 or 11:30, but there was often more music in the courtyard out behind, in my experience generally a blues singer. Weekends at Preservation Hall were among the most memorable days and nights of my life. I could hardly make myself get back in the car on Sunday night.

As the summer passed, we spent some time planning how to inaugurate a permanent relationship between Harvard and Tougaloo, not knowing that we were already too late. The previous year, Barnaby Keeney, the President of Brown, had moved to create an institutional relationship with Tougaloo, which was announced publicly at Brown that fall, and Brown sent a professor of Sociology, Harold Pfautz, to represent the university officially.[12] He arrived in August, not long before the end of summer school. We were crestfallen. There went our plans. Little did I know that I would return to Brown four years later and have an opportunity to extend my relationship with Tougaloo College far into the future.

Brown's relationship with Tougaloo, while it brought the college a good many educational benefits, was not without problems, one of which remained unknown for a good many years. By the time we arrived at the beginning of the summer, President Beittel had resigned and was just cleaning out his presidential desk. We believed that powerful people in Mississippi had forced him out. It was well known that the state legislature had tried to get rid of him. Years later, however, it was discovered that it was Brown University's then president, Barnaby Keeney, who had decided that Beittel's active involvement in the civil rights struggle was bad for Tougaloo and, perhaps, for Brown. So Keeney had arranged with the Ford

[12] The only opposition to the Brown-Tougaloo relationship came from a professor in the History Department, Forrest McDonald, the head of Barry Goldwater's presidential campaign organization in Rhode Island. According to McDonald, such a relationship was "immoral," because "it encouraged Negroes to aspire to goals which they could not achieve in the present makeup of Southern society." (*Providence Evening Bulletin*, November 4, 1964, p. 50.)

Foundation and other important donors to make future grants for Tougaloo conditional on Beittel's resignation.[13]

How successful were we in our three months-plus at Tougaloo? For me and no doubt for most of the visitors, it was a memorable experience. Some of us feel that it changed our lives very dramatically, others that it was the best thing we ever did. I guess I feel that way. Just to be able to say "I was a part of that," however small, had a quite disproportionate effect on my life. John Mudd put the matter in his usual straightforward way, writing later in a letter to me recalling the summer that, despite some reservations about the way we set about our teaching, "our presence was part of the sea change in the culture of Mississippi and the South. There were many pebbles cast in the water that summer, with profound ripple effects. None in isolation were definitive. But each contributed."[14]

How, in more practical ways, had I changed? Realizing, permanently, the depth and power of racism's role in American history and politics was a part. Gaining a new and deeper sense of the relativity and subjectivity of cultural viewpoints, something also fostered by the study of Russia, was another. I was also more balanced in my assessment of the United States. Those sound abstract. It's hard to know. Small insights came frequently. John Woodford remembers "the statement of a young man deemed hick even by rural Mississippi standards. I had agreed [in class] with some students who dumped on television in the 'Vast Wasteland' discourse of the day. He raised his hand and said he looked at TV every chance he got. He'd read every book in his humble school and there was no library nearby, so he ... relied on TV to learn about people, culture, history and the country at large; without it he'd know even less ...."[15]

From a purely pedagogical perspective, however, it was a reality

[13] Dittmer, *Local People*, pp. 234-236.

[14] Mudd, letter to the author, August 26, 2003.

[15] John Woodford, email to the author, January 22, 2004.

check for most of us. We came to realize that neither our fascination with ideas nor our political points of view were very readily transferable to African-American students in Mississippi. Our sense of being "liberators" was naïve and somewhat condescending. Too often we displayed, I'm afraid, what Walker Percy called "the post-Christian piety of the sociology major."[16] Nor was our effect on our students invariably remarkable or in most cases durable. Some few diverged from the careers they might have had, in favor of more adventurous ones in the North, but I think some of these young people went from project to project and may have had an even harder time finding their feet than they would have if they had stayed in Mississippi or emerged from it in some other way.

What the northern students among us largely did was bring them the syllabi from the undergraduate courses that had turned us on. The reading list we threw at them—Max Weber, Rousseau, Marx, John Stuart Mill, Hobbes, Plato—was not given sufficient context and often seemed quite unrelated to the daily problems of their lives. So although the summer was an important milestone for most students as well as faculty, I suspect that the curriculum we worked so hard on was among the least significant aspects of the summer's activities for the large majority of the students.[17] In retrospect we realized to a greater or lesser degree that our ideas, outside of our own contexts, did not travel particularly well, and that social change would be a longer and more arduous process than we had supposed and less dependent on "great books." Allen Graubard wondered in retrospect why it didn't occur to us to put together projects "where student interest and experience could be key in developing active participation and hence 'relevance'." Part of the answer is that we were just emerging from the top-down fifties.

[16] Walker Percy, "The Fire This Time," *The New York Review of Books*, Volume 4, No. 11, July 1, 1965.

[17] That was the opinion of Polly Greenberg, who was not part of our group. See *The Devil Has Slippery Shoes*, London, Macmillan, 1969, pp. 332-334.

And yet, there is some testimony that for some students, the events of that summer were connected to deeper narratives of change. Marion Gillon, who came North to Harvard and now works on teacher certification for the state of Massachusetts, told Mudd that "I still remember the courses I took; I still remember the discussions. ...Riding around Mississippi in an integrated car was a major thing; doing things that hadn't happened before. ...These were more important than the academic." Another activist, Arverna Adams, who was not actually at Tougaloo, told Mudd, in slight contrast, "I think the academic part was important. We can't change life without changing ideas....It's not true that the ideas didn't connect. ...I know from myself and other students that we were in a search to liberate ourselves from a society we considered unjust. ... What drove the civil rights movement? It was ideas and thoughts from many different cultures."[18] John Woodford agreed. "If intelligent and learned people come to your bailiwick and treat you with respect and take you seriously, a lot of learning and developing goes on beyond classroom dimensions, and some of the learning detonates in time-release fashion. So I'd say the ... Harvard volunteers' 'fascination with ideas'... were transferable to many Tougaloo students and in fact hit fertile soil."[19] At least in some cases, sometimes. But pessimists can always find something to whine about. The deep South is a far less oppressive place racially than it was in those days, to be sure. But as another Harvard roommate, Jack McNees, recently reflected, while the explicit segregationist politicians like Stennis and Eastland are gone, Trent Lott's unguarded remarks praising Strom Thurmond remind us that those times may not be as far away psychologically as one might hope.[20]

[18] Marion Gillon and and Arverna Adams, quoted in John Mudd's letter to the author, August 26, 2003.

[19] John Woodford, email to the author on January 22, 2004.

[20] "I want to say this about my state," said Senator Trent Lott at a social gathering late in 2002. "When Strom Thurmond ran for president, we voted for him. We're

Around the end of August, most of us headed on, either north toward school, or, in my case, to New Mexico to reestablish contact with my girl friend, Sarah. Only John Mudd and Elaine DeLott stayed on, Mudd to focus his extraordinary energy and idealism on a series of other projects, including especially, the first head start group in Mississippi, the Child Development Group of Mississippi (CDGM).

proud of it. And if the rest of the country had followed our lead, we wouldn't have had all these problems over all these years, either." See "Lott apologizes for Thurmond comment," <CNN.com/INSIDE POLITICS>. Tuesday, December 10, 2002.

Sarah Gleason, c. 1970

Marriage and the Sixties

Return to graduate school entailed, to say the least, an abrupt shift of gears. Academia and Cambridge for a while seemed quite unreal. Cops, astonishingly, paid no attention to me. Nobody glared at me on the street or stared at my shoes (outside agitators wore different footwear from Mississippians and could be thus identified). I wasn't living in a largely black world. For days I felt at loose ends and purposeless, but gradually Russia began to reassert its fascination, and academia began to feel natural again. The principal project remaining for me in graduate school was my dissertation—an enormous, but on the whole, welcome challenge. There was also my first experience with regular teaching.

My provisional models for a dissertation remained two: the books of Andrzej Walicki and Martin Malia. I was steeped in their work. Between the two of them they defined my initial academic ambitions. Both men worked in an idiom that might best be described as the social/psychological history of ideas, but with differences. What I wanted to do, as I was beginning to understand by the early mid-1960s, was to write the most acute intellectual biography or group biography possible. I wanted to root even the most idiosyncratic personal characteristics of my subjects in the social circumstances of their lives, starting with class, but going as far beyond it as I could. My models for biography were heavily literary, but I thought they could be reconciled with sociology and the history, at least, of philosophy. This may seem like squaring the circle today, but I believed then that something like that could be done.

Despite similarities in their work, the difference between the two scholars were several. Walicki emphasized the sociological, Malia the psychological. What was common was their effort to connect pure biography with some larger structure. As I returned from the South, I was mulling over attempting an extended study of the Slavophiles[1] and their intellectual influence on writers like Dostoevsky and Tolstoy and a number of lesser writers, thinkers and critics, but even as I settled in back at Harvard, Andrzej Walicki's magisterial study of the Slavophiles arrived in the mail with a friendly inscription from the author. As I struggled through it in Polish, virtually one word at a time, I realized that I did not yet know nearly enough to write such an ambitious study. Even had Andrzej not scooped me, it would have been ten or fifteen years before I was ready to venture on an undertaking of such scope. So I gradually narrowed my topic until I had decided to examine the first generation of the Slavophiles, using a biographical study of the most innovative Slavophile thinker, Ivan Kireevsky, as a framework.

Who were the Slavophiles and why was I interested in them? They were a self-conscious group of Russians drawn from the intellectual generation born between 1800 and 1810, who in the 1840s and 1850s collectively imagined the first coherent formulation of Russian identity, at both the cultural and the personal level. Most of them, not all, received their early education in the spirit of the European Enlightenment but became converts to romanticism. Significantly, they were on the cusp of that great change from the world of Enlightenment "rationalism" to romanticism, just as I was on the cusp—although I didn't know it yet—of the change from the American fifties to the turbulent sixties. Abetted by their vantage

[1] *W Kręgu Konserwatywnej utopii*, Polish Academy of Sciences, 1964. The English translation, published by Oxford University Press (New York) in 1975, is entitled *The Slavophile Controversy*.

point, the Slavophiles put a set of ideas into circulation that are still powerful beneath the surface of Russian culture almost two centuries later. The most fateful aspect of their intellectual synthesis was the largely negative basis for defining Russia: Russian identity was fundamentally different from, and in most important respects, superior to European identity. This was a central Slavophilic premise – Russia was not European. Even today, the argument over whether or not Russia is really part of the Euro-American world continues, although sometimes in the form of parody and caricature, and nowadays with diminishing intensity. For the first time, Russia is really wide open to a variety of Western influences, from literary classics to the most awful pornography. Never has "the West" been so powerfully present in Russian culture, for better and for worse, as toward the end of the first decade of the new century.

The Slavophile arguments about Russia's superiority to Europe were an ingenious and extreme version of contemporary German assertions about the superiority of their romantic *Kultur* to the classic *Civilisation* of the French. The German and even more the Russian theories centered on a romantic critique of Enlightenment rationalism and industrial modernity, which they linked to it. The Slavophile critique of Russian development took the form of an exaltation of pre-modern agrarianism, which their nation had preserved: in particular the Russian village and its inhabitants. The German romantics demonized the French as the progenitors of rationalism and revolution. The Russians demonized the entire "West" as the creator of soulless industrial civilization. This was natural, given the degree to which Germany was less industrialized than either France or England. Russia was still so preindustrial that whether Russia belonged to modern Europe at all was hotly contested.

Rather than accepting earlier assertions that European civilization was unitary and the Russians were merely more backward in its assimilation than the nations of "the West," the Slavophiles elevated the pre-capitalist and integral communalism of the Russian peasant village into an assertion of Russian distinctiveness and superiority to the other nations of Europe. Characteristically, Russian assertions of religious and cultural superiority were based on fears of inadequacy and wounded self-esteem, far more than on genuine cultural self-confidence. Part of what educated Russians feared in the nineteenth century was that their national identity was plausibly based on a brutalized and superstitious peasantry. After the French Revolution, Europeans had gradually accepted that national identity had to be derived not from the opulence or achievements of the upper-class minority, but needed to be grounded on the broad strata of the population that corresponded more closely to what French revolutionary thinkers meant by "the people." This meant that any nineteenth-century effort to say who "the Russians" were had to accept the peasant-ness of Russia and find ways to affirm it. This the Slavophiles did.

The roots of Russian superiority, they asserted, lay in the purity of Russian Christianity and in the religious traditions of the East Slavs. The Roman Catholicism and Protestantism of the West, on the other hand, were perversions of the true spirit of European Christianity, which—after the medieval Christian schism between East and West—had been preserved only within the Orthodox Church, and most particularly within its Russian variant. The world of classical antiquity had corrupted Catholicism by introducing the rationalism of pagan antiquity into Christian culture, largely through Aristotelianism and Roman legal traditions. The Protestant Reformation had not provided the needed corrective to Catholic authoritarianism epitomized, the Slavophiles believed, in the papal dictatorship. Instead it had deprived the rebellious Protestant churches of authority and organization altogether, while failing to provide a comprehensive, inclusive basis for the unity of the Church.

The result of Slavophile discussions and polemics with the rival "Westernizers" was the exaltation of an alleged Russian communalism, exemplified by the "conciliarism" (*sobornost*) of the Orthodox

Church and the collective institutions of the Russian village. Both stood in sharpest contrast to Western Europe. The Slavophiles alleged that in the early days of the Orthodox East, the entire Church had participated in decision-making and thus virtually encompassed society. This positing of authority in the entire Church was a bit vague and the method of transmission even more so, but at least it contrasted with both major Western denominations.

It was the German romantic critique of the French Enlightenment that gave the first generation of romantic-minded aristocratic intellectuals the tools to create the ideological edifice that came to be called Slavophilism. The Slavophiles were hostile to secularism, individualism, cosmopolitanism and formal representative government. Like the German romantics, they exalted pre-modern communalism, religion and patriarchal-monarchical tradition. Expressed in a rather schematic sociologism, Andrzej Walicki had examined how romanticism had migrated East in a finely detailed and erudite study completed in his late twenties and early thirties—a major achievement, it seemed to me, that became my scholarly starting point.

Martin Malia had a similar, although less explicit conception of the intellectual development of Slavophilism. He focused, however, on the so-called "Westernizers," those rival intellectuals from a less uniformly upper-class background, who wanted Russia to continue to embrace the progressive thought of Western Europe. His account of the acceptance of German romantic doctrine by the Russians was even more vivid and acute than that of Walicki, if less comprehensive. This quarrel between the Westernizers and the Slavophiles was the premier intellectual event of mid-nineteenth-century Russia. Laying out and analyzing this struggle for the soul of Russia was my first project as a historian and its afterglow has dominated much of my career.

Malia's interest in the dispute began in an attempt to ascertain how the Westernizers came to found what he called "Russian socialism," the beginning of real left-wing politics in Russia. There was a close connection between the first generation of Slavophile conservatives on the right and critical Westernizers on the left. Early Russian ideas of peasant socialism owed much to the conservative Slavophile hostility to industrialism and urban factory life, adding an additional complexity to their rivalry. Malia demonstrated an acute understanding of the psychological dimension of the quarrel between Westernizers and Slavophiles in his splendid biography of Alexander Herzen, the great nineteenth-century man of letters so venerated by Isaiah Berlin. It appeared in 1961, just after I returned from my year in Europe to enter graduate school, and I immediately fell under its spell.

Apart from my admiration for Malia's and Walicki's work, there were some personal reasons why I was so drawn to this problem area. The quarrel between the Slavophiles and the Westernizers resonated with elements of my own biography. I was in many ways a respecter of tradition (though I resisted this realization for quite some time) and was becoming more so as I embarked on my family's third generation of the academic experience. As a result, I found it easy to sympathize with the Slavophile idealization of the past, although I was determined not to be taken in by it, as some Slavophile scholars had been. I was and would continue to be torn between liberal individualism and communal/collective points of view, between individual development and romantic and collective identities. In terms of literature and aesthetics generally, I was on the cusp between the Edwardian and Georgian generation of Rudyard Kipling and John Buchan on the one hand, and the modernist rebels against the Georgian world, on the other. I was simultaneously a proponent and a resister of secularism, who managed to identify with Stephen Daedalus and Bilbo Baggins, Stravinsky and Sibelius. And I was much drawn to ideologically minded groups of friends with intellectual missions. This academic "band of brothers" fantasy was to be an important but gradually passing phase of my intellectual development, no doubt rooted in the struggles of an academic brat to harmonize his egoistic need for self-assertion with his equally powerful need for group appreciation, support and solidarity. James Billington had already during my undergraduate years semi-facetiously imagined me and my friends as Russian intellectuals. I continued to cherish rather idealized pictures of group intellectual life, awkwardly harnessed to contrasting fantasies of individual achievement and recognition. The Russian intellectual "circle" was not merely a scholarly interest but had deep psychological resonance for me. It was a fantasy which appealed both to the traditionalist and the modernist sides of my evolving personality, both to hobbit-lovers and to sympathizers with the Students for a Democratic Society.

Teaching was also a new thing for me. What was it? How did you actually do it? How much did you impose your own ideas and structures on students? Or was it better to simply serve as a friendly guide? To what degree did you link the subject to contemporary issues and points of view? To what extent did you attempt to remain within the confines of the past? With bright Harvard and Radcliffe students perhaps you just showed them the books and more or less got out of the way. To what extent did you adopt a teacherly or professorial persona? How egalitarian should you try to be? I am still grappling with many of these questions at the end of my career. You make choices, but there are no final answers.

At the beginning I may have unconsciously identified teaching with showing off. At the same time, however, I imagined drawing out talented students in a cleverly unobtrusive way, helping them to develop their diverse talents, rather as my high school art teacher had done. I was hard put to decide between altruistic indirection and self-assertion. Was I going to be a midwife or an authoritative doctor?

For two years I struggled with these issues as a tutor in the Harvard undergraduate honors program known as History and Literature. I assigned students my favorite books. I gave a kind of mini-course on nineteenth-century French and Russian novels in a social and political context, figuring out the French side hours—or minutes—before the beginning of class. I tried to be very egalitarian, a sort of elder brother who had been away at school and had returned to enlighten his younger siblings. I succeeded to some degree. I was popular with my students, among whom I was known as "Tom Tutor." But a great deal of my initial success was due to my youth, my closeness in age to the students I was teaching. I did not yet have to face the challenge of the steadily advancing age gap between teacher and students. I was not pompous or bossy, but I didn't know nearly as much as I thought I did. The flip side of my broad interests was a certain superficiality.

"Tom Tutor", 1963

I also taught in an introductory social science course, known in the Harvard system as "Soc. Sci. 3." In that capacity I had to give three lectures on the origins of the British Labor Party. These were my first lectures, and I worked on them and worried about them for months. I read voluminously, and ultimately produced three finely edited texts of over twenty pages apiece, which I read out loud to a slightly somnolent audience of about a hundred students. In order to come close to getting everything in, I had to read very fast, and the effect was much like that of a speeded-up tape recorder. I had a number of what I believed to be hilarious and apposite jokes, but I sped through them at such a rate that the students never knew anything intended to be humorous had been said. Many of them gave up trying to take notes. Digesting this experience was my first lesson in lecturing. Among the things I learned was that you have to indicate to students absolutely clearly through body language, pregnant pauses, or facial expressions that a joke is coming. Otherwise most of them will miss it. Even more fundamentally: There is an enormous difference between a polished written text and a good lecture. It takes a long time to realize the limited amount even the most conscientious professor can pack into a fifty-minute lecture and have it stay with the students.

In the summer of 1963, I also served as a course assistant to Arthur Mendel, a most pleasant and casually democratic visiting professor from Michigan. One of my students in the course was a dazzlingly beautiful editor of *The Harvard Crimson*—the Fashion Editor, I think—who came in late almost every time and sat down next to me and talked nonstop throughout the lecture. "Hey Tom, did I tell you that my grandparents were East European Jews who settled around Boston in 1903, etc., etc." Mendel looked down at me questioningly as the conversational flow continued. I later explained to him as well as I could that I just couldn't get her to shut up. Mendel was understanding. "Yes, and she's quite a babe too, isn't she?"

But this beautiful editor did almost no work and flunked the course. I went on a brief trip after summer school and when I got back, I soon encountered her in the large main reading room of the Harvard library. To my surprise, she had gained an enormous amount of weight. And she immediately burst into tears and began to accuse me, between sobs, of taking advantage of her. People started to look at me angrily, and I suddenly realized that they thought I was the father of her soon-to-be-born child. I had only been away for a week, however, and it soon transpired that she had merely gone on an eating jag when I flunked her.

Felicia Kaplan, the indefatigable matchmaker, introduced me to my wife-to-be, Sarah Fischer. She didn't actually mean to do so. She intended Sarah for one of her numerous godchildren. But I overheard her trying to set him up over the phone and intervened, pleading my case. "Why don't you ever find me attractive women," I whined, exhibiting the ugliest characteristics of a second-year graduate student, caught in the toils of seminar papers and suffering from enforced academic solitude. It worked. I got to ask her out.

I provided a characteristically academic first date—the Harvard Dramatic Club's production of *Henry IV, Part I*; but we went down to a beach at Cape Cod on our second. After a summer apart we got serious in the fall of 1963. At the same time, I left the womb of the Kaplan house to room with John Casey, then in his second year at the Harvard Law School, in a house on Francis Avenue, a mecca of liberal Harvard faculty families and people like them. Somewhat confusingly, my new landlord was also a Kaplan—Justin Kaplan, the biographer of Mark Twain—married to the novelist, Anne Bernays.

John Casey and I roomed together for three years, while John was deciding whether he would give up law for writing fiction. It was not a rapid process, but writing gradually won out. It was helpful when Peter Taylor, the novelist and short-story writer, spent a year at Harvard, along with his poet wife, Eleanor, and encouraged John to take the plunge. The high prestige of the writer's vocation among his friends may have helped counterbalance the prestige of law within his family.

The new (for me) Kaplans lived in a spacious house on a quiet street not far from Memorial Hall. They had a little dog named Olive, who would go out to pee very early most mornings. John's room abutted her favorite locations on the side lawn and he would often be waked up by her barking at 6:00 or so in the morning. Drugged with sleep he would stagger out onto a balcony-like structure outside his window and fire everything that came to hand at Olive. Hours later, when I woke up, I would see the lawn covered with our stuff: books, tennis rackets and balls, water glasses, pans from the kitchen. Olive, who never suffered any damage or stopped barking, would be long gone.

A survey came out midway through Casey's second year at law school, indicating how much work students were putting in to achieve certain grade levels. John was doing extremely well, in view of the work he was putting in. After graduating, he passed the DC bar exam, but that was his last gesture in the direction of a legal career, except for legal references in some of his short stories that later appeared in *The New Yorker.* Throughout most of our time together, he was dating a beautiful and brilliant Radcliffe undergraduate, Andrea Petersen, active in Harvard theater, and she and John and Sarah and I were often a foursome. John was a voracious reader, a scintillating conversationalist and an insomniac. I might have done better on my preliminary exams in History if I had had a less fascinating roommate. Andrea and I were also simpatico. She was from a German and German-Jewish family and many of the dilemmas of modern Germany were embedded in it. We communicated seriously and humorously in and out of German, which I found most appealing.

Sarah was beautiful and shy. Four years younger than I, just finishing her junior year, she felt herself almost in a different generation for awhile. With time that changed, of course. She had a lovely straightforward quality which won my heart immediately.

John Casey and Andrea Petersen, 1963

My approach to this new relationship, however, was to assume that she would be delighted to make a ceremonial entry into my world, which meant reading all the books I liked and becoming friends with everyone who was my friend. It also meant liking modern jazz, *The Lord of the Rings*, Ezra Pound, Henry James and God knows whatever other idiosyncratic and contradictory enthusiasms my head was stuffed with. And of course, Russian history. She was willing to try these things out, but like any normal person, she drew her own conclusions.

Sarah's resistance became active and passionate when I "lent" her Martin Malia's biography of Herzen, my current favorite book. It was of particular importance to me, as I was planning in my dissertation to do for Kireevsky and the Slavophiles what Malia had done for Herzen and the Westernizers. I fantasized my book on the shelf right next to Malia's, with a similar but color-contrasted dust jacket. I imagined conversations in which people linked the two books together as the duo that had brilliantly redirected the field of Russian intellectual history, etc., etc. At first Sarah temporized.

But weeks went by and she hadn't read it. I began to pressure her: "You must read it. It's important to me that you read it!" Finally she rebelled. "I don't want to read it! I'm not interested in it," she shouted. Her exemplary forthrightness became a permanent influence on my education. But at the time, this event was traumatic in the extreme. NOT INTERESTED IN IT! She had failed to adopt my interests and enthusiasms. Not only that, she didn't like every one of my friends as well as I did. She found bebop noisy and Victorian fantasy literature tedious. I was forced to confront the paradox of falling in love with someone whose tastes and enthusiasms were quite distinct from mine, in certain cases very different. Eventually this led to a healthy breach in the armored and vociferous egoism of my personal and cultural enthusiasms. Out of this conflict ultimately grew a life-changing respect for difference. But in the short run, it was painful. We continued to go out together, but there were struggles. I was not confident enough in my own taste not to need reinforcement from my girlfriend. My intellectual and romantic interests were for a time painfully distinct, if not absolutely contradictory. We were separated for four months in the summer of 1964, then together over the winter. Our relationship blossomed.

Over the summer of 1965 I went to work in the Russian Library in Helsinki, Finland, for four months. It was one of the great Russian collections in the world, and far easier to access than libraries in Moscow or Leningrad. In theory a copy of every book printed in Russia between 1809, when Finland became part of the Russian Empire, and 1918, when it achieved independence, was in the library. In addition, it had complete runs of many periodicals I needed to read. I also wanted to decide about marriage. So, too, did Sarah, but characteristically I thought of it as my decision.

—⁓—

My three months in Helsinki were wonderful although I missed Sarah and became more accustomed to solitude again. I was a novice enthusiast about Scandinavia, about Finnish architecture and especially about saunas, which I looked forward to experiencing as often as possible. So only a day or two after my arrival I enquired at a downtown hotel as to where I might find a good one. No doubt with some degree of malice, the clerk at the desk gave me directions. "Take the number such-and-such streetcar across the bridge; go three stops; walk across the field on your left and you're there." I did so and came to a rather fancy and quite extensive two-story building next to a small lake. There was no sign at the entrance. I walked in. There was nobody at the desk, but I had no difficulty finding the locker room. I picked a locker and undressed. Naked men were going in and out of the hot room. I grabbed a towel, a bundle of birch twigs, and followed along. Several pleasant-looking men some years older than I were there. We chatted as we steamed, beat each other with birch twigs, showered, and steamed again. I told them about my summer plans. They all spoke good English. Afterwards we swam in the freezing lake outside and then sat in chairs alongside it. A woman came by with a tray of cognacs in snifters. "Wow," I thought to myself. "Scandinavian social democracy. Bring it on." Then we showered again and dressed. As we were finishing up, one of the pleasant businessmen I had been chatting with said to me with a smile how much he and his friend had enjoyed making my acquaintance and having me as his guest. But, he informed me in the friendliest way imaginable, I had walked into a private club. I was embarrassed but felt just wonderful physically and walked back to town. I never found the clerk who had sent me to this exclusive men's club, but ultimately I was grateful to him despite his clearly mischievous intent.

Several days later, I moved into a youth hostel for the summer. I got a very good rate on a basement room. An old man with a cat had lived there for months, if not years. If I would agree to scrub the room with disinfectant and could stand the smell, management said I could have the room at half price for the remainder of the summer. I would and I could. I didn't have a grant for the summer, and the price was right.

Even so, I soon ran out of money. I hunted for work at the university and found just what I was looking for. A man phoned the youth hostel and asked for me. "I understand you have an American voice," he said. I did. We met for coffee, and a very rewarding three-month relationship ensued, one we renewed periodically in the years that followed whenever I went in or out of Leningrad through Helsinki. My benefactor was Karl-Joachim Ahlsved, known as K. J. or Kalle, and he worked for the very large forestry faculty at the university, which was much larger than academic departments like history or philosophy. Although he had scientific training, his great interest was scientific-technical translation.[2] His English was excellent, but not native, and I was able to help him with the final version of scientific papers to be published in English or delivered at international conferences in English. I also put the finishing touches on two film soundtracks and read them aloud for the final versions. *The Vertical Decomposition of Peat Cellulose in Pine, Spruce and Birch Swamps* was one. The storyline sounded like an unpublished novel by Joseph Conrad: poor Pete Cellulose, living alone in a swamp, always on his feet (vertical) and gradually going mad. The other was entitled *Male Flowering*. I never ran into either one in Boston or New York film festivals. But I still have the texts, battered and yellowing, on a shelf in the attic.

The "white nights" in Helsinki and Leningrad, where I also visited, were wonderfully disconcerting. Around the June equinox it really never got truly dark at all. The long, long, never completed sunsets were enticing but melancholy. The days had no boundaries but flowed into each other. On the overnight ferry to Stockholm the party never ended. I took it more than once.

Helsinki, with its nicely designed garden suburbs and lack of urban sprawl, reinforced my faith in socialist planning. I knew at

[2] Kalle has had a fine career. A recent Google search reveals that he has realized one old ambition: to produce a multi-lingual (English, Finnish, Swedish and Russian) dictionary of forest terminology.

some level that building an apartment complex in Finland must necessitate a great deal of red tape, but I never seriously questioned whether it was worth it. Helsinki was also the cleanest city I had ever seen, and full of fine modern buildings, design outlets and fascinating small museums. I spent as much time as I felt I could wandering around and I traveled by bus to picturesque cities and towns, like the old capital, Porvoo.

At the end of the summer I accompanied Kalle Ahlsved and some of his scientific friends, most of whom were microbiologists and swamp foresters, almost to North Cape at the top of the Scandinavian peninsula. Reindeer were much smaller and more moth eaten than I had expected; herds of them frequently crossed the dirt roads inside the Arctic Circle. The mosquitoes, on the other hand, were much larger, and after dark, millions of them invaded our campsites, whining like fighter planes. From the Arctic Ocean, I hitchhiked down the coast, along the misty fjords, through some of the most beautiful country in the world, and over to Oslo, where I met my parents. When I returned to New York, Sarah met me at the airport and I proposed on the spot. Being away from her for four months had done it. I had missed her more and more.

I asked John Fischer for his daughter's hand in the family living room in White Plains. My request was made after she had accepted me and I suppose it was a mere formality. He said yes, but drily suggested that elopement would spare us all unnecessary ceremony. Things like weddings took time away from work, and so did the families that followed. We were married in June of 1966, in a Unitarian church in White Plains, which seemed to my increasingly royalist parents excessively plain. Sarah's matron of honor, Rina Solomon, was a childhood friend and Harbison, Casey, Field and Chris Clague, my oldest friend, with whom I had lit fires as a six-year-old, stood up for me. We honeymooned briefly in Randolph Center, Vermont, in a rambling, slightly down-at-the-heel mansion lent to us by Sydney and Jameson Parker. Then back to Cambridge, Sarah to a teaching job, me to my dissertation.

Sarah Gleason, c. 1970

My Harvard friends and I were really on the cusp of the sixties, generationally speaking, not entirely part of them, perhaps especially so in my case. Partly this may have been because of a kind of group commitment to straightforward Enlightenment views. Partly it was a simple matter of age. In fact, what became known as the sixties actually seemed to begin about 1965 and end about 1973, and I was already a little too old to consider myself a part of "youth" in the passionately generational system that was emerging around 1967-68. Probably more significant was the fact that despite periodic spasms of self-hatred, I had never repudiated my background and really remained a Cold War liberal at heart. Suspicious of Marxism, anarchism and the demonization of Washington, I had tuned out a certain amount of the early anti-war movement and its activities. I did not join such early anti-nuclear organizations as SANE (Committee for a Sane Nuclear Policy). This was partly because of my intense focus on academic activities, but it was also because I did not feel the same clarity about the evils of American foreign policy that I did about the evils of segregation. This was, in turn, partly because there was an aura of pro-Sovietism that seemed to me to hang like a cloud over such organizations—or, if pro-Soviet is an unfair term, insufficiently anti-Soviet might be better. I liked Professor Stuart Hughes personally. He was one of the very few faculty members in the Harvard History Department who seemed to talk pleasantly and naturally to graduate students. But there was an anti-anti-communist aspect to his campaign for the Senate in 1962 which kept me from volunteering, as so many of my friends did. His candidacy was roundly rejected, even by Massachusetts liberals.

As the sixties—whatever the boundaries of that period actually were—developed, I began to intuit the limitations of my sympathy with the growing radicalism of young Americans, and I was ultimately embarrassed at how rapidly I seemed to be turning more conservative. It took me a good deal longer to develop some perspective, to begin to get a historian's take on those years. For a time, things just seemed to get more radical every day. Clothes became weirder, as students began to advertise their political and personal identities through what they wore. Sexual encounters became more casual, something of which I failed to take full advantage. The word "fascist" to describe mild conservatism became commoner than ever. To some degree contemporary history seemed to me—scrutinized through my trick Russian lens—to be recapitulating the development of Russian radicalism after 1848. My fixation on these two eras—similar and yet so very different—eventually led me to undertake a history of early Russian radicalism as seen through the lens of the American sixties a century later.

As undergraduates in the fifties, my friends and I had considered ourselves socialists, but definitely of the democratic variety. Like the "New York intellectuals" that we looked up to, our socialism was by and large quite compatible with liberalism, although even in the late fifties there were nuanced differences among us that became more pronounced with time. Even then, Jack McNees and

Allen Graubard chafed at Cold War liberalism and clearly hoped somehow to escape its limitations. By the early sixties they seemed to have moved further along this path, as had Jack Womack. Jack McNees wrote me in June, 1961 from Oxford, *inter alia*,

> I don't suppose there's any strict logical incompatibility between liberal institutions and a thoroughgoing socialist revolution (I'm talking about the transitional process now; ultimately, of course, on my understanding of "socialist," there is a strict logical mutual entailment); but I can see how, in most probable historical situations, there would be tremendous risks, at least, in trying to have both at once: widespread illiteracy among the underprivileged would make even the fairest, free-est elections "anti-democratic" in a deeper sense, and in places like Cuba, at least (and Iran), it is no vulgar Marxist misnomer to call the existing judiciary and organs of opinion "class tools". Which isn't to deny that Castro sometimes goes too far...".

The idea of transcending liberalism or escaping from it, even temporarily, made me nervous. While more or less accepting this as a likely future, I tended not to dwell on what specifically it might mean. In fact I couldn't imagine it. As well, being more and more engaged with Soviet history and experience, I was clearly more anti-Soviet than most of my friends and was not opposed to the idea that the Cold War had been forced upon the United States and that Stalin represented a great danger to civilized life. These beliefs were unquestioned at the Russian Research Center and I accepted them wholeheartedly, if uneasily. I certainly never regarded the Cold War as a smokescreen to justify and conceal American imperialism. But I was not eager to draw attention to this sort of difference with my friends. In many left circles of the day it was okay not to be pro-Soviet, but to admit to being anti-Soviet was to move quite far to the right. So I remained rather discreetly anti-Soviet. For a long time the differences with my friends remained mostly implicit. In retrospect I came to realize how guilty I felt about being so anti-Soviet.

We were also fifties people in the way we accepted (moderately) radical politics and the artistic avant-garde as natural bedfellows, as well as assuming an important connection between political and artistic integrity. But both artistic and political integrity would become steadily, even agonizingly, more complex as the sixties wore on. I think we also shared a general perception that may have been as much a piece of Harvard arrogance as a generational marker. Graduating from Harvard around 1960, it seemed to me and many of my contemporaries that smart people were going to run the world over the next generation or more, and those smart people were largely academic: scientists, social scientists (the word was just becoming fashionable), even people in the humanities. I assumed that they would be on the Left. The experience of the Kennedy administration should have begun to temper this absurd optimism, but it didn't, much.

After the lurch to the left during the sixties, the world has resolutely moved the other way for more than thirty years. I have often thought that the Saint-Simonian socialists in the 1830s might have drawn similar conclusions about the role of science and socialism and the forging of a new elite, which were also vanquished by the march of time. Part of my view of the future direction of the world was no doubt merely a characteristic generational historical consciousness: young people often see the world of the future as getting more and more like it already is. It is hard for them to imagine a decisive political or cultural turn in another direction. I can remember Allen Graubard laughing loudly at the mere idea of a right-wing youth organization. It seems to me, in 2009, that we were expecting Barack Obama's presidency—but we were almost half a century early. We had no idea of what the country was going to have to go through before he could get here.

Civil rights was an issue that at least initially did not force a breach between liberalism and radicalism. But with the coming of black power of course it did, and so did the development of the Viet Nam War. I was still at Tougaloo when the Gulf of Tonkin episode took place. I remember watching on a small black and white television set as small and larger boats maneuvered for some advantage that I couldn't grasp. I sensed that something momentous was happening, but I failed to grasp just how momentous it would prove to be. The escalation in Viet Nam would shake my somewhat jerry-built world to its foundations.

When I returned from Helsinki I involved myself in wedding preparations and in writing my dissertation, which took me almost exactly three years. On the dissertation front, I was anxious about Richard Pipes' reaction to my topic. As he was Harvard's historian of modern Russia there was no question of anyone else directing my dissertation. Pipes seemed not personally hostile to Andrzej Walicki, but I had heard him make remarks critical of sociology, which he seemed to feel was a completely different enterprise from history, whereas I thought of the disciplines as near neighbors. However, he accepted my topic without demur. I thought he was hardly aware of who I was, beyond another member of the large squad of graduate students he then had working with him. But in the aftermath of my choice of dissertation topic, he gave me a copy of the two-volume set of Ivan Kireevsky's works dating from 1911. It was a beautiful volume. The books were hard to come by and I was overjoyed to have them. But despite the generosity of the gift, our relations remained formal and rather remote. One of his talented women graduate students would occasionally breast feed her baby in front of him, apparently quite unself-consciously. This appeared to draw favorable attention, but was not in my repertoire.

As the anti-war movement began to pick up steam after 1965, I felt more and more ambivalent. I had no doubt that the war was a mistake but I was unable to believe what seemed to me the fringier theories that were gaining wider and wider circulation. I could not accept that the substructure of American capitalism made an increasingly voracious American imperialism inevitable. As I watched the American working class become more and more nationalist and supportive of the war, however, the idea of even a potential radicalism of the American proletariat became less and less plausible. If you clung to a Marxist orientation, you had to resort to more and more complex theories of mystification to explain why proletarian thinking was moving so resolutely in the wrong direction. False consciousness seemed more powerful every day. More plausible than any sort of traditional Marxism, but still not entirely convincing to me, was Herbert Marcuse's idea that consumer capitalism deprived Americans of the ability to envisage alternatives to the status quo. This formed the crux of the left-wing version of totalitarian theory associated primarily with the Frankfurt School that I would later write about. The end result was that I began to feel increasingly out of sympathy with the steady shift to the left among my contemporaries and those slightly younger. I later wrote an op-ed piece entitled "Next Time Let's Not Spell America with a K," but was never satisfied enough with it to try and publish it.

Furthermore, the demonization of Washington that took place in academia seemed wrong to me, occasionally preposterous. I had grown up there. I knew, I thought, that these people were not fatally corrupted in some mysterious way simply because they worked for the government. Nor were they "evil", nor particularly cynical, nor different in any fundamental way from academics. The wrongness about the war that dominated official Washington seemed to have much more to do with a mis-application of the "containment" paradigm by the Washington establishment, and with the arrogance of power that Senator Fulbright spoke of, than with capitalist structures or the pressure of purely economic interests. On the other hand, American "national interest" seemed parochial and willfully misguided at best, and thousands of Asian peasants were dying because of it. Surely the U.S. could live with a communist North Vietnam. Surely Vietnam was not really a domino. And yet I knew how pleased the Soviet Union was with what they called "the correlation of forces". Although sometimes expressed in philosophically arcane Marxist terms, this abstraction merely meant that the world was going their way. But sometimes my viewpoint would crumble.

Maybe the Sovs were right. Maybe I was a part of the rotten system, rather than a sophisticated, realist critic. I was often at sea.

On the other hand, neither my father nor, after my marriage, my father-in-law was sympathetic to my political attitudes, relatively moderate though they may have been. My own father was vociferously horrified by the political radicalism he read about in *The Washington Post*, although of course he didn't actually see much of it living in Georgetown and working at the State Department. Our political quarrels grew steadily worse in 1966 and 1967. Family visits to Washington became more and more strained, with my mother's health declining and my father more and more irritable and—it seemed to me—politically obsessed. Dinner table arguments about Viet Nam were constant. Both of us ended the meals angry. My father was sometimes in such a rage that he had to leave the table in the middle of dinner. He persisted in defining what divided us politically as my willful failure to understand how dreadful communism was. He simply had no interest in my criticisms of American foreign policy. Our inability to agree even on what we were arguing about drove us both crazy.

He wasn't sure that I wasn't under some kind of communist influence. He was angrily certain that my radical, left-wing friends were responsible for my anti-Americanism. He told this to an acquaintance who taught at the Harvard Law School, who availed himself of his connection with Ben and Felicia Kaplan to invite himself over to meet me. He and his wife spent two uncomfortable hours with me in the Kaplans' living room, trying to find out, with no great subtlety, about my politically extreme friends and opinions. I was temporarily mystified, then when my father confessed, furious. Felicia Kaplan just laughed at the idea that I was any sort of real radical. The term "Establishment" had by this time been taken over from the British and lightly adapted to fit America's more mobile society. Gradually I came to realize that my father felt he had earned an honorable place in it, through his Harvard, Episcopalian and Washington connections, and he was angry and upset to find his son appearing to turn his back on the assured place in the middle echelons of that "Establishment" that had been bequeathed to him. Ironically, the very issues we were concerned with—social mobility and above all, the Viet Nam War—would fragment that socio-political world beyond repair.[3]

Only later did I realize how disappointed my father was with the winding down of his own career. He had failed to achieve a return to the intelligence community after his interlude in London. Allen Dulles had not even bothered to answer his letters. On balance he had not enjoyed his editing job at the State Department Historical Office, although he had done it well enough. My mother had had a series of small strokes and was by now not well enough to travel, except for short distances to destinations where good care could be relied on. As the end of his life loomed, my father also felt religious doubts. He felt abandoned by God, as well as by the Harvard History Department and the Central Intelligence Agency, institutions on which he had lavished his devotion. What a troika! His wonderful wife was receding further and further into illness, his daughter into serious medical problems of her own, and his son—and the world at large—were being swallowed up by an incomprehensible radicalism. Whatever his suppressed doubts about American institutions he rallied to their defense. Despite his son's academic specialty, the young man clearly didn't understand how dangerous communism was—but weren't academics like that? Their knowledge of the world was untested by experience and therefore worse than worthless, because of their pretensions. And thus my father slid into his own version of Fathers and Sons. And in his frustration and misery, a man who had never uttered a racist word to me said things I never expected to hear on his lips: "Why are all your friends Jews?" he asked angrily. Twenty-four hours later he would

[3] For one take on this process, see Geoffrey Kabaservice, *The Guardians. Kingman Brewster, his Circle and the Rise of the Liberal Establishment*, New York, Henry Holt, 2004.

be saying quietly that he couldn't understand why God had failed to send him grace or adequate faith, despite a lifetime of faithful religious observance. But we were both so caught up in the struggles of the time that it was only gradually that I realized the depth of his personal crisis.

I never had anything like these awful screaming arguments with my new father-in-law, John Fischer, but there were parallels. Although more liberal than my father, he too was a defender of the Viet Nam War, at least in public, and my criticisms of Johnson, MacNamara and the Bundy brothers made him quietly angry. He had been a speechwriter for Adlai Stevenson and looked up to the Democratic Party establishment in Washington in a way not unlike my own father's attitude toward the intelligence community. Some of his annoyance, at least, at his difficult son-in-law was understandable. Passionately anti-war, although in a non-Marxist way, I must have been in his face a good deal—and he couldn't get rid of me, because I had married his daughter!

Fischer was from Oklahoma and thought of himself as a southerner as well as a westerner. He was a very private person. On one occasion I told my in-laws that, as an admirer of the writer Eudora Welty, I had written her a letter, asking her to meet with our group when we were in Mississippi a couple of years earlier, and she had not replied. Doubtless some indignation crept into my voice as I related this. Fischer, who knew Welty, didn't say too much, but every bit of his body language indicated a deep sympathy for her failure to write.[4]

I felt quite unappreciated in the Fischer household. Some part of this was because of my own insecurities. Reading back over the

[4] The distinguished critic, novelist and teacher Monroe Engel also wrote her before coming to Mississippi. Welty did write him, remarking that she would very much like to talk with him but that "she couldn't talk to him in her parents' house." When Monroe met her in Cambridge some years later and introduced her at a Harvard lecture, neither made reference to their failure to connect in the summer of 1964. I quote from Engel's email of June 30, 2008.

accumulated correspondence of that period, I failed to espy in John Fischer's letters most of the critical and judgmental attitudes that I remembered. Perhaps he just didn't make them in print. Perhaps I exaggerated them; young people are often so easily offended. I was hard on my father-in-law as well as my father. In one of his stories about his own family John Updike observes how easy it is to appreciate people afterwards. The hard trick is to love them when they're right there, in front of you.

Anyway, like a lot of other anti-war but fundamentally moderate liberals I felt very squeezed. I was not ready to sever ties with American society in any general way, a step symbolized for me by draft card burning, something which I brooded about doing. Why didn't I do it? Why was I such a coward, I asked myself? At the same time I couldn't defend what the American government was doing. I had a student deferment. After I finished my dissertation I would lose it. Would I be drafted? If I were, would I serve or go to jail or Canada? I didn't know, but I felt that terrifying choices lay just ahead in my life. I was so uncertain that I didn't know what to say to Sarah, so I didn't say anything, which, in time, she understandably resented. It looked like a typical case of male chauvinist failure to consult. I began to be haunted by the idea that the decision to join the civil rights movement had been easy—too easy. We might never get such a softball again. American public opinion had been primarily supportive of voting rights and public accommodations issues in the South, however passive or unreconstructedly racist in its own, regional ways. You risked your life in Alabama or Mississippi, but of course you could always leave the region if you were no more than a well-intentioned visitor, like me. But on the question of opposition to the war, the choices were steadily getting more drastic. The U.S. needed major reform. How was that to be achieved by an increasingly polarized country? But how could polarization be avoided? Ultimately I came to think that my moderation was a potent source of isolation. I never experienced more than the most modest body warmth from the sixties, yet I felt unable for many years to be at home in my former life, or to feel its continuities. My Victorian boyhood had receded, temporarily as it turned out, into the distant past.

On January 19, 1968, our son was born: Nicholas Abbott Gleason. We drove to the hospital in the small hours of the morning. Sarah and I had gone through a series of drills known as the "Lamaze method" in which I participated in Sarah's preparation for the baby's birth by doing breathing exercises and panting. The presumption of the instructor would be that the father should be present at the birth of the child, but as it turned out the Boston Lying-In-Hospital did not allow it.

At the time of Nick's birth we were house-sitting for the Kaplans, and as soon as we brought him home from the hospital on a cold, late January day, the furnace failed. We kept him warm at night by turning on the electric oven and placing his basket near its warm mouth.

Tom and Nicholas Abbott Gleason, 1970
Photo by Sarah Gleason

Carrie Tower, Brown University, Providence, Rhode Island

Brown University

I WROTE MY DISSERTATION MOSTLY AT NIGHT, beginning often with a visit to Harvard's extraordinary Widener Library early in the evening, followed by four or five hours of intermittent scribbling. Days were largely given over to teaching, more general reading on political romanticism, nineteenth-century sociology, and—after Nick was born—child care. Sarah bore the brunt of the burden, however, along with her nursery school teaching. My consciousness had not yet been raised about the "politics of housework." In actual fact, the pamphlet of that name was the first piece of feminist literature I vividly remember reading, sometime around 1970. It had an immediate impact on my thinking, being so simple and jargon-free. Our domestic arrangements just weren't fair. But that came later. I managed to get my thesis done and turned into a book before my first major attack of conscience. Some women would surely say that men manage these things well.

My major distraction was spy literature and thrillers, which sometimes punched a big hole in my evenings. This kind of fiction provided a special psychological antidote for me to the day-in, day-out grind of writing a book. I finished the Eric Ambler and Graham Greene novels that I had not yet read and devoured the John Le Carré tales as soon as each one of them came out. I enjoyed being storm-tossed in the sea of German and Russian romanticism, slightly remote as it was, but there was a real-life excitement in the history of the Cold War that I longed for. In addition, as sixties radicals came increasingly to see the Cold War as a smokescreen for domestic conservatism or foreign imperialism, I became more and more interested in the twentieth century, Stalinism and the Cold War, in whose midst I had very self-consciously grown up. I continued to have difficulty squaring my memories with the Washington of the New Left. However plausible I then thought some of their criticisms of American foreign policy might be, most New Left people clearly had no concrete idea at all what Washington was like. I thought I did. Thrillers and spy literature were a bridge, of a kind, between these clashing contexts. Graham Greene's dark fictions of the forties and fifties connected English leftism of the thirties with the present, but Eric Ambler's chilling stories about the communization of Eastern Europe in the late forties reminded me reassuringly that it wasn't merely American cold warriors who hated and feared Stalinism.

The dissertation chapters slowly increased in number and, with great effort, intricacy. Toward the end, I began to develop some momentum and came to feel that I was riding a wave, if a small one. I tried to fuse the systematic sociologism of Walicki with the psychological acuteness and intellectual vivacity of Malia, and hoped to use biographical accident and incident to inform a narrative that I struggled to keep fresh, personal and as full of story as possible. I tried to squeeze every ounce of biographical material out of the sources I had, to root generalizations about my rather melancholic Slavophile subject in the tissue of Russian romantic society and its literary culture. By the spring of 1968, it was essentially done.

In the end I was a little disappointed. It wasn't as big a book, didn't send its tentacles as far out into the streams of Russian cultural history, didn't illuminate as broad a swathe of its cultural surroundings as I had hoped it would. I had discovered what many another journeyman has learned: that it is easier to write a decent monograph than to illuminate an era. I didn't feel my book had the electricity of Malia's *Herzen*, its range, or its masterful aura. And I had gradually come to feel that the history of religious thinkers

Sarah and Tom Gleason with Nick, 1968

in the nineteenth century was a bit removed from the fascination and terror of contemporary American-Soviet relations. My readers, Pipes, Edward L. (Ned) Keenan and Barrington Moore, Jr., accepted it, but with few comments—the Harvard way—leaving me at sea about how good it actually was. It was at least good enough to be published, three years later, as *European and Muscovite* in the Russian Research Center monograph series at Harvard University Press.

A lot of time has passed since then. The Russian radicals, on whom everyone was then focusing, have receded again, as has the Russian revolutionary movement, now known almost entirely for its demonic side.[1] The Slavophiles remain, however, as an early and very important stage in the evolution of the currently hot subject of "Russian identity" My choice of dissertation topic has looked better and better to me as the years have passed. In the post-Soviet world it has finally had some appreciative Russian readers, who have visited me from time to time.

Meanwhile, a young man's thoughts turned to employment. Those were halcyon days for academic jobs—1967-68 was almost the last of the really good years. There were plenty of excellent jobs out there in both European and American history. An acquaintance of mine in the Harvard career placement office actually asked me to come in and pretend to interview with a campus recruiter. He came to Harvard dangling before graduate students various jobs at the University of Wisconsin campuses other than Madison, the one where everyone would have been eager to go. She was afraid that nobody would show up to interview for other Wisconsin state university jobs and she thought the interviewer was a nice guy whose feelings ought not to be hurt! I went and chewed the fat with him for forty-five minutes. Nobody else was there. Nowadays there would have been any number of candidates for such openings. The University of Wisconsin at Milwaukee. Wow!

I was still thinking of jazz, and living in New Orleans continued to be an enticing fantasy. I wrote letters to Tulane and to Louisiana State University's New Orleans campus, asking if they had a job for me, but not surprisingly, I never received a reply since neither had advertised a position in Russian history. I imagined myself dividing my professional life into thirds; one third devoted to Dostoevsky and the Slavophiles, another third to Stalin and Soviet tyranny, and

[1] Perhaps the Tom Stoppard trilogy of plays, collectively called *The Coast of Utopia*, will revive some of that earlier magic.

a final third to Preservation Hall and the Eureka Brass Band, one of the last of the New Orleans street bands with which I hoped to be a regular marcher. We would live in the French Quarter, and I would write on New Orleans jazz as well as Russian history. I continued to add books to my collection of studies of jazz musicians and black music generally.

Brown was among several schools interested in me and they ultimately came through with what seemed a handsome offer in those days: something on the order of $9,000 a year for salary, plus benefits. And the possibility of tenure. "Job talks"—demonstration lectures in which the novice showed what he or she was made of before an audience of local faculty and graduate students—were not *de rigeur* in those days. That was probably lucky for me, given my primitive lecturing technique, in which I lurched inexpertly between literature and pedantry, stand-up comedy and hysteria. All my lectures exceeded the speed limit by plenty. Fortunately, I merely came down to Providence and had lunch with the chairman of the History Department, Donald Rohr, and the editor of the journal *Daedalus*, Stephen Graubard. They had in hand only a letter from Richard Pipes, I believe, but in those high and far off times, a single letter from a well known male professor could get someone a job. There was nothing resembling affirmative action pressure on behalf of women or minorities. All that would change quite quickly over the next decade. I got the job and turned down an offer of an instructorship from Harvard, which essentially entailed taking discussion sections in Pipes' lecture courses. "You get out of Cambridge!" said my father severely. He whose heart was still there. And I did, to my everlasting benefit. I realized only later and gradually how much I profited from having my own shop for the first six or seven years of my career, and at a first-rate university.

Providence was a place that I recalled from the earliest days of my childhood, as it was only thirty-five miles from Spring Farm. If my father or uncle or other family members were taking the train to Washington during World War II, they left from Providence rather than Boston. So I carried an old but deeply engraved 1945 memory of the platforms of its railroad station at 7:00 PM of a summer evening, with coaches and sleepers and steam locomotives puffing South, usually carrying my father, while my mother sniffled on the platform. And then the drive back to the farm in the gathering darkness.

Except for the arrival of the Interstate Highway System, nothing much seemed to have changed when we arrived in August of 1968. Old memories did well up: of traffic jams in Kennedy Plaza, for instance, on U.S. 44, which was the most direct route between Cape Cod and the farm in the days before the interstate system. When we passed through town, usually in August, it was always hot, and the traffic was bumper-to-bumper, with radiators boiling over all around us in a gigantic oval of traffic in the heart of downtown Providence. There was no such thing as automobile air conditioning in those days. Perhaps my un-thought-out attitude could be summed up by saying that Providence was not a place where you went voluntarily, but, sometimes passing through couldn't be avoided.

On the other hand, we had friends who knew people at Brown and the Rhode Island School of Design (RISD) and had good things to say about resident artists and jazz clubs in Providence, not to mention the architecture. There was a club called Pio's, reputedly a mob spot, but all sorts of major musicians had played there. The Celebrity Club, one of the first thoroughly integrated jazz joints in New England, had shut its doors, but Bovi's Tavern in East Providence had a big band every Monday night. Boston was an hour away, New York not much more than three. Cape Cod and the islands were as near Providence as Boston.

In some ways, Providence reminded me of Boston and Cambridge a generation or more earlier, especially the College Hill area around Brown and RISD. The housing stock was similar; so were the old wrought iron fences and the big slabs of slate set into the old brick sidewalks. The older parts of the East Side resembled Beacon

Hill. Everything was smaller and less grand and more run down, although far from the moldering gothic of H.P. Lovecraft's stories about Providence, which had thrilled and scared me in my early teens. Wonderful old mills surrounded the downtown and ran right up against the small suburban edges of Providence and Pawtucket. So I had an open mind as we sat in a spacious rented apartment with our variously assorted pieces of furniture in a pile in the middle of the room. It was a steamy August day and my academic career was about to begin in earnest. There was a lot of exploring to be done on a number of fronts.

We soon discovered that Providence had already moved a considerable distance from the depths of its post-industrial doldrums. The beautiful eighteenth- and early nineteenth-century houses on Benefit Street had been mostly renovated, thanks to the efforts of visionary restorationists like the architectural historian and *grande dame*, Antoinette Downing, and the founding members of the Providence Preservation Society. PPS had been in existence for only twelve years when we came to Providence in 1968, but much had already been done. There was a stirring in the air, a sense that the precious housing stock which we saw all around us would be saved and restored sooner or later. I rejoiced to see these old buildings, which looked (and smelled) like the old farmhouse in which I used to spend summers. Eventually we bought one of them.

Wonderful old things continued to vanish, however. During my first few weeks at Brown, when I knew nobody, I used to walk most days at lunchtime from my office down College Hill and, crossing the Providence River (then covered over by what the *Guinness Book of World Records* said was the largest bridge in the world—not lengthwise, but in terms of area) I would gawk my way down Weybosset Street. There I would have lunch at the almost deserted lunch counter of the Weybosset Market, an old food emporium, pre-super market, but larger than a mom and pop store. There was sawdust on the floor; ancient fans whirred overhead; a butcher in his white coat cut up meat for his infrequent customers. This, my favorite lunch spot, was demolished around 1970, as stores of all kinds continued to desert the old downtown for shopping centers and suburban malls.

A different fate was reserved for Dana's, a wonderful second-hand bookstore run by a most elderly couple. I believe Mr. Dana was a descendant of Richard Henry Dana, author of *Two Years Before the Mast*. Dana's was in the basement of the Wilcox Building, where there was a serious fire in the early 1970s. The bookstore was technically saved, but the water damage was so extensive that Mrs. Dana was forced to dispose of her water-logged stock and go out of business. Dana's had wonderful nineteenth-century children's books. I managed to find a first edition of *Siberia and the Exile System* (1891) by one of America's first Russian experts, George Kennan, great-uncle of the distinguished diplomat for whom I would work a decade later. The book only cost me $10.00 and I had the pleasure of presenting it to the Kennan Institute in Washington D.C. years later, to replace their copy, which oddly enough had been damaged by water.

Virtually the first person we met in Providence and certainly our first friend was a beautiful and loquacious graduate student in German history named Margaret Lavinia Anderson. We were sitting in the living room of our first apartment with our small store of furniture and our many boxes of books piled in the center of the room when she swept in, clad in a trench coat, and, sitting on a kitchen stool, regaled us with local lore for an hour. She had a radiant smile, a slight lisp and congenial political opinions. She had come to Brown to work with the great German historian, Klaus Epstein. The latter, however, had been killed in a traffic accident in Germany the previous June and been replaced by my colleague-to-be, Norman Rich. Peggy, as she was called, was our initial guide to all things at Brown. I still had the psychology of a graduate student, and felt more at home among them than with faculty. A strong liberal, a strong Christian and a committed philosemite, Peggy eventually found happiness in a marriage with another distinguished

German historian at Stanford, James Sheehan. From Brown she took her Ph.D. to Swarthmore and then on to Berkeley. She was and is the most dedicated teacher of undergraduates I ever knew and probably the kindest person.

The small Brown History Department was on the move, although it gathered itself slowly. One professor I knew of was an old antagonist of my father named Carl Bridenbaugh. He was a well known scholar of colonial America and a famous curmudgeon, who didn't like Jews or liberals and demanded a great deal of deference from all and sundry. He was reputed not to admit Jews to his graduate seminar, on the theory that if your forebears had not been part of early American history you didn't have the right qualifications to study it.[2] Unless, of course, your ancestors had been members of one of the very early Jewish congregations, such as the one in Newport, R.I., whose Touro Synagogue was world famous. When he dined out, if there was silver cutlery on the table, he would shamelessly check to see if it had markings.

I soon experienced his famous bad temper. Not long after my arrival, I was talking to another new colleague and mentioned that the great Harvard historian of all things American and naval, Samuel Eliot Morrison, had changed his mind, according to the *MacNeil/Lehrer NewsHour*, and come out against the Viet Nam War. I made the mistake of referring to him as "Sam Morrison." Bridenbaugh, who was passing by, interrupted furiously. "What right do you have to call him 'Sam'?" he barked. I was quite taken aback. I replied (thinking quickly, I thought) that I meant no disrespect, any more than I would if I had referred to President Kennedy as "Jack

[2] Bridenbaugh had been the President of the American Historical Association in 1962, and in his presidential address he had made disparaging mention of the "many of the younger practitioners of our craft" who are "products of lower-middle class or foreign origins." These snobbish remarks were almost universally interpreted as anti-Semitic. See "The Great Mutation," *American Historical Review*, Vol. 68, No. 2 (January, 1963), pp. 315-331. The most pointed remarks are on p. 328.

Kennedy". I then made the mistake of adding that I had known Morrison through my parents. Bridenbaugh was livid. "Well, you leave that 'Sam' business to your parents," he shouted and stormed off. Several colleagues subsequently stopped by my office, which was in a broom closet on the second floor of Prospect House, and told me not to give Bridenbaugh's rudeness a thought. "We've all felt the lash at one time or another," said Bryce Lyon, a medieval historian and one of the luminaries of the department.

His colleague, Donald Rohr, was the chair who hired me. Rohr published a small monograph on German liberalism, but scarcely anything else. All his energy, and it was considerable, went into his European history survey, from the early middle ages to almost the present, which was one of the most popular courses at Brown, and deservedly so. Rohr kept up with European historiography, but always with half an eye on what might be assigned in his lecture course. He read an enormous amount and rarely assigned the same books twice in either History 1 or History 2. The course was redone virtually from stem to stern every year and his lectures were always changing.

Many students told me that Donald Rohr was their ideal of a mysterious being called the archetypal Ivy League Professor. I don't believe that in my time there was any such thing, but clearly Rohr projected a mix of urbanity, erudition, self-confidence and humor that many undergraduate students who admired their faculty liked to believe was characteristic of the exalted educational world in which they now found themselves. His humor could be delightful. When students at some point in the mid-1970s complained about the faculty-student ratio at Brown, Rohr went to the Guinness Book of World Records and discovered what the most extreme faculty-student ratios in the world were—one faculty member to every 25,000 students—as I recall, in a non-American university that shall be nameless. No one made direct comparisons, but Brown's problems assumed a less dire aspect.

I could detect little difference between the students I had taught at Harvard and those I encountered at Brown, although of course I was looking for differences. At the end of my first few years, however, I became aware that there seemed to be fewer self-conscious eccentrics at Brown than at Harvard, and perhaps less overall flamboyance among students. And Brown was distinctly less snooty than Harvard. There was much less of the pervasive belief that everybody on the faculty except a few old has-beens was a genius. And it was a smaller world than Harvard: a large village, not Gotham. But when the student radicalism of the sixties engulfed both institutions, distinctions were even harder to make.

That first year at Brown I spent almost every afternoon and night writing lectures, since I only had about three weeks between finishing my dissertation and the start of the fall semester at Brown, and a good deal of that period was taken up with the move and establishing ourselves in our rented apartment. At least five nights a week and sometimes six, I was back in my office by eight or eight-thirty in the evening and would generally work on my lectures until I went to sleep some time after midnight, usually still sitting at my desk.

I was mightily helped by a wonderful jazz radio show, presided over by a local leprechaun named Fred Grady, whom I later met a number of times. Fred had the standard relaxed, hip jazz announcer voice of the period, and listening to his show made me feel more at home than anything else in my first year or two in Providence. It began at eight or nine in the evening on an AM station, WXTR, when Fred signed on with a Count Basie recording of "Satin Doll." After working for hours and finally falling asleep at my desk, I would generally wake up around 4 AM, to hear him sign off with another Basie rendering of the late night ballad, "Li'l Darlin'", in a wonderful arrangement by Neal Hefti. Night after night, Fred's music and his relaxed chatter kept me going. Later he lost his show on WXTR, but re-surfaced on a smaller station across the Massachusetts line in Taunton, which fortunately my radio would pick up. So for some five years Fred helped me most week-day nights with my lectures.

Sometimes I would call him up during his show and we would talk. We also met at a small and seedy jazz record store called Carl's Diggings on North Main Street, another Providence institution for jazz lovers where I would go every week or two to check out new discs. Fred had a heavy hand on the bottle, as Sydney Parker used to say, and did not live to a ripe old age, but at his death he left his fabulous record collection to Brown's radio station, WBRU, and I mourned his passing.

My first lectures were somewhat traumatic. As I prepared frantically, I was haunted by a hypothetical undergraduate critic, the product of my lunatic anxiety. He was well informed, well dressed in some modish, historical English sartorial style and he knew an enormous amount of Russian history. I imagined him asking all sorts of penetrating questions, focusing relentlessly and condescendingly on omissions and flaws in my lectures. "Well, Professor Gleason, if you know so much about Metropolitan Hilarion's *Sermon on Law and Grace*, what about the connection with Byzantine allegorical exegesis, and also while we're on the subject...?" Having discovered this arcane weakness in my own lecture, I would rush off to the library and attempt to plug the hole. In the event, my tormentor proved to be entirely imaginary and the questions I actually received from students were mostly quite manageable. The very first one was from a student whose room had a hole in the plaster wall, and he wondered where he could get a map the size of the one I was using in class, which would nicely cover it up. My terrors gradually dissipated.

Actually, I was inadvertently the cause of some embarrassment to one of my students in that first year. There was a historical rumor, which appears to have been started at the time of the death of Catherine the Great, that she died having sexual intercourse with a horse. It seems to have been started by her Polish enemies. As far as I know, the tale did not appear in print until far into the twentieth century, but, instead, had been passed on by word of mouth for generations. But I had never heard it. So when a student asked his apparently uninhibited young professor whether it was true "about Catherine and the horse," I was mystified. I asked him to explain. He was unwilling to do so. But I made him, and the merriment was general, partly at my expense, and partly at his.

I soon discovered that the Brown History Department was torn between European and American factions, which also corresponded roughly to a political split, the Americanists on the left, the Europeanists on the right, including in their number Carl Bridenbaugh as a kind of renegade from his lefty Americanist colleagues, Jack Thomas and Bill McLoughlin. But the new appointments, who came about my time refused to take part in the ongoing civil war. There were Europeanists—Anthony Molho (Renaissance Italy), David Underdown (early modern England), Norman Rich (modern Europe, especially Germany), and Burr Litchfield (early modern continental Europe)—and Americanists Gordon Wood (Colonial) and Howard Chudacoff (the urbanist). None of us joined the combatants. Political divisions continued to simmer in the department, but the European-American war came to an end because there was only the old guard left to fight. Officers with no enlisted men—a Gilbert and Sullivan situation.

Some fifteen years older than I, Underdown became a particular friend. We had lunch together two or three times a week for better than fifteen years before he moved to Yale. To an eavesdropper, his companionship might have seemed a blend of anecdote (often cricket-related), historiography, European and occasionally world politics, the craft and methodology of the historian, and reminiscence. These elements were seldom truly separable but ran together in a complex design which made sense at the time but could never be perfectly recalled afterwards. Like other representatives of the moderate English Left of the early and mid-twentieth century, Underdown was a highly—although never ostentatiously—ethical person, driven above all by an ideal of fairness. I used to fantasize that having regular lunches with W.H. Tawney must be very like this. I also connected Underdown with my almost cultish devotion to Orwell. When he left Brown for Yale, I very much felt I was losing a big brother (not, of course, in the Orwellian sense). Perhaps that helped me out of my long, lingering adolescence. In his casual, indirect, understated way, Underdown was a force in my upbringing, and I will always be grateful to him for that. After he left, his office across the hall from me was taken by the German historian Volker Berghahn, whom I also found particularly simpatico in departmental affairs and in general. All three of us were among the notable "softs" in the department supporting – often reflexively—more egalitarian styles and behavior. We were usually the last to give up on students and wash them out of the program. Gordon Wood, by contrast, was always trying to raise our standards—which very often meant washing more graduate students out of the program—and sooner. Of course he had a career of great distinction, something reflected in the use of his name as a symbol of erudition in Ben Affleck's and Matt Damon's *Good Will Hunting*. Late in his career, political conservatives—notably Newt Gingrich—praised his work vociferously and even sought him out at our History Department. Wood is a person of deep and genuine good nature, however, and rarely if ever held our political disagreements against me.

But my principal intellectual interlocutor, the man whose intellectual interests were closest to mine, was another American historian, John Thomas, known as Jack. He also had a deep interest in the relationship between intellectuals and larger publics. His wonderful wife, Patty, was a fine watercolorist and art historian who taught at Simmons College in Boston and the Rhode Island School of Design. Jack and I were members of the same fifties generation, but we inhabited different parts of it. Jack was an early fifties guy, coming of age right at the end of the Second World War, liking swing rather than bebop, pre-Pollack and De Kooning, already becoming political in the late forties, ten years before me. I was on the cusp between the fifties and the sixties, a mess of inharmonious radical and conservative impulses, but inspired by the civil rights movement and anti-war sentiment. Both of us were critical of the buttoned-up fifties, but formed by the era nevertheless, Jack at the beginning and me at the end.

Jack and I used to argue about whether there was actually a generational entity that could be called "the forties" that Jack might belong to. Was some notion of "the forties" a useful historical periodization? Did World War II create a generation in the U.S., something with its own contours? Or was it just a massive world event? Those historians and journalists who have written about "the greatest generation" have made a good case, but Jack didn't buy it. After a few drinks he once told me that Bugs Bunny was the most plausible representative of the no-man's land between the thirties and fifties. Bugs had lost the radical spirit of the thirties but was not yet part of the tranquilized fifties. He was excitable and implicitly anarchist but had no ideological direction. His carrot-eating was ultimately apolitical.

But Jack was more than a thirties lefty coming of age a little bit late. He showed little trace of Marxism in his thinking. With his populist outlook and his belief in what he called "the commons," Jack was by instinct as well as through the reach of his scholarship a utopian socialist, like the men he studied and wrote about so wonderfully well. He believed in an "Alternative America," the title of one of his best books. Jack's intellectual generosity with colleagues, and especially with students, provided a kind of bridge between his underlying socialist impulses and the intellectual world we inhabited on a daily basis. He recognized no private property in ideas. They formed a kind of "commons" too, where everybody could graze their animals, or, to put it more concretely, take what they could use from the common store. Their only obligation was to use creatively what they took and to introduce their students, in turn, to "the commons."

Jack was a curmudgeon, and even his closest friends felt the sting of his anger from time to time. He knew he had a temper and tacked a figure of a bomb with a lit fuse, dressed as a man, to his office door, as if to warn visitors that he could go off at any time.

Jack was a formidable fighter, but he was a big man, and humble enough to learn from others. He was also a secular man, in every way, perhaps, but one. He believed in giving and gave things away to his students in a way which any serious Christian would instantly recognize and with which she would identify. Jack may have been at his very best when he had your text on his lap and was suggesting what you might do to improve it. In those moments we were all his students and very grateful to be.

Even before we arrived in Providence, Rhode Island had become a more attractive destination for us. That was because John Casey, my old buddy from St. Albans and Harvard, was marrying a native of the state and they were buying an island in Narragansett Bay. His wife-to-be was Jane Barnes, whom my sister and I had known in Washington back in the fifties. Janie was an enthusiast about literature, tennis, friendship and life in general, and quickly became a close friend, along with John. She was a loving rebel against her parents and the rather traditional social life they lived, both in Rhode Island and in D.C., where her father, Tracy, was one of the key early operatives of the Central Intelligence Agency. After the Barnes family moved from Providence to Washington, their beautiful house on George Street was bought and torn down by Brown to build the dormitory and fraternity complex that was christened the "Wriston Quad" after President Henry Wriston.

The island John and Jane bought was called Fox Island, a small dot in Narragansett Bay, within sight of the Jamestown Bridge. The Caseys commuted from nearby Wickford in a slightly battered Boston whaler. Tracy Barnes was by this time gone from the CIA and he and his wife lived in a beautiful renovated barn, more or less directly across the water from Fox Island. There was much traffic back and forth, and the Caseys often entertained in Jane's parents place, known always as "the Barn." It was an ample, comfortable building, held together by the old beams, full of paintings, old and new, and Washington memorabilia. I was particularly struck by the pictures by the famous Portuguese-American artist, Vieira da

Silva. The senior Barnes knew many foreign service officers who had served in Moscow, so I had the pleasure of re-meeting Charles Bohlen and his wife, a year or so before Bohlen's death. Bohlen was a classmate of my father at Harvard, and like him a heavy smoker. Both men died of cancer in 1974. Bohlen was a charming and vivid raconteur; but like my father he found writing difficult, and there was some joking about having to lock him in his house to get him to write his memoirs. I had known his daughter Avis at Harvard where she was also a student of Jim Billington. At the Barn, we also met Llewellyn "Tommy" Thompson and his lively and charming wife. For me, visiting the Barn was like being transported back to an easier-going version of my parents' house in Washington, where the Cold War was always on the front burner.

There were many great parties, both on Fox Island and at the Barn, some of them involving Duncan and Mopsy Kennedy, special friends of the Caseys, with whom wonderful, swirling arguments took us far into the night. An occasional visitor was John's friend Bill Keough, a Harvard-educated writer and author of a wonderful book about violence in American literary humor. Keough, the son of a Boston cop, was a *raconteur extraordinaire*, especially about Irish subjects. In his youth he had the hands of a surgeon, too. I remember once at the end of a long evening of revelry, Keough and I performed a heart transplant on a peach. As I recall the evening, which ended in a haze, the operation was successful but the patient was eaten by the doctors. Neither of us, to my knowledge, ever operated again. On a later evening at our house he was talking about a singles bar he had been to after his first divorce. The name of it was Raffles—only Bill called it Wrinkles. It was an ironical story, but with a good deal of pathos, about being a middle-aged man among "the gods and bods." Bill was a wonderful performance artist, like Richard Pryor and Lily Tomlin, whom he admired so much. His life ultimately ran aground on the twin shoals of alcohol and bi-polarism.

Sometimes the revelry took place in the Caseys' small house on the island. Electricity there was provided only by a small generator, which would be turned off before we went to bed each night. One stormy night, not long after moving in, John woke up and had to go to the bathroom. In the utter darkness of a moonless night, he found his way downstairs to the only toilet in the house. Proud to have done it in pitch darkness, he began to relieve himself, noticing with pleasure as he did so the reassuring sound of rain on the roof. "But wait a minute," he caught himself. "It's not raining." Although he had performed flawlessly in finding his way downstairs to the bathroom, he told us the following morning, he had not seen in the dark that the top lid of the toilet was down.

Slowly but surely, the world of Brown began to absorb my energies. But for the first few years, I went almost every week to the Russian Research Center at Harvard for at least a day and intellectually it remained my principal home base. I still felt like a Cantabridgian, partly for old family reasons, but particularly because of the Russian connection. Under the genial aegis of Adam Ulam, intellectual commuters like me were made very welcome at the Russian Research Center. And as long as the Cold War raged on, the Center was one of the two or three greatest concentrations of resources in the world for the study of the Soviet Union in its confrontation with the United States. "Gleason," Ulam would roar as I walked into his office. "Come to coffee!" And then would ensue some thirty or forty minutes of gossipy, sometimes rambling conversation, but often with nuggets of information or crucial flashes of intuition that would have been hard to find anywhere else. And lunch with colleagues would take place in the wonderful lunch room, presided over by a brilliant African-American chef with the wonderful name of Curlie Mae Black. She provided us every day with a menu which owed much more to the ribs and red beans of the American South than to anything connected with Russian cabbage soup or chicken Kiev.

And it was as much at Harvard as at Brown that I saw the sixties come to a head and flame out in the early seventies. By early April of

1969, opposition to the Viet Nam War, to on-campus recruiting by companies like Dow Chemical, and to ROTC had been growing on the Harvard campus for weeks. On one of my Cambridge Thursdays, I walked through the Yard and saw a solitary figure, who turned out to be the philosophy professor Hilary Putnam with a bullhorn in his hand. He was addressing an indefinite but indubitably student audience. "I give you a blank check," he intoned several times, to nobody in particular, or perhaps to everybody. It seemed to sum up the times.

I continued on to the Russian Research Center, where I stopped in to see Adam. I learned from him that Students for a Democratic Society (SDS) was planning to pay a visit of inspection to the Center some time that day. Adam was very anxious, but not without gallows humor. "Don't ever forget, Gleason," he kept repeating to me, with a shudder, "there's *no such thing* as a bad boy." This slogan, popularized by Father Flanagan of Boy's Town, a famous orphanage of the fifties, seemed to Adam to sum up the foolishness of current beliefs and the naiveté of those progressives who believed that liberal students were a force for good in the university. I argued with him, but as much out of habit as conviction at this point. As the day passed, the raid failed to materialize, but Adam grew more and more anxious. "I'm going to paint my ass green and head for the hills," he proclaimed with a ghastly smile. In Adam's heavy Polish accent, it seemed ominous, touching and funny.

Around this time, serious disruption of classes at Harvard began. Our mutual friend, the vivacious and intellectually omnivorous sociologist, Alex Inkeles, was so traumatized by a Columbia student who repeatedly invaded his classroom—and, as I recall, disrobed—that he moved to Stanford not long afterwards. He had lost his taste for the physical environment of Harvard. Like others, he couldn't bear to be excoriated and stigmatized for his liberal beliefs, especially from the Left. He simply could not imagine the possibility of a sustained and personal attack from that quarter. The fact that what seemed such militant hatred came from a graduate student contributed to the impression of generational war which was so widespread.

A few days later, on April 9, came the seizure of the main Harvard administration building, University Hall, by SDS. Deans were shoved downstairs, jostled, and one was physically carried out of the building. Files were rifled and false letters of admission were written to a list of students found in one of the offices.[3] Then, the following day, came the famous "bust" by the police that caused an argument that has lasted well over a generation. Few faculty members at the time supported the building takeover by SDS, but opinion was largely negative about the university's decision to have several hundred police break the doors of University Hall down at five in the morning on April 10 and "bust" the students, with considerable minor violence. Some forty-one students were somewhat bloodied. Two policemen were bitten.[4]

In the subsequent faculty meeting, the redoubtable Alexander Gerschenkron, for whom I had the utmost respect, made the most widely discussed speech. It was a response not merely to the building seizure and bust, neither of which had he actually seen, but to his growing hatred of "utopian" thinking and the cruelties that this particular kind of idealism could engender. In that respect, it anticipated a major motif of the neo-conservatism of the next twenty-five years. But the major impulse was provided by the "criminal" behavior of radical students, which Gerschenkron regarded as virtually unmotivated. His speech was a defense of Harvard and was widely and correctly regarded as the most memorable public utterance of that time by a faculty member in any more or less public arena. It was not merely about the bust at Harvard, but about the

[3] Nicholas Dawidoff, *The Fly Swatter. How My Grandfather Made His Way in the World*, Pantheon, 2001, p. 310. This is an admiring but conscientious and balanced biographical memoir of Alexander Gerschenkron by his grandson.

[4] One of the more recent and widely noticed accounts is Roger Rosenblatt's faux-modest *Coming Apart: A Memoir of the Harvard Wars of 1969*, Little-Brown, 1997.

vulnerability of universities in the age of student radicalism.

Gershenkron famously retold a Hans Christian Andersen story entitled "The Most Unbelievable Thing." It was the story of a cultivated king who had a daughter, whose hand in marriage he promised to the man who should accomplish "the most unbelievable thing" in the arts. A handsome young man who had invented a marvelous, striking clock, which was adorned with a train of allegorical figures, celebrating in gesture and procession the great intellectual and spiritual feats in human history, seemed to be the winner. But just as the prize was about to be awarded to the handsome young man, upon whom the princess was already smiling, another candidate came forward, described as a "lowbrow," or in one translation a "working man," and smashed the clock with three blows of an axe. The smashing of such a magnificent artifact was even more "unbelievable" than its creation, or so the judges felt compelled to rule. The happy ending in the story is somewhat contrived. The allegorical figures returned in spirit and confounded the lowbrow villain just as he was about to marry the princess.

Gerschenkron let Harvard off the hook entirely for the troubles through which the university had been going. The students, he charged, had attacked Harvard only "because it was there," as thieves might steal an object merely because it was lying around and could be stolen. No mention of the university culture that gave such a low status to teaching and where, members of the faculty were wont to boast, "every man (and perhaps the few women as well) was a star."

The speech had an enormous impact, especially coming from such an eminent and intimidating scholar, who had fled from Nazism and was widely given credit, therefore, for having a special appreciation of the fragility of social institutions confronted with violence. His lengthy speech was discussed for days and weeks and probably had more impact on faculty opinion than any other utterance. A few critics did note, however, that although student violence against administrators deserved to be condemned, the Harvard

SDS students were not really comparable to the Hitler Youth, a distinction Gerschenkron ought to have acknowledged.

For all its distinctive pathos and rhetorical effectiveness, Gerschenkron's speech seemed to me at the time to give off the odor of a certain special Harvard egotism. An implicit theme of the speech was: "We who are the smartest people in the world need a place where we can nourish our talents and pursue our ambitions. This is Harvard's essential mission." Having reflected on this a good bit, I have concluded that it was not entirely fair to Gerschenkron, who surely thought of Harvard as a kind of community, but one, I think, that existed almost entirely for people he judged to be the brightest and best, according to his extraordinary and exacting standards, rather than one where people of diverse views learned from one another.

In reflecting on Gerschenkron's speech, Stephen J. Gould put it another way: "there never was a clock like that." Monroe Engel, a teacher of creative writing in the English Department and subsequently a friend, deplored the comparison with Weimar Germany.[5] We and our work are so important, Gerschenkron seemed to be saying, that we need and deserve to be taken care of by elite society with a special kind of solicitude. We are the people who create the miracles of these wonderful artifices, the clocks that do everything. And suddenly, through no fault of ours, the vandals are at the gates. They will smash this wonderful thing that we have created, that is in fact "us." This seems to me narcissism at a very high level, but narcissism all the same, and of a type that probably flourishes most luxuriantly at Harvard. Adam Ulam disagreed vehemently with me. Gerschenkron had expressed Adam's views exactly.

Until the speech, I had never questioned Gerschenkron's bearing or ambitions. If it was intellectual arrogance, I felt, like most everybody I knew, that he was entitled to it because of his extraordinary intellect and attainments. But I couldn't help thinking,

[5] Dawidoff, *Fly Swatter*, p. 322.

after the lengthy round of discussions that followed, how self-cultivation and personal ambitions dominated the cultural world so utterly at Harvard, at least among those who prospered most greatly there. Harvard University wasn't merely "there" for "criminals" to smash. It was in varying ways and to various degrees complicit in what had occurred. Indirectly relevant, I think, is a judgment by a recent student of the problem. At large research universities during the Cold War, "administrators responded to the concerns of undergraduate students—large classes, alienation from professors and from the university as a whole—by treating them as symptoms of a failed adjustment to college life."[6]

Never before or since have I seen such intellectual polarization in our small university worlds, not only over the bust at Harvard, but over charges that Harvard, Brown and the rest of them were complicit in racism, in the Viet Nam War, in the class divisions in American society. Even among the older generation, among people whose orientations were fundamentally similar, there were deep and painful splits. I remember an evening on which Sarah and I returned to Cambridge for a buffet supper at Ben and Felicia Kaplan's house. I stood and listened as two of the more senior Harvard Law School professors, Ben Kaplan and Louis Jaffe, talked with great seriousness about rethinking their courses, about introducing different perspectives, about going back to reexamine the first principles of what they taught and how. "Maybe we really are just corporate types," said Ben. "Maybe they [the students] are right." He glanced over at me with a half smile on his face, but his eyes were serious. Neither Kaplan nor Jaffe had been radical within the context of the Harvard faculty, but unlike so many on all sides of the controversy, they were disposed toward introspection and self-questioning. Suddenly Derek Bok joined the group. Although soon to be Harvard's new president, he was still Dean of the Law School

[6] David Engerman, "Rethinking Cold War Universities: Some Recent Histories," *Journal of Cold War Studies*, Vol. 5, No. 3 (Summer 2003), p. 92.

at that point. Although not exactly angry, he was vehement. No need to rethink anything fundamental, especially not for reasonable, thoughtful men like Jaffe and Kaplan, he said. Responses to the crisis varied deeply even among the most mainstream Harvard faculty members and administrators, I thought to myself. There were an awful lot of people who thought Harvard was pretty great just exactly the way it was.

There were of course, lighter moments. I remember hearing from several friends about a highly charged faculty meeting, during which a student had jumped to his feet and shouted "Fuck you, President Pusey." One of the professors returned from the faculty meeting to his house, where a large reception was starting up. He told his wife about the scandalous occurrence at the faculty meeting as the guests began to arrive. We will call his wife Nora. She was so stirred by what had happened that she told each guest the story as he or she arrived at the front door. But not being familiar with the expression that the student had used, she told each new arrival how the student had shouted "fuck on you, President Pusey." Finally her husband, mixing drinks across the room for the guests, lost patience. "No Nora," he shouted in exasperation, "not fuck *on* you, fuck you, Nora!"

I was more intimately involved, of course, back at Brown. During my first year of teaching, Ira Magaziner, then a senior, was engaged in restructuring the Brown curriculum, in the institutional context of a year-long seminar with the future provost Paul Maeder and a faculty-student group. Magaziner knew very well who his friends and enemies were among the students, and especially the faculty, and he was engaged with them on a daily basis. This had been his world for several years. I was too junior for him to bother with. By the end of the year his proposal, which laid the basis for Brown's "New Curriculum," the so-called "Magaziner-Maxwell Report," was finished. On May 8, 1969, it was presented to the faculty and, over the objections of a small group of faculty conservatives, accepted.

For a major American university the reforms were fairly radical.

Distribution requirements were abolished. The number of courses required for graduation was reduced from 32 to 28 (although students were required to pay for 32). Pluses and minuses were eliminated, and any course could be taken for a grade of SATISFACTORY (or NO CREDIT). If the student's performance was judged not to be satisfactory, no failing grade was recorded. They were merely denied credit, and no record of their lack of success was entered on their final transcript. Freshman seminars called "modes of thought" were devoted to explicating disciplinary methodologies. The concept was excellent, but there were never enough offered and they were never successfully integrated into the curriculum.

In the years immediately following the reform, particularly in the early 1970s, many idealistic students did extremely good work for a grade of satisfactory, plus a written "course performance report" from the professor. With the passage of time, however, the excitement of the de-emphasis on grades waned. Professional and pre-professional ambitions made a comeback, and grades were needed for students to "distinguish themselves" at Brown and keep their upward trajectory going. By the 1990s, the grade of SATISFACTORY had become in almost every case a fall-back position for students who feared a letter grade. Even a grade of B was a defeat for some students, who would take an S rather than risk a grade other than an A appearing on their transcript. In the competitive culture of the century's end, the educational virtue of the satisfactory-no credit option had disappeared.

Partly as a result of his curricular reform activities, Ira Magaziner was selected to be a Rhodes Scholar and set off for Oxford, where he met a fellow Rhodes, Bill Clinton, his subsequent escort into national politics. During his time at Brown, Magaziner had developed both a political style and a slightly hang-dog sixties charisma that he determined to test beyond the gates of academe. Part of his style and substance was positioning himself short of the extreme Left, where part of his argument could be to those on his Right: choose me, or deal with the dangerous Left. It must be said, however that he appreciated the importance of hard work, careful preparation and, within limits, patience. It was a canny social idealism.

During his senior year, and later at Oxford, Magaziner and a number of his friends developed a scheme for local reform that became known as the Brockton Project. The idea underlying it was to find a community that had a constituency of working people and needed help from a cohort of well-connected young idealists. The method was to move in and establish oneself as a serious contributor on a relatively long-term basis and see what kind of reform could be achieved by taking over grassroots organizations and positions. The political agenda was democratic but definitely anti-capitalist, a somewhat ironic fact, in view of Magaziner's later success as a business consultant. Brockton was a tough, working-class Massachusetts town south of Boston that had been deserted by the shoe industry some two generations earlier. Several dozen Brown graduates of the early 1970s spent a year or more in Brockton. Ultimately they had to give it up. What had been relatively easy to achieve in an academic community turned out to be much harder with the more diverse and recalcitrant populations of a hard-luck manufacturing town. It was also a matter of how much time to devote to such a project. Within a couple of years these very ambitious kids were launched on their career trajectories.

I had arrived at Brown on the eve of tumultuous changes, which would ultimately redound to the University's competitive advantage but only after a certain amount of chaos. A major contributing factor was executive instability. During what became a period of dizzyingly rapid turnover, there were four presidents in four years, if you count acting ones.

After I had been teaching for only three months, Brown's small black student cohort (sixty-five men and women) walked off campus and pledged to stay away until their demands were met. The previous spring, Brown had committed to a series of improvements in the numbers and status of black faculty and students. The students believed that the university had not moved effectively to meet its commitments. After a period of negotiation, the university agreed to admit an annual entering class at Brown which reflected "at least" the percentage of blacks in the general population, and appropriated more than a million dollars to make it happen.[7] The results were remarkable and immediate. In 1968, thirty-nine black freshmen had come to College Hill. A year later, following adequately funded recruiting efforts, one hundred and thirty-five black freshmen enrolled.[8] By 1972 there were 417 African-American students at Brown, representing 8.9% of the student body.

Questions of gender also moved to the front burner during my first year of teaching. The issue of parietal hours for women undergraduates, increasingly irksome to students of the period, had been festering for several years, along with the larger issue of university supervision of male-female relations. Connected to this issue was the matter of the federative status of "Pembroke College in Brown University" and whether it should be replaced by complete integration of the two institutions. In response to student pressure in November 1969, Acting President Merton Stoltz appointed a twelve-person committee to study "all facets of university life affecting the women of Brown University."[9] That same year, the first co-ed dorms were established, and full integration was achieved in July of 1971. "Pembroke Dead at 78" proclaimed the *Brown Daily Herald*.

The world of co-ed dorms and completely unsupervised sexual relationships and arrangements was not always a happy one, however. I remember accompanying one undergraduate woman to see a dean over her living arrangements. Assigned to a triple with two

[7] Monte Bailey, Ed., *Black Student Life at Brown* (n.d., n.p.), p. 15.

[8] "Blacks at Brown," *Brown Alumni Monthly*, December, 1972, pp. 3, 5.

[9] Stoltz's letter quoted in Jesse Marmon, *In the Best Interests of Women*, Senior Honors Thesis, Brown History Department, April, 1997, p. 53.

other women, both of her roommates had moved their boy friends in by Christmas and she had to try and sleep surrounded by two couples, often engaged in sexual activities, without much regard for the comfort level of their third colleague. In fairness, it was not difficult to secure relief for her in this poignant situation.

The coming of spring, in those years, generally presaged renewed political activity. In 1969, the administration unfortunately chose Henry Kissinger and an alumnus, the former American ambassador to Guatemala, Nathaniel Davis, to receive honorary degrees, and there were demonstrations against both. The spring of 1970, my second year of teaching, was as stormy at Brown as elsewhere. By early May, the university was already in reaction against Nixon's invasion of Cambodia and the resumed bombing of North Viet Nam. There had been a one-day strike on April 15. On April 29, a Navy recruiter was prevented from interviewing potential sailors. After agonized deliberations, the University Council suspended for one semester the students who had blocked the recruiter.

When word came of the shootings at Kent State on May 4, the university community reacted immediately and directly. The following day, three thousand students—more than half of the undergraduate body—gathered at the hockey rink and voted to go "on strike," as the terminology then went, meaning they would not attend class. With considerable faculty encouragement, including new assistant professors like me, a resolution calling for immediate withdrawal of all U.S. forces from Indo-China was passed. A twenty-one person Strike Steering Committee was also elected. The faculty, meeting separately, voted to suspend "normal academic functions" for the rest of the semester. Striking students were allowed to complete the semester without penalty.[10]

[10] According to the student newspaper (*Brown Daily Herald*, Vol. CIV, No. 61, Wednesday, May 6, 1970), p. 1, students were given three grade options: (1) take an incomplete; (2) take the final examination and receive a letter grade; (3) take a grade of S(atisfactory) if they were in good standing, without doing further work in the course.

On Monday, May 11, a "Free University" opened, replete with teach-ins on American foreign policy, Marxism, Latin America, Southeast Asia and many other subjects, relevant and not so relevant.[11] On the same day, the faculty voted to allow the students a two-week "moratorium" from school the following fall, to encourage them to engage in electoral politics and proper democratic activities in the run-up to the election.

Four days later, two students at Jackson State University in Mississippi were killed by police, who claimed to have been fired on from somewhere in a crowd of demonstrators. That kept the pot boiling at Brown and around the country. On May 23 and 24, delegations of faculty and students went to Washington to discuss the political situation with Senator Claiborne Pell and other members of Congress who, as I recall, listened patiently. The "free university" remained open in theory all summer. The first "commencement forums" took shape as teach-ins that spring, but have continued in morebourgeois form at Brown commencements down to the present day.

Marches and demonstrations continued for several years longer, and I participated in many teach-ins, usually to talk about the Cold War or the significance of U.S.-Soviet relations (or the lack thereof). I remember Brown and Rhode Island School of Design students marching around the local bank three doors down from the History Department in a conga line of some three hundred shouting "Take the bank ... Take the bank!"

One of the most fascinating aspects of those years was to meet smart kids in their radical phase and then see them evolve subsequently into solid citizens and distinguished doctors, lawyers or scholars. At the very beginning of my first year of teaching I was approached by three radical roommates who wanted me to direct an independent study for their benefit on the Russian Revolution.

[11] Richard Dannenfelser et al., "Chronology of the Brown Strike," University Archives, John Hay Library.

I suggested that they take my lecture course, which spent a lot of time on the Revolution. Uh-uh. The three were well known campus lefties and they wanted something created just for them by this new young prof. So I did it. Two of the three have had distinguished careers and gradually evolved into respectable centrists. Rich Feinberg, who used to sign his letters to me with revolutionary slogans, subsequently took a Ph.D. at Stanford in Latin American politics and later served on President Clinton's National Security Council. David Kertzer was the most formidable of the three. He was (and is) ferociously intelligent and in those days smiled infrequently, at least in the presence of professors. He was quite tall and had an enormous Afro-like head of hair (which he called an "Izro") and asked extremely hard questions, generally from a far left position. From Brown he went on take a Ph.D. in Anthropology at Brandeis. He then taught for some years at Bowdoin before returning with his talented lawyer wife Susan to Brown, where his distinguished scholarly career has flourished and at this writing he is Provost of Brown. He is slightly embarrassed by his early views and will refer to himself as an ideologue if I kid him about signing letters to me *avanti popolo*. We were almost all of us caught in the undertow of ideology in those days.

Radical costumes and demeanor gradually changed of course, diminishing in intensity and sometimes adding a satirical or even comic dimension or descending into eccentricity. At the very tail end of this tragi-comic period we had a rather slight kid on campus usually wearing a black suit and top hat. Doctor Death, as he was known, looked more like the Mad Hatter. By the late seventies or early eighties he was a mere campus character. The first time round as tragedy, the second as farce.

Marxism was hitting the skids too. A very bright, somewhat disheveled student named Bob Tashman was one of my favorite dialectical opponents in those days. He later became a long-time staffer for *The New York Review of Books*, and sadly died much too young. We argued endlessly about radicalism, always with good humor. One day, as I was sitting talking to another student in office hours, Tashman banged on the door and without waiting to be invited in flung it open and skidded across the floor. He was very upset. "Professor Gleason," he shouted, with a wild, stricken look on his face. "There's just no such thing as a Marxist ethics! There's just no way!" He repeated this lament several times before noticing that there was another student present and departed as quickly as he had arrived. I had the impression that he was weeks getting over the shock of this unwelcome conclusion.

Of course over time came considerable change. Student radicalism had always had a narcissistic dimension to it, and that steadily increased during the 1970s and early 1980s. Faculty radicalism had always had a medieval aspect to it. As student and faculty radicalism increased, university administrations longed increasingly for efficient and hierarchical models. So as time passed, the faculty, student body and corporation at Brown developed almost wholly different conceptions of what the university was. To the professoriate, the university was wherever the faculty sat down and whatever they said—not dramatically different from the time of Abelard. The student view was increasingly a consumerist one—the university was like an intellectual Benetton store. And the administration gravitated toward a hierarchical, corporate model. The diversity of these essential conceptions did nothing to make conflicts about how to run the university easier to resolve.

The Gleason family: (left to right) Tom, Nick, Sarah, and Meg, July 1998

Family and Friendships

EXPERIENCING THE AMERICAN SIXTIES and their backsliding sibling, the seventies, as a young person with a family was quite different from experiencing the slightly earlier period as an under-twenty-one year old protected by parents and university walls. It turned out to be anything but a purely academic experience. In fact, I quickly realized just how academic my previous experience had been. Now everything mattered!

For people who were seventeen or eighteen in the late sixties, the coming of this new era deepened the turmoil and upheaval of adolescence. For those of us who were ten years older, it both deepened and prolonged it—I am tempted to say unnaturally, although there was really nothing "natural" about how earlier American generations experienced adolescence. As I look back, perhaps the dominant memory I have is of the terror of post-college life during the Viet Nam War, especially after my marriage, when I'd been out of college almost a decade. I felt I was on my own in some new and important way, for which I was not prepared. Of course, I found no one with whom to share these rather inchoate feelings. In fact I tried not to understand what I was actually experiencing, not to take it in. My public persona was one of amused and bemused competence. But beneath this self-assured surface were terrible uncertainties.

Among the most difficult issues was the impossibility of separating the political and public from the private. Everything for me was political, but nothing was entirely political. Things that

I experienced as agonizingly private—above all, family relationships—were constantly cropping up in the middle of experiences that I would once have supposed were purely political. Of course I had always nodded wisely when people said that "everything was political." People reared in an atmosphere saturated by Marxism felt obliged to believe that even if they were not Marxists, as I wasn't. But real life seemed totally different from the cliché I had thoughtlessly ratified. Within both academic life and family life, virtually all priorities were called into question and had to be worked out all over again, by some composite and unclear method that you couldn't discover in advance. I usually blundered into things through this part of my life. That was how I got along. From blunder to blunder.

For instance, I agonized for more than a year about whether I would serve in Viet Nam if drafted, or go to jail, or go to Canada, but most of my agony I did not share with Sarah or anyone else, partly because I was not only terrified by the situation, but by my own indecisiveness. I planned to tell Sarah what I had decided to do once I had made up my mind. I justified this to myself as protecting her from my indecisive agony, but my discomfort was also a source of embarrassment to me. I was in a familiar place. I couldn't stomach what I saw as the pointless slaughter in Viet Nam, and I didn't believe that North Viet Nam's relationship with either China or the Soviet Union was simply that of a satellite. In my view, there were no dominoes ready to fall. But I also couldn't bring myself to consider seriously severing relations with my country. There was much talk of going to Canada among people I knew, although no one I knew well actually went. Other people obviously felt something similar to what I felt. But how many, I wondered? I was usually too buttoned up either to ask or to tell. I was afraid of finding out that I ought to go to Canada and then losing face with myself if I didn't. I was haunted by what seemed my cowardice. Sarah, as I came to understand later, felt that she had been excluded by my characteristically male behavior that took for granted the right to make important decisions solo. In fact I was paralyzed by my inability to decide what to do.

And fairness! At home, fairness turned out to entail real sacrifices for which I was quite unprepared, despite my blithe assumption that I was a fair person. When I look back on this aspect of the late sixties, I recall reading that pamphlet called *The Politics of Housework* and abruptly deciding that I had to do more around the house.

Characteristic, I'm afraid, that I should read a booklet and then decide myself what I was going to do. Sarah had different memories of the same period. She recollected broaching the idea that we share regularly in getting dinner on the table and my being in a rage for some time after. No doubt there is some truth to both memories. Both highlight some things and obscure others. I suspect that her version was more central to our situation, however, than mine. I have little doubt that I trotted out the standard male argument: I provide more of the money and put in the very long hours that support us, so you do more of the cooking. Cleaning occasioned the same kind of struggle and after trying students we eventually hired a married Portuguese couple to come in once a week. This provided a different kind of discomfort, as hiring a working class couple with little spoken English to vacuum our house seemed too close to our parents' bourgeois ways. But we felt forced into it, as it provided a way out of a conflict that had mobilized a deep stubbornness in both of us. An example of how established patterns "replicate themselves," as academics like to say.

Until we were well into the sixties I had little idea of what a mandarin I had remained … or become. I had evolved from an unconscious preppie mandarin into a scholarly/artistic mandarin, which turned out to be not much better, mixed as it was with scholarly ambition just beginning to be seriously tested. I considered myself a (small-d) democrat, and I was in some ways, but not in the most important ones. An unsympathetic critic might have accused me of "being a democrat" without understanding that being a democrat was more than holding an intellectual/political position. I had to behave like one, which turned out to be quite different from winning an argument about democracy in a college bull session. It could mean not doing things that you really wanted to do. I didn't figure that out either. I had to live through it.

Then there was the quality issue. I had emerged from the educational process up to that point with a general idea that everything had to be the best: the best painting(s), the best performance of Beethoven's "Seventh Symphony", the best history of Russia. That was part of my unconscious mandarin-ism. I was periodically terrified of my own ambitious standards of which I expected to fall short, although I continued to impose them on others as well as myself. And when I criticized things as less than the best, it was often not a personal judgment, but the application of a learned "high" or elite standard. For Harbison, recognizing good musical performances was part of going to work. For me it was more like showing how smart and hip I was. I was all too ready to loudly whisper a litany of criticisms as soon as a piece of music had been played or the lights had come on in the movie theater. That had not been regarded severely by my undergraduate band of brothers, most of whom were ready critics and likely enough to do the same thing.

Although I rejected with horror my father's ideal of becoming a Brahmin, in the sense of "Boston Brahmin," I was not at all conscious of the cross-cultural links between brahmins and mandarins. (The vague term "elitist" was not yet in wide circulation.) But surely I had a terrible cluster of discordant attitudes with which to enter marriage, particularly since almost nobody knows how to be married without a lot of practice, and even the couples best suited to each other have a great deal to learn. Humility is essential. Best of all is to appreciate how little you know. Mandarins are sure to have a very hard time—and likely to give other people a hard time, too. After all, what on earth was "the best?" Maybe an answerable question in some areas of the arts, maybe not. But in marriage? And anyway I was barely an aspirant mandarin at marriage, as I soon found out. To say that I was a journeyman would be generous. But I was on a journey, for sure, or perhaps a trip, as we used to say.

In retrospect, I think there was a coldness and a measuring quality about our self-consciously highbrow academic culture back in the fifties that embarrasses me now. A sort of Bread and Circus shopping trip out into life, rubbing elbows with other self-confident and slightly officious shoppers. Or a museum trip with Michael Fried in which you'd better not like the wrong picture. Of course, I didn't have to put myself on the line as Fried did when he staked his precocious reputation on the major importance of the stain painters. I was just showing that I knew what was going on, that I was hip.

Needless to say, I didn't have an idea that there was anything the matter with that at the time. Getting art right was a high ideal, at least to aspire to. When I got it wrong (or was told so authoritatively) I felt crushed, gritted my teeth and vowed to do better next time, something I had long been accustomed to doing. I had no idea how such a cold, lofty and perfectionist ideal would relate to a real life. What would it be like to run it up the flagpole in a family situation? I had gotten in the habit of thinking back on my prep school and upper-middle class family life and feeling superior to that square old world. Now I knew, or so I thought, what really smart people were like. I had, in fact, been provisionally accepted into the Ludwig Wittgenstein Smart People Cooperative—I stress the "provisionally". If I was uneasy about this aspect of things (and I think I was), it was below the level of consciousness, like a barely noticeable ache—faint and faraway.

I'm glad I can't remember all the things I said and did in the name of high standards. This issue was present but muted at home and more out in the open (if less charged) in the Brown History Department. Over time in both arenas I gradually came to realize how much repressed personal malice, jealousy and unexamined feelings of self-doubt could present themselves, sometimes thunderously, in the name of high standards. "Look," says a colleague angrily, "this kind of work would simply be unacceptable at Yale or Harvard." Or, on another occasion, "Her [cultural history study] is pretty thin gruel. It's showy at best." I'm not sure at this distance whether I actually pointed out how odd a dish "showy thin gruel" must be. It was easier for me to discern these things at work, where my sympathy for those who needed help made steady progress against the strutting patrolman inside me who was so worried about maintaining high standards. I can honestly say that developing as a teacher and colleague helped me develop as a human being—and finally as a husband.

In time, my tendency to side with the underdog and outcast began to triumph over my mandarin assumptions—not that they were always in opposition to each other. Increasingly, I erred on the side of giving students one more chance, or I discerned good qualities in a much larger range of written work, some of which I would earlier have considered disorganized, undeveloped or one-sided. Some of my less inhibited colleagues grew impatient with me. I was considered "soft"—one of the usual charges brought against liberals—even by my buddy Jack Thomas. "Gleason, you've gotta draw the line somewhere." Over time, as I developed into who I wanted to be, "drawing the line" became harder and harder for me to do. Of course, sixties orthodoxy aside, I had to admit that education inevitably involved the imposition of standards. This balancing act became how I was trying to live my professional and personal life. I never found a generalizable solution.

Part of this was a matter of age. Older guys, such as I was gradually becoming, are likely to become mellower about standards. Part of it was the era. The spirit of the sixties was quite hostile to abstract standards, especially those imposed from above by the powerful on the relatively helpless. But mostly it was a conflict within me. I never became comfortable "drawing the line."

As Sarah and I began our married life, all these things were out there, waiting to snare us. Life was so unexpectedly concrete! I had little appreciation of the high incidence of failure in life, or the subtle interrelationships between failure and success. Certain failures might actually reveal the road to success. I had trouble accepting people unless I admired them without reservation—at which point I was likely to try to become them. My ideas about nurturing existed, but initially they were abstract and largely embryonic. Fortunately, my experiences as a teacher moved me along.

"To Speak of Woe That Is in Marriage," is the title of one of Robert Lowell's greatest poems, and we had some woe. To begin with, I thought almost entirely about bringing Sarah into my world. Lucky girl. In Victorian times, people used to talk about "Lady Bountiful," a character from an eighteenth-century comedy who was the embodiment of philanthropy and benevolence. She operated very much above the fray. As the aristocratic age passed, the term turned into a sneer. Lady Bountiful became insufferable. I acted for a while like a kind of Lord Bountiful in my marriage, and Sarah understandably resented my bestowing on her the gift of my likes, dislikes and inclinations.

Compounding matters, I had since undergraduate days come to think of myself as living a kind of group life, in Sherwood Forest, or at Camelot—yes, no kidding, but it was too corny to be expressed in public. Much more than I realized, membership in my band of brothers promoted various kinds of imposture. I was living the lives of various people more or less simultaneously. I had an underdeveloped existential sense of my own life and a much too theoretical sense of what I wanted it to be. Key details were missing that would have helped me put flesh on it and make it realizable. In today's academic jargon, you might say I was "overtheorized."

Talking. Issues like talking too much, interrupting, and not hearing her out quickly became big issues between Sarah and me. I had always been an arguer. I was schooled to be a critic. Professionally I lectured on historical subjects for a living. Everybody in my Harvard group talked, interrupted, disagreed, criticized. Feelings sometimes got hurt, but that was rarely clear or obvious, and the universally accepted conversational model was the free-for-all.

Living after college with John Casey, a wit and raconteur of no mean proportion, probably heightened my tendency to make virtually no distinction between social life and performance art. But lecturing and explaining could ruin people's pleasure, distract them, prevent them from making up their own minds. Almost inevitably in my case it involved condescending to people, asking pedagogical sorts of questions, expecting smart answers. Sarah recalls crying quietly in the car coming home from movies while I droned on critically to a friend about the film. When she suddenly turned on me once and shouted "I'm not a graduate student," I finally shut up. Could that have been the first glimmering of understanding? I said I was sorry and meant it. There was a turning point somewhere around then—or at least the overdue run-up to one.

Many of our early differences were revealed in our relations with animals. That gave us a small reservoir of experience before we had to turn our full attention to the raising of children. Cat experience was less charged. For me it began with my winsome companion, Sabrina, named after Audrey Hepburn in an early movie role. She saw me through graduate school, and tolerated my long hours in libraries. Sabrina was a calico cat—tricolor that is—of the kind sometimes known as a "money cat." She was lovable, but as far as I knew, penniless. After marriage, there were small, charming cats like Sabrina and strong, silent, tough cats, like the Bogart-ish Jerry, who liked to nap on a neighbor's porch with his Irish wolfhound friend, and the chronically angry Scrat, whose bad temper kept him alive for almost twenty-four years. He acted like someone who had suffered a terrible act of violence that had soured him forever on humanity. But if anything like that actually happened it was certainly not on our watch. Sarah loved him, in spite of his anger. He softened in his later years. The last we saw of him was on a bright Labor Day morning, a very old guy blinking peacefully in the warmth of the sun. Then he slipped away and never came back.

Our first dog was a black Labrador whom I named Merlin. I wanted my dog to be a powerful wizard and, like God, I assumed the right to name him. Merlin was the well-bred son of John Casey's yellow lab, Bonkers, and he had the classic lab personality: eager to please, full of goodwill, not very subtle, a lover of tennis balls and swimming, preferably simultaneously. In fact, Merlin liked any form of athletics involving a ball and once made a mad dash on to the field to grab the lacrosse ball during a game between Brown and Penn. He returned it when he understood his mistake.

Sarah and I had some of our early disagreements over Merlin. They were about rules and authority. I was deeply ambivalent about rules, of course. With people, I was on the whole not a "rules man"—but with dogs I turned out to be, sort of. I wanted my dog to run free, but I thought he would have to be trained, so that he could be free. (On reflection, that sounds like a social science explanation of Canino-fascism: the dog forced to be free, etc.) But of course I had never trained a dog before and had little idea of how to do it. Like our marriage, it was trial and error. I wasn't as steady as I might have been, or as patient. Better at theory than practice. Better at arguing for training than doing it.

Sarah didn't have a developed position on dog rules, but she instinctively felt my training was too rigid, coercive and mean. Neither of us had really investigated how a dog would change our lives, and Sarah at the time was the principal care-giver for our young son, Nick. Thus occupied, it's not surprising that she reacted by declining to cooperate in my rather *ad hoc* training process. We had arguments about how often to use the leash, whether to make Merlin heel, and how much obedience to try and compel. We were often on edge with each other when Merlin was with us. Since we were seeing each other in new ways in relation to our dog, it was not difficult to feel disappointed in the co-dog trainer that each of us had married. I was surprised and resentful that Sarah did not share my attitude toward "training" and my conviction that authority—with respect to dogs—had to be certain and consistent. Somewhere around a bend in the road, tolerance and cheerful acceptance of difference were still ahead of us.

No wonder there are so many anecdotes in which people who marry late joke about having skipped their first marriage, the playful assumption being that it would have ended in divorce. If I had had a practice round—in golf terms maybe six holes out of eighteen, with some mulligans—I might have done better at understanding what marriage was going to require of me, a variant of what it requires of everybody who makes it work. In retrospect, I clearly needed training myself. "Trainer, train thyself!" It was ultimately my own inconsistency about rules which most undermined our dog's consistencies. I needed to be loved in spite of my own inconsistencies, forgiven and gently encouraged to do better. Marriage turned out in the end to be an admirable training ground for both Sarah and me. We taught each other, over time, how to be good trainers. Although we could never agree on precisely the same set of rules, we got close enough. Although an ordeal, my early married years were of immense importance in helping me grow up. Sarah was my best and most important teacher.

This was the late sixties and the world around Brown was a bit anarchistic. There was not yet a leash law in Providence. So the not very well-loved Merlin lived his own life, connecting from time to time with our family, sleeping in on the couch, after I'd abandoned it and gone to bed. Who knew where he spent his days? One afternoon Sarah and I were walking up toward campus and at an intersection we looked around the corner and saw Merlin a block away, trotting in the other direction, with what looked like a small leg of lamb in his mouth. Where had he gotten it? Where was he going with it? Would he share it with friends or just hide out somewhere and consume it?

Almost every day, a pack of some ten or a dozen dogs played on the Brown main campus which was known confusingly as the Brown Green. Some had owners living nearby. Some lived now and again in dormitories. Some were day students. Merlin seemed to know them but never became part of their radical pack. Most people around Brown enjoyed their presence, which seemed like a canine, parody of the human sixties. These dogs, of all different breeds and sizes, lived communally. They had tuned in, turned on and dropped out. They were attending Brown, but only occasionally went to class. They had a sixties look too—bandanas, long hair, unkempt. They shunned all authority, were unembarrassed about nudity, relied on others to clean up after them, had sex whenever they felt like it and generally lived in their own world with no thought of tomorrow. They made love not war.

When we moved back from Washington in the summer of 1982, Nick and Meg wanted another dog. I did too, and Sarah didn't object. This time—not wanting to repeat our experiment with a handsome purebred—we paid a family visit to the Animal Rescue League. A negotiated compromise produced Dinah, a somewhat runty shepherd-whippet mix. I did manage to train her to heel and wait for me at street corners. She came to work and even to the library, where she would simply lie down outside the revolving door and wait while I picked up books or did whatever I did in there. I tried not to stay inside longer than twenty minutes when she was with me. She was a celebrity there, where her faithfulness in waiting for me outside without a leash became one of those conventional dog parables that are mostly the same but seem new as they pop up again and again. The library staff would bring treats and rush to feed her and pet her while she was waiting, so these delays could be pleasant for her, especially in warm weather. She also went to the History Department almost every day, where she was similarly welcomed.

Everybody loved Dinah. Students were pleased when she came with me to lectures and lay by the podium. She was often "in" during office hours and only the most caninophobic (or allergic) students objected. Wearing her heart on what approximated her sleeve, she had no enemies and many friends. John Casey was rueful. His handsome purebred had not been a success, but here was this spindly, cowardly mutt that everyone loved. No accounting for tastes.

She needed the leash only in unfamiliar downtowns or in

Dinah and Tom, 1983
Photo by Sarah Gleason

situations when she was likely to become anxious. She was timid and had a few phobias. Once a week the trash barrels came out onto the street to be picked up by the city, and this changed landscape freaked her out. She never got used to trash day. The only thing more terrifying was thunder and lightning storms. When the thunder began—or even before anyone else could hear it—she would get as far down in the house as she could and start to dig. If the storm lasted a while she could go right through drywall partitions and even have an impact on stout floorboards. On one occasion we were called in St. Petersburg, Russia (then still Leningrad) by a Providence dog sitter, who hoped we could calm Dinah down and get her to stop digging in a corner of our basement during a storm in Providence. We tried it over the phone, unsuccessfully.

Dinah was wholly domestic and felt that her leash and especially her collar were not badges of servitude, but symbols of belonging—her membership in our family. She never violated rules, except when terrified, which was not infrequently. When her collar was taken off—it rarely happened, usually for bath purposes—she would stare at it beseechingly until it was put back on. She would scream and wail with pleasure when any member of the family returned after even the shortest absence. I would have preferred it if Dinah had been as brave as Mother Wolf in *The Jungle Book*, but she wasn't, so I continued my education in acceptance.

She spent most of her time with me around the university, but she gradually came to have an especial affection for Sarah. When we would occasionally have to split up in the middle of a walk, she would be so badly torn she would seem on the verge of a breakdown, eyes bulging, head rapidly swiveling back and forth, as the distance between us widened. But if given a choice, she more and more often chose to go with Sarah, as if afraid of losing her. . . .

In her old age, Dinah spent most of her time on a small rug, at the foot of a philodendron that year after year hung off a table in our living room. One night in the early spring of 1999, we heard her moaning; she had slipped and fallen in the ground floor bathroom, drinking out of the toilet, and fractured her pelvis. She couldn't move without great pain. Sarah slept with her on the living room rug for several hours. In the morning we brought her to the vet on a makeshift stretcher, where she ended her days. We were devastated. Her ashes lie under a statue of St. Francis in our little garden.

Dinah saw our family through Nick's and Meg's overlapping sets of adolescent years and helped me learn to let other people tell their stories too and to let the lives of others unfold on their own schedule. Dinah could be coerced or shamed so easily that my revulsion against those methods grew steadily. Learning to keep quiet has thus far eluded me; it helped me to remember, however, that Bobby Doerr's No. 1 was mounted on the wall in Fenway Park, along with Williams' No. 9 and Yaz's No. 8. He was in the Hall of Fame too and Williams called him "the silent captain of the Red Sox."[1]

School was easier than home. Showing off was much less hazardous in class, and one has greater leeway in less essential relationships. Students mostly liked having the professor step up and take over the narrative, even at the height of the sixties. Students may have wanted their turn but rarely did they really want equal time. Knowing this, when questions were raised about the proper roles of teachers and students, I could always spend time negotiating about egalitarianism or parsing our differences. I had been an advocate of greater classroom egalitarianism in the fifties, and I could pass a lot of time in game-playing with students while I tried to figure out how far I wanted to go down that road. At the height of the sixties, a minority of students really had a radical agenda for the classroom order and structure. I discovered that I really didn't, but I wasn't uptight about discussing it. Most students were happy enough with just that.

I liked my students too and genuinely wanted to become their "big brother." Pun intended, I guess. Big brother, any way you sliced it, was a more stable role and an easier one than husband. I was trying to figure out what I was doing, which at first amounted to creating an illusion of mastery. Fortunately or unfortunately, mastery (note the gendered term) is far more appropriate in the classroom than in marriage and less obnoxious. But power and control didn't come overnight and as they did they satisfied me less and less. Wit was a source of joy to me, and mine could be wounding. Gradually, though, I learned either to turn my instinctive, out-of-nowhere humor on myself or on neutral subjects. Things improved. Gradually

[1] Years later, David Halberstam wrote a touching tribute to the Red Sox of my childhood (and his), entitled *Teammates*. It focused on Doerr and Williams.

I ceased to blurt out wounding barbs without meaning anything more than a snappy comeback.

Russia of course was my thing and during the seventies it absorbed my attention almost totally. Competitive sports—tennis and golf—practically disappeared from my life, and I became a runner, as I had briefly been in prep school. It was what I did for recreation, but it was also a metaphor for how I lived. Sarah remembers me as absorbed and neglectful at home, struggling with my first books. I would fall asleep on the couch downstairs, and wake up there in the middle of the night and stagger sleepily upstairs to bed. I generally reverted to "comfort reading" late at night: Damon Runyon and Sherlock Holmes stories. Father Brown and the adventures of Bilbo and Frodo Baggins were about as far from the Soviet Union as it was possible to get. I took refuge in my semi-secret Edwardian inclinations. The conflict between my sentimental Edwardianism and my modernist side gradually hardened into a split that I realized I would have to live with, a split that I would never overcome. After an evening retreat, I was back to Eastern Europe in the morning for calisthenics with the New Soviet Man.

Despite my sympathies for Russian culture, I discovered that I was positioning myself as an outsider-critic of Russia. I continued to work on Slavophiles and nationalists, but I was certainly a "Westernizer" who spoke in terms of the classic dichotomy among intellectual Russians and the people who studied them. I felt drier and more Anglo than the Russians I was teaching or writing about. I was tempted to make fun of them, but almost always with some sympathy, because of the soft-heartedness buried under my assumed dry wit. I was anti-utopian too. The study of Russian history can erode the optimism of even the strongest liberal. I remember being struck in the middle of a lecture I was giving on Catherine the Great by the degree to which my subtext was that the best laid plans of all sorts of critters either fail or result in monstrous deformations. Then, thinking that over, I realized how many of my lectures reluctantly pitted my increasingly chastened point of view against the hopefulness of Russians, especially intellectuals, whom I "knew" would be disappointed in the end. I was slow to realize that this process was also about my own life.

Another factor may have been that my Russian language skills were always a bit less developed than they should have been, in part because I never immersed myself in Russia the way I might have. Fortunately, my German and French were good and I could write fluently. In the arts, I knew a little about a lot of things. I tried to compensate for my insufficiencies with things I did well, which had the effect of making my view of Russia seem even more "Western" – emanating, perhaps, from some indefinite space close to the English channel, a consequence partly of relying a little too much on style and imagination, rather than immersion in Russian sources.

After some five years at Brown my first graduate students had arrived, beginning with Stephen Frank, an irreverent and apparently casual kid from a small town in upstate New York. The first one in his family to go to college, let alone graduate school, his facetiousness masked a powerful intellect and a growing scholarly ambition which gradually worked free of its inhibitions. I was initially frustrated by his casual flippancy, but soon became aware of what a self-protective mask it was. After laboring over his dissertation for many years, he produced a deep and original study of Russian peasant legal consciousness in the nineteenth century, and received tenure at UCLA. Then came Dave Pretty, a complicated refugee from Columbia, the New York Yankees of the Russian Studies world. After settling down, he eventually produced a massively researched study of the peasant roots of worker violence in late Imperial Russia.

More graduate students arrived when Patricia Herlihy—a devoted teacher and a fine scholar—arrived to share the responsibility for teaching Russian history at Brown. Chris Ely produced a superb account of how Russians came to treasure the apparently flat, drab physical world in which they found themselves, and how they learned to paint it. In reading Ely's thesis, I had a powerful sense of our being caught up in a common intellectual enterprise. I'm grateful to Chris for confirming the essential bond between teachers and students. Steve Seegel was a whiz kid from upstate New York. Using cartography and the study of map sequences, he studied the relations between Russia, Poland and emergent Ukraine during the period between the French and Russian Revolutions. Andrew Gentes, a tough kid from New Hampshire, alternately found me a good buddy and a tyrant, and produced a massive study of the colonization of Siberia. Elisa Gollub, my last Ph.D. candidate, is writing a comparative study of collective farms from different regions of Russia, during the exit from communism. A laid-back Californian, she put on her boots and lived in different parts of rural Russia for a year, emerging a stronger and more self-reliant person and a scholar of great promise.

Over the years, a steady stream of my undergraduate students went on to have careers connected with Russia, some in government, communications or banking, most in academia. This wonderful group began with Jon Purnell '70, who did an MA at Harvard and joined the Foreign Service. After serving in Moscow, Washington, D.C., and other places, he retired as the U.S. Ambassador to Uzbekistan and left the service in 2007. Jon's appealing roommate Chuck Partington, on the other hand, seems to have been one of the many who got lost in the counter-cultural tides of the sixties and early seventies. Living with us for a few months, he was Nick's first Brown student friend, and he and I and Sarah laid out the little garden back of our old house, bought in 1970.

One of the great advantages as well as pleasures of living in an academic community was the steady movement of students through our house, from which our children derived all kinds of benefits. Chuck lived on our top floor for a few months, and a boon companion he was! He was so enamored of the history of science and philosophy that he would wander into our bedroom any time of the day or night, intending to read us a stimulating passage from

Wittgenstein's *Philosophical Investigations* or Newton's *Principia* without much attention to what we were doing. He had played varsity soccer at Brown, and was a man of real scholarly ability, humor, and capable of deep, almost naive affection, mixed with self-doubt.

"Be direct, be direct, I whisper to myself" he wrote in an overdue letter to us, after he had moved to the Bay area. "I have proved to be a poor friend, a debtor without a conscience, a non-existent correspondent who has made the most of the three thousand miles separating us. So the wretch. I regret it." After exclaiming about a picture Sarah had sent him of Nick sitting with his new little sister, Meg, whom Chuck had barely met, he asked how Nick was.

> I often wonder about him. How has the Fox Point (public) School worked out? Is he happy? So many questions, so little do I know. How I love that child. Wretched were the books I sent but they were the best I could find in this bibliophobic city, where Kerouac serves as Homer and Ginsberg the finest flower of Eastern civilization, where children are weaned on astrological charts and the colored dots of nutritional calendars.

A few months later he again wrote, to talk about books he was reading, ask about Sarah's dawning interest in photography, and about Nick. He hoped school was not too "hellish." He wanted to know how Nick got on with Meg. "Such a beautiful little girl. Give them both kisses for me." He concluded on a down note. "I am easily recognizable, though I no longer smoke and am about fifteen pounds lighter. An ulcer plagues me occasionally. I have no biography and have stopped searching for one."

A few years later (about 1976), Chuck paid us a visit, then a few weeks later he sent Nick a book and a letter, just before I took Nick (aged nine) on a trip to the Caucasus and Soviet Central Asia. "I enjoyed seeing you again, Nick" he wrote. "You are so much older, so much more grown up than when I left (so am I, I suppose). We both looked very different to each other. But I think we tend to notice the differences most at first. The changes which have taken place surprise us and part of what we knew so well is gone. But some things change more slowly, and some things never change at all. It takes longer to see what hasn't changed sometimes, I think." When I last heard news of him he was living on a commune in Virginia, after a stint in Vermont. He was still working as a carpenter, as he had in San Francisco, and writing. After that, we gradually lost touch with him.

Joe Augustyn, who got his MA with me in 1971, went into the CIA. Catherine Theimer Nepomnyaschy '73, it seems to me in retrospect, spent many months and even years of her undergraduate time working to get her future husband Slava out of the Soviet Union, an effort involving professors like me, journalists, diplomats, *New York Times* reporters and, perhaps, Gandalf and Elrond behind the scenes. This sustained project was ultimately successful, and today Cathy writes brilliant essays on modern Russian literature and administers the Harriman Institute at Columbia University.

Olga Andriewsky '76 did her Ph.D. at Harvard and is currently chair of the History Department at Trent University in Canada, where she writes on Russian and Ukrainian identity. From the Ukrainian community, she gave me my first sense of what the children of émigrés might be like as students. She was beautiful, hardworking and reserved, somehow appearing a kind of guest in the chatty, privileged world of Brown, with its attenuating radicalism. After getting a Ph.D. at Berkeley, Lisa Kirschenbaum '86 has had a distinguished scholarly career, with important books on Russian experience of childhood in Stalin's time and domestic life during the catastrophic World War II siege of Leningrad. Fran Bernstein '87, a lively member of a delightful and inseparable troika of Russia-oriented undergraduates, got her Ph.D. at Columbia and now teaches Russian history at Drew University, with special interests in gender and medical history. Her equally talented friend, Kate Brown, became a banker, and—despite the efforts of her former teacher to re-direct her—the third member of the troika, Amy Kellogg, works for Fox News out of London after serving in Moscow and Jerusalem. Debra Javeline '89, an intrepid battler for students on financial aid at Brown, did a political science *cum* demography Ph.D. at Harvard and now teaches at Notre Dame, as does the gifted young German historian, Lauren Faulkner, Ph. D. '09, with whom I also worked extensively. Nicholas Breyfogle '90, a talented Canadian student of Russian imperialism and non-Russian nationalities, did his graduate work at the University of Pennsylvania and now teaches at Ohio State. Eileen Kane '94 was a lecturer at Princeton after finishing her Ph.D. there and is now teaching Russian and Middle Eastern History at Connecticut College. This intrepid adventurer journeyed through Siberia in the winter of her senior year, investigating a reclusive community of Old Believer religious schismatics for her honors thesis. And Cinzia Solari '97 is pursuing her Ph.D. in Russian sociology with Victoria Bonnell at Berkeley. Perhaps the best in-class conversationalists I ever taught, her written work deals with the complex inter-relationships across the porous barrier between the prosperous Western Europe and the impoverished former Soviet Union.

Not entirely surprisingly, jazz played a big role in my academic as well as private life. One day in the spring of 1970, a tall, lanky, curly-haired undergraduate with a ready grin dropped by my office, and said he had heard that I was into jazz. He was, too. His name was John Lax, and he turned out to be a most interesting character and an important figure in my life. Jazz was our first bond, but far from our only one. His parents were distinguished mathematicians associated with New York University's Courant Institute. His father, Peter Lax, was and is a world-class mathematician. His mother, Anneli, was a very considerable figure in mathematics pedagogy. Peter Lax was a Hungarian Jew, his wife German. They were refugees from Hitler, and were cosmopolitan Europeans to the core.[2] Their son John, born and raised in the U.S., was not surprisingly

[2] Peter's father (John's Hungarian grandfather) was the doctor who attended Bela Bartok at Mt. Sinai Hospital in his last illness.

John Lax, c. 1976
Photo by Sarah Gleason

less Europe-oriented in both personal style and intellectual interests. His ran to history, literature and music, rather than science. A devoted son, he was nevertheless moving gently away from his parents' world, and in search of something of his own. I think he wanted quite consciously for that "something" to be definingly American. Although John had his share of rueful, ironic humor and could do shtick, his straightforward, extroverted optimism differentiated him somewhat from his parents.

We became close friends almost immediately, having as we did connections to Eastern Europe and black American culture which both dovetailed and contrasted. No doubt this constellation of Jewishness, jazz, history and Eastern Europe linked our friendship psychologically with my old Harvard gang, with whom relations were attenuating at various rates of speed, but remained powerful in my memory. We exchanged music and jokes. We often just hung out. John was a talker, like me, but Sarah minded it less with John, not being married to him. She and I and the kids visited John's family summer place in upstate New York at Loon Lake, where John and I laid out a tennis court together. Our friendship derived some of its power for me from continuity. The old set of Harvard relationships were subject to the pressures of differing careers, interests, regions, to say nothing of family lives. But here was some new growth.

The echoes, and in some cases more than the echoes, of my group of undergraduate friends have remained with me all my life and in some cases grown stronger. Learning how to combine academic and intellectual friendships with emotional relationships, marriage and family began there, in that place. It was a process not unlike learning to reconcile the Edwardian, sentimental side of myself with the aggressive, competitive aspiring wit who also inhabited my skin. Later, as we entered old age, some of us began to draw closer again, conscious both of our diverse life trajectories but also of the common, unifying experience of our early friendship and how shaping it had been for us.

In his senior year, John Lax produced a wonderful honors thesis: a profile of the black jazz musician in the Chicago of the 1920s and his experience, discussing the employment situation, the dual black and white union structure, crime, club owners and their clubs, corruption. It was based not only on wide reading in primary and secondary literature but on eight fine oral interviews with survivors of that time and place.[3]

[3] A portion of John's dissertation was published in the *Journal of Jazz Studies* (June, 1974). The eight interviews are housed in the Oral History Research office (OHRO) at Columbia University. See also Burton W. Pettis, "Speaking in the Groove: Oral History and Jazz," *The Journal of American History*, Vol. 88, No. 2 (September 2001), p. 8.

After graduating from Brown, John embarked on his Ph.D. in American History at Columbia, and by 1978 was well launched on his dissertation with William Leuchtenberg, a great student of Franklin Roosevelt's world. The subject was to be the American Legion, but in February of 1978, while passing through Chicago on his way to the Herbert Hoover Presidential Library in Iowa, John was killed by a drunk driver. I got the news on a Sunday morning in the kitchen, with my mother finally on her deathbed at the farm. I will never forget that bleak, miserable February morning. John was twenty-seven. A wonderful graduate school friend of his, Bill Pencak, now a history professor at Penn State, took over the project and using John's material turned it into a book.[4] Pencak was really the author but John was very much present in it. Had Pencak not resurrected it, John's fine foundation never would have seen the light of day.

John's death devastated his family and friends and produced an aching void in all of us. It is a sadness that I have never entirely gotten over, perhaps because it foreshaowed the inevitable losses to come. His fiancée, Martha (Marnie) Greenwood, then in medical school, was devastated. So was his roommate, Tom Bryson, to whom he was very close and Tom's wife, Antonia Levine, who had been a friend of John since their schooldays at Fieldston. And Betsy West, who became a friend of all of ours at Brown and who went on to become an important figure in broadcast journalism. And Glenn Whitmore, an aspiring poet who once got his car stuck in one of the big campus gates at Brown very early in the morning.

John's death had the effect of cementing us all together in a group with a void at the center, and for the most part these friendships have lasted for some thirty years. The common relation to Brown no doubt helped, and the fact that Betsy West and Tom Bryson retained

[4] William Pencak, *For God & Country. The American Legion*, 1919-1941, Boston, Northeastern University Press, 1989. See also John Lax and William Pencak, "The Knowles Riot and the Crisis of the 1740s in Massachusetts," *Perspectives in American History*, Vol. X (1976), pp. 163-214.

strong Rhode Island family connections would have brought them back to the state in any event.

A few months before John's death another quartet of students graduated from Brown who also became long-term friends of Sarah's and mine, after an undergraduate period of friendly rivalry between the girls and the boys. The women both went on to have acting careers. Eve Gordon moved steadily away from history toward theater during her four years at Brown. She was scheduled to do an honors thesis with me on English writers fighting on the Republican side in the Spanish Civil War. When she got into the Yale Drama School she dropped by my office to tell me she was bagging her honors thesis in history. Theater was the thing. But I shamed her into doing a good, long piece of work in only a couple of weeks and graduating with honors in history, before going on to Yale and a career in movies and television. She was in Barry Levinson's *Avalon*. I taught her classmate Kate Burton in Russian history courses, and we joked about whether she would get to Moscow as a star of Chekhov's *Uncle Vanya* or as the first woman ambassador to Russia. Uncle Vanya won out and Kate is one of the best, most versatile and intelligent actresses in American theater. She is also a woman of transcendent Celtic charm and good nature.

The men in the class of '77 were Bob Sloan and Oren Jacoby. Both were into jazz, Russia and theater. Sloan, as he was known, was a gawky beanpole of a man who improvised episodically on bass clarinet and acted in either comedy or avant-garde things. Jacoby was sometimes an actor, usually a theater director and very much involved in Russian studies. He was also the nephew of dixieland jazz guitarist and entrepreneur, Eddie Condon, author of *We Called It Music*, a side-splitting classic account of early jazz. Since graduating, Sloan, a picaresque intellectual, has been a teacher, a jazz journalist, a writer of mystery stories and cookbooks. His son Nate, a good jazz piano player, graduated from Brown in 2008. Jacoby is a very successful documentary filmmaker on jazz (Duke Ellington and Benny Goodman), the political transition in Russia, the Irish in America, anti-Semitism in the Catholic Church and much else. The rivalry between these pairs of friends was generally friendly, and the links were strengthened when Oren Jacoby and Betsy West got married. In general, women were playing an increasingly central role in the networks of friendships that formed around us at Brown, as opposed to earlier times at Harvard in which the central relationships were likely to be among men, with women relegated to auxiliary girlfriend roles.[5]

All through the 1970s our children were growing up, a constantly developing factor in my efforts to figure life out at home and in school. Nicholas Abbott Gleason, first Nicky and then Nick to us, was a shy but adventurous little boy. At something like three years of age he got up early one morning, tried to slide down the banister from the second floor, fell a story and a half onto the concrete basement floor and fractured a vertebra. We rushed him semi-conscious to the hospital where he was placed in a body cast for more than a month. Fortunately all his bones and tendons returned to their original locations. The following year, we were sitting in our postage stamp back yard when all of a sudden we heard his piping voice from high in the air. Nick and a slightly older neighbor had climbed a railing-free fire escape to the third floor of a neighbor's house and he was waving to us from above. "Hi mom," as they say in pro sports.

Our nice old house was located on a kind of approximate boundary line—between what was known as the East Side of Providence, where most people were white and well-to-do, and a neighborhood known as Fox Point, where most people were from the collapsing

[5] Brown had women historians before I arrived. The celebrated historian of early modern Europe, Natalie Zemon Davis, had been briefly on the Brown faculty in the 1960s, but there were no women faculty in my early days in the History Department until Mary Gluck arrived in 1978. She had the unenviable role of trailblazer. Her position (and mine, in a different way) was greatly strengthened when the scholarly and irrepressible Patricia Herlihy came to Brown to join me in Russian history.

Nick and friends, c. 1973
Photo by Sarah Gleason

Portuguese empire, in particular from the Azores and Cape Verde. Kids at the local elementary school who didn't speak English were known as "Portugees," a usage Nick soon picked up, and about which we questioned him closely. Nick had some white friends from the "East Side," where he went to nursery school, but the majority of his friends were local kids from Fox Point—all more streetwise than Nick and many older than he. He soon joined them in the local public elementary school.

Both Sarah and I felt very conflicted about Nick's education at Fox Point School, which seemed to be moving rather slowly, but Nick usually enjoyed his Cape Verdean and Azorean friends, many of whom spent long hours at our house, playing with what they regarded as Nick's great toys. Occasionally, they would beat up on him, too. These were tough kids, who knew how to fight. Nick didn't. I, of course, worried that Sarah and I might be sacrificing

Nick's welfare to our ideological convictions, but he came through this experience unscathed. These kids, many of whom belonged to the large Gonzales clan, also went with us all over Rhode Island in the back of our beat-up old station wagon. One of Nick's particular friends was somewhat older, three or four years at least, but loved going on trips with us in the car, virtually anywhere. He and Nick made a peculiar machine, something between a portable radio and a pencil sharpener, which they kept in the car between trips. When they were on the road, I could hear the machine whirring along in the back and the two boys humming tonelessly, over and over again, "Grinding up girls, grinding up girls, grinding up, grinding up, grinding up girls." There were hours of fun in this pastime.

Nick also had a number of imaginary friends, over whom he had more control than the tough neighborhood kids with whom he otherwise largely hung out. His principal "friend" was Snucky, but there was also Tick-a-tick and Rack-a-Rack, who sometimes seemed to have bodyguard functions. At Fox Point (now Vartan Gregorian) School, Nick's best friend was Seth Handy, another nice middle-class kid, who struggled with the educational milieu and, like Nick, eventually went to private school. They would hustle by "Manny's Ringside Lounge" on their way to school, a hangout for tough, older boys.

Margaret Gleason—Meg—was born in the fall of our third year in Providence. Highly sociable, she was drawn to the arts almost from day one. I read to both Nick and Meg a lot, even after they could read to themselves, but I was not always careful enough about what was coming along on the next page. Nick and I were working our way one evening through an old collection of English folk tales I hadn't read before, and I launched into a very short one called "Mr. Miacca." It turned out to be about a child-eating ogre, and it scared both of us, Nick half to death. The effect lasted for awhile. Some years later Nick remarked to us that "everybody's afraid of something. I happen to be afraid of a psycho child killer." No more explorations in unknown folk tales after that. Good-bye, Mr. Miacca! Back to Northumberland or wherever you came from. As I was writing this I discovered that Mr. Miacca is famous enough to have his own home page. How many other ogres can say the same, I wonder.

After some travels, of which more later, Nick went to Stanford followed by several years of searching. Having decided that he needed further credentialing and increasingly interested in life in the inner city, he moved to Roxbury and went to Harvard Business School. While still in school, he founded CitySoft, a company created to train kids from Roxbury and Bedford-Stuyvesant in the use of computers so that they could be employed as programmers and other kinds of techies. Nick and CitySoft, now considerably evolved, are currently based in San Francisco.

By the time Meg was born, we were well settled in a nice old house near the Brown campus, with wide floorboards, ancient appliances,

Tom reading to Meg, 1974
Photo by Sarah Gleason

charmingly antique bathrooms and fireplaces all over the place. No doubt living in it reinforced my archaic side, since the ambience was so like the farmhouse in which I spent summers growing up. Meg was even more receptive to my Edwardian literary side than Nick, and also to the visual arts. While Nick was devoting himself to sports, she attended children's art classes at the Rhode Island School of Design and produced her own illustrations to the Beatrix Potter classics we were reading, not to mention wonderful clay figures, and boxes full of found objects, in the manner of modernist sculptor, Joseph Cornell.

Our kids were not particularly close when they were little, and in view of my own experience with sibling rivalry and its deleterious consequences, I tended to worry about it. I was open enough about the sources of those worries that both kids said to me at various points along the way—and with varying degrees of impatience—that I wasn't to foist my own experience onto them. I was reassured about them, and struggled to take their good advice. During adolescence, as it turned out, their rivalry reduced itself to a residuum, and as adults they are close friends.

Connections were continuously developing between our closest student friends and our children. For students who wanted a semester off, a few months living in our guest room and helping look after our kids in exchange for room and board turned out to be a great arrangement for all concerned. Wendy Strothman '72, after Brown a publishing ace with Beacon Press and Houghton Mifflin, and now a renowned literary agent, was the first to do it. She was followed by Betsy West '73, a media person, first as a TV news producer and and now as a Columbia professor. Then came Mary Chaffin '75, a deeply good-natured Southerner with a passion for Russia which has today developed into the central focus of her legal career. Mary was a great anecdotalist, and her animal fable about the dangers of curiosity, "The Wide-Mouthed Frog", kept us in stitches. These relationships attenuated the boundaries between family and friends and between generations. It kept us all close. My students of that

Meg and Nick, mid-1970s
Photo by Sarah Gleason

era were just about equidistant between Sarah and me on the one side and our children on the other.

One day when Mary was off, another sitter brought Meg home from play school. "Meg says she has a berry up her nose," the sitter confided to me as she took off, "but she doesn't." "Yes I do," said Meg confidently, and she did. So I took it out. Presently Meg spoke again. "I have another berry in my nose, Daddy." And she did. This one had to be extracted with tweezers. I knew these small, hard blue berries. They came off a vine on a chain-linked fence surrounding a Brown parking lot. "I have another berry in my nose" said Meg a moment later. This one wouldn't come out at all and eventually entailed a visit to the emergency room, where Sarah and I felt we were becoming regular customers after Nick's various misadventures. Meg's cheerful equanimity was finally shaken, but not for long. She went on to attend Classical High School, Harvard, the Rhode Island School of Design, and is currently a sought-after events designer in New York.

Balancing my domestic struggles with writing and teaching proved difficult. It was not made easier for me by the fact that I was more successful at school than at home and probably found refuge there from my long struggle to change myself into a more nurturing husband and less of a pedagogue. Home life eventually changed for the better, but the struggle was lengthy and consuming. As might be expected, Sarah and I differed over many child-rearing practices. TV was a major issue. In theory I was more rule-oriented than Sarah, but as usual real life was different. Partly because I enjoyed watching TV with the kids, I didn't seriously enforce the ground rules we struggled to agree on. Sarah, by contrast, did not share my theoretical interest in rules, but sensibly regarded TV-watching as an activity that demanded regulation. For awhile there seemed almost nothing we could agree on except that "The Wide-Mouthed Frog" was great stuff.

As these problems were becoming more acute, my father was diagnosed with lung cancer and died quite rapidly in the fall of 1974. Our relations had been improving. My father continued to think of me as impious and ungrateful, but then his take on the sixties was that the whole world had gone crazy, so I was no longer in the vanguard of the horrors of the time, as I had been a few years earlier. I was merely suffering from the general insanity. I had a job and I was doing things he knew about and approved of: writing and teaching. Our relations were a bit stiff and correct, and we never talked politics. But the crisis of a few years earlier had eased. My mother was beginning to suffer from weakness and incipient dementia, either from a series of small strokes or, as I now think, from Alzheimer's, a term not widely known in the seventies. My parents, I think, sensed that they were becoming more dependent on me, rather than the other way around, which subtly changed my father's attitudes.

For the preceding three years, in part due to my mother's frailty and lack of mobility, my parents had taken their summer vacation with us, on Block Island, in a charming converted barn that we rented from one of my Harvard professors, Monroe Engel, and his wife, Brenda. It was beautifully sited on a hillside, with a spectacular view of Long Island Sound. Although my parents paid the rent and the kids had a great time, it wasn't all that much fun for me, but it was especially hard on Sarah. My mother was turning into a real invalid and my father's arch-Victorian style baffled Sarah, rather than provoking the playful reaction he was after. There wasn't much communication, and I felt caught in the middle. Sarah took the lead in running the household. I was trying to write some and keep my parents going. The surface of the water was calm. Discontents were forced down toward the bottom, as had become our wont.

My father behaved extraordinarily well in the last few months of his life. I hope that I can do as well. His affairs were in extremely good order and he was considerate and gentle with everybody. We had our first intimate conversations, and I realized the depths of his disappointments. I did not expect any bouquets or messages from God, the CIA or Harvard, but it brought a lump to my throat to hear his solemn and mournful confessions of how the priests of the temples at which he worshipped had failed him. I spent as much time in Washington as I could that fall: teaching on Mondays; flying to Washington Monday night, returning to Providence Tuesday night; teaching Wednesday, then going back to Washington for the weekend. I was almost certainly the most difficult challenge my father had ever faced and we never achieved anything like a stable or serene relationship until the very end of his life. There were obviously qualities that many of his friends saw in him that in our relationship were diverted from their normal course or obscured. "I had known him first as a bright medievalist in Cambridge," Arthur Schlesinger, Jr. wrote in his obituary:

> When I encountered him again in Washington in 1943 he was now Lieutenant Colonel Gleason in charge of the Current Intelligence Staff in the Office of Strategic Services. His incisiveness and skepticism made him a first-class intelligence officer as his urbanity, kindness and unfailing sense of the comic in life made him a first-class boss ... Quietly, without egotism or fanfare, Ev Gleason contributed valuably to our knowledge of recent American diplomatic history; scholars will long be in debt to him. He was, in addition, a man of rueful wit and immense, diffident charm who will be greatly missed by a wide circle of friends.

Years later, I discovered an ironical aspect to his passing. Although the CIA was no longer interested in him, its—and his—enemies were. One of the Venona Documents, intercepts of Soviet intelligence communications, revealed that Iurii Andropov, doubtless guided by staff, had decided in the summer of 1974 that several veterans of the Eisenhower/Nixon administration might be recruited. The four were Patrick Buchanan, William Safire, the economist C. Fred Bergsten and my father.[6] Was this mere coincidence, or had he indicated some bitterness in conversation with others, which had somehow found its way back into the Soviet world? I doubt it. The other three potential recruits were equally implausible targets, particularly Buchanan and Safire. Had my father lived to learn about his bizarre designation as a promising agent for Soviet intelligence, I suspect that in addition to anger and indignation, he would have felt more than a trace of satisfaction that he was still regarded as an important enough figure for a Soviet leader to go after.

In the aftermath of my father's death, two extremely difficult

[6] Christopher Andrew and Vasili Mitrokhin, *The Sword and the Shield: the Mitrokhin Archive and the KGB*, Basic Books, 1999, p. 211.

questions were posed immediately. What should happen to my mother and what should be done with the Washington house? Taking an invalid into our house with two young children would have put enormous strain on our household. I was not prepared to consider a nursing home. Life seemed to be presenting me with another impossible dilemma. Then came a break in the clouds. My mother's brother, Charles Abbott, and his wife offered to take her into the old "Big House" in Pomfret. As I have had occasion to mention, my uncle was often a hard man, but he loved his older sister dearly and I never heard them disagree. My mother, I know, defended me from his bullying, but never in my presence. After describing the proffered accommodations in some detail, he ended his letter to her, written on New Year's Day, 1975, as follows:

> The sun has come out after the snowstorm last night. The cows — for a week or so now—have come back up to 10 ... The boys at the barn are slaughtering hogs today. Emma's [the nanny] Scotty puppy has recovered from the "shits" she had yesterday & is as much under foot as usual ... The children also think it would be good for Mummy and me to have you around. Think about it.

Written like the Tory squire he aspired to be. My mother accepted the offer with joy.

This generous act served more than one good purpose. It gave my mother an assured base of operations, but it also restored relations between two wings of the family. I was enormously grateful to my aunt and uncle. Our political differences and history of conflict became trivial confronted with this magnanimity. Since the farm was only an hour from Providence, it also made it possible for me to actively cooperate with her regime there, paying the bills and seeing her frequently, as well as restoring her to a familiar ambience. "I feel that I'm moving back in with my parents," she told me as she settled in her new-old room. These were almost the last coherent words she spoke, as dementia overtook her. She clung to life for almost four years and her grandchildren visited her from time to time, but she was a faint shadow of the loving and resourceful presence of the old days. She lay in bed, misery and terror in her eyes and said nothing during our visits, only stared at me. It was awful. But when I skipped a week and didn't go, I felt even worse, and my aunt was quick to remind me of my neglect.

The storms of 1974 in my personal life blended oddly with the national drama of Richard Nixon, over whom my father and I had quarreled so bitterly. I inherited the signed photographs that I used to take down from the walls and hide from the old man on visits to Washington—Nixon must have given him half a dozen over the years. The absorption of Watergate passed too, leaving the nation sore and divided, nursing grudges that would flare again in the future. Absorbed in my marriage, my work, my invalid mother and my growing children, I was becoming sick of politics and thought as little as possible about them for some time.

The sixties and early seventies in a university had its lighter side, of course, and thinking about it relieved my somber mood. I marveled—for the first time it became obvious to me, how could that be?—at the power of youth culture in America: how quickly, in this case, it could transform kids from various incarnations of American Gothic into little hippies, Captain Americas, Che Guevaras or Vietnamese guerillas. One minute they had buzz cuts and limp gabardine slacks, the next minute they had some new identity, a costume or costumes to go with it, or at least hair well down their backs. These transformations could be effected in what seemed like hours.

The clothes thing could cut more than one way, however. I felt a stubborn, undoubtedly reactionary, loyalty to the way I had dressed since prep school: chinos, oxford button-down shirts with no tie, leather jackets. I stuck with that. Some went further in opposing the clothing Zeitgeist. Jack Womack, the Marxist chairman of the Harvard History Department, was deeply ambivalent about the counter-culture, which he saw as far too flighty and romantic. He used to wear a three-piece suit and tie when he taught, to emphasize that he was not currying favor with the students. His radicalism was about labor and economics, and his impulses were not about to be satisfied by long hair or Che Guevara outfits. But he often wore cowboy boots with the suits.

I remember one rural North Carolinian transformed in no more than a few days into a previously unknown superhero of some sort. He once burst into my office, in full regalia, and shouted to me to come with him: we were going out to East Providence and do guerilla theater. "What are we gonna do exactly?" I enquired cautiously. "You and some other guys are going to lie down in the parking lot and be Asians who we've bombed," he enthused. "Yeah? How they gonna know we're Asians who've been bombed?" I asked, feeling unusually un-Asian. "Simple. We're going to pour ketchup on you, and you're gonna lay as still as you can." A certain grouchiness overtook me at the thought. It was a hot day and I really did have students waiting to see me. "Man, I can't make it," I said, somewhat shamefacedly. "I really gotta see these students." It's the moment when, after years of temporizing, my apostasy to the spirit of the age became clear to me.

As the Viet Nam War drew to its dreadful close, the Brown campus nevertheless continued to be highly political, with a constant round of teach-ins and political speeches. Despite my developing revulsion at politics, I was still active on campus, but I noticed myself moving steadily away from the moderate Left into the sort of liberal position that I still occupy. I had generally occupied the right wing of the Left in the political position of the early seventies, attacking the war, but basing my criticism on the proposition that George Kennan's policy of containment could not be applied mechanically in Asia, scarcely a radical view. I was embarrassed in the company of colleagues who continued to assert what they thought of as revolutionary Marxist points of view, while living thoroughly privileged and tranquil bourgeois lives. My embarrassment at their unconscious hypocrisy was simultaneously permeated with guilt at my moderation and my abandonment of critical spirit. A reaction against the most extreme elements of the sixties was beginning to take shape all around us, and I was as usual divided. Part of me was simply appalled at the Weather Underground and part of me was afraid of what an anti-sixties reaction would be like. My fears would be amply justified.

Radical students and faculty passed around all sorts of books about American malfeasance and oppression, and of course male oppression of women as well. There was Norman O. Brown's *Life against Death* and Herbert Marcuse's *One Dimensional Man*. The point of "The Myth of the Vaginal Orgasm" was that women didn't need men to have rewarding sex. Particularly for a historian of Russia like me, it was easy to draw analogies between what was happening around us and the beginnings of the Russian revolutionary movement a century earlier. The radical Russians in those days had books like that too, books that were often more talked about than read, but that the hip were required to know about. Clothes were key identity symbols. Long hair and dark glasses were de rigueur at radical student parties in the Russian 1860s too, as were working-class or peasant outfits. Then as now, radical professors mentored radical students. Who were the Marxes and Marcuses of the Russian 1860s? What was revolutionary social life like? The speed with which a radical left appeared after the Crimean War approximated the radicalization I had just lived through during the Viet Nam War.

The comparisons I found myself using in class more and more —while trying not to troll for easy laughs—eventually led to a book about those parallels. *Young Russia* was a long essay which talked about the radicalization of Russia in the 1860s, as seen through the lense of the radicalization of the U.S. in the 1960s, as best I could discern it while it was unfolding. The book was a lot of fun to write and it was published and got me that more-or-less total job security, called "tenure."

In the process of writing it I consciously tried to make my style more colloquial and less academic; I was helped in doing that by the services of probably the best editor around, Elisabeth Niebuhr

Sifton, then of Viking Press, earlier a classmate of mine at Harvard. She helpèd me cut the first draft of my book by almost twenty percent and her shrewd guidance helped me realize that I was a better raconteur than an analyst, but that the two were not mutually exclusive as I had tended to assume. I tried to get more Orwell into my style and less Henry James. In doing so, I became aware of how hard it was to assimilate Orwell's plain style. My favorite essay was one about his schooldays entitled "Such, Such Were the Joys." I tacked the first sentence up by my typewriter, in those pre-computer days, to remind me to keep my style deflationary:

> Soon after I arrived at Crossgates (not immediately, but after a week or two, just when I seemed to be settling into the routine of school life) I began wetting my bed.[7]

Writing a book of this type raised, especially in those days, the issue of objectivity. Wasn't I merely writing a little essay which might be amusing, at best, but wasn't really history? By linking the two eras, wasn't I distorting "the facts"? My tactic, for better or for worse, was to deal with the objectivity question by stressing that I was not objective, and by admitting the personality and politics of the author as a factor in the book's viewpoint. By admitting one layer of subjectivity, of course, I was not dealing with the question of either unconscious or hidden motives at deeper levels. American historians of Russia—especially writing during the Cold War—often had anti-utopian motives, for example, the semi-conscious goal of showing what happened when people who wanted to change society abandoned traditional ethical restraints. I was almost certainly part of that tendency, although I only gradually realized it—for the first time, vividly, during a lecture on Catherine the Great, for some reason. In the years since then, writing more or less openly to

[7] George Orwell, "Such, Such Were the Joys," reprinted in *A Collection of Essays*, Harcourt, Brace, Jovanovich, New York, 1953, p. 1.

demonize the Russian revolutionary movement has become quite acceptable, even *de rigeur.*

But I didn't want my account to appear simply as an attack on the Left or straightforwardly against utopianism. I was afraid that such an account would simply constitute a veiled defense of the existing order, something I was very anxious not to write. I wanted to saddle the Russian imperial government and society with their share of the responsibility for the extravagance of the Russian Revolution and its remarkable cast of characters. And this historical effort was connected to my personal desire to balance my critique of the radical Left in the United States with a critique of American society and official American policy that stemmed from my ambivalent attitude toward my own times. But what an involved, elaborate point of view! God, I used to say to myself, "Do you have to qualify everything like this? Can't you make even one simple, straightforward statement about something?"

At the time, then, I found a kind of relief in turning the times I was living through into a history book. But deep down I felt a little uneasy about it. I was not responding to the ethical challenges of my faltering belief in radical egalitarianism, but turning those challenges into an interesting game at which my cleverness helped me to excel. I found that I was beginning to feel quite at home in academia, which made me uneasy. I called the book *Young Russia*, but in looking back it is clear that I had begun to condescend a bit to youthful follies, although I consciously tried not to do so. I was becoming a middle-aged American writing about "young Russians" of a century ago. At times my own youth seemed almost as far away.

As I concluded *Young Russia* and was promoted I was experiencing a certain restlessness. I was doing okay, I was at home at Brown, but Rhode Island seemed increasingly like a small pond. I was about to get a chance at a larger body of water.

Tom Gleason and George Kennan, 1981
Photo courtesy of the Wilson Center

The Kennan Institute and the Wilson Center

With tenure achieved and my essay on radicalism nearing completion, Sarah and I were sitting around at about nine one evening in the spring of 1979, when the phone rang. It was my old Harvard History tutor, James Billington. After Harvard he had been for a time a member of the History Department at Princeton and was now the director of something called the Woodrow Wilson International Center for Scholars, housed at the Smithsonian Institution in Washington, D.C. This well known think tank had been established by Congress in 1968 as a "presidential memorial" to Woodrow Wilson and for that reason received a good bit of its budget through congressional appropriation. That fact was completely lost on me as Billington explained the center to me over the phone, but it became important to me later, with my baptism of fire as a fundraiser. It was nice to have Congress supplementing my amateur efforts.

Why Billington was telling me all this soon became clear. I was being offered the job of administering a major piece of the Wilson Center. It was an exciting moment for a young scholar who would like to try out his fins and flukes in a bigger pond. The Wilson Center, Billington reminded me, had a section devoted to Russian politics, history and culture, called the Kennan Institute for Advanced Russian Studies. I had heard of it, but not much more than that. It was not precisely named for the George Kennan who had been ambassador to the Soviet Union and Yugoslavia and had written remarkable history and memoirs. Confusingly, "the Kennan," as folks in the Russia business called it, was actually named for a cousin of his grandfather, who had virtually the same name. (The younger Kennan had a middle name, "Frost". His forebear was simply George Kennan.)

The first George Kennan was almost as interesting as his greater descendant. He had begun as a kind of nineteenth-century traveler and adventurer, caught up in what Theodore Roosevelt called "the strenuous life." As a young journalist he had traveled across the face of Russia and Asia covering a failed attempt to lay telegraph cable across Siberia and the Pacific Ocean to the United States. He came close to death on more than one occasion through sickness, starvation or the North Siberian winter. He was best known, however, for having later written *Siberia and the Exile System*, a seminal study of the Tsarist practice of sending political and other criminals to Siberia. He ended his career as the closest thing the United States had to a Russian expert during the Woodrow Wilson era. As I discovered, the similarity in names was far from a coincidence. The Kennan Institute was in fact a monument to both men. The younger Kennan was seventy-six when Billington called in 1979; he died a full quarter century later at the age of 101.

The former administrator of the Kennan Institute, a talented historian of about my age named S. Frederick Starr, had left. Would I like his job, Billington asked? Of course this prospect had to be thoroughly gone over with Sarah, but I was pretty much instantly in favor of this adventure and Sarah fell in with my plans. She had just finished an MA in Museum Studies at Brown and eventually landed a job at the National Trust for Historic Preservation in Washington. I made a date to visit the Kennan Institute in the next few days and flew down to Washington.

I was excited at this prospect. Because of the Cold War, in which I had been caught up virtually since early childhood, Russian history was much more than an academic field of study. It was at the very root of the whole of contemporary politics. By working at the

Smithsonian Castle, 2006

Kennan Institute, I would not only educate myself and become a better scholar. I would also move into that border area where my academic interests could merge with the nation's major political preoccupations.

The Woodrow Wilson International Center for Scholars was then housed in the wonderful "Castle" building on the Mall—the original Smithsonian Institution building, a charming pseudo-medieval *schloss* roughly halfway between the Washington Monument and the U.S. Capitol. The Castle housed a multiplicity of entities, with a grand exhibition hall on the ground floor and the offices of the head of the Smithsonian, Dillon Ripley, in one part of the third floor. The Wilson Center occupied most of the rest, and some of the next floor up. Its upper floors were accessed by a Victorian elevator which never exceeded the speed limit. In order to enter the building you had to have your pass with a photograph clipped on to your shirt or jacket to get in. That seemed quite grand at the time, long before the age of terrorism made such precautions commonplace. Right close to the side entrance, which we often used, was a beautiful old carousel, which gave a welcome carnival air to the whole building and environs. In back was a lovely garden, screening the building off from the non-stop traffic on Independence Avenue.

The Wilson Center was devoted to international studies, organized by "areas." This was not just a geographical or spatial reference, but referred to the so-called "area studies" movement which emerged during and after World War II. For its practitioners it was an article of faith that the deepest kind of knowledge could only be had by studying the history, language(s), anthropology, economics and politics of a region together. Something like that still seems right to me, although "area studies" went out of style long ago. Foundations will virtually throw you out of the building if you say "area studies" out loud in their precincts. It's "been done" and there is no use telling them you think it's still worth doing. One of the great failings of American foundations is their endless search for novelty. If a "methodology" has been in operation for awhile, it is almost by definition not worth supporting—or even insupportable.

Inside the big box of the Wilson Center were some smaller boxes, devoted to the study of other things, including, but not limited to, the various "areas." There was also a lively journal, the *Wilson Quarterly*, a small office devoted to media outreach, and then the five "area" programs: the "Kennan Institute" for Russia, and similar entities covering Eastern Europe, Latin America, China and the United States. A reasonably well funded fellowship program supported a certain number of distinguished academic visitors for each program on an annual basis. The director, James Billington, ruled over this variegated federation, aided by an assistant director, a manager and sundry lesser bureaucrats.

The Kennan Institute was *primus inter pares* within the Wilson Center, for several reasons. It had been the Wilson Center's first area program—and George F. Kennan, even then the premier American diplomat, was Chair of the Academic Council which exercised an oversight role over the management of the Kennan Institute. And Billington, of course, was a Russian historian and author of an ambitious and durable cultural history of Russia, *The Icon and the Axe*, to which I had made an indirect research contribution in my younger days.

I knew just about this much when I arrived at the Smithsonian Castle on a day in mid-December of 1979 and was shown upstairs via the truly antique elevator into Billington's office. The next several hours were spent in touring the premises, a process which included introductions to several future colleagues, who directed the various area programs. They were then known as "secretaries" of the programs they managed, in the parlance of the Smithsonian. The director of the whole Smithsonian, Dillon Ripley, was also called the Secretary. The title was a badge of honor, not an emblem of servitude. The term "program director" did not come in until the 1990s.

As I moved from introduction to introduction, I began to feel a certain unease. Some people were cordial enough. Others seemed quite cool. By all odds the coolest was a man whom I was quite unprepared to encounter there: Woodrow Wilson's grandson, the former dean of the National Cathedral, Francis B. Sayre. As I dimly recalled, Sayre had preached at my graduation from St. Albans, but as I soon discovered, he had resigned as dean a few months before my visit and was now some kind of special assistant to the Director of the Wilson Center. I well remembered Sayre's heavily gracious manner and mellifluous speaking voice, and I had a vague recollection that he had become controversial several years earlier as a result of his emphatic criticisms of Zionism and Israeli practices.

I spent a few moments alone with each of my new acquaintances, the general idea—put forward explicitly—being that they could and would speak more frankly in the absence of the director. As I recall, Sayre was the only one who did so. In a somewhat agitated way, he gave me some disconcerting information. The parting between Billington and my predecessor, Fred Starr, had not been particularly amicable and, Sayre indignantly informed me, had taken place with George Kennan away in Germany. Wait until George got back! Not only that, Sayre clearly suspected that I knew all about what he regarded as a plot and that I was a co-conspirator of some kind.

I was flabbergasted. I assured Sayre that I had no inkling whatever of the relations between the founding fathers of the Kennan. But he continued to eye me with schoolmasterly severity until I was fetched away for my next interview. I had no way of even starting to comprehend the circumstances of Starr's departure to Tulane where he became some kind of senior dean. At the end of my interview schedule, I was ushered into the small but well appointed Kennan Institute Library, where I encountered a member of the Kennan Institute Academic Council, a group with which I was to meet frequently over the next several years. He was an Indiana University history professor, whom I knew only by reputation. He was distinctly ill at ease in my presence. I was already under a cloud, it seemed, and I hadn't even started work. I hadn't even been hired.

It was not until my next trip down to Washington, a week or so later, that I met the famous George Kennan. By that time—the end of 1979—I had encountered him several times before. Accompanied by Billington, I had heard him lecture on Soviet foreign policy at Harvard in the spring of 1960, lectures which became part of a classic account of Soviet foreign policy, *Russia and the West under Lenin and Stalin*. And I had heard him give a seminar at Harvard's Russian Research Center (now the Davis Center for Eurasian Studies) at some point toward the end of the 1960s. He had taken up with gusto the possibility that Josef Stalin had, early in his revolutionary career, given evidence to the Tsarist police incriminating his Menshevik colleagues in the Caucasus, in order to smooth the way for the Bolsheviks in their power struggle with their radical rivals. Kennan had been interested in this appealing proposition for some time. Imagine—young Stalin as a Tsarist agent! What a movie it would make, too. But his case that day remained highly circumstantial, as he readily conceded, and convincing evidence has never been found that Stalin was at any time an accomplice of the Tsarist police.

On both occasions I had been bowled over by Kennan's erudition and articulateness, but also by somewhat more fugitive qualities: a certain air of command, his aristocratic bearing, the way he inhabited his handsome suits, his intellectual confidence and quickness, his responsiveness to questions, even his erect posture. I still considered myself a leftist bohemian in those days, but every time I saw Kennan I thought, "Wouldn't it be something to be like that!" He seemed a character out of my romantic Edwardian era, like the hero of a John Buchan thriller or a member of Woodrow Wilson's cabinet—aristocratic, but somehow the opposite of a stuffed shirt. I couldn't believe he had felt out of place, as he had proclaimed in his memoirs, in the 1920s Princeton of Scott Fitzgerald. He looked as if he could have handled Fitzgerald without breaking a sweat.

I had read, I believe, every word that Kennan had published up to that point. The thought of working with him for several years was thrilling and it had been a major factor in my quick decision that I wanted this job. The idea that he might regard me as an imposed and inadequate substitute for Fred Starr, however, or even a usurper, was intolerable. Kennan's actual relations with Billington remained a mystery to me at that point. But the thought that he might think me some kind of conspirator against his interests rather than the disciple I longed to be left me desperate to demonstrate my good will.

I needn't have worried. I met with Kennan and several members of the Kennan Institute Academic Council in a cavernous

Georgetown house belonging to one of Kennan's friends on a dark afternoon in late December, with snow threatening. Billington was not present. Kennan was the soul of courtesy, if not quite the soul of warmth. There was not the slightest indication, however, that anything was amiss, and by the end of our two-hour discussion, I found myself speculating about something which later became a virtual certainty. However much of a controversialist Kennan might be in policy or doctrinal matters, he disliked quarreling, had a horror of it, even. His persona contained plenty of miracle, mystery and authority. Employing it, together with the faintly condescending courtesy he habitually displayed to younger scholars, he was confident of winning me over. He was right.

I took in another vivid impression of Kennan that day. At seventy-six years of age, Kennan was still genuinely and deeply interested in history, not only Soviet history, but also much of the political history of Europe generally, starting from quite far back in the nineteenth century. At the mention of some new book or historical argument, his face would brighten up, almost dramatically, and warmth would pervade his patrician, slightly husky voice. "Ye-es," he would begin, and his stiffness would largely vanish. The other youngish professors were in as much awe of Kennan as I was, but as they realized Kennan's depth of knowledge and unfeigned interest, conversation took off, bouncing between discussions of new historical literature and contemporary Soviet politics. Not until this introductory session was drawing to a close did Kennan resume his normal reserve, and the rest of us resume our posture of friendly but marked deference. That day, and ever after in Kennan's presence, all tendencies to take over a conversation stuck in my throat, and I noticed that this was the customary experience of other big talkers as well. Around Kennan I became, in a phrase my friend John Casey often employed, "a nice young man."

Kennan was a memorable and entirely unique figure in my experience. Despite the respect in which he was held (especially in public) by official Washington, he was increasingly regarded as insufficiently anti-Soviet, especially after the Reaganites began to pour into Washington. But Kennan was anything but an ordinary man of the Left—and certainly not a liberal. I never heard him criticize Africans or Asians, but he certainly thought that Northern Europeans and to some extent their offshoots in the United States were the great progenitors of creativity in the world and had been since the eighteenth century. He told me several times with great seriousness that nothing great or important had yet come or probably ever would from tropical climates or their inhabitants. He was far from a Democrat—or even a democrat—in politics and believed deeply in the rule of "wise men." It was not clear whether "wise women" could ever be part of Kennan's ruling group, or how these venerable male leaders would actually achieve these leadership positions. Surely they would not be elected! If Kennan was a "peacenik," as was occasionally alleged in Reagan's Washington, he was the most unusual one to be found anywhere between the East Village and Haight-Ashbury. Although I couldn't say that Kennan was a racist, his conversations with me and others—to say nothing of his later writings—indicate that he believed himself to be descended from "good stock," and that such things were of significance in the world.

My predecessor, Fred Starr, was almost as intimidating as George Kennan, but in a rather different way. Starr was a Princeton Ph.D. of Jim Billington's and had written a good book on the "undergovernment" of the Russian provinces in the nineteenth century. It was not, perhaps, a spellbinding topic, but Starr wrote well and made the reader understand the importance of Tsarist Russia's deficiencies in personnel, both quantitatively and qualitatively. But Starr was more than just a good historian. He was and is a polymath. Starr's most notable talent, from my highly personal perspective, was that he was an excellent jazz musician. An active member of a band for many years, Starr played traditional New Orleans clarinet, and was also a considerable scholar of traditional jazz. He did period arrangements for his various bands, which were, however, anything but pedantic. He was also very knowledgeable about Russian art and architecture and had written an excellent treatment of the Soviet modern architect, Konstanin Melnikov. A book he was just then finishing up on jazz in Russia is still by a good margin the best book on the subject. And while he was at Tulane, in subsequent years, he wrote a good deal about the architecture and history of New Orleans, in addition to its music.

I could never understand how Fred was able to do so much writing while administering the Kennan and pursuing his numerous other interests. I certainly couldn't, but Fred always made light of his accomplishments. Given his orientation to the arts, I always hoped we would become real friends, but I never managed it. Despite a talent for gregariousness, Fred always seemed to me a kind of lone wolf. His attitude toward Washington—and, perhaps, toward life—reminded me a little of the ambitious young man in Balzac's *Père Goriot*, who stood on a hillside outside Paris at night, looked down at the city, bathed in light, and challenged it to a duel. So far Fred was ahead in his challenge match with Washington.

Starr gave every evidence of being deeply at home in Washington, and he also spoke with confidence about the intricacies of current United States-Soviet relations. He made me feel like the archetypal country mouse. Following him was going to be a formidable assignment. I quailed but—except for a few dark moments—never wavered about going through with it. Somehow I'd make the transition. After all, I'd grown up in Washington.

Many questions began to occur to me almost from the moment I accepted the job in the spring of 1979. Did I know enough about post-1917 Russia? Were my language skills sufficient? Would this be a major turning point in my career? How long would I stay? Did I want to leave academia for some kind of administrative post or posts? I had no idea at that early stage. Howard Swearer, then president of Brown, was a Ph.D. in Soviet politics from Princeton, and interested in Russian and Cold War history. After some coaxing he gave me a year and a half leave, with an informal assurance that if

I wanted an additional year away, I could have it. If I stayed longer than that I would have to resign from Brown. But I could see no further ahead than beginning to learn these new ropes.

—~—

On a warm August afternoon that summer I had one of my few epiphanies. We had rented a beautiful house on the wild side of Block Island. Sarah was in Providence; Nick, Meg and I had just returned from the wonderful Mansion Beach, named for a summer hotel that had once stood there before a fire had swept it away. I was drinking a gin and tonic, listening to a Count Basie jam session, cooking fish for supper. A slight breeze blew through the kitchen. Stan Getz finished his solo. I felt an extraordinary surge of well being. Washington suddenly felt easy. I stopped worrying ... at least for a while.

—~—

When I formally began in January 1980, however, my anxieties had returned with a vengeance. I walked into my beautiful old-new office with considerable trepidation. I knew that I was regarded by some—including my critical secretary—as a poor substitute for the glamorous, multi-suited Fred Starr. By contrast, I usually wore sports jackets and chinos, and down-at-the-heel shoes. I made an early decision to continue to do so, with suits reserved for special occasions. From time to time, ads for sales at Brooks Brothers would mysteriously appear on my desk, no doubt from local well-wishers. They tried, but I was beyond help. My intuition, however, was that I would do better to stick to my academic style, rather than try to become a three-piece suit man or an omnicompetent bureaucrat. This way, I thought to myself, at least I'll leave them laughing.

Blair Ruble did his best to help me negotiate the ways of Washington. Blair, a University of North Carolina BA with a political science doctorate from Toronto, was a research associate at Kennan and knew his way around. He was a good scholar, well versed in labor and urban history, knowledgeable about art and architecture. Most important of all, he took official Washington seriously, but with a grain of salt and often a twinkle in his eye. He soon became my deputy and has been director of the institute now for the last eighteen years, dealing calmly and competently with the tumultuous events connected with the end of the Soviet Union and the transition of the Kennan Institute from a benevolent auxiliary force in the Cold War into an advocate for and adviser to the newly emergent Russia. We were both mild rebels against the hierarchical culture of the Wilson Center. That hierarchy was asserted rather lightly at the Wilson Center. It was often barely perceptible, but Blair and I preferred to do without it as well as we could.

I was also indebted to Mike Lacey, who ran the American Studies program, and who was known as "Jim Billington's fundamentalist." What this meant essentially was that when senior staff conversations got too high up into the aurora borealis of appearances and image-making, Mike would bluntly remind us that our fundamental obligation was to high-level and jargon-free scholarship. This made Michael a most valuable man, as did the long list of exemplary conference volumes edited by him and produced by his office. When overcome by the heady atmospherics of our jobs, Lacey and I would play hooky at a nearby seafood restaurant and drink as many beers as it took to restore our essential good nature.

The 1980s culture at the Wilson Center—quite Washington in most ways—was not accustomed to hide its light under a bushel, so what I regarded as self-deprecating humor of the appropriate kind for me was seen by my secretary and to a lesser extent by others as a ruinous confession of failure. My jokes about not knowing what I was doing embarrassed her even more than my lack of influential friends and acquaintances. My coming had brought with it a sharp and, in her view, entirely unmerited diminution in her own status, which she quickly and indignantly communicated to me. After several months of sustained chilliness the Smithsonian authorities helped us get a divorce on grounds of incompatibility, and she went to work for a law firm. She was replaced by Rosemary Stuart, a young, efficient and delightful graduate of the University of Virginia, who could genuinely endure my eccentricities with a smile; our Kennan troika became a quartet when Mark Teeter, a Slavist with excellent Russian, a droll sense of humor and a profound love of baseball, came on board as an editor of some of our various publications.

I rode a bike to work, which bemused some and displeased others. Riding my ancient, brown, three-speed bicycle was in fact one of my great pleasures. At first I commuted from temporary quarters in Cleveland Park by bus and metro, but after we moved into my parents' old house in Georgetown, I could come and go conveniently, if with more effort, on a bike. From high on the hill in Georgetown, just across the street from the front entrance to Dumbarton Oaks, I would coast down the hill, across the bustle of M Street to the canal. Taking a left on the canal, I rode along the towpath, across Rock Creek, to the Mall, then down the Mall, a mile or a bit more to the Smithsonian. It was about a four-mile ride. Of course, going home was a brutal uphill ride most of the way, and in the summer heat of Washington I was wringing wet by the time I got back up to the corner of 31st and R Streets. Fortunately the head of Dumbarton Oaks was a genial medieval historian whom I had known at Harvard named Giles Constable, and both he and Alexander Kazhdan, the distinguished Byzantine historian resident at Dumbarton Oaks, were generous with invitations to cool off in the institution's elegant swimming pool, surrounded by beautiful potted plants and flowering vines.

While I was figuring out my new and political frame of reference in the Wilson Center and scrambling to learn as much as I could as fast as I could about contemporary U.S.-Soviet relations, my bike spent the day tethered to the wrought iron fence surrounding the Castle, patiently awaiting my return. There it attracted the attention of the head of the entire Smithsonian, the illustrious Dillon Ripley, even more aristocratic and accustomed to command than

George Kennan. "Jenkins," snapped Ripley to the security guard who guarded the back entrance near the carousel. "Who owns that piece of junk?" "That would be Mr. Gleason," said the guard noncommittally. Of course Ripley had no idea who I was. "Well you tell him to park that thing somewhere else," said Ripley. But there was no other place to park it, and eventually Ripley had a bike rack constructed for me, between the Castle and Independence Avenue, next to the Victorian Garden. He did so, I believe, without knowing precisely who I was. There was one other bike commuter to the Castle at the time and the two of us had the glittering new bike depot entirely to ourselves.

Ripley was a far cry from the hustlers who have been at the helm (and in the pants pockets) of the Smithsonian in recent years. He made highly effective use of pageantry in keeping the Smithsonian in the forefront of people's consciousness when he was director. He was also a fabled fundraiser and the Smithsonian went through a major period of expansion under his leadership. Ripley loved birds, and was an ornithologist of great accomplishment. Alone among the people I met in Washington at this time he appeared completely unafraid of either the executive or the legislative branch of government. If Ripley did not care to greet a visiting Congressional delegation, rumor had it he would arrange a bird watching expedition to the Himalayas and be completely unavailable.

The first five months I was at the Kennan Institute, Sarah, Nick and Meg remained in Providence in order for the kids to finish out their school year. I came home as many weekends as I could. In Washington, I was a boarder in the house of my mother's college roommate, Elizabeth Coonley Faulkner, known to her legion of friends as "Bussie." My family, the reader may recall, had lived next door to her and her architect husband for a year during World War II. She was recently widowed and pleased to have a man in the house. She was a delightful hostess, the embodiment of cordiality and tact, unselfconsciously at home in her upper-class world and beloved by everyone who knew her. A great deal of her time was taken up, during the months I was in residence, with the troubles of the blue-ribbon private Madeira School out in McLean, Virginia, and its headmistress, the beleaguered Jean Harris.

Bussie, whose daughter Celia had gone to Madeira, was a former chair of the Madeira board, and her daughter-in-law Alice, married to her son Avery, was the current chair and a dignified and effective spokesperson for the school in its hour of travail. Night after night, I returned from the Kennan to find the past and present elite of the Madeira School assembled at the Faulkners, trying to figure out the mysteries of the unfolding melodrama that was absorbing much of the nation: the apparent murder of a physician in suburban New York by the prim and meticulous headmistress of Madeira, Jean Harris. Had she really had a passionate affair with the "diet doctor," Herman Tarnower in Scarsdale, the staid members of Madeira's board asked each other incredulously, and then murdered him? This violation of a number of WASP codes (including, of course, that of murder) was particularly difficult for the elite of Madeira to grasp, since Jean Harris had just thrown four students out of Madeira for a little pot-smoking and had been known to scold students in public for leaving a piece of orange peel on the well manicured lawns of the school. There were several questions to be sorted out. Had she journeyed from Washington to Scarsdale with gun in purse to do her faithless lover in or to kill herself somewhere in his vicinity? And what was the nature of the drama that had taken place once she was there, that led to his being fatally shot? The tawdry details were probably as painful for Madeira as the larger drama of Dr. Tarnower's death: the headmistress of Madeira discovering the underwear of her younger rival hanging up to dry in Tarnower's bathroom and blowing him away.

Bussie would greet me amiably, of an evening, but with a preoccupied air. Had I had a good day? How was that nice Mr. Billingsley (James Billington)? Often she would have some tasty snack for me to eat, despite my repeated reminders to her that I was to be on my own at lunch and dinner. Having plied me with macademia nuts (which we called Academia Nuts), she would disappear behind closed doors, where I was never invited to accompany her. The fact that I studied an episodically violent culture and was learning more each day about Stalin did not persuade these elegant ladies that I could contribute to their deliberations—not that I made the case openly or at length. Nonetheless, my curiosity was thwarted. Eventually Jean Harris was convicted and spent eleven years in a New York state prison before being pardoned by Governor Mario Cuomo in 1992. By and large the alumnae of Madeira rallied to the school exactly as Bussie and her daughter-in-law had hoped they would, and the school, now some three decades on, would appear to have put the episode far behind it, despite two movies about Mrs. Harris, one of them starring Ellen Burstyn as the beleaguered headmistress. In more recent times a whole TV series could have been constructed around this very American relationship and its melodramatic end.

In June of 1980, Sarah and the kids joined me in Washington and we reclaimed our house from the tenant to whom we had rented it after my mother moved back to Spring Farm. It was a pleasant, strategically located row house in Georgetown. Although rather dark and sandwiched between two larger dwellings on either side, it had a nice little garden out behind. Our tenant was an apparently amiable psychiatrist, who nevertheless left behind him a string of unpaid bills, some going back to the time he had taken occupancy almost five years earlier. The day we moved in I received a letter from the District of Columbia informing me that approximately $1200 was due for water and that if I didn't pay up, our water would be turned off. We also discovered that the daily consumption of water averaged 450 gallons. It turned out the doctor had been recently divorced, and was having a mid-life crisis. Suffering from angina, he would take extremely lengthy early morning showers to calm himself down before going off to see patients, one of whom he had just married. Unfortunately the tiled walls in the bathroom were not adequate to withstand this onslaught and eventually the seeping water destroyed the wall in the downstairs hall underneath the shower.

In addition, the tax bills on the house had been delivered to him in Washington and he never forwarded them to us, so we had five years worth of unpaid taxes outstanding. The government of the District of Columbia was threatening to take possession of the house if we didn't pay up immediately. ("Well," commented a friend to whom I indignantly related this detail, "didn't you wonder up there in Providence why there seemed to be no D.C. taxes to pay?") Two days after I moved in, the phone went dead in the middle of the morning. I managed to find a neighbor who would let me call the phone company. The doctor had also failed to pay his phone bill. His new wife, a product of the mid-life crisis, came by that afternoon to pay the bill.

Our tenant had also told the neighbors, prior to our return, that the house was haunted by my father's ghost. Had he seen the ghost? Well, no, continued the neighbor, but he had heard him creaking about on the top floor of the house, occasionally rolling things around on the floor that sounded like large marbles or ball bearings. Our next door neighbor, the divorced wife of a CIA East German specialist, had also heard some strange noises, and told me that it sounded like rollerskating. My father had not played marbles in many years and I had never seen him on roller skates. Why would he take up such pastimes in the other world? In addition—and apparently conclusively for the doctor—it turned out that liquor and cigarettes had been disappearing from the house, and it was known that my father was fond of both. The latter point was true, but it eventually turned out that one or both of the doctor's sons had developed the very same tastes.

Georgetown had become even more posh during the years of my absence. Boutique stores had mushroomed. A gigantic Safeway market was nearing completion nearby. Hordes of tourists were roaring up and down Wisconsin Avenue in buses. The student population seemed to have doubled. But the old landmarks were intact: Montrose Park still had nice clay tennis courts available on a first-come, first-serve basis, and Dumbarton Oaks Park, the wild garden, was still beautifully maintained. But there was no more climbing over the walls of Dumbarton Oaks at night. Barbed wire had been placed on the top of the wall now and guard dogs roamed the premises after dark.

At the age of 40, it was very strange to move back into the house in which I had grown up. Sarah and I slept in the master bedroom, and it took me a long time to rid myself of the feeling that I was usurping my father's position. What with all the talk of the bourbon-drinking ghost in particular, I half expected—especially on our first couple of nights in the house—to have my father translucently stroll into the bedroom and order us out. At odd moments, I seemed to have somehow re-inserted myself into his life and career. But the ghost never came, and we never heard the mysterious ball bearings on the floor above us. After a while I got used to it, but Sarah never lost the feeling that she had been billeted in someone else's house, surrounded by alien furniture, china and books.

The Kennan Institute was definitely a bully pulpit and as time passed I became known, at least by name, to almost every American academic in interested in Russia. It took time for me to adjust to my new role. There was an enormous amount to learn, especially about the contemporary Soviet Union. Every Wednesday, the Kennan would host a lunchtime speaker to address some aspect of Russian history or Soviet politics or U.S.-Soviet relations. This was followed by lunch at a special table in the Smithsonian lunchroom downstairs at the Castle. Scary at first, as I gained self-confidence it became fun to choose a weekly speaker and preside over an informal lunchtime discussion afterward. At last my gift of gab was unequivocally useful. The big challenge was paying for lunch. The Smithsonian dining politburo insisted that I collect individually from all visitors who were joining us and pay the authorities one lump sum, rather than have the waitress or waiter bill each guest. On some occasions there were as many as forty guests at several very big tables. I rarely got the bill exactly right. On some occasions I would manage to collect more than we all owed collectively, but I was much more likely to forget to collect from a guest and lose money as a result. On Wednesdays, I tried to remember to bring extra cash with me.

Knowing very few significant government figures, I initially sought the advice of Jim Billington and other knowledgeable people about whom to invite to the lunchtime discussions. Eventually and with mixed results, I began to choose people on my own. On more than one occasion I found obscure figures whose interests seemed to promise much, but who turned out to have debilitating stage fright or vacuity or the mumbles. I soon realized that choosing speakers, introducing them and keeping them to the allotted time period was an art, if not precisely a fine art. Russian-language meetings were a particular hazard. Whereas someone with better language skills would have spoken extemporaneously, I often tried to conceal the shortcomings of my spoken Russian by memorizing introductions and brief speeches. Nonetheless, my knowledge of Soviet history and the Cold War grew apace.

Among those occasionally present after the election of Ronald Reagan in November, 1980, was my former teacher, Richard Pipes, who was a member of Reagan's National Security Council. Pipes had been a prominent member of the famous "Team B," that had criticized the National Intelligence Estimates prepared by the CIA on the Soviet Union as dramatically understating Soviet defense expenditures and paying insufficient attention to its malevolent political culture. This exercise had brought him additional attention from Washington hardliners and eventually membership on the National Security Council. On one occasion, his wife Irene accompanied him to an event at Kennan. "Why Tom," she exclaimed incredulously when she caught sight of me in this exalted milieu. "I had no idea you were in line for such an important job."

No one is surprised by the presence of young conservatives these days, but coming as I then was out of post-sixties academia, I must admit to having been amazed by the legion of dark-suited conservatives who arrived with the Reagan administration. Sometimes they sat quietly along with everybody else, but every so often some one would walk out, muttering "disgraceful, disgraceful!" if a speaker seemed insufficiently critical of the Soviet Union or inadequately supportive of Israel.

My national status in my field changed almost overnight. Instead of simply being an assistant or young associate professor with one book and a couple of articles to my credit, I became someone with resources, who, if approached properly, could agree to put on conferences and award fellowships. Every young Russianist who aspired to take part in such activities—and that meant most of the better ones—needed to know who I was. This led to a surge of unearned fame, or at least notoriety. To be sure, the authority of the Wilson Center stood behind the Kennan Institute, especially in financial matters. But even that was complex, since I did a good deal of fund-raising myself—with very mixed results, I must add.

A national fellowship program was one of the Wilson Center's principal activities, and so a variety of "fellows" came to rest at the Kennan Institute, as with the other programs, for periods of time ranging from a month to well over a year. The money for the fellowship program was appropriated by Congress. Among these fellows were a variety of American academics who were quite at home in Washington, and used their time to good effect to write monographs on Soviet history, economics or politics. Because of its location and resources, the Kennan Institute during the 1980s may have equaled or even briefly eclipsed the traditional leaders in Russian Studies—Harvard, Columbia, Berkeley. But there were also a good many Russian émigrés, who were less uniformly productive. Many of them clung to their roost at the Kennan Institute, well beyond their allotted fellowship time, to avoid going out into the cold, cruel world of ordinary America.

Working with, and caring for, this sort of person, was sometimes tedious, but occasionally an adventure. I remember on one occasion a resident émigré Russian historian of science came to my office in high excitement, saying that he had an invitation to give a lecture at the University of Pittsburgh. But where was Pittsburgh and how could you get there? We figured out that the best way to go was on the bus, and arrangements were made to have a Russian-speaker meet the bus in Pittsburgh, as our scholar, whom I shall call Dr. Popov, spoke no more than three words of English and understood four. So I dropped him off at the DC bus station in the early afternoon on the day of his talk and hoped for the best.

Around eight o' clock that evening, Dr. Popov called in a semi-hysterical state. He had dismounted from the bus in a small town in Virginia, not in Pittsburgh. No one met his bus, no one spoke Russian, and there was no sign of a university. It turned out that Dr. Popov had bought a ticket to Petersburg, Virginia, instead of Pittsburgh. I should have gone in with him and bought the ticket. The episode was like something out of *Pnin*, Vladimir Nabokov's droll collection of anecdotes about a Russian professor's futile efforts to adapt to American academia.

We had many famous Russian visitors: some were Soviet officials, others were dissidents like Andrei Sinyavsky. Most stayed only a few days, but there were some exceptions. The most famous Russian writer we hosted was the formidable, talented Vasilii Aksyonov, who emigrated in the wake of the severe criticisms and arrests incurred by the literary miscellany, *Metropol*, with which he had been deeply involved. Getting Aksyonov as a fellow was a coup for both the Kennan and the Wilson Center. To celebrate, Aksyonov had a party in his new apartment, to which I was invited. While struggling along in Russian, talking with some guest, I stepped up to the bar for another shot of alcoholic assistance. But just beneath the table, hidden by the swathes of the table cloth, was an enormous dog poop, placed there by Aksyonov's nervous cocker spaniel puppy. I didn't miss it, and was forced to do a soft shoe routine on one foot to the bathroom, excusing myself in Russian all the way. Not putting my best foot forward, but hopping on it! My worst foot didn't bear thinking of. As he watched me, Aksyonov was bemused by the tribulations and efforts of his administrative caretaker. He died in July 2009, in the aftermath of an automobile accident.

In addition to the money appropriated by Congress, the various programs, including the Kennan Institute, had to raise additional funds for such activities as short-term fellows, academic conferences and other kinds of meetings. Most of the grants that Fred Starr had procured for the Kennan Institute at its inception in 1975 had run out by 1980, or were on the point of doing so. We were in much less solid financial circumstances than I had thought, or contrived to believe when taking the job. To be fair, Billington had on several occasions informed me that I would be expected to raise my own salary. I agreed, but without understanding how challenging a proposition this would be. Within a few weeks, however, I had come to understand how urgent fundraising was; with almost no experience and deep trepidation I set out to learn how to do it.

First came the vital matter of how to approach grant-giving institutions and which ones were likely to be the most receptive. Where did the Kennan Institute have an advantage in competing for funds? Maybe it was with grain traders, because of their economic connection with the Soviet Union. Maybe it was communications people? Some foundations still funded area-studies programs. Then there was the matter of demeanor. Was I a humble supplicant, a competent professional, a big shot or some mysterious blend of the three? If a person were too humble he would register with the funders as insignificant. But appearing to be arrogant was just as bad. I had an idea that I ought to be able to convince people that they were lucky to be able to give money to the Kennan Institute—call this the Harvard model—but I found doing so difficult in practice. Waiting in well appointed antechambers to see representatives of CBS or Archer Daniels Midland, with almost no previous experience, I initially found myself simply hoping to get through the next half hour credibly, never mind actually persuading them to give me the money. Slowly, however, I developed some self-confidence.

One of the first people I approached was the CEO and chairman of the board of Pepsi Cola, Donald Kendall. I flew to New York and took a cab to PepsiCo's opulent headquarters in Purchase, complete with a well maintained sculpture garden. I was courteously received and ushered in to see the boss. Kendall was a large, ruddy man with a mane of white hair and the intimidating appearance of someone who ate professors for breakfast even though he didn't much like the taste. Despite being in most respects a committed conservative, Kendall was interested in the Soviet Union. A confidant of former President Nixon, he enjoyed sharing his ideas for the Kennan Institute. In his opinion, it should become the premier venue where American business people could meet in private with Soviet officials and make deals. Kendall had already made a big one. Pepsi Cola distributed Stolichnaya vodka in the U.S. and in return a certain amount of Pepsi Cola found its way onto Soviet shelves. My prepared speech about the importance of bringing scholars to Washington as Kennan had prescribed froze on my lips. But I had enough sense not to raise the faintest protest about Kendall's view, and just nodded agreeably. Once more, I was "a nice young man." After I made my pitch, Kendall threw me a contemptuous glance, said he'd think about it, and our interview was at an end. He did in fact contribute, but less than he had given in his previous five-year grant to Fred Starr.

More than a year later, I put on a conference at the Kennan with two of my colleagues from graduate school, Peter Kenez of the University of California, Santa Cruz, and Richard Stites of Georgetown. Our subject was the complex process through which Russian culture was transmuted into Soviet culture in the years immediately following the Russian Revolution. What had changed? What remained the same and what was the mix of new and old? The conference was considered a success, and Indiana University Press published the proceedings as a book, entitled *Bolshevik Culture: Experiment and Order in the Russian Revolution*. More than a quarter century later it still remains available from the press and has generally been considered an influential volume in our generation's emerging interest in the social and cultural history of Russia/USSR, especially among Anglophone scholars and from an anthropological point of view. But Donald Kendall hated it. His ire fell especially on an essay by one of my female colleagues entitled "Village Women Experience the Revolution." If there was ever a subject that Donald Kendall felt could be left out of consideration by any organization he was supporting, this was it. He wrote an angry letter of protest to James Billington and brought the obnoxious essay up in conversations repeatedly. But his small grant of $15,000 came in three discrete bites, so the problem of continuing support for Kennan from PepsiCo was left for the next Secretary to address. I never enquired as to whether that support was forthcoming.

The Donald Kendall relationship exposed a serious difficulty that has plagued the Kennan Institute over time, particularly when it was staffed by liberal academics like me. The people with the money very often—but not always—had little or no interest in the scholarship we were turning out unless it had a direct bearing on political and economic issues on the front burner between the United States and the Soviet Union. When the Cold War ended, the Kennan Institute was still grappling with that challenge. As for me, I felt that after dealing with Donald Kendall I had been permanently immunized against intimidation by anybody in the academic community.

I was fortunate to inherit from Fred Starr a number of conferences, some emanating from the government side, some from academia, most of which were securely funded. The secretary of the Kennan Institute presided over these, and in some indirect way got credit for staging them, even though in many cases he had to do little more than smile, greet participants and provide space. Several of the conferences were particularly good. One focused on the so-called "second economy" in the USSR—basically the black market; another on Soviet natural resources in the world economy; and a third on nationalism and social change in the Caucasus region. My

Joseph Biden speaks on U.S.-Soviet relations at Kennan, 1981
(left to right) Tom Gleason, Joseph Biden
Photo courtesy of the Wilson Center

contribution to these conferences was largely ornamental, but I learned a good deal, both about the subjects under discussion and about how to run a conference. Hosting them gave me confidence in my ability to function in this milieu. The Castle was a charming facility for such events, especially the library of the Wilson Center. It looked out on the Mall and exuded a scholarly atmosphere quite unusual in Washington. The faint melodies emanating from the carousel outside were just audible and added to the charm.

My institutional position at the Kennan Institute exposed me to an often amusing pantomime conflict between my two bosses. Billington was adamant that the Kennan Institute, despite its name and genealogy, was merely a division, or a "program," of the Wilson Center. And indeed he had hired me, and I was a member of his "senior staff" (a corporatism that was gaining ground even in academia by 1980). But to George Kennan, I was the director of his Institute. Although I had been hired by Billington, I worked for Kennan. Of course, my awe of Kennan was such that I gloried in having people believe that he was my boss. He confided in me that the growing influence of the Kennan Institute was reinforcing his hopes and dreams that one day it would be independently endowed. I was flattered, despite the fact that Kennan's hopes were divulged to a fairly large number of confidants. Billington, of course, knew of this and repeatedly reminded me of the "real" state of affairs. The Kennan was a division of his shop. The two of them never had an open confrontation on the matter. Kennan was deeply averse to quarreling about anything, and Billington was keenly aware of Kennan's prestige and how awkward any public or semi-public disagreement would be. The two men treated each other with extravagant courtliness in public but complained politely about each other in private.

Kennan's hope that his institute would deepen official Washington's knowledge of how Russia and the Soviet Union operated was never really realized. It was a utopian vision. Washington was about politics, and academics could affect it only at the margin, unless they were chosen by politicians to act as their spokesmen. Some Washington officials did learn more about the Soviet Union by coming to Kennan Institute events, but by and large they were people already disposed to learn more. On the other hand, a number of academics learned more at the Kennan about how American politics actually worked which was indisputably a good thing. Overall, the entire academic field of Russian/Soviet studies was enriched by the presence of the Kennan Institute. I learned an enormous amount. Like so many others, I was de-provincialized by my time there. But I also became reacquainted with the deep alienation that the Viet Nam War had created between academia and Washington. The brass at the Wilson Center respected scholarship, but there was a barely disguised sense that many, if not most, academics were a bit out of it. "Academics" made us worldly folk smile.

James Billington had lost none of the boyish charm and good looks that had characterized him in his younger days, but he had added to them a good deal of sophistication and worldly ambition.

He was a churchgoer and a conservative, and saw the world very much in religious terms, but this did not rule out personal ambition—his hopes, for example, of becoming ambassador to the Soviet Union. He was relatively tolerant of my liberalism, however, so long as it didn't rile conservative members of his board, like the neo-conservative lawyer and diplomat, Max Kampelman. I engaged in a certain amount of self-censorship in Kampelman's presence, which was probably not necessary, as I was a bit below his radar screen. Kampelman was then chairing a number of delegations affiliated with the Conference on Security and Cooperation in Europe. He was also a member of the Committee on the Present Danger, an influential anti-Soviet lobby, of which Richard Pipes was also a charter member. This was the seed-time of the neo-conservative movement, although I had not yet become aware of the term. But I was of the view that the American government was quite anti-Soviet enough.

The CIA had played a variety of roles on the periphery of my life. Through my family and by growing up in Washington, I had a distant acquaintance with the first generation of CIA leaders: Kermit Roosevelt, Frank Wisner, Tracy Barnes, whose children I also knew. And, of course, my father had been part of the secret conversations which had led to the Agency's founding. Like most liberals of my generation, I was suspicious of the CIA and regarded some of its activities—like the overthrow of Prime Minister Mohammed Mossadegh of Iran—as tragically misguided. The prevailing demonic view purveyed by some sixties radicals had always struck me as much overdrawn. The CIA was an agency of the United States government set up for very specific purposes. One might deeply disapprove of those purposes, think them misguided, badly executed or whatever, but I had known from early on that there was no particular villainy or viciousness about being an intelligence agent, beyond the existential hazards of an agent's life and work, as depicted, for example in John Le Carré's *The Spy Who Came In From The Cold*. CIA employees were no less intellectually honest (if no more so) than my academic colleagues, and their view of the world was generally similar.

It was satisfying to confirm that CIA specialists on the Soviet economy like Grey Hodnett or Douglas Diamond shared views that were generally indistinguishable from leading academicians. They mixed readily with them at Kennan Institute conferences on the Soviet economy. Of course, conservative critics like Richard Perle and Richard Pipes were already critical of the CIA for insufficient anti-Soviet fervor. They claimed that the CIA analysts focused too much on Soviet "capabilities" and ignored the Soviet Union's messianic and malign intentions. The Soviet military budget and its percentage share in the overall Soviet economy were vital parts of this matter (although they were in fact extremely difficult to determine, in view of the almost total unreliability of published Soviet statistics). For most students of the Soviet economy, as a young scholar has recently observed, "the size of the Soviet economy was a proxy for the Soviet military threat."[1]

I knew that I had a lot to learn about the Soviet economy, so among the first places I went to visit from my new Kennan office was a couple of small, crowded rooms in the Commerce Department that were generally known as "Murray's Shop." Murray was Murray Feshbach, who was alleged to have more statistical information on the Soviet economy than anyone else in town, especially demographic data. A 1974 Ph.D. from American University, Murray had experience analyzing the Soviet social, economic and ecological system that went back to the late 1950s. His title when I met him was a mouthful, even for Washington. He was Chief of the Foreign Demographic Analysis Division of the U.S. Bureau of the Census in the Commerce Department. He retained this post, with several stints as a guest scholar at the Wilson Center, until 1981 when he took a position in the Economics Department at Georgetown

[1] David Engerman, *Know Your Enemy: The Rise and Fall of America's Soviet Expert* (unpublished manuscript).

University and moved his enormous collection of data into his big new office there.

Murray was no slouch as an analyst and even better as a sleuth, but his most important contribution was as a collector of data. Everything he had was part of a laboriously accumulated trove that ranged from his Soviet data to an extensive mineral collection housed in his Silver Spring home. All Washington students of the Soviet economy as well as visiting specialists from universities across the country came to Murray's Shop at Commerce to see what he had. As most collectors do, he loved to display his treasures: data on industrial sites, infant mortality, life expectancy, alcoholism.

The Soviet experience had an enormous impact on the rest of the world, of course, but for its own inhabitants, especially the Russian ones, a central part of its legacy has been an ongoing crisis which is partly economic, partly ecological, and partly epidemiological. These interlinked problems were becoming quite clear by 1980. The crisis was caused by decades of headlong industrialization, terrible pollution, extravagant consumption of alcohol and cigarettes, increasing infant mortality, healthcare failures and that most enduringly Russian of problems, poverty. It resulted from doing things coercively from the top down. Not only has infant mortality gotten worse and worse, in recent decades male life expectancy has fallen to approximately fifty-nine years for a child born today. Female life expectancy is seventy-three. This gender gap was—and is—the widest in the developed world. The Russian crisis is deeply rooted, and, thus far, the collapse of the Soviet Union has had no significant effect on the statistics or their general tendency.

At a deeper and more ideo-philosophical level the crisis is linked to an attitude that exalts the conquest of nature, rather than accommodation with it. One finds this to some degree in all modern industrial societies, but it is more pronounced in Marxist states than in Euro-American ones. Surrendering to the forces of nature was considered, in Marxist circles, to be a form of reactionary passivity. "Natural" barriers were to be stormed and broken down, not accommodated. Traditionalist and phenomenological critics of communism like Vaclav Havel and Alexander Solzhenitsyn had been pointing to this crisis for several years. As Solzhenitsyn wrote more than thirty years ago:

> [The Soviet Union] had to be dragged along the whole of the Western bourgeois-industrial and Marxist path in order to discover ... from progressive Western scholars, what any village graybeard in the Ukraine or Russia had understood from time immemorial and could have explained ... ages ago ... that a dozen worms can't go on and on gnawing the same apple *forever*; that if the earth is a finite object, then its expanses and resources are finite also and that the endless, infinite progress dinned into our heads by the dreamers of the Enlightenment cannot be accomplished on it. All that "endless progress" turned out to be an insane, ill-considered, furious dash into a blind alley. A civilization greedy for "perpetual progress" has now choked and is on its last legs."[2]

No critic can claim sole credit for identifying the maladies so deeply present in late Soviet and post-Soviet society, but Murray Feshbach certainly did the most to track them down, connect the dots, and present the disturbing results to his professional colleagues. Murray has pursued his prey with his extraordinary single-mindedness since the mid-1970s. He was a Kennan Fellow while I was there, and the Wilson Center became a second home to him while he was making his transition from government to academia. He became a minor celebrity for his exposition of the Soviet Union's demographic, economic and ecological troubles.[3] Murray

[2] Aleksandr I. Solzhenitsyn, *Letter to the Soviet Leaders*, New York, Harper and Row, 1974, pp. [illegible]

[3] For an early instance, directed toward a large audience, see Christopher Davis and Murray Feshbach, "Life Expectancy in the Soviet Union," *Wall Street Journal*, June 20, 1978. An influential early statement was "The Soviet Union: Population Trends and Dilemmas," *Population Bulletin*, Vol. 37, No. 3 (August, 1982). His most magisterial synthesis is (with Alfred Friendly, Jr.), *Ecocide in the USSR:*

enjoyed his role as a seer and occasionally assumed a Delphic manner, which contrasted amusingly with his enormous good nature and his gigantic store of information.

Another person we met in Washington in 1980 was a friend of Murray Feshbach, named Norton Dodge, the pre-eminent collector of Russian dissident art. Norton has since become better known than he was then, partly because of *The Ransom of Russian Art*, a vivid if somewhat slapdash book about him by the famous journalist John McPhee. Norton's enormous collection of between eight and ten thousand pieces has been rounded off and given to the Zimmerli Art Museum at Rutgers University. It is far and away the largest and most representative collection of works of "unofficial" or "underground" art created during the Soviet period—art which did not conform to whatever the reigning canon of socialist realism that may have prevailed at the time.

By the time I met Norton Dodge, he was about fifty years old, and had been traveling for years back and forth to the Soviet Union, buying the work of dissident or underground artists. Somehow he had managing to bring their paintings, prints, pieces of sculpture and unclassifiables back to his estate in St. Mary's County, in southern Maryland. His period as an active collector was about over by then, although friends and acquaintances of his and the artists still procured works for his collection which had become famous among Soviet artists. Having your work in Norton's collection was generally considered the only hope for a Soviet modern artist to gain fame, fortune or both. Of course, a major part of Norton Dodge's fascinating story was how he got this art out of the Soviet Union, as these unorthodox works were regarded by the Soviet government as criminal, and emphatically not for export.

Health and Nature Under Siege, New York, Basic books, 1992. For a brief statement of the current status of Russia's crisis, see *Russia's Wrong Direction*, Council on Foreign Relations, Independent Task Force Report, No. 57, New York, 2006, pp. 67-69.

Norton used a variety of method. Some were simple, like sticking paintings flat in suitcases, or rolling them up inside politically orthodox posters which could be taken out legally. Others were more elaborate. Foreign embassies were not supposed to use the so-called "diplomatic pouch" to send material of this sort, but they would sometimes do so anyway. Occasionally, Norton would seek the assistance of foreigners less likely to stir up suspicion than he was. He even bribed employees of the Ministry of Culture to help him exporting them. Sometimes, he shipped art hidden inside articles already cleared for departure from the Soviet Union. Back at Cremona Farm in Maryland, he housed his remarkable collection not only in the large country house where he and Nancy, his charming wife, lived much of the time, but also in refurbished chicken coops and in sheds that had been built to cure tobacco or store feed corn.

Dodge had engaged in extraordinary feats both in finding these works and in positioning himself at the center of a network of the artists who created them. It was amazing that this portly, balding academic with an enormous mustache and imperfect Russian managed to do all this in the midst of active police surveillance. McPhee quoted Norton's own account of "finding your way around, finding apartments in the outskirts, stumbling through all this, and after midnight asking yourself, How do you get back? When you add it all up, you wonder how you did all that."[4] The "getting back" was particularly important and difficult for such a conspicuous foreigner. It often involved sneaking back pictures in the middle of the night to one of the specially designated Intourist hotels where all foreigners were required to stay, and which were under varying kinds of surveillance, twenty-four hours a day. There is a bit of a mystery here, as Norton did not appear to have the skill of a James Bond. As Norton's wife Nancy put it, "How could you ever get around the

[4] John McPhee, *The Ransom of Russian Art*, New York, Farrar, Strauss and Giroux, 1994, p. 36.

Soviet Union if you can't beat your way out of the St. Louis airport."[5] In reading McPhee's account I wondered whether the KGB really cared as much about this type of lawbreaking as about other illicit activities that they were more effective in stopping.

Several writers have pointed out that Norton Dodge did more than spend several million dollars to accumulate a large number of individual works of art. According to McPhee, "what Dodge had evidently assembled was not so much of an era as the era itself. It was the whole tree—the growing cambium with the dead wood. If his motive was higher than money it was also higher than the aesthetic level of any given work. He had released into the general light a creativity whose products had been all the more concealed because they were untranslatable and awkward to move. With it, he had released the creators."[6] That is, the sum total of the works he brought out amount to a richly detailed portrait of middle and late Soviet society as seen through its self-appointed illustrators. Without Norton, much of this illustration would never have seen the light of day.

Norton, like Murray Feshbach, is a man of great originality, although this has not been universally recognized by his circle of friends and acquaintances. He began his career as a student of the Soviet economy about a decade or so ahead of me in graduate school at Harvard. He wrote the first study of the singular importance of women in the Soviet economy. After taking his Ph.D. he accepted a position in the Economics Department at the University of Maryland and began to play the stock market, both for himself and for others, who morphed into clients. He hired knowledgeable colleagues to aid him in investment decisions as well. He soon acquired enough money to resign from the Economics Department and indulge what had become his full time passion: collecting the

[5] John McPhee, *The Ransom of Russian Art*, New York, Farrar, Strauss and Giroux, 1994, p.105.

[6] Ibid., p.19

contemporary art rejected by the Soviet authorities.

This art was of a peculiar kind. It was recognizably modern and had connections with the mainstream of European and American art of the twentieth century. But it was—borrowing from the student language of today—a bit "random". For a Soviet artist active, say, in 1975, Cezanne, Picasso, Kandinsky, Salvatore Dali, Jackson Pollock and Andy Warhol could all seem contemporary. The work of Soviet painters incorporated icons, academic art from earlier times, book illustrations, comic books, tarot cards, graffiti and many other things. The quality was wildly variable. Soviet modernism was influenced by the Western art that had been seized by the Soviets and carried home as spoils. It was then used in an art world with no real canon.

Most Sundays in 1980 and 1981, Norton would serve a delicious brunch at Cremona to his friends and to anyone else interested in Russia, especially in Russian art. As the secretary of the Kennan Institute, I had a standing invitation. It was great fun to drive down as a family which we often did, sometimes combining a viewing of new acquisitions with brunch and a swim. Oysters, of which Norton was enormously fond, were an additional attraction.

It was fascinating to be taken through portions of Norton's enormous and varied collection. He generously loaned the Kennan Institute some of his pictures, including Vladimir Nemukhin's "Poker on the Beach,"[7] which was stylistically somewhere between Hans Hofmann and Philip Guston, and a painting by Alexander Sitnikov, a decorative neo-cubist.

Our son Nick was immersed in Sherlock Holmes stories at the time, so conversations about Holmes and Watson were recurring. In the car going home one Sunday, as Sarah and I were digesting both what we had eaten and what we had seen, Meg, who had an excellent sense of the satirical, suddenly remarked in that slightly portentous Holmesian idiom: "The Strange Case of Norton Dodge."

[7] Reproduced in McPhee, *Ransom*, p. 22.

Both Nick and Meg seemed to enjoy their time in Washington, accommodating the great cast of characters with equanimity, as kids tend to do, and enjoying the Cathedral schools.

The National Security Council was, of course, my father's old shop and no doubt I had a special feeling about it. By 1980 it had become vastly larger, more like a research institute for the president than the small staff it had been in my father's time. Under President Jimmy Carter, I became acquainted with some intriguing intellectuals and politicos, whose influence would extend well into the future. Two quite distinct factions vied for President Carter's ear on policy toward the Soviet Union. One was the détente-minded group led by Secretary of State Cyrus Vance and ably seconded by Marshall Shulman, formerly of Harvard and Columbia. The harder-line group was led by Zbigniew Brzezinski, with whom I had only the slightest acquaintance, and two of his Ph.D.s from Columbia, Madeleine Albright and General William Odom, with whom I became quite friendly and whom I deeply admired. Bill, with characteristic lack of self-regard, simply introduced himself to me one day after someone's talk at the Institute. Around the same time, but under entirely different circumstances, I got to know his wife Anne, a historian of Russian decorative arts based at the Hillwood Museum. Bill and Anne were an intimate part of the most congenial social circle that we encountered in Washington. Conversations in the Odom household were notably broadened and enriched by Anne's sympathetic presence. Her interest in Russian decorative arts and antiquities afforded welcome relief from exhausting political disputes and offered a providential escape into the world of icons, enamels and porcelain.

My perspective on the Soviet Union was somewhere between Brzezinski's hostility, aggravated by his Polish nationalism, and Marshall Shulman's tendency to lowball Soviet aggressiveness. Also on the Carter National Security Council was Al Friendly, Jr., whom I had known both at St. Albans and Harvard, a talented linguist and writer, and an experienced staffer on Capitol Hill, whose job for the NSC was dealing with the press. Plagued in his later years by depression, Friendly was an exceedingly able man who never quite found his groove. He was a man of considerable wit and large vocabulary, but who had trouble appearing sufficiently populist for Ronald Reagan's Washington.

When Reagan succeeded Carter, Albright was out of a job, and so she accepted a fellowship at the Wilson Center. She was not formally affiliated with the Kennan Institute, but her interests ran to Eastern Europe, and from a regional point of view she was one of us. She was "studying" the Polish and Czech press, but had no great ambition to produce a major scholarly work. She was newly divorced and spent lots of time around the Castle. I found her great fun to talk to. Just as I was heading back to Brown in the second half of 1982, Madeleine was coming to the end of her fellowship. Would I, she asked, be willing to write her a reference? I was flattered. Of course, I would. So, I wrote a letter saying how much she knew and how smart she was. She used the letter to apply for a position in the Government Department at Georgetown. I knew Angela Stent, the departmental chair and a vivacious former student of Adam Ulam. She phoned me up. Albright may be interesting, agreed Angela, but she has no publications to speak of. Well, now that she's out of government she'll produce some, I argued. And besides, she's going places! Little did I know how right I was. Madeleine got the Georgetown job and, on becoming Secretary of State, she put Angela on her Policy Planning Staff, working on Russo-German relations, which was her specialty. Years later when Angela and I met in Washington at a memorial ceremony for Adam Ulam, we had a chuckle about how we had helped Madeleine Albright's career along.

Disciplined though he was, Bill Odom enjoyed the cloak-and-dagger aspects of his career. Among other exploits, he eluded agents sent out to shadow him in both Germany and the Soviet Union, and he smuggled Solzhenitsyn's memoir, *Gulag Archipelago*, out of the Soviet Union. Bill was the most energetic talker that I ever knew outside of the academic community. He was plain-spoken, indeed blunt. When he returned from a trip to China as part of a political and military delegation, he deprecated Alexander Haig's view that the United States might "play the China card," if sufficiently provoked by the Soviet Union. Fresh from viewing the Chinese military close up, Bill exclaimed unceremoniously that the so-called China card "is a deuce".

When I talked to Bill on the telephone, I would invariably discover about ten minutes into the conversation that I had been walking in a big circle throughout the first floor of the house. It was impossible for me to sit still and either listen to Bill or try and get my two cents worth in. Of course, moving my feet around in a circle didn't enable me either to counter Bill's arguments or think of new ones of my own. I was simply carried along physically by the effort and excitement of talking to him. Bill, a man of deep moral principle, passion and unusual candor, died of a heart attack in the early summer of 2008. Zbigniew Brzezinski said in his eulogy of Bill:

> His intellectual horizons were wide and his mind creative. He wrote books ranging from authoritative studies of the Soviet military to ambitious examination of the new Post-Cold War American Empire....He enjoyed teaching and was a superb teacher, truly loved by his students. I was struck by how much time he was prepared to devote to prolonged, informative, and relentlessly challenging discussions, conducted in Bill's spirited debating style of "take no prisoners"—which nonetheless stimulated intense loyalty among those exposed to it. And yet despite that combative style, he encouraged independent judgment, not only in academia, but also in the disciplined military setting—making it clear to subordinates that if they had a reasoned case to make, they should not fear to speak up.[8]

Many of my arguments with him in those days dealt with whether the so-called "totalitarian model" was the best framework for understanding how policy was formulated and executed in the

[8] *The Middlebury Magazine*, Fall, 2008, p. 92.

Soviet Union. The totalitarian model and the comparison with Nazi Germany upon which it rested had dominated Soviet Studies since the early 1950s, especially among political scientists who liked models. In the 1980s, the model was challenged by scholars who gave greater account to local and regional variations and who located revolutionary impulses coming from below, as well as from above. The most notable champions of the latter view were Sheila Fitzpatrick, a University of Chicago history professor, and her then husband, Jerry Hough of Duke, a political scientist. Both were Kennan fellows during my tenure. The argument raged for a long generation, dividing students of the Soviet Union into those who believed centralized politics and ideology were driving the entire Soviet enterprise and those who believed that social change and other developments within the Soviet Union were emerging from society itself. This argument eased only with the demise of the Soviet Union, and it seems fair to conclude that the adherents of a "totalitarian" point of view had somewhat the better of the argument. At any rate, no one argued more passionately for the totalitarian model than Bill Odom, or with greater effectiveness.

At the time I was as usual positioned in the middle. The totalitarian model struck me as having a major flaw. The "model" was constructed from a comparison of the experience of National Socialist Germany, Fascist Italy and the Soviet Union. It seemed redundant to compare the Soviet Union to such a model since the Soviets were so instrumental in its creation and development. There was a limit to how much you could learn by looking through this kind of lens.

Both Odom and Brzezinski came to occupy a very different place in the political spectrum in recent years than they did before 1991. Both were strongly opposed to American policy during the second Iraq War. In the post-Cold War world, Brzezinski's sense of kinship with Polish patriotism has become much less of a factor in his foreign policy views, yielding to a realism that rejects the liberationist ambitions of George W. Bush, especially his religious messianism. Once Soviet zealotry was taken out of the equation, Odom's realism became fully as astringent as that of Brzezinski. Both had zero sympathy for the neo-con tendency to bring Cold War attitudes into the new conflicts in the Middle East.

It was not long before my time in Washington was up and the big choice loomed before me: Should I stay longer at the Kennan Institute, and then—most likely—move into academic administration, or should I return to academic life at Brown? Without much hesitation I chose the latter, opting for academia over Washington. My father had made the opposite choice in 1950, and I had long thought he made the wrong one. I knew I would miss the regular contact with students and faculty colleagues and the time to write. Sarah was not crazy about life in Washington and was disappointed to have been unable to launch a career in the extensive museum world of Washington. Meg was happy to go where we went. Our challenge was Nick who loved St. Albans, and we had a long struggle over whether he could remain as a boarder. Finally one of the fine young St. Albans teachers intervened and told us, "Nick can't decide. He can't make the choice. He needs you to do it for him." So Nick came back to Providence and enrolled as a ninth-grader at Moses Brown School, a choice we never regretted. Meg rejoined her wonderful cohort at Nathaniel Greene Middle School. They both readjusted beautifully to Rhode Island, but like Sarah and me they were more cosmopolitan when they returned than when they left.

There was a little party for me just before we departed. George Kennan came down from Princeton to say good-bye. To make the occasion particularly memorable I threw my back out the night before and had to reply to toasts uncomfortably immobilized in a straight-backed chair.

I returned to Brown a changed person. I had much greater professional self-confidence, and felt I could legitimately teach the entire span of Russian and Soviet history. I was also much more attuned to contemporary Soviet politics and Soviet-American relations. If I still felt a provincial at heart, I no longer doubted my ability to function in the capital.

Boris Klinč, Fire Hard at the Class Enemy, *1933*
from the exhibition: Views and Re-Views: Soviet Political Posters and Cartoons *at Brown University, 2008*
Jo-ann Conklin and Abbott Gleason, curators

Gorbachev and Totalitarianism

Sarah and I flew from Moscow to Zurich after I had finished lecturing to a group of American tourists in the Russian capital. We were going on back to the United States, but would take an extra two days to see Zurich, a city neither of us had visited. It was late August of 1988, and the end of the Soviet Union was some three years away. Moscow was already suffering from food shortages. There was less and less in the stores. For over a year, the streets had become increasingly crowded with people selling—or trying to sell—anything they could. People shopped at poorly supplied farmers' markets. Makeshift kiosks were everywhere, mostly purveying booze of unknown origin and provenance. I recall leaving a friend's apartment and heading for the nearest Metro stop one morning. At the top of the stairs a slim, middle-aged woman was sitting on the ground, with a kitten in her lap. Her head was down, so that she made no eye contact with passers by. She appeared to be deeply ashamed. When I returned, some seven hours later, both the woman and the kitten were still there, position and demeanor unchanged. No takers.

Sheremetevo Airport had been a madhouse when we left. It was hot and steamy and the lines were immensely long. Many people were not waiting their turn for ticketing or baggage check. They simply butted into a spot as near the head of what passed for a line as possible. Those guards who had shown up for work were even slower and less friendly as they checked documents. The floors were filthy. I thought—as I often did—of Pushkin's remark after reading Peter Chaadaev's famously bleak description of Russia in the early 1830s, "God how sad our Russia is."

The contrast with Zurich was extraordinary. There the sun shone in an azure, cloudless sky. Everything was quiet and orderly at the airport. The city seemed extraordinarily prosperous, but without ostentation. It was a conservative, rather prim and bourgeois show place, entirely without apology for the injustices of its system, which were quite visible to the interested eye. Wealth dominated. There were poor people and shabby corners, but even these were tidy and discreet in a Swiss way.

Mikhail Gorbachev had just gone the other way, also changing planes in Zurich, on his return to Moscow. I imagined him observing the chaos at the Moscow airport as he was whisked through. "Surely," I thought, "he sees the contrast with Zurich in *at least some ways* as we do." No doubt Gorbachev's more or less frequent trips to the West had an impact on his reformist thinking. He had traveled abroad far more than previous Soviet leaders. No Westerners knew at that time, I believe, how early Gorbachev and his inner circle had come to the conclusion that radical reform of the Soviet Union would be necessary. "Everything has gone rotten here," Eduard Shevardnadze told Gorbachev apparently as early as 1984, an interesting year for this remark.[1]

Russia continued its most spectacular travails for well over a decade after 1991. There was an attempted coup, a corrupt privatization process and the emergence of the so-called "new Russians." Actually, many of them were the same old Russians, but their wealth was certainly new. Toward the end of 2008, Moscow had pockets of enormous, ostentatious wealth. Spectacular malls emerged downtown and gated communities in the burgeoning suburbs. Although other parts of urban Russia showed increasing prosperity too, progress was extremely uneven. The inequality was awful, and democracy seemed far away. While the worst appears long over, for

[1] Archie Brown, *The Gorbachev Factor*, Oxford University Press, 1996, p.81.

many Russia remains a place of desolation, despite its wealth. A graduate student of mine who spent some weeks in the countryside near the city of Nizhny Novgorod on the Volga in the fall of 2007 was devastated by the poverty, drunkenness and hunger she found there. Despite being knowledgeable and theoretically astute, she was ill-prepared for what she actually encountered.

I sampled Russia during many summers during the 1990s, although never for more than a few weeks at a time. I saw Intourist, the Soviet tourist organization that ran special hotels for foreigners, disappear, like its parent organization, the Soviet Union. For the first time, I was thus able to rent an apartment in Leningrad, the double doors of which were supplied with no fewer than five locks. Shortly thereafter, I was astonished when the city reverted to its original name of St. Petersburg. Repudiations of Lenin and the revolution were still breathtaking to me and other scholars. How far might it go? Restoration of the monarchy? It sounds fantastic again now, but in the late 1990s nobody could foretell what might happen.

To me the most surprising development of the transition from the Soviet Union to Russia ("transitology" as it came to be called) was the fact that Russia's incipient capitalism was so permeated by criminality. It was almost as if the Soviet vision of capitalism as a violent criminal conspiracy had been deliberately realized by some malign Russian demiurge. Perhaps it was really not so surprising. After all, crime is one of the demonic extremes of individualism (although not without a dimension of collectivity), and that was what the successful in the world—like the United States—were preaching to the Russians. Then, too, behind the Russian commitment to the communal had always lurked a secret lust for its opposite.

I had several experiences with Russian criminals, but more farcical than frightening. I was guiding another group of tourists on a trip to Moscow and what was then still Leningrad in 1990, when a criminal gang got hold of the skeleton key to our hotel bedrooms.

Everybody in the tourist group who had not chain locked their doors—as it turned out, some forty people—lost wallets, purses and other valuables. Being accustomed to old-time Soviet hotel security where burglars were among the few things tourists never worried about, I had not bothered to chain-lock my door either. I awoke about 4:00 A.M. that night to discern through the gloom that a man was rifling through my pants pockets. I blurted something out and raised myself groggily to a sitting position. "Pardon," the intruder said politely in a French accent and bolted out of the room with my wallet. The victims all straggled into the lobby to assess what had happened. I then had to phone Sarah and have her cancel all my credit cards. On another occasion, in the wide-open atmosphere of the transition, I was swarmed by gypsies on Moscow's Arbat Street. I fought off my first Russian mugger in the early 'nineties, but a group of young men from Central Asia got me a few years later. Both muggings were encounters in St. Petersburg.

Perhaps even more astonishing than the collapse of the Soviet Union—if that was precisely what it was—was that it took place with minimal loss of life. But things were certainly harrowing for many Russians and some foreigners, as the "Russian mafia" began to fill the vacuum left by the Soviet state and police structure. A Brown student who had probably (and accidentally) seen a transaction he ought not to have witnessed, "fell to his death" from a high rise. At about the same time, a young American named Ken Kalfus wrote about an experience which seemed to me to epitomize the complex lawlessness which had overtaken the former Soviet Union by the latter 1990s. He went to visit a couple he knew who lived in a small community on the outskirts of Moscow, and they told him the following story. One winter day, an expensive Western car roared down their small side street at about sixty miles an hour, killing their German Shepherd and dragging its body along the street for some hundred feet. Then the car screeched to a halt and the driver leapt out and not only did not apologize but was in a rage, claiming damage to his car. When the couple tried to pull the dog's body out from under the car, a shoving match ensued, and the driver demanded the Russian equivalent of $300. Failing to get it, he left, but promised he would be back.

That evening, three big four-wheeled vehicles arrived, carrying several men with shot guns. They stopped on the street and got out with their weapons. They mis-identified the couple's house, so they fired a number of rounds into the wrong house, doing a fair amount of damage. They then interrogated neighbors at gunpoint to find the owners of the dog, but everybody clammed up like Sicilians who had taken a vow of *omertà*. The entire community, however, was now in terror about what was going to happen. The couple sent their daughter away to stay with relatives.

The next day they went to the police, a rather obvious idea to a Westerner, but much less so in Russia. The cop they talked to was sympathetic and told them that the really important thing was to find out of which gang they had run afoul. The helpful policeman was able to do this, and he arranged for a representative of the gang in question to come to the couple's house. The gang rep arrived in a BMW, accompanied by a colleague in an Audi. He threatened the couple and said they would simply have to pay. "Do you think you run the region?" he asked the dog owner. "Are you so brave?" Then he and his escort drove away. The driver who had killed the couple's dog returned the next day and demanded $12,000, but after a great deal of raging and threatening, he settled for the $300 he had demanded originally. The couple really had no other option than to pay up.[2]

This anecdote suggests the depth of the lawlessness that attended the birth of Russian capitalism and the demise of the old system. No wonder people made endless jokes about the "Wild East." A great deal of what passed for police work around the turn of the 21st century was either free-lance extortion or—as in the Kalfus'

[2] The full story in Ken Kalfus, "Far from Normal: Scenes from the New Moscow," *Harpers*, December, 1996, pp. 53-62.

anecdote—mediating between the criminal bosses and their enemies or victims. The situation is much improved today, but the best security in Russia is still private. Body guards are still necessary for anyone above a certain income level. And pity the critical journalist or politician who cannot or will not pay for protection—known, in Russian, as "a roof."

The collapse of the Soviet Union had an impact on organized crime far beyond Russia, although many of its most spectacular scenes were played out in Moscow. It has been described by a knowledgeable observer as "the single most important event" affecting the vast increase in global crime between 1990 and 2008.[3] The buccaneering privatization affected global crime and criminal activity in multiple ways, involving gigantic flows of money and goods all over the world. The drab Russian capital was transformed—for some—into "a breathtaking Babylon of guns, enterprise, money, violence, and fun."[4]

Despite the criminality and chaos which attended the end of the Soviet Union, it may have been the most remarkable event of the twentieth century and was certainly the most amazing international event in my lifetime. The sheer magnitude and rapidity of the Soviet collapse took everyone by surprise, especially following the glacial decline of the Brezhnev period, which itself was by no means clear to everyone and took a long time to register even with keen-eyed observers. Some social historians may have been influenced by their demi-Marxism into believing that the Soviet system was more rooted in the subsoil of society than it was. A frequent charge leveled by my generation of scholars against their conservative senior colleagues was that the oldsters overemphasized purely political power. That general view does not seem very convincing to me now. But both generations saw the Soviet Union as far stronger than it turned out to be. As an eminent Polish economist remarked

[3] Misha Glenny, *McMafia*, Alfred E. Knopf, New York, 2008, p. 52.

[4] Ibid., p. 53.

to me, the Soviet dictatorship turned out to be a mysterious "black box," even to insiders.

Neither liberals nor conservatives wanted to err on the side of seeing the Soviet Union as weaker than it was. Conservatives were always ready to pounce on liberals who didn't understand how powerful the Soviet enemy was. The proposition that the Soviet Union's underpinnings were so weak that the polity might collapse relatively quickly was simply not discussable in mainstream political circles in Europe or the United States during the eighties.

Another important point. The Soviet collapse took place in a very conservative time, not only in American politics and political culture, but globally. Free market liberalism or "neo-liberalism" was riding high. Friedrich Hayek, Ludwig von Mises and especially Milton Friedman had marginalized John Maynard Keynes. Social democratic points of view commanded ever less support and respectable Leftists were circling the wagons close to the political center. Just as this worldwide economic tendency played some role in the downfall of the Soviet Union, it also provided the context for what had happened, and for what was believed to be possible in the future. The collapse could be understood as—and was considered to be by many conservatives—the most spectacular triumph of the new economic order.

The fact that so many highly trained people failed to predict the collapse of Soviet Union damaged the credibility of Sovietologists. Why was so much invested over so many years to train so many specialists—"polar bear watchers," as my colleagues at the Chinese embassy used to call them when I was at the Kennan Institute—who couldn't foresee such a major thing as that the Soviet Union wasn't going to make it? As Robert V. Daniels put it, "Was Sovietology as it was pursued in the USA invalidated because it failed to predict the collapse of Communism?"[5]

[5] Robert V. Daniels, "American Soviet Studies and the Grand Surprise of 1991," in Cox, *Rethinking the Soviet Collapse*. Richard Pipes, rather mysteriously to me, blamed the moral relativism of Sovietologists for the failure of Sovietology to

Of course, there are considerable differences between saying that "the Soviet Union collapsed" and saying that "Russia evolved through a Soviet phase and out the other side of it" which is how we tend to treat "Communist" China. According to Daniels, "the so-called 'collapse' of Communism is another formula that needs to be reexamined. Collapse is a facile popular image of what was actually a complex, step-by-step, and still incomplete process of change in the society or societies of the Soviet Union. Moreover it obscures the elements of continuity in the successor regime and their problems."[6] Still, I can't help but feel that—however true Daniels' reflection may be—there is something a little defensive about it.

In fairness, I have to admit that the two extremes among scholars and Sovietologists came a little closer to "getting it" right than respectable left-center opinion, of which I was a part. Commentators who for one reason or another regarded the Soviet Union as an "aberrant" or abnormal polity in some broad or *systemic* way were a bit less surprised at its demise than those who regarded it as a variant of a "normal" modern state, if a distinctly unpleasant one. Why should dissident Marxists, on the one hand, or hard-liners like Richard Pipes and Martin Malia on the other, have somewhat more accurately sensed the fragility of the Soviet Union than my more mainstream colleagues? Merely to formulate the question may suggest a part of the answer. Trotskyists and dissident Marxists, on the one hand, and right-wingers, on the other, had clearer and more definite ideas about what kind of state can (or should) survive in our world. For many political conservatives and old-fashioned economic liberals, no state can deny the market and survive for

foresee the end of the Soviet Union. He appears to mean by this assertion that American students of the Soviet Union tried to see the Soviet Union more as scientists than as moralists. But seeing things as accurately as possible and avoiding scholarly wishful thinking is surely our obligation. See Richard Pipes, *Vixi. Memoirs of a Non-Belonger*, New Haven and London, Yale University Press, 2003, p. 89.

[6] Daniels, "American Soviet Studies," in Cox, *Rethinking*, pp. 12-13.

very long. The Soviet Union clearly did deny the market, and paid the supreme penalty.

For non-Soviet Marxists, especially those of a Trotskyist point of view, the Soviet Union was the outcome of a "failed" or "betrayed" revolution.[7] It was, therefore, fated either to revert to some kind of capitalism, or eventually experience a "real" revolution. From both of these opposing perspectives, the Soviet Union was "unnatural," and so it was less surprising to either of these special cadres that the Soviet Union passed from the scene. Most of my contemporaries, by contrast, had a much less dogmatic attitude about what state forms might be sustainable. The Soviet Union had managed to survive the Nazi attack in 1941. How could it succumb in what we might legitimately call peacetime? Many right-wing Republicans credited Ronald Reagan with single-handedly bringing the Soviet Union down by playing the "Star Wars" card and challenging it to a duel over defense budgets. Stephen Cohen, the left-liberal journalist and historian, also saw the Americans as responsible, but primarily through their promiscuous offers of bad economic advice. It became clear during his torrential accusations that he preferred what had to be a murky idea of liberal communism to the demonic capitalism that actually ensued.[8] But both the Right and the Left substantially overestimated American influence. The failure of the Soviet Union was largely caused by internal insufficiencies in an economy increasingly dominated by globalism.

My generation of Sovietologists, Kremlinologists and just plain students of Russia was about as politically divided as my generation was generally—defining my generation as people who came of age during the fifties, but were still young enough to have experienced

[7] Terry McNeill, "... those who focused predominantly on the core contradiction at the heart of the Soviet system were more likely to anticipate the system's implosion than those who did not.", Cox, *Rethinking*, p. 52.

[8] *Failed Crusade: America and the Tragedy of Post-Communist Russia*, W.W. Norton & Company, Inc., 2000, 2001.

the sixties directly when they were still more or less young. The difference between my generation as a whole and my generational cohort that was specifically concerned with Russia is that our understanding of changes in political culture was based on our understanding of the Soviet Union and its fate. In trying to understand the various generational mentalities and the conflicts between them—among these Russianists specifically—you can start with the common and rudimentary division between those who were known as hard-liners and those, such as myself, who were known, by contrast, as soft-liners, moderates or some other nebulous term. In assessing how people regarded the end of the Soviet Union, one also needs to factor in the very different worlds of Washington and the universities. The distrust that the Viet Nam War sowed between them has not been entirely overcome to this day.

Hard-liners were more common in Washington; soft-liners, by and large, in the universities. Having said that, the hardest of hard liners tended to be editorial journalists and academics rather than CIA analysts or others in the corridors of power. Many of them were future neo-conservatives like Paul Wolfowitz or Richard Pipes. While hard-liners and soft-liners were generally aligned respectively with conservatives and liberals the fit is imprecise. Many of the first generation of neo-cons had Trotskyist backgrounds and many others were Wilsonian idealists who wanted to bring democracy to benighted totalitarians or authoritarians. Finally, my generation's teachers were predominantly (but by no means entirely) Russian or East European émigrés, and we, by contrast, were largely home-grown products. Although there was no uniform émigré political point of view, a great many of those teachers had, broadly speaking, been "driven out" of Eastern Europe, a fate that many of them believed their more fortunate American students would never fully comprehend. Although the significance of that is unclear, they were probably right.

Why people were more or less hostile to the Soviet Union varied enormously, but in a general way, the more conservative you were, particularly on economic issues, the more anti-Soviet you were likely to be. By contrast, the more sympathetic you were to efforts to alleviate poverty and work actively toward social justice, the more complicated your attitude toward the Soviet Union was likely to become, and the more reluctant you were to see it as wholly evil.

When I was in college and immediately afterwards, I couldn't help noticing how so many intellectuals of my parents' generation had begun on the very far Left in the 'thirties, and then moved to the far Right. Most of the first generation of neo-conservatives began as Communists or Trotskyists and moved—more or less continuously—all the way across the political spectrum after the World War II. This pattern was repeated in a less extreme way by my own generation, although notably not among students of Russia. How come? Those who made that transition from Left to Right invariably say, "We wised up." Those like myself who did not participate in that seismic shift, tend to attribute such dramatic changes in view to the personal instability of the ideological migrants, as well as to the shift of the American political spectrum to the Right between 1945—say—and 2005.

What precisely was—or is—a "hard-liner"? During the Cold War it was usually limited to one's attitude toward the Soviet Union, and did not imply broader political or temperamental differences. Back then, "hard-liner" referred to someone who was harshly, publicly and relentlessly critical of the Soviet Union, almost invariably on ideological grounds. I choose those words carefully, because there was good reason for any normal person passionately to criticize the Soviet Union for its deeply anti-democratic political system and for the monstrous crimes committed by its leadership, particularly by Stalin. But most "hard-liners" tended to have a passionate commitment to a rival philosophical system, often a purist version of laissez-faire capitalism, and were prepared to advocate relatively risky policies in opposition to the U.S.S.R. Most wanted to bring the Soviets down. In national and civilizational terms, they were often people who believed that we wore white hats and the Soviets were, as Ronald Reagan's speechwriter put it for him, "the focus of evil in the modern world". Folks like me who had experienced the American South in the 1960s were likely to think that cruelty, harshness—indeed "evil"—were globally distributed.

The two most prominent hard-liners of the older generation—people some fifteen or twenty years my senior—were Richard Pipes of Harvard, my dissertation adviser, and Martin Malia of California-Berkeley, whom I had known as an undergraduate and whose book on Alexander Herzen had served as my first scholarly model. But their paths to the Right were quite different and to some degree illustrate the differences between the émigré professoriate and the homegrown conservatives, many of whom had unpleasant experiences during the university struggles of the sixties. In what became a major cliché, Irving Kristol defined a neoconservative as a "liberal who had been mugged by reality."

Pipes' wealthy Polish-Jewish family had to flee the Nazis and was subsequently unable to return to a communist Poland. I think it more than likely that his family situation disposed him to see Nazi and Soviet authorities as virtually identical thugs and goons. A deep belief in the central importance of private property to proper social development was fundamental to Pipes' conservatism.

Martin Malia, on the other hand, began life as a conventional American liberal, growing up in a middle-class Irish-Catholic family near New Haven, attending Yale and going into the Navy after graduation. In France in the late 1940s, he flirted with socialism, but he was always anti-Soviet. He was still a moderately Left person when I knew him at Harvard, a decade or so later, as he was turning his Ph.D. dissertation on Herzen into a book. He did not become a strong ideological conservative until he crossed swords with the gladiators of the "Free Speech Movement" at Berkeley in the 1960s. Malia experienced the radicalism of the sixties in Paris as well as in the exhausting negotiations with the Left in Berkeley, and one knowledgeable student of the period believes that his politics are best understood as an "opposition to French gauchisme."[9]

Conservatives like Malia and Pipes tended to have a rather schizoid view of the Soviet Union. On the one hand, the Soviets were doomed to failure in the age of capitalism, middle-class democracy, the global economy and the "end of history." On the other hand, the Soviet Union was an ideologically inspired totalitarian state, and therefore static, unable to develop in any really favorable way and extremely dangerous. That this souped up, ideologically driven mega-state could implode so peacefully into chaos, and then slide into a corrupt but less thoroughgoing despotism surprised most staunch conservatives. In 1947, George Kennan—throughout most of his career a solitary and extremely keen-eyed observer—had presciently written that if "anything were ever to occur to disrupt the unity and efficacy of the Party as a political instrument Soviet Russia might be changed overnight from one of the strongest to one of the weakest and most pitiable of national societies."[10] In his memoirs, published in 2003, Richard Pipes told his readers that in 1951 after writing his dissertation on the question of the various nationalities that formed the Soviet Union, he "was left with no doubt that should the central authority in Russia weaken again, as had happened in 1917, the empire would fall apart."[11] Of course, that is not quite the same thing as having a document from 1951 to demonstrate his prescience.

When Pipes and Malia said that the Soviet Union was a "totalitarian state," they referred to a polity in which modern technological advances had made possible a far deeper, broader and more thoroughgoing state control over the citizenry than had been

[9] David Engerman in an email to the author on May 20, 2008.

[10] George Kennan ["Mr. X"], "The Sources of Soviet Conduct," *Foreign Affairs*, Vol. XXV (July, 1947), pp. 566-582.

[11] *Vixi*, p. 74. Of course, neither Kennan nor Pipes nor any other well-informed observer, so far as I know, actually expected that this would happen in his lifetime. The single exception might be Andrei Amalrik, a dissident who suggested that the Soviet Union might perish in a conflict with China.

possible under earlier dictatorships. Historically speaking, the Soviet Union and Nazi Germany were the two principal examples of "totalitarianism" in the modern world, with Italy—where the term originated—often thrown in as well. By the time I was in graduate school, the term "totalitarian" was applied exclusively to communist states. Theorists of totalitarian states generally described them as inherently expansionist, uniquely invasive and intolerant of any individual's "private sphere." They were self-perpetuating states that were especially impervious to externally produced change. Karl Deutsch, the distinguished political scientist, wittily distinguished between totalitarianism and democracy by noting, "In a democracy ... everything that is not forbidden is permitted. Under an authoritarian regime, everything that is not permitted is forbidden; under totalitarianism, everything that is not forbidden is compulsory."[12]

Pipes' view that the Soviet Union was "totalitarian" was undergirded by his analysis of Imperial Russia and, before that, medieval Muscovite society. The pre-conditions of Russian despotism in Pipes' ingenious analysis went back almost to the beginning of time. Geography and economic development played a central role in this syndrome. Russia was vast, cold, and northerly. It had a dispersed and poverty-stricken peasant population. Agricultural techniques were primitive and grain yields low. The inefficient nature of this rural economy drove Russia continually to expand in lieu of improving productivity, which impelled Russia to adopt a rudimentary bureaucratic despotism to deal with recalcitrant neighbors. All this began unfolding centuries before Peter the Great modernized Russian imperialism. In his principal early work, Pipes considered Imperial Russia comparable to the Hellenistic states that developed out of the rule of Alexander the Great. In his study of the Russian Revolution, Pipes wrote that Russia in the early twentieth century "resembled an 'Oriental despotism.'"[13]

[12] Carl J. Friedrich, *Totalitarianism*, p. 309.

In addition, the political sovereignty of the tsars took the form of a "patrimonial" power over all their subjects, which strongly implied "a 'proprietary way' of looking at political authority."[14] Surveying Russian history, Pipes argued that strong centralized political power effectively constituted ownership. With no essential difference between sovereignty and ownership, any kind of real independence for society from the political structure would be extremely difficult, if not impossible. How can property—even baptized property[15]—achieve independence from its owner, save by a complete overturning of the socio-political order? The growing challenge to the Russian government in the nineteenth century, first by individual members of the intelligentsia, eventually by a revolutionary movement, led to a retaliatory government modernization of this patrimonial power, largely through the expansion of executive and police powers. These expanded powers, especially the devolution of authority to provincial governors to administer summary justice to political criminals produced what Pipes understood to be a strong tendency toward totalitarianism in Russia some half century before the Russian Revolution. But precisely how the leap was made from step-by-step government centralization of the late Imperial Russian government to Soviet "totalitarianism" remains unclear.

Russia had never had the multiple sources of political authority characteristic of much of Central and Western Europe in the early modern period. As Russian society became increasingly

[13] Richard Pipes, *Russia under the Old Regime*, Charles Scribner's Sons, New York, 1974, p. 24. Pipes, *The Russian Revolution*, Alfred A. Knopf, New York, 1990, p. 53.

[14] *Russia under the Old Regime*, pp. 22- 24. Some of the points in my paraphrase of Pipes' and Malia's views were put with particular felicity by Timothy Abbott in an unpublished paper, "The Debate Within," written for my seminar at Brown in 2000.

[15] The phrase "baptized property" was used by Alexander Herzen to describe Russian serfs before they were emancipated in 1861. Pipes regarded serfdom as merely an especially onerous form of a broader Russian bondage.

monolithic, the Bolshevik seizure of power in 1917 was merely, Pipes believed, the culmination of a centuries-old historical process marked by a failure to systematically safeguard private property. In the late Imperial police state, the political opposition—particularly Lenin's Bolsheviks—grew correspondingly extreme.

Martin Malia, by contrast, found the source of Soviet totalitarian communism not in the depths of Russia's past, but in the ideologies of the West—especially the inheritance of the French Revolution and the eighteenth-century *philosophes*, Jean-Jacques Rousseau and, above all, Karl Marx.[16] Russia had always been less socially and economically developed than the nations of Western Europe, but was not—Malia maintained—different in any essential way.[17] Malia attributed Russia's plunge into communism to the radical Enlightenment philosophy of Western and Central Europe, and—more specifically—the rise of extreme egalitarianism and the utopian idea that egalitarianism could be realized through force. Jean-Jacques Rousseau believed there was "a general will," a collective public understanding of historical development that could be detected—to all intents and purposes imposed—by a "philosophical" elite. Rousseau's "general will" was not an empirical "will of all," a simple majority of individual wills that could actually be counted. The presumption of a "general will"—even worse in its Marxist variant than in the original Rousseauist one—meant that a small, empowered political group could bring its own ideologized "truth" into the political leadership of a revolutionary nation if it could persuade or compel people to accept it—which was precisely how a totalitarian point of view was brought into Russia and institutionalized in the rule of the Communist Party. Malia's highly intellectual analysis did not take sufficient account of the soil in which communist ideas actually developed in Russia. He concentrated

[16] Malia was influenced here, I believe, by the Polish philosopher, Leszek Kołakowski.

[17] Martin Malia, *Russia under Western Eyes: From the Bronze Horseman to the Lenin Mausoleum*, Cambridge MA, Harvard University Press, 1999.

instead on the development of Jacobin ideas among Russian radicals.[18] Despite Malia's effort to make the Russian intelligentsia the agent of transmittal from generation to generation[19], in my opinion Rousseau's and even Marx's utopianism cannot bear the weight that Malia's analysis ultimately laid upon them, Some serious and careful sociological analysis of the host society must be invoked to explain why these ideas found such ready acceptance.

Interestingly, Pipes and Malia—who led the intellectual Right to which members of my generation had to respond—disagreed profoundly about how history worked. Malia stressed the role of ideas and minimized the importance of institutions. Pipes' position was paradoxical. Although, contrary to Malia, he believed that Russian traditions and institutions played the decisive role in that country's tragic destiny, he shared Malia's detestation of intellectuals. While Malia saw bad ideas as all-powerful with Lenin and Stalin, Pipes saw the Soviet leadership as crudely self-interested and only interested in ideas to conceal their opportunism. He considered them "functionally illiterate."[20] Although Malia was by no means a Slavophile, he—like those nineteenth-century romantics—attributed Russia's troubles to evil Western ideas. From his very conservative position, Pipes instead saw Russia's troubles as largely home grown, a view he shared with the anti-Slavophile "Westernizers". Neither analysis was wrong, but both were one-sided, overly deterministic, and tended to be monocausal. Both Pipes and Malia discounted the actual political struggles in Russia during and after 1917. Both believed that the totalitarian conclusion was inevitable, albeit for entirely different reasons.

Malia was fascinated by Russia. He liked being there, and traveled there often except during a long stretch during the middle of

[18] For Pipes' criticism of Malia, see *Vixi*, p. 82.

[19] In certain respects Malia's view was anticipated by Jacob Talmon. See his *Origins of Totalitarian Democracy*, Praeger, New York, 1952.

[20] Cited by Abbott in "The Debate Within," p. 20.

his career when he was denied a visa for political reasons. Pipes disliked Russia, as well as the Soviet Union. His remarks about Russia were often belittling, especially during informal conversation, as I well remember. Malia was an adventurous individual with a limited interest in American politics. In his deepening opposition to everything Soviet, Pipes eagerly supported the most conservative American politicians. The two men disliked each other with some intensity. Perhaps their mutual hostility originated in their rivalry for the Russian history position at Harvard, which had gone to Pipes, allegedly because William Langer, the most powerful and influential Europeanist in the Harvard department of that day, had decided that Pipes would be the more productive scholar—which he was.

Despite differing over why Russia became totalitarian, Pipes and Malia—along with another important conservative, Robert Conquest—were united about the continued relevance of the totalitarian paradigm. They thus opposed the majority of my generation of scholars who either denied the paradigm altogether or understood the Soviet Union as having evolved to a point that the concept of totalitarianism was no longer useful. Both were intensely hostile to the American 1960s, the period that had such a strong influence on so many of my contemporaries and me. Both Pipes and Malia were superb linguists, both wrote vividly (and at times with eloquence) and both were ambitious. Neither lacked self-confidence or *amour-propre*. In addition, neither had a devouring interest in the majority of their students, so they were relatively free to go where they wished, whether to Warsaw or Washington, and do what they chose.[21] Pipes was on Reagan's National Security Council, after heading the notorious "Team B", which criticized the CIA for basing its analyses of the Soviet government on uncertain statistics,

[21] The index to Pipes' memoirs does not, so far as I could tell, contain the name of a single one of his graduate students or a single detail about any of their careers.

while failing to comprehend the evil mindset of the Soviet leadership, which Pipes believed he himself entirely grasped. Malia spent much time away from Berkeley involved in the intellectual politics of Paris and doing investigative journalism about Solidarity, the Polish trade union. Pipes allied himself early on with the neo-conservatives.

The totalitarian "syndrome" or "model," to which both men subscribed, strongly presumed that the Soviet Union could not evolve in a liberal direction and was unlikely to lose power. The essential attributes of the model had been laid out—in surprisingly diverse fashion—by the political philosopher Hannah Arendt, and the political scientists Karl Friedrich and Zbigniew Brzezinski. Until the mid-fifties, the term "totalitarian" had been more of an epithet than an analytical term. The more precise academic model maintained that the Soviet Union was quasi-permanent, or if it did fail it would happen in some unforeseeable way in the mists of the future. That the Soviet Union had evolved and, in limited ways, become more open after Stalin's death in 1953 may have been the most difficult point for adherents of the totalitarian model to concede. They tended to acknowledge marginal, fragmentary improvements but little more. They believed that the Soviet Union under Brezhnev was not *significantly* different from what it had been under Stalin.

Malia claimed that he learned that "communism is mortal" as he watched the struggles of Solidarity with the Polish government in 1981-82. It is unclear when or if Pipes came to a similar conclusion. Other hard-liners, like Jeane Kirkpatrick, gradually abandoned the idea that totalitarian states were stable and permanent forces of evil. She saw Mikhail Gorbachev as simply giving up the enterprise of making the world totalitarian.[22] Unlike previous theorists, she was willing to conclude that a totalitarian state could simply collapse because a leader emerged who thought it was too difficult

[22] On Kirkpatrick's evolution, see Abbott Gleason, *Totalitarianism*, Oxford University Press, New York and Oxford, 1995, pp.208-209.

to maintain. Kirkpatrick's assessment that that Gorbachev was a "sport" in the system was not a very convincing explanation of the end of Soviet totalitarianism to those of us who believe that things happen for reasons.[23]

The center-right position was occupied by scholars like my friend and mentor, Adam Ulam, who thought the Soviet Union a singularly nasty place and was willing to call it totalitarian, but really didn't mean anything very systemic by the term. On one occasion he marveled to me at how ideological Pipes' views were. Robert Conquest, whom I came to know with pleasure at the Kennan Institute, was somewhere between Ulam and Pipes. He was a strong conservative, but a quite untheoretical one. Like Ulam, he was happy to call the Soviet Union totalitarian, but he was not interested in analyzing the term. He was, however, highly antagonistic toward liberals whom he thought glossed over Stalin's crimes and determined to oppose such antics at every turn. His conservatism did have, like Malia's and especially Pipes', a strong free-market component.

Conquest knew I was a liberal, but one who was not inclined to shrink the numbers of Stalin's victims—which, in fact, do seem to have been lower than he originally thought. Conquest was quite willing to leave politics aside and talk about poetry. He loved regaling me with lurid tales about the great poet Philip Larkin, whom he knew well, and with whom—along with their friend Kingsley Amis—he enjoyed free-wheeling, "blokish"[24] conversation and pornography. Conquest had no interest in social theory, but he had pretty good instincts about how things happened, which may have served him better. He was a good poet and a witty writer of limericks, which he could produce at the drop of a hat.

The most dedicated opponents of Pipes and Malia were two men

[23] Webster's *New World Dictionary of the American Language* defines a "sport" in this sense as "a plant or animal showing some deviation from the normal type."

[24] Larkin's biographer Andrew Motion uses this term but it seems to have originated with Larkin.

whom I knew slightly less well: Professor Leopold Haimson of Columbia University and Professor Moshe Lewin, whose career in America was spent at the University of Pennsylvania. Both were close to Marxist in outlook, and believed that social development determined political structures. Both were resolute enemies of the "totalitarian" point of view, which rested on the primacy of imposed, top-down radical politics over socio-economic developments. While their personal experiences and intellectual evolution differed markedly, they ended in contiguous positions.

Haimson was born in 1927, in Brussels. His parents were middle-class Jewish immigrants who had met in political exile in Manchuria, a major center of Russian émigré life after the Revolution. They moved to Berlin and then fled the Nazis to Belgium. Haimson attended Harvard where he studied with the first great teacher of Russian history in the United States, the émigré Michael Karpovich, who also taught both Pipes and Malia. Haimson had grown up speaking French with his parents at home, and was initially most interested in French history. On the basis of his brilliant undergraduate work at Harvard, Professor Crane Brinton arranged for him to become a member of Harvard's prestigious Society of Fellows after the war. Like Malia, Haimson was very much at home in France, but his French influences were quite different. Most notably, he became a great admirer of the social historian Ferdinand Braudel, whose influence on him he described as "profound." Braudel was above all a student of social structures and material influences over the *longue durée* of history.

Influenced though he was by Braudel, Haimson was much more interested in "individual agency." Working with anthropologists like Margaret Mead and with psychologists and even psychoanalysts had no doubt disposed Haimson to invoke categories like "consciousness" and "spontaneity," in which Braudel had little interest. The most significant influence on Haimson's views was probably his long study of the Mensheviks, which—according to his conservative critics—predisposed him to a rather schematic and abstract form of Marxism. His long, two-part article published in the *Slavic Review* in 1964-65 had an enormous influence on my contemporaries, pushing many of them toward a Menshevik interpretation of war and revolution. In a recent interview he described himself as above all interested in the "connections between social and political pressures in late imperial Russia."[25]

Moshe Lewin's biographical trajectory was dramatically different. Born in 1921 in Wilno/Vilna/Wilnius (pick one), Poland, Lewin fled to the Soviet side when the country was partitioned by Germany and the Soviets in 1939. He worked on a collective farm during the World War II and also served in the Red Army, emigrating to Israel when the war was over. He received his bachelor of arts degree at Tel Aviv in 1961 and his doctorate at the Sorbonne in 1964. It was only after teaching at the École des Hautes Études in Paris and at the University of Birmingham in England that he came to the United States, where he taught at the University of Pennsylvania from 1978 until his retirement in 1995. His presence, along with that of the versatile and erudite Alfred Rieber, made Penn one of the top places to study Russian history in the United States between the mid-sixties and the mid-nineties.

I saw Haimson frequently at conferences and academic meetings between the late 1960s and the early 1990s. He was a considerable figure among those in my cohort who believed that political institutions grew out of society and its complexities, rather than being imposed from above by a political elite. At a theoretical level, this position was not totally incompatible with Pipes' view, but Pipes saw the Russian evolution as having ended in a static Soviet totalitarianism, while Haimson, Lewin and their admirers believed that Russia and the Soviet Union continued to evolve. As a consequence, they felt it was important to continue analyzing the development of the Russian/Soviet body social and to determine how that affected the state, or—in Marxist terms—the political superstructure. The

[25] Interview with Leopold Haimson, *Kritika*, Vol. 8, No. 1, Winter 2007, pp. 3-11.

events which led up to the Russian Revolution, the consolidation of Soviet power, Stalinism and later destalinization were part of a long developmental continuum, stemming ultimately from Russian social and economic backwardness, a view widely shared by Sovietologists and Russian historians. Richard Pipes and Moshe Lewin believed in different versions of it, but Malia believed that Russian backwardness, while undeniable, was far less important than the ideas of the French Revolution. Despite their differences, Pipes and Malia saw the Soviet political structure leading inevitably to the icy grip of totalitarianism, while Haimson and Lewin saw a constant interplay between the economic/social substructure of Russia and its political superstructure, extending right through the Soviet period and out the other side.

Malia read Soviet historiography almost entirely to attack it, while Pipes picked up odds and ends of information from it. The Haimson cohort took Soviet historians and their work quite seriously. My old friend Daniel Field was considerably less Marxist than Haimson, but worked closely with a number of Soviet scholars and spent a year as a Fulbright professor at Moscow State University. His study of peasant monarchism, *Rebels in the Name of the Tsar*, was much admired by the social historians, of which he considered himself one, although he was more interested in both political history and literature than many of them. Ronald Suny, then of Chicago, William Rosenberg of Michigan, Stephen Cohen then of Princeton and Reginald Zelnik of California-Berkeley were even more critical of the "totalitarian" school than Field.

In his analysis of Soviet history, Moshe Lewin began not with ideology, or with Lenin or Stalin, but with a concrete analysis of evolving social structures. He was at pains to point out that the society from which Stalinism emerged was very primitive. There was an enormous layer of poorly collectivized peasants and a working class made up of a subset of these peasants who had been brought into the cities and put in factories at a time when they were accustomed to using their hands rather than machines. Those in management and the state apparatuses were also new to their positions, which they learned on the job.

Despite the horrors of collectivism, the purges and World War II, Lewin saw Soviet society gradually becoming more and more complex, more differentiated and better educated in the post-Stalin period. It could no longer be governed by the primitive "age-old despotism" that culminated in Stalinism. New groups of educated specialists had emerged: writers, teachers, professionals. By Brezhnev's time, the Soviet bureaucratic ruling class could no longer govern effectively, yet it prevented these new groups from claiming positions of political influence. This conflict is what produced Gorbachev and the reform momentum: The driving force was congeries of new social groups fighting to emerge from the stifling political conformity of the Brezhnev era. It's interesting to note that for Lewin the Communist Party was of secondary importance—it was merely the summit of the old bureaucratic elite. I myself had trouble believing that the connection that Lewin made between social forces and Gorbachev's reform politics was so central. Gorbachev, it seemed to me, consulted people whom he regarded as talented and innovative and began to make his changes in a more-or-less top down way. In this unprecedented situation, he was groping.

A third historian during this period of methodological struggle should also be mentioned, Sheila Fitzpatrick. She championed the social history and social science methods associated directly with the French *Annales* School in much the same way that Haimson did, but she focused on a somewhat later period—Stalin's time above all.[26] Several years younger than I, Fitzpatrick has been the most productive English-language student of Russia of my generation.

[26] See her interview in *Kritika*, Vol. 8, No. 3, Summer 2007, pp. 479-486. Although she championed the French *Annales* school, her historical practice was probably more influenced by the English Marxism of her teachers, most notably Edward Hallett Carr.

For years she was widely admired by younger, left-leaning scholars and often reviled by conservatives.[27] Her father was a prominent Australian radical, Brian Fitzpatrick, an historian, politician and an independent Marxist. I always thought of her as a leftist and certainly influenced by Marxism, although she has recently described herself as "the skeptical child of Australian Old Left parents." She maintains that as a young scholar she "was not New Left or any other kind of Left," but does (I imagine with a wry smile) concede that "the milieu was familiar."[28] Her genealogy was certainly regarded with suspicion by some conservatives. Maintaining that Stalin's rise to power was facilitated, if not brought about, by a "revolution from below" of radicalized workers in search of material security and political influence, Fitzpatrick saw their success and their subsequent purging of those they replaced as a tough form of "affirmative action." This view stirred the wrath of the conservatives as much as any claim made by the Russianist political Left in my time. She eventually moved unobtrusively away from the Left positions she had staked out as a young scholar. Instead of stressing a complex congruence between Stalin's positions and popular attitudes, she analyzed various kinds of everyday forms of popular "resistance" to Stalinism itself. She traced her changing views not to conservative attacks on her, but to the opening of the archives and the availability of new evidence of popular hostility to Stalin's officialdom. Fitzpatrick's political leftism had a limited influence on the way she framed historical matters, however, and less and less with the passage of time. She is in many ways a positivist, a great gatherer of information who was cautious in her generalizations, especially as the sixties receded into the past.

These were some of the principal scholars in the political wars

[27] For her own point of view on many of these controversies, see her "Revisionism in Perspective: A Personal View," *Slavic Review*, Vol 67, No. 3, Fall, 2008, pp. 682-704.

[28] "Revisionism in Perspective," p. 685.

over the meaning and development of the Soviet Union in the 1980s, during the time I was the Secretary of the Kennan Institute and after I returned to Brown. They inhabited rather different worlds. One would miss significant things about them if they were simply categorized as, say, "six professors" or "six Russian historians with different views on what Soviet history meant." Richard Pipes, for example, regarded himself as a luminary, an aristocrat, albeit one whose ample talents had taken him far. He went to few academic conferences, seeming to regard them as a bit grubby. Late in his career he came to the Russian Research Center (later the Davis Center for Russian and Eurasian Studies) less and less frequently. He seemed to regard himself as cut from quite a different cloth than the run of the professoriate, although in my experience he always remained proud of his status as a Harvard professor. He could be vindictive, and made punishing critiques of the "revisionists" on the Left, for their crude intellectual errors and stylistic vulgarity, but he also had a strong aesthetic side which he rarely revealed publicly. He was not a modest man. When an interviewer gushingly suggested that he had brought down the Soviet Union, he gracefully accepted some of the credit. A fascinating character and an enormously productive scholar, he was the darling of conservatives like A.M. Rosenthal of the *New York Times*, and a sworn enemy of the liberals.

One may locate Moshe Lewin at the other extreme. He had seen the horrors of the twentieth century close up in a way that none of the other five had, even Pipes, and the experience had not left him soft on liberals, tolerant of conservatives, or patient with people he regarded as fools. When I first arrived at the Kennan Institute, he was on the advisory board, which is how we first met. Lewin was quite cognizant of the Kennan Institute's resources and wanted to share in the bounty. Although he never spoke of it to me, it was clear he did not care for Billington, whom he probably regarded as a muddle-headed conservative. Lewin's initial take on me was that I was Billington's creature and for several years he treated me with unobtrusive disdain. Eventually he relented sufficiently to call my book on totalitarianism a "reasonably balanced presentation" by which "readers are quite well served."[29] But in the company of a relatively small number of people whom he liked and trusted, he could apparently be charming and funny. His dedication to his research was awesome, and not merely in the casual way that young people use the term—it really inspires awe. He occasionally frightened American students with his mordant and often relentless criticism. He found nurture difficult.

Leopold Haimson had a good deal in common with Lewin intellectually, but was quite the opposite in character and personality. He was warm-hearted and could be positively sentimental. He loved our mutual friend Alexander Erlich, for his rectitude and purity. He cultivated friendship, but had a strong sense of his own agendas—two attributes that were occasionally in conflict. His presentation of the development of historical mentalités at conferences was often lengthy, sometimes interminable, but these expositions provoked considerable interest among younger scholars. He liked nothing better than to take a seminar group from Columbia University's Harriman Institute out to a Chinese restaurant dinner afterward and continue the discussion until the more far flung of his colleagues had to head for home.

Widely admired by many of my slightly younger contemporaries, Sheila Fitzpatrick—in my experience—was a relatively subdued or contained person, much focused on her work. Without engaging in feminist rhetoric, her determination and focus and her year-in-year-out productivity made her sponsorship and support particularly attractive to women scholars, but surely also to some men. When she married Professor Jerry Hough, a Duke political scientist who liked to compare Soviet society and non-Soviet Western societies in ways conservatives found abhorrent, they were regarded initially—and quite unfairly—as the classic Stalinist couple in the

[29] *Slavic Review*, Vol. 57, No. 2 (Summer, 1998), pp. 425-26.

field. During the period of her marriage to Hough, Fitzpatrick produced her most political and controversial work.

These were the *dramatis personae* whom I got to know at the Kennan Institute and among whom I spent the middle years of my career. The two sides did not actually encounter each other very often. Pipes launched his thunderbolts from conservative journals like *The National Interest* or as op-eds in the *New York Times*. Malia wrote for the journal *Daedalus* and often for the *New York Review of Books*. The social historians published primarily in trade journals like the *Slavic Review* and the *Russian Review*. They were a commanding presence at national and regional meetings of the American Association for the Advancement of Slavic Studies, known as the "Triple A, Double S," and were often at the Kennan Institute, both as fellows and board members. Adam Ulam, who occasionally attended the AAASS, called it the "triple ass," but did not really turn up his nose at it. Malia would also attend on occasion.

The struggle between the social historians and the adherents of the totalitarian point of view was well under way by the time I returned to Brown in 1982. As an intellectual and cultural historian, I found myself more interested in the vocabulary employed by these gladiators than by who was "right"—or whose assumptions were at least more plausible. Capitalizing on a famous upcoming anniversary, I wrote an article about these controversies entitled "'Totalitarianism' in Nineteen Eighty-Four," which led Oxford University Press to ask me to write a book-length study of the concept of totalitarianism. I accepted the offer. In writing the book, I tried to contextualize the concept, seeing it as neither true nor false, but as a particular way of analyzing the mega-states of the twentieth century, albeit a valuable one, at least for a time.[30] This project meant that I set to work on a book which ultimately tried to

[30] "'Totalitarianism' in Nineteen Eighty-Four," *The Russian Review*, Vol. 43 (April, 1984); *Totalitarianism: The Inner History of the Cold War*, Oxford and New York, Oxford University Press, 1995.

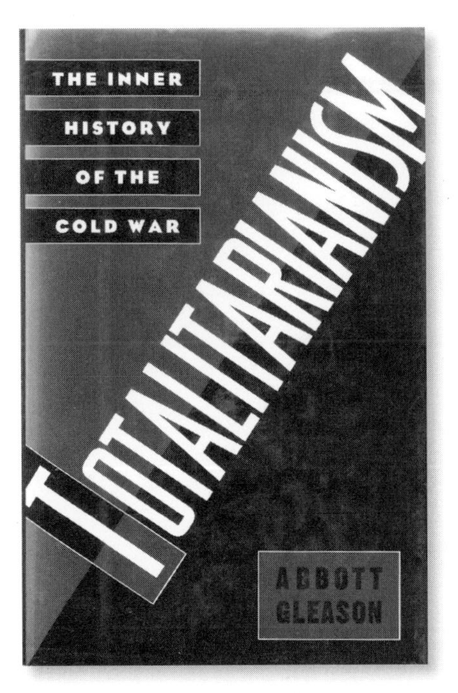

Totalitarianism *by Abbott Gleason, 1995*

fuse two rather disparate goals: on the one hand, describing and analyzing the interpretive disputes among my colleagues; on the other hand, the term 'totalitarianism' itself had a much longer history. The study quickly became a labor of love and took me almost a decade to complete, since during this period I was departmental chair for three years and also helping get Brown's Watson Institute for International Studies off the ground.

In line with my growing conviction that scholars—historians above all—should not ignore the subjectivity of their viewpoint, I couched my introduction to *Totalitarianism* as partly a memoir, trying to describe the disputes among my father's generation and mine over the meaning of the term. This kind of introduction occasioned a certain amount of criticism, among both reviewers and my colleagues. My longtime friend, the distinguished Colonial

American historian Gordon Wood, told me severely that history was one thing and a memoir quite another. An Australian historian of Italian Fascism claimed to be "troubled by my moments of confession," which he suspected of being "Clintonic"—whatever that might mean. Presumably it was not a ringing endorsement.

In some sense my new project meant that I was concerned with what the Soviet Union was, for something on the order of a decade, between 1984 and 1994. In fact, my investigation of terminological and methodological disputes coincided in unexpected and interesting ways with the last days of the Soviet Union. I had the good fortune to be studying decades of scholarly arguments in Europe and America about how to describe the place, precisely as it was coming to the end of the road.

At the beginning, I was very cautious in my estimate of Gorbachev. How could this system, so effectively closed, produce a radical reformer? For a year or so after 1985, I was far from convinced that this man was different in any essential way from his predecessors. In retrospect it seems to me that my views were much too deterministic. I thought the Soviet Union simply couldn't in any rapid way break out of its long history as a closed society—and over the long haul I'm afraid this fate has befallen Russia, even though Soviet institutions have been swept away. My impression was reinforced by Gorbachev's initial efforts to conceal the nuclear disaster at Chernobyl in 1986 and by his clumsy attempt to change Soviet drinking habits by fiat.

Another factor in my slowness to grasp Gorbachev's importance may have been my own professorial caution—a narrow empiricism that contributed incrementally to my growing reluctance to take risks. Although much less so than in earlier generations, specialized academia discouraged large-scale studies of social systems. The Welsh Trotskyite Michael Cox maintained that if we train people to be "narrowly academic specialists ... we should hardly be surprised when they fail to come up with genuine insights. Small-scale thinking about small-scale problems is unlikely to come up with large-scale theories about the way systems in general function and malfunction."[31]

Between 1987 and 1991, a period of only five years, things moved very fast indeed in the Soviet Union. I spent a summer talking to Russians in Moscow and St. Petersburg and exploring in amazement the empty shelves of Soviet food stores and other frightening signs of systemic disaster. But lacking an ideological view pointing to an impending collapse, I found it difficult to imagine that somehow the next step would be taken. I thus found myself constantly behind the eight ball. Many of my colleagues, especially those with liberal views like mine, had long seen the Soviet Union as evolving toward an increasingly open, pluralistic society, with increasing political participation and a slowly improving welfare system. As the chaos deepened, scholars who had expected a continuing Soviet evolution toward openness and pluralism fell silent, or changed the focus of their research. While hoping for such progressive developments, I had been a good deal less sanguine than the social historians. But I certainly never expected such a rapid delegitimization of the system.

I came to believe—as did a number of others—that the heart of the Soviet crisis lay in something that neither George Kennan nor anyone else had really foreseen at the beginning of the Cold War: the inadequacy of the Soviet statist economy and the inability of the Soviet political structure to deal successfully with the modern challenges of information, innovation, productivity, prices, and so on. By the early 1990s, the international system had little use for a state predicated on Stalinist industrialization: a smokestack economy grounded in the material of a peasant society. The great achievement of Stalinism, paid for at such a tremendous price, was to control rather than stimulate the agricultural economy, to move millions of peasants to cities and to create (very quickly) second-rate versions of Pittsburgh and Detroit.

[31] Michael Cox, *Rethinking the Soviet Collapse*, pp. 4-5.

Tom Gleason with Jack Matlock, the last U.S. ambassador to the Soviet Union, 1996

Photo courtesy of the Kennan Institute

The Soviet political and economic system had great difficulty in doing things that became increasingly important during the Brezhnev era. It could not bring information to people quickly. It could not generate economic innovation. It could not compete with the United States, Western Europe or Japan in either quality or quantity of production. Most seriously of all, from an economic point of view, the Soviet system could not generate a price mechanism. This meant that the prices paid for virtually everything in the economy remained arbitrary, so that no realistic combining and deploying of resources for profit was possible. None of the Soviet reforms attempted after Stalin's death ever resolved this problem.

The Soviet Union and its East European client states remained largely outside the world market, while becoming gradually ensnared in its financial apparatus and dependent on it economically. The challenge of privatization and the open market could only be addressed after the dissolution of the Soviet system.

In a more general way it seemed to me that Stalinist industrialization tended in some ways—though not in all—to leave society behind, a conclusion which I guess put me in the company of the older and more conservative analysts. Under communism, the Russian economy and Russian society did not change and develop together. Certain sectors of society remained rather archaic and static, politically and economically, even as the Soviet leadership pushed the industrialization process from above. In the Soviet Union and to a somewhat lesser extent in Eastern Europe, people's political, economic and cultural attitudes remained partly frozen even as their countries, one way or another, became more developed. Technocrats and intellectuals changed the most, workers and peasants least. Geographical differences were considerable.

It is easy to exaggerate the archaic nature of Soviet society. If portions of Russia in particular had not been better educated, more Western in orientation, and more secular and rationalist in their beliefs, Gorbachev would not have gotten so much support. Even so, the persistence and re-animation of archaic Russian points of view was very clear. Envy, social and political passivity, something approaching hatred between status and ethnic groups, was more widespread than in the West. Personal ambition, as opposed to the desire for security and stability, was understandably absent. A peasant tendency to prefer "leveling down" persisted. There was little confidence that a rising tide would lift more boats. Even in Russia today, what are described as political parties are little more than clientelistic networks formed around individual leaders. Lenin sometimes said that communism was all a matter of cadres. The Soviet Union perished partly because of a shortage of the right kind of cadres.

My book on the phenomenon of "totalitarianism" ended shortly after its subject. Although the label of "totalitarian" has continued to flourish, it is used mostly on the political Right and has come to mean something between "repressive," "liberal" and "very unpleasant" to the neo-conservatives. In the end, totalitarianism was much more fragile than it appeared to be back in the apocalyptic days of Hannah Arendt and George Orwell.

Tom Gleason, c. 1990

Photo by John Forasté

Scribble, Scribble, Scribble

I always thought he [Lionel Hampton] was older than he said he was.
Well he plays on that boy shit, you dig ... That motherfucker is old, Jim.
He's not as old as Coleman Hawkins?
No, nobody's that old. Not even Albert Nicholas.
Have you seen Albert?
Yeah, he's in Copenhagen.
That's my man. He sure is sweet.
He kills me.
He loves you.[1]

The academy is a curious place. Time moves more slowly and more swiftly there. Time moves more slowly because more time is visible. Professors know figures long dead more intimately than they know their neighbors ... They and their students read ruins, hieroglyphics, layered rocks, dark matter and old books. They read the alien and the enemy.[2]

—Anne Norton

Sometime during 2001 I began to have a major problem with my tennis game. I couldn't seem to throw the ball straight up in the air and so I really couldn't serve. The ball would either slide off my finger tips and I'd hit it down into the net, or my arm would unaccountably jerk and the ball would fly backward over my shoulder. I gradually lost control of how high I threw the ball. I was not

[1] Interview with Dexter Gordon. Arthur Taylor, *Notes and Names: Musician to Musician Interviews*, Da Capo Press Edition, New York, 1993, p. 9. Albert Nicholas was an old New Orleans clarinetist who played in Europe for many years. He was many years older than the bebop musicians talking about him here. I heard him once in Heidelberg, in 1961.

[2] Anne Norton, *Leo Strauss and the Politics of American Empire*, Yale University Press, 2004, p. 21.

completely surprised by these developments. I had always had trouble with my serve, even back when I was quite a decent prep school and college player. But I was embarrassed. Over the course of the next three years, the situation progressively worsened, and I was somehow slow to grasp that I was losing the proper use of my left arm. As the downhill process continued, I found myself coming almost to hate my tennis dates, which now involved a major struggle. But I kept on playing. I couldn't face the idea that I might simply be too old, and no other explanation occurred to me. It didn't occur to me that something might be medically wrong. I was embarrassed playing doubles, but at least then I had a partner who could serve. So I struggled on, overcoming my aversion to my increasingly poor play and schooling myself to be apologetic but casual about it. No big deal.

I still dreamed—literally dreamed—of playing soccer. The dreams came only every so often, but quite regularly. Even after coming to Brown I had played weekends on an outfit based in Cambridge made up of former college players. But in 2003 when I tried playing in a pick up game at a picnic, I very quickly found myself on the ground. I didn't seem to hold my liquor as well as in the old days. I staggered more easily. Sarah had her misgivings. I started to develop a tremor in my left hand. About a dozen years earlier, in 1991, I had had my first brush with medical crisis at the age of fifty-three. Prior to that, I had always lived at peace with my body. It was a so-so body—not what I would have liked, but good enough to get around in. Like a five-year-old Camry that needed some dents and scratches taken care of. We also had one of those.

Vartan Gregorian had just become the new president of Brown. I had known him, although not really well, for some years. He was looking for a provost and I was chair of the History Department. He had become a tenured member of the department when he became president, and we joked about my being his boss, as well as he being mine. The search committee asked if I would like to be considered for the provost position, and I said yes. The provost, incidentally, is the academic officer who for all practical, administrative purposes runs the university, while the president deals largely with fund-raising, and retains the right to final decision-making, except in cases in which that rests the with trustees.

I had always had an ambivalent attitude toward academic administration. I often thought I could get things done as well as anybody, perhaps better, but when I was chair of the History Department, I was often bored with the ongoing administrative tasks. I longed to be reading or writing or going for a run. It was hard not to be cynical about the clichés and posing that institutional leadership demanded. And I was awfully thin skinned and a bit too much of a worrier. To be good at that kind of stuff you have to leave the job dilemmas in your office, but I usually brought them home with me, even the little ones. Nor did I have a real educational agenda for Brown. My picture of myself as educational leader was much too general and abstract, and too wrapped up in thoughts of how it would seem to others.

So in fact I was really paralyzed about whether I wanted to be provost. Sometimes I would have additional fantasies about going on to become a college president after being provost of Brown. Other times I would think about the regimen of meeting after meeting after meeting, day in, day out, and my heart would sink. Not enough to keep the mind alive. Surely I'd be tempted to start smoking again. Or grow to hate coming to work … or worse. I was afraid to go for it and afraid not to.

Things came to a head one Sunday morning. I was sitting at the kitchen table, drinking coffee and ostensibly reading the *New York Times*. In fact, I was trapped in the coils of my indecision. Motionless. Suddenly I couldn't take in the words on the newspaper. I could still see them but I couldn't understand them any more. My body seemed to be filling up with some opaque material. I felt a stab of fear and spoke to Sarah, but the words came out thickly and were virtually unintelligible: "Call 911". Sarah looked at me uncertainly. Was I being funny? Suddenly she realized I wasn't. Everything became blurred. Could I keep on breathing? Then I was in the truck, in the emergency room, on an IV. My whole right side was paralyzed. I was having a major stroke. Would I die, I wondered? The doctors and nurses looked at me—pityingly, I thought. Then, soon after reaching the emergency room, I began to move my right arm again. My ordinary consciousness returned. I had no idea of why or how—any more than why or how it had been so intensely lost.

Gregorian came to see me in the hospital the next day. Nothing had to be said. My body had informed both of us that I should not be provost. My rival, a biologist and an old friend got the job. It was hard on him, and it would have been even harder on me. I returned to my writing and my teaching with relief. My administrative ambitions were gone like a puff of smoke.

In 2003 my body rebelled again. In-ho Lee, my distinguished friend from graduate school, had become head of the Korea Foundation, following her stint as ambassador to the Russian Federation. She was the first woman in Korean history ever to be ambassador to a major foreign country. The foundation, at her initiative, invited me to spend ten days lecturing at various Korean universities. I did. It was a delightful experience. I had, for the first and I assume last time in my life, a limo—well, at least a dark colored car—a translator and a driver. I anticipated with pleasure how this list of Korean universities would enliven the tedious precincts of my CV.

But on my way home to Providence via Chicago, I didn't get up often enough from my seat, and when I debarked in Chicago, I found myself disconcertingly short of breath. I could not breathe and talk at the same time. I went to a medical aid station, established in the airport to deal with the current SARS crisis, and turned myself in. It was a good thing I did so. I had embolisms in both lungs, and spent a week in a nice Catholic hospital near O'Hare, watching television. I had always meant to watch "Seinfeld" and now I got the chance. I enjoyed it, but not enough to become a regular viewer after getting out. The embolisms finally dissolved.

When I got out of bed to take a leak or to walk down the hospital corridor, I felt unsteady on my feet. I never fully regained my balance. My tennis game was even worse that winter and I fell a few times. I also lost a lot of weight and was tired almost every night. I cut back on alcohol, but it didn't seem to make any difference.

In the fall of 2004, Sarah and I spent a weekend with a doctor friend outside New York. We put in a long afternoon at the New York Botanical Garden, a favorite site. Our friend observed me closely. At the end of our visit, she took Sarah aside and told her that she thought I had Parkinson's. A neurologist soon confirmed her preliminary diagnosis.

My first sensation was relief. I knew what I had. After a period of adjustment, I set to work learning more about the disease. That turned out to be difficult. I quickly discovered that although there were some common symptoms that almost everybody had, their relative severity and the development of the disease for each patient varied enormously. It seemed to me that Parkinson's was not a single illness, but a cluster of illnesses, each with a kind of family resemblance. Quoting from a classic account of the disease, the anthropologist-neurologist Oliver Sacks described the various symptoms as "a constellation, [in which] seemingly unrelated phenomena form a definite and constant 'assemblage' of symptoms. ... this constellation or syndrome we now call 'Parkinsonism'".[3] A tremor, for instance was almost invariable. I had one, but it was, and has remained, very slight. But my energy level is much less than it used to be, and dressing and undressing—buttons and socks, in particular—go very slowly. A good night's sleep is a receding memory.

After discovering that I had Parkinson's, the first practical consideration I had to face was whether I could continue teaching, or should I retire? I simply couldn't imagine what that would be like.

[3] Excerpts from *Awakenings* by Oliver Sacks, <www.academia.info/literature/alexanders_feast/awakenings /excerpts.htm>.

What would I do all day? Would I get depressed? Would I be able to continue writing history? Then, did I want to write more history? Students liked me and their warm feelings about my teaching fed my self-esteem. Could I do without that? What would I do?

As it turned out, I decided to stop lecturing, and—on balance—was glad I did. I had taught all of Russian history, lecturing on everything from the emergence of the Slavs as a definable Eurasian culture all the way through to the end of the Soviet Union. Partly because of my professional dilettantism—my breadth of interests, as I phrased it to myself—I had never been able to keep fully up to date with important new scholarship for the entire field. As a result, I often found myself being able to spend at best an hour or two tweaking my last year's lecture, or reading a new article or book on some aspect of the wide range of political and cultural problems my chosen lecture subject might be covering that day. I had a bad conscience about that. Even if last year's lecture was tarted up a bit and went over perfectly well, I increasingly felt I was just fooling my students. Like me, my lectures were aging and not any too well. I was eager for something new, which would still draw on areas of experience and expertise. My analytic capabilities were slowly eroding, but my descriptive powers seemed much as they had always been.

Retirement, as it turned out, enabled me to focus my teaching on individual students, and on projects that particularly interested me—such as an undergraduate honors thesis on the Czechoslovakian rock group, the Plastic People of the Universe. The band's intransigence, combined with Communist hostility to their bohemianism, helped to inspire the Charter 77 resistance to the communist government. My student, Brian Corcoran, learned Czech and went a couple of times to Prague, just for an undergraduate honors thesis. Christina Koningisor, a good-natured dynamo with a love of travel and a lawyer's gift for argument, traveled to Sierra Leone to investigate how the local people were relating to the Constitutional Court established there after the genocide—an experience she recounted in a memorable essay for Brown's Royce Fellowship program.

Working with left-wing Israelis and several of Brown's few Palestinian students, I improved my knowledge of the Middle East—unfortunately, just as my memory slowly lost altitude and my declining energy made mastering new areas and themes more difficult. But the situation of Palestinians under Israeli occupation reminded me vividly of African-Americans in the South back in the 1950s and 1960s. I took up their banner with enthusiasm. I kept thinking that somebody would come along and insist, "You're a Russian historian! You can't do this stuff." But nobody did. I continued to freelance.

Earlier in life I had adopted the pose of a stoic, partly out of enthusiasm for Camus' work, and partly out of a political/aesthetic sense that it suited me. It also seemed the opposite of my early bad-little-boy self. The result was that I had some experience with stoicism when it became necessary on an everyday basis.

I also discovered that Parkinson's often produced bizarre results. In a small number of cases, unexpected musical talent can emerge. My musical interest remained strong, but nothing new in the way of talent has appeared so far. I found myself singing ballads and carols, but my voice, alas, was the same old one. I sat down at the piano, but the result was the same. On the positive side, I didn't suffer from the addiction to gambling that occasionally afflicted Parkinson's patients under medication. Nonetheless, music has become even more central in my life. It helps me to keep a rhythm and tempo in what I try to do which is much more difficult these days.

Old age, especially combined with Parkinson's can be embarrassing and sometimes shameful. You lose control of your body. I can't go around a corner without bumping into the door jamb. I come downstairs like I'm walking on eggs. Reading demands more focus and tires me out sooner. There is less you can do for people, which causes the ego to suffer. On an unpredictable timetable, you lose various abilities, capacities and ambitions. Some things have been easy to give up. Biking and jogging were major forms of exercise for many years. But I don't miss them—especially the jogging. I don't exactly miss tennis and squash, but I miss loving them and my long lost ability to play them quite well.

Curiously, despite diminished capacities you remain—or feel that you remain—the same person. At the end of my third year of retirement, I was medically stable, but doing analytical work was becoming more difficult. It called for greater effort and wore me out quickly. Shifting gears intellectually was harder. So was remembering names, especially out of context. Sometimes it seems as if a translucent veil has been drawn between my consciousness and the outside world. My gait is more labored. I have lost "the silent music of the body."[4]

Nevertheless, accepting that most of life's adventures—except the big one, of course—are past has been less difficult than I thought it would be. There is more satisfaction in becoming a spectator than I thought there would be—watching birds at the feeder, seeing my children's lives unfold, watching the Red Sox deep-six the Curse of the Bambino... My world is shrinking. Isolation, resignation, acceptance prevail—but I think I can deal with that.

When I look into the mirror I see my parents—as they were in old age, not when they were young and healthy. This confuses me. Why only now do I find the full extent of their connection with me? These are people that I loved, was exasperated by, sometimes hated, established my independence from, came back to take care of, grieved for. How peculiar that I have become them. Or at least become more deeply aware of my resemblance to them. What a paradoxical thing our youthful revolts are! Remembering Eliot, "And the end of all our exploring will be to arrive where we started." With greater knowledge? Perhaps.

[4] William Harvey, quoted in "Kinetic Melody: Parkinson's Disease and Musical Therapy," Oliver Sacks, *Musicophilia: Tales of Music and the Brain*, Vintage Books, Random House, New York, 2008, p. 270.

So, now academic life goes on in a slowly attenuating version of its accustomed way: articles, reviews, a final book, graduate students finishing up: "Scribble, scribble, scribble, Mr. Gibbon, eh?", as George III is supposed to have said to the great historian of late Rome. Now Louis, our third dog, is getting a little old and stiff himself. He accompanies me to my last university office, located in Brown's Watson Institute for International Studies, an institution which I helped shape over the years.

After recounting J.R.R. Tolkien's (not very dramatic) youthful struggles, his talented biographer, Humphrey Carpenter, concludes "and after this, you might say, nothing really happened." He then goes on to describe the circumscribed existence of an English university philologist, caught up in an "ordinary suburban life, bringing up his children and tending his garden."[5] The irony, of course, is that during this lengthy and superficially somnolent period, Tolkien wrote *The Hobbit* and *The Lord of the Rings.* I wrote some things too, but, alas, nothing like *The Lord of the Rings.* In some respects, though, the dichotomy between the excitement of writing about totalitarianism and living in a tranquil academic community with its Trollopian ups and downs becomes even more striking. As I write these words, I have to concede that I still don't know how to make a normal human being interested in the routines of academic life.

John Keats romanticized regular reading, but references to traveling in the realms of gold have lost whatever power they once had over us. I gravitate more toward the account of academic life provided by my grandfather's student, Jack Hexter, in an essay, famous long ago, entitled "The Historian and his Day." Hexter described his days as "grimly uniform", despite the fact that he clearly enjoyed them. With only slight exaggeration, he reported that "from one in the afternoon to midnight with time out for dinner and domestic matters I read things written between 1450 and 1650. I vary

[5] Humphrey Carpenter, *Tolkien*, New York, Ballantine Books, 1977, p. 124.

the routine by writing about what I have read on other days."[6] Still, I was on to something long ago when I signed on to the academy. I needed an education and I got it.

After almost a decade of searching, Nick married a lovely woman and moved his business, CitySoft, from Boston to San Francisco. In 2006, when we were visiting, he gave Sarah and me a remarkable album of music called *Old and in the Way.* Being nearly sixty-eight and having just decided to retire, I liked the title. The music was bluegrass, but with Jerry Garcia of the Grateful Dead on banjo. The album had been recorded in 1973, and it was great. It swung, almost in a jazz sense, and it had pathos, which I was just beginning to be able to accept. As I listened, rock and bluegrass finally came together for me—albeit more than a quarter century late. The last interior wall of the Fortress of High Standards had finally been breached. Blackbeard the Pirate (Jerry Garcia) was staring fixedly at me, but with a grin on his face. I tried to grin back. "Deathbed conversion," I muttered, hoping it wasn't, quite.

[6] J.H. Hexter, "The Historian and his Day", *Political Science Quarterly*, Vol. 69, No. 2, June, 1954, p. 225.